THE ENCYCLOPEDIA OF
CLASSIC
MYTHOLOGY

THE ENCYCLOPEDIA OF
CLASSIC MYTHOLOGY

ARTHUR COTTERELL

LORENZ BOOKS

This edition is published by Lorenz Books

Lorenz Books is an imprint of Anness Publishing Ltd
Hermes House, 88–89 Blackfriars Road,
London SE1 8HA
tel. 020 7401 2077; fax 020 7633 9499;
www.lorenzbooks.com; info@anness.com

This edition distributed in the UK by The Manning
Partnership Ltd, 6 The Old Dairy, Melcombe Road,
Bath BA2 3LR; tel. 01225 478 444; fax 01225 478 440
sales@manning-partnership.co.uk

This edition distributed in the USA and Canada by
National Book Network, 4501 Forbes Boulevard,
Suite 200, Lanham, MD 20706; tel. 301 459 3366
fax 301 429 5746; www.nbnbooks.com

This edition distributed in Australia by Pan
Macmillan Australia, Level 18, St Martins Tower,
31 Market St, Sydney, NSW 2000
tel. 1300 135 113; fax 1300 135 103
customer.service@macmillan.com.au

This edition distributed in New Zealand by
David Bateman Ltd, 30 Tarndale Grove,
Off Bush Road, Albany, Auckland
tel. (09) 415 7664; fax (09) 415 8892

A CIP catalogue record for this book is available
from the British Library.

Publisher: Joanna Lorenz
Editorial Manager: Helen Sudell
Project Editor: Belinda Wilkinson
Designer: Nigel Soper, Millions Design
Illustrators: James Alexander, Nick Beale,
Glenn Steward

Frontispiece: *The Forging of the Sampo*
by A Gallen-Kallela.
This page: *The Rape of Ganymede*
by Peter Paul Rubens.

Author's Note

The entries in this encyclopedia are all listed
alphabetically. Where more than one name exists for a
character the entry is listed under the name used in
the original country of origin for that particular myth.
Names in italic capital letters indicate that that name
has an individual entry. Special feature spreads
examine specific mythological themes in more detail.
If a character is included in a special feature spread it
is noted at the end of their individual entry.

10 9 8 7 6 5 4 3 2 1

CONTENTS

PREFACE

THIS COMBINED ENCYCLOPEDIA of mythology contains the three outstanding traditions of Europe – Greek, Celtic and Norse. They form the core of European mythological thought, the early ideas and notions which underlie our present-day consciousness. For the stories related in Greek, Celtic and Germanic myths touch upon the fundamental issues of existence. They reveal the power of love, with its accompanying anxiety and jealousy; the conflict between the generations, the old and the new; the violence of men, especially on the battlefield or in single combat; the mischief of the trouble-maker, bored by the steady pace of everyday events; the sadness of illness or accidental injury; the mystery of death, with a variety of after-life possibilities including rebirth; the effect of enchantment upon the mind and body; the challenge of the unknown, whether a voyage into uncharted waters or a quest for a sacred object; the personal danger of a contest with a monster, even a beheading game; the sadness of betrayal and treachery, not least within a family or a group of colleagues; the cycle of fertility in human beings and animals, plus the growth of plants; the horror of madness with its disruption of human relations; the incidence of misfortune and luck, plus the whole issue of fate; the relation between human and divine, between mankind and the gods; the creation of the world and the origins of society; and, last, but not least, the nature of the universe.

Different myths tackle these great questions in distinct ways. But heroes and heroines find themselves in unrelated circumstances facing the same basic problems in Greece, Ireland and Scandinavia. The Athenian hero Theseus successfully confronted the Minotaur on Crete, but later abandoned his helper, the Cretan princess Ariadne. Full of his success against the bull-man, Theseus forgot the agreement made with his father about changing the sail of his ship from black if he escaped death himself. As a result of this moment of carelessness, Theseus' father committed suicide by leaping from the Athenian acropolis when the black sail was sighted. So in Ireland the inability of Cuchulainn to stop and think for a moment led to his killing of Conlai, his own son by the Amazon Aoifa. In Norse myth, however, it is the pride of the gods or their opponents, the frost giants, which causes disasters to occur. Unlike the Greeks

NESSUS, a wild Greek centaur, tries to abduct Heracles' new bride while ferrying her across the River Evenus. (THE RAPE OF DEIANIRA BY GUIDO RENI, CANVAS, 1621.)

A CELTIC DEITY, possibly Dagda, dangles two warriors high above his head, and thus reveals his awesome power, while the warriors in turn lift two boars, showing their supremacy over animals. (GUNDESTRUP CAULDRON, GILDED SILVER, C. 100 BC.)

and the Celts, the German peoples of northern Europe did not develop a heroic tradition of any significance. The great hero was Thor, the slow-witted but honest champion of the gods. He delighted the tough Northmen, who appreciated how his allergy to frost giants naturally led to skull-smashing encounters in fields and halls. Yet those who undertook raids as Vikings had a more suitable patron in Odin, the one-eyed god of battle and the inspirer of the dreaded berserkers.

Usually myths reveal an interwoven pattern of circumstances outside the control of both mortals and gods. Fate and destiny in European mythology are almost beyond manipulation. Attempts may be made to slow down the operation of fate's decrees, sometimes to thwart them entirely, but they never work. Odin can do nothing about his future death at Ragnarok, the doom of the gods. The Celtic sun god Lugh cannot save his son Cuchulainn on the battlefield. And even immortal Zeus, the chief god of the Greeks, has a duty to see that fate takes its proper course. He cannot control events.

The tangled web of difficulties which besets Theseus can thus be traced to a number of actions, but one stands out clearly: the refusal of King Minos of Crete to sacrifice the white bull from the sea to Poseidon, its real owner. In consequence of this sacrilege Minos' wife Pasiphae was consumed with passion for the beast, and her mating with it led to the birth of the bull-man known as the Minotaur: hence Theseus and his combat with the strange creature. The Athenian hero's entanglement with Minos' family did not stop with the abandonment of Ariadne and the death of his own father, however. For Theseus married Phaedra, another daughter of Minos. She too was cursed with an illicit passion, not for an animal this time, but for her stepson Hippolytus. Before Theseus learned the truth, he banished honest Hippolytus on Phaedra's denunciation of his evil intentions, and then lost his exiled son in a chariot accident.

The abiding interest of mythology, European or otherwise, is its frankness about such basic human drives. It could almost be described as sacred literature undisturbed by theologians. The raw and ragged ends of existence are still visible in its tales of both men and gods.

SIGURD, the great Norse hero, helps his mentor, Regin, re-forge his wondrous sword. With it, Sigurd slew the dragon, Fafnir. (WOOD CARVING, 12TH CENTURY).

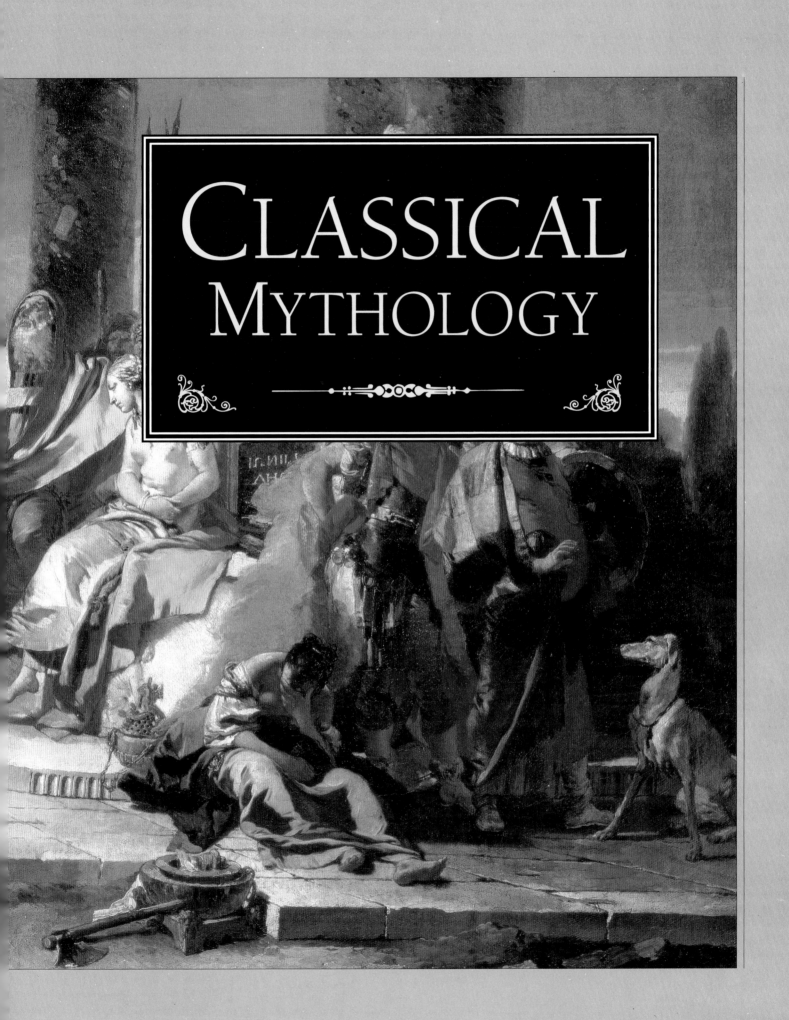

CLASSICAL
MYTHOLOGY

INTRODUCTION

THE ANCIENT GREEKS WERE THE great myth-makers of Europe. They even gave us the name by which we refer today to the amazing stories told about gods, heroes, men and animals. Around 400 BC the Athenian philosopher Plato coined the word *mythologia* in order to distinguish between imaginative accounts of divine actions and factual descriptions of events, supernatural or otherwise. Although he lived in an age that was increasingly scientific in outlook, and no longer inclined to believe every detail related about gods and goddesses, Plato recognized the power that resided in myth, and warned his followers to beware of its seductive charm.

The strength of Greek mythology, like all active traditions, lay in its collective nature. Unlike a story composed by a particular author, a myth always stood on its own, with a plot and a set of characters readily under-

MARS AND NEPTUNE, two gods of ancient Rome, ride over the Eternal City, guarding its military and maritime interests. At left, an airborne putto above Mars bears his horse's helmet, while Neptune's putto carries a seashell, symbol of the god's dominion over the waves. (MARS AND NEPTUNE BY PAOLO VERONESE, CANV.)

ANCIENT GREECE

stood by those who listened to the story-teller or dramatist making use of it. When, for instance, the Athenians watched the great cycle of plays that Aeschylus staged about the murder of Agamemnon, they were already aware of the main characters and their actions. The audience knew how the House of Atreus, Agamemnon's father, was fated to endure a terrible period of domestic strife. Not only had Atreus and his brother Thyestes been cursed by their own father, Pelops, for killing his favourite child, their half-brother Chrysippus, but a bloody quarrel of their own had also added to the family misfortune. A dispute over the succession to Pelops' throne at Mycenae led Atreus to kill three of Thyestes' sons, although they had sought sanctuary in a temple dedicated to Zeus, the supreme god. Even worse, the murderer then served the bodies of his nephews up to his brother at a banquet, after which he dared to show Thyestes their feet and hands. Atreus paid for the outrage with his life at the hands of Thyestes' surviving son, Aegisthus, who later became the lover of Agamemnon's

wife Clytemnestra during his absence at the Trojan War.

All this would have been familiar to the Athenians before Aeschylus' treatment of the myth began with Agamemnon returning home from the Trojan War. Some of the audience doubtless recalled an even older curse laid on Pelops himself by the messenger god Hermes. Pelops had provoked the god by refusing a promised gift to one of his sons. Nothing that Aeschylus included in his plays was unexpected: neither the murder of Agamemnon, nor the revenge of his son Orestes, nor Orestes' pursuit by the Furies for shedding a mother's blood. What would have fascinated the audience was the dramatist's approach to these tangled incidents, his view of motive, guilt and expiation. For that reason another dramatist was able to tackle the same story later in Athens during the fifth century BC. It needs to be remembered that such drama remained very much part of ancient religion. Today we cannot expect to appreciate the full meaning of these performances, but we are fortunate in having the raw materials from which they were made, the myths themselves.

Myths retain much of their power, even when told in summary, as they are in this encyclopedia. Because Greek myths were fashioned and refashioned over so many generations, they acquired their essential form, a shape that had been collectively recognized for longer than anyone could remember. Even now, we continue to be fascinated by the stories of Oedipus, the man who murdered his father and married his mother; of the Athenian hero Theseus, slayer of the strange bull-headed man, the Minotaur; of the great voyager Jason, who sailed across the Black Sea to distant Colchis in order to fetch the Golden Fleece; of Agamemnon, the doomed leader of the Greek expedition against Troy; of cunning Odysseus, one of the bravest of the Greeks and the inventor of the Wooden Horse, the means by which Troy was taken; of the hapless Pentheus, victim of Dionysus' ecstatic worshippers, who included his own mother; of the unbeatable champion Achilles; of the labours of Heracles, Zeus' own son and the only hero to be granted immortality; and many others. As Greeks living before and after Plato evidently understood, myths were fictitious stories that illustrated truth.

The Romans were no less impressed by the range and interest of Greek mythology. Indeed, they adopted it wholesale and identified many of their own Italian deities with those in the Greek pantheon, even adopting others for whom they possessed no real equivalent. The unruly Dionysus gave Rome considerable trouble. This god of vegetation, wine and ecstasy was by no means a comfortable deity for the Greeks, but the Romans were more deeply disturbed by his orgiastic rites. In 186 BC the Roman Senate passed severe laws against the excesses of his worshippers. It is likely that several thousand

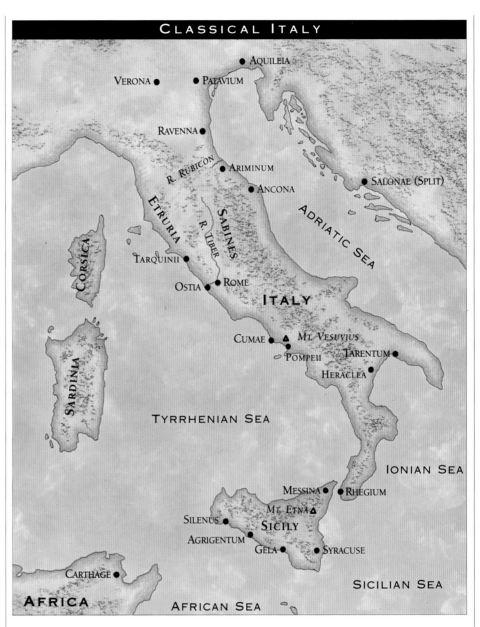

people were executed before the cult of the native wine god Bacchus discarded those aspects of Dionysus which met with official disproval. This taming of a Greek god, albeit Thracian in origin, could stand for the entire process by which Greek and Roman mythology merged in the second century BC. There were just too many myths for the Romans to resist, although they chose to impose a typical restraint on Greek extravagance.

Roman heroes could never compare with Heracles, Jason, Theseus, Perseus or Bellerophon. Something synthetic can be felt in the story of Aeneas, the leader of the refugees from Troy. His adoption as a founder-hero made him of particular concern to the first Roman emperor Augustus, but *The Aeneid*, the epic poem about Aeneas written by Virgil in the 20s BC, turned out to be a balanced celebration of Roman authority rather than an exciting heroic narrative. The hero heeded the call of duty and abandoned the woman he loved, as Roman heroes were expected to do in every myth.

ACHILLES was the son of King Peleus of Thessaly and the sea nymph *THETIS*. He was the greatest of the Greek warriors, although in comparison with *AGAMEMNON* and the other Greek kings who went on the expedition against Troy, he appears to have been something of a barbarian. His anger was as legendary as his prowess.

The uncertain nature of Achilles is apparent in the story of his birth. Both *ZEUS* and *POSEIDON* wanted to have a son by the beautiful Thetis, but *PROMETHEUS*, the fire god, had warned them that her offspring would be greater than his father. Anxious to avoid the emergence of a power superior to themselves, the gods carefully arranged the marriage of Thetis to a mortal. Because she was so attached to Achilles, Thetis tried to make him immortal by various means. The best known was dipping the new-born baby in the Styx, the river that ran through *HADES*, the world of the dead. Since Thetis had to hold him by the heel, this one spot was left vulnerable and at Troy brought about Achilles' death from a poisoned arrow shot from the bow of *PARIS*.

Achilles learned the skills of warfare from *CHIRON*, leader of the *CENTAURS*, who also fed him on wild game to increase his ferocity. Under Chiron's care Achilles became renowned as a courageous fighter, but his immortal mother knew that he was doomed to die at Troy if he went on the expedition. So Thetis arranged for him to be disguised as a girl and hidden among the women at the palace of King Lycomedes on the island of Scyros. The Greeks felt that without Achilles their chances of beating the Trojans were slim, but no one could identify the hidden hero. At last, cunning *ODYSSEUS* was sent to discover Achilles, which he did by means of a trick.

Having traced the young man to Scyros, Odysseus placed weapons among some jewellery in the palace. While Achilles' female companions were admiring the craftsmanship of the jewels, a call to arms was sounded and the warrior quickly reached for the weapons, giving himself away. Unmasked, Achilles had no choice but to sail for Troy.

There he bitterly quarrelled with Agamemnon, the leader of the Greeks. It may be that he was angered by Agamemnon's use of his name to bring *IPHIGENIA* to Aulis, for she had been told she was to marry Achilles, whereas Agamemnon intended to sacrifice

ACHILLES, relaxing beside his tent with his companion, Patroclus, welcomes his comrades, Odysseus (centre) and Ajax (right), who implore the moody hero to return to battle where he is sorely needed.
(ACHILLES RECEIVES AGAMEMNON'S MESSENGERS, BY JEAN-AUGUST INGRES, CANVAS, 1801.)

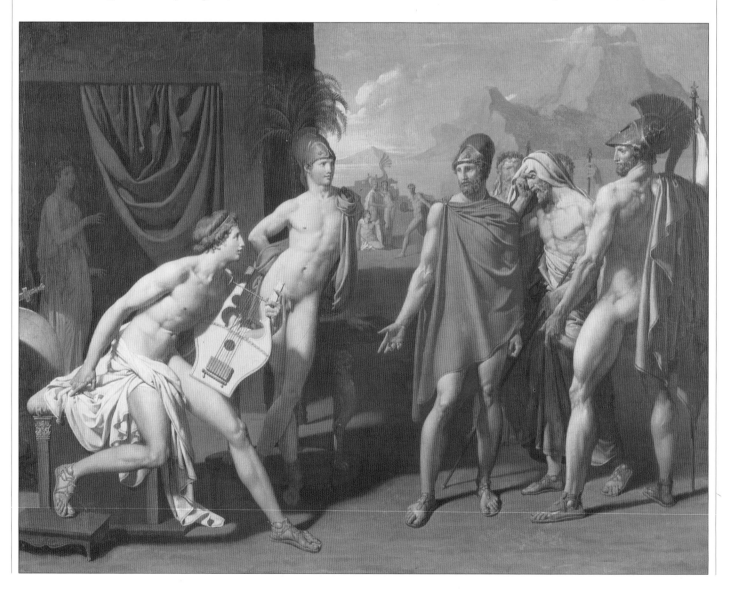

her to the goddess ARTEMIS, to ensure a favourable wind for the Greek fleet. For a long time Achilles stayed in his tent and refused to fight the Trojans. He even persuaded his mother to use her influence with Zeus to let the tide of war go against the Greeks. But Achilles was roused to action by the death of Patroclus, his squire and lover, at the hands of the Trojan HECTOR. Patroclus had borrowed Achilles' armour, which had been forged by the smith god HEPHAISTOS, and entered the fray, but he came up against Hector who easily defeated him.

In brand-new armour Achilles sought out Hector, who asked for respect to be shown for his body if he was defeated. Achilles refused, slew Hector with his spear and dragged the Trojan hero round the tomb of Patroclus for twelve days. Only Thetis could persuade her son to let the Trojans recover the corpse and arrange a funeral, a serious obligation for the living.

Back in the fight, Achilles struck fear into the Trojans, of whom he killed hundreds. But his own life was coming to an end, which he

ACHILLES falls beneath the Trojan walls, shot by Paris. The sun god aims his arrow straight for Achilles' heel, the only mortal part of the hero's body. In some myths, Apollo guided Paris' bow; in others, the god shot the arrow, as seen here. (APOLLO SLAYS ACHILLES BY FRANZ STASSEN, WATERCOLOUR, 1869.)

ACTAEON was a young Greek hunter who unluckily chanced upon the pool where Artemis and her nymphs were bathing. In outrage, the virgin goddess turned him into a stag and he was torn apart by his own hounds. (ILLUSTRATION FROM DICTIONARY OF CLASSICAL ANTIQUITIES, 1891.)

had been warned about by his steed XANTHUS, before the FURIES struck the divine creature dumb. An arrow from the bow of Paris, guided by the god of prophecy APOLLO, gave Achilles a mortal wound. Heroic yet also arrogant, Achilles was the mythical figure most admired by Alexander the Great. At the commencement of his Asian campaign against the Persians, the youthful Alexander participated in funeral games that were held at Troy in memory of Achilles. (See also HEROES)

ACTAEON was the son of a minor royal god and Autonoe, daughter of CADMUS. A Greek hunter trained by CHIRON, he offended the goddess ARTEMIS and paid with his life. There are several reasons given for his terrible end. Actaeon may have boasted of his superior skill as a hunter, or annoyed the goddess by seeing her bathing naked. To stop his boasting, Artemis turned him into a stag and he was chased and devoured by his own hounds. But these faithful animals were broken-hearted at the loss of their master, until Chiron carved a statue of Actaeon so lifelike that they were satisfied.

AEGEUS was the son of King Pandion of Athens, and father of the hero THESEUS. Having twice married without begetting any children, Aegeus went to consult the Delphic Oracle but received only the ambiguous answer that he should not untie his wine skin until he reached home. When he sought advice from his friend Pittheus, another ruler, the latter realized that the oracle had foretold how Aegeus would father a heroic son. To secure the services of such a man, Pittheus made Aegeus drunk and let him sleep with his daughter Aethra. When Aegeus understood what had happened, he placed a sword and a pair of sandals beneath an enormous boulder. He told the princess that if she bore a son who could move the rock, he was to bring these tokens to him in Athens on reaching manhood. Thus it was that Theseus grew up and was eventually reunited with his father.

Meantime, Aegeus had married the sorceress MEDEA, whose magical powers had given him another son, Medus. It was for this reason that Medea did everything she could to thwart Theseus. At her

suggestion Theseus was sent to fight the wild bull of Marathon, which he captured alive. Once Aegeus recognized his son, Medea returned in disgust to her native Colchis on the Black Sea. But bad luck continued to dog Aegeus and eventually caused his death. For it was agreed that Theseus should travel to Crete with the seven girls and seven boys sent as tribute each year to feed the MINOTAUR, a bull-headed man. If Theseus was successful in his dangerous mission to kill the Minotaur, the ship bringing him home was to fly a white sail; if unsuccessful, a black sail would signal his death. Returning to Athens after an incredible adventure in the Labyrinth at Knossos, Theseus forgot the agreement to change his sail from black to white, with the result that, upon seeing the vessel with its black sail, Aegeus threw himself off the Athenian acropolis to certain death.

AEGEUS, looking out to sea, sees his son's ships returning home, all with black sails hoisted. Thinking that his son had died, Aegeus hurled himself into the sea, afterwards named the Aegean. (ILLUSTRATION BY NICK BEALE, 1995.)

AENEAS was a Trojan hero and the son of Anchises and *VENUS*, the Roman goddess of love. He was the favourite of the Romans, who believed that some of their eminent families were descended from the Trojans who fled westwards with him from Asia Minor, after the Greek sack of their city. Upstart Rome was only too aware of its lack of tradition and history in comparison with Greece (there was a notable absence of a glorious past peopled with mythical heroes and gods), so the exploits of Aeneas conveniently provided a means of reasserting national pride. It was not a coincidence that the first Roman emperor, Augustus, took a personal interest in the myth.

During the Trojan War Anchises was unable to fight, having been rendered blind or lame for boasting about his relationship with Venus. But young Aeneas distinguished himself against the Greeks, who feared him second only to *HECTOR*, the Trojan champion. In gratitude *PRIAM* gave Aeneas his daughter Creusa to have as his wife, and a son was born named *ASCANIUS*. Although Venus warned him of the impending fall of Troy, Anchises refused to quit the city until two omens occurred: a small flame rose from the top of Ascanius' head and a meteor fell close by. So, carrying

Anchises on his back, Aeneas managed to escape Troy with his father and his son. Somehow Creusa became separated from the party and disappeared. Later, Aeneas saw her ghost and learned from it that he would found a new Troy in distant Italy.

After sailing through the Aegean Sea, where the small fleet Aeneas commanded stopped at a number of islands, the fleet came to Epirus on the eastern Adriatic coast. From there it made for Sicily, but before reaching the Italian mainland it was diverted to North Africa during a sudden storm sent by the goddess *JUNO*, the Roman equivalent of *HERA*, who harassed Aeneas throughout the voyage. Only the timely help of *NEPTUNE*, the Roman sea god, saved the fleet from shipwreck. At the city of Carthage, the great trading port founded by the Phoenicians (which was located in present-day Tunisia), Venus ensured that Aeneas fell in love with its beautiful queen, the widow *DIDO*. Because of her own flight to Carthage, Dido welcomed the Trojan refugees with great kindness and unlimited hospitality.

Time passed pleasantly for the lovers, as Aeneas and Dido soon

AENEAS gazes in wonder at the decorative temple in Carthage, while Dido, the queen, welcomes him to her exotic kingdom. Around them, pillars, doors and beams are made of bronze, while the fabulous walls are decorated with the famous tale of Aeneas and the Trojans.
(*ILLUSTRATION BY NICK BEALE, 1995.*)

became, and it seemed as if Italy and the new state to be founded on its shores were both forgotten. But watchful *JUPITER*, the chief Roman god, dispatched *MERCURY* with a message to Aeneas, recalling him to his duty and commanding him to resume the voyage. Horrified by his intention to leave, Dido bitterly reproached Aeneas, but his deep sense of piety gave him strength enough to launch the fleet again. Then the weeping queen mounted a pyre which she had ordered to be prepared and, having run herself through with a sword, was consumed by the flames.

When the Trojans finally landed in Italy, near the city of Cumae, Aeneas went to consult the *SIBYL*, who was a renowned prophetess. She took him on a visit to the

AENEAS and his comrades battle with a flock of raging harpies who hover above them in the sky, waiting to carry off the weak and wounded. Beside Aeneas shelter his family: his blind father Anchises, his wife Creusa and their two sons. (AENEAS AND HIS COMPANIONS FIGHT THE HARPIES BY FRANCOIS PERRIER, CANVAS, 1646-47.)

AGAMEMNON watches coolly as his daughter, Iphigenia, is offered as a "sacrificial lamb" to appease the anger of Artemis; but at the last moment, the goddess herself relented and, descending from heaven, she carried Iphigenia off to Taurus. (THE SACRIFICE OF IPHIGENIA BY GIOVANNI BATTISTA, TEMPERA, 1770.)

underworld. There Aeneas met his father's ghost, who showed him the destiny of Rome. Anchises had died of old age during the stay in Sicily, but his enthusiastic outline of the future encouraged his son. Aeneas also saw Dido's ghost, but it did not speak to him and hurriedly turned away.

Afterwards, Aeneas steered for the mouth of the River Tiber, on whose river banks the city of Rome would be built centuries later. Conflict with the Latins, the local inhabitants, was bloody and prolonged. But peace was made when Aeneas married Lavinia, the daughter of King Latinus. It had been foretold that for the sake of the kingdom Lavinia must marry a man from abroad. The Trojans, in order to appease Juno, adopted the Latins' traditions and language. (See also *VOYAGERS*)

AGAMEMNON, according to Greek mythology, was the son of *ATREUS* and the brother of *MENELAUS*, king of Sparta. He was married to *CLYTEMNESTRA*. From his citadel at Mycenae, or nearby Argos, he sent out a summons to the Greeks to join the expedition against Troy. The cause of the war was the flight of Menelaus' wife, *HELEN*, to that city with *PARIS*.

However, the Greek fleet was delayed at Aulis by contrary winds. Agamemnon then realized that he would have to make a human sacrifice in order to appease *ARTEMIS*, the goddess of the forest and wild animals. His daughter *IPHIGENIA* was therefore sent to Aulis under the pretext that she was to be married to the Greek champion and hero *ACHILLES*. According to one tradition, Iphigenia was sacrificed, but according to another, she was saved by Artemis herself and taken to Taurus to become a priestess in the goddess's temple.

Clytemnestra never forgave Agamemnon for Iphigenia's loss, and she took Aegisthus for a lover during the ten-year siege of Troy. Aegisthus was the son of Thyestes, the brother and enemy of Atreus,

Agamemnon's father. On her husband's return, Clytemnestra at first pretended how pleased she was to see him. Thanking the gods for his safe return, Agamemnon crossed the threshold of his palace, ignoring the warning of his slave *CASSANDRA*, the prophetic daughter of *PRIAM*, the defeated Trojan king. He then retired to a bathroom in order to change his clothes. Clytemnestra quickly threw a large net over Agamemnon and twisted

AJAX heads off the Trojan onslaught with typical might and courage. Beside him, his brother, Teucer the archer, aims his bow at the Trojans who, with flaming torches, hope to set the Greek ships alight. (ILLUSTRATION FROM STORIES FROM HOMER, 1885.)

it around his body, rendering him an easy target for Aegisthus' axe.

AJAX was the son of Telamon of Salamis and, like *ACHILLES*, was a powerful aid to the Greeks in their assault on Troy. After Achilles' death there was a contest for the armour of this great warrior, which had been forged by the smith god *HEPHAISTOS*. When *ODYSSEUS* was awarded the armour, Ajax became mad with jealousy. He planned a night attack on his comrades, but the goddess *ATHENA* deceived him into slaughtering a flock of sheep instead. In the light of dawn, Ajax was suddenly overwhelmed by a fear of his evil intentions, and fell on his sword and died.

ALCESTIS, according to Greek mythology, was the daughter of King Pelias of Thessaly. When she was of an age to marry, many suitors appeared and her father set a test to discover who would be the most suitable husband. Alcestis was to be the wife of the first man to yoke a lion and a boar (or, in some versions, a bear) to a chariot. With the aid of *APOLLO*, the god of prophecy, a neighbouring monarch named Admetus succeeded in this seemingly impossible task. But at the wedding he forgot to make the necessary sacrifice in gratitude to *ARTEMIS*, the goddess of the forest and wild animals, and so found his wedding bed full of snakes. Once again Apollo came to the king's assistance and, by making the *FATES* drunk, extracted from them a promise that if anyone else would die on Admetus' behalf, he might continue to live. As no one would volunteer, Alcestis gave her life for him. *PERSEPHONE*, the underworld goddess, was so impressed by this complete devotion that she restored Alcestis to Admetus, and they had two sons who later took part in the Greek expedition against the city of Troy.

ALCESTIS (below) welcomes her suitor, Admetus, who arrives in a chariot drawn by lions and bears, while Alcestis' father, Pelias, looks on in disbelief. Admetus was the only hero to yoke the beasts, so winning the hand of Alcestis. (ILLUSTRATION FROM STORIES FROM GREECE AND ROME, 1920.)

ALCMENE was the daughter of Electryon, son of *PERSEUS*, and the mother of *HERACLES*. She married Amphitryon, king of Tiryns, near Mycenae in the Peloponnese. Alcmene refused to consummate her marriage to Amphitryon until he had avenged the murder of her brothers. This the king did, but when he returned he was amazed to learn from Alcmene that she believed she had already slept with him. Amphitryon was enraged until

ALCMENE (right) was one of the sky god Zeus' many lovers, but was punished for her infidelity by her angry husband, Amphitryon, who here is portrayed setting alight a pyre beneath her. She was saved by a heavenly downpour sent by Zeus. (ILLUSTRATION BY NICK BEALE, 1995.)

the seer *TIRESIAS* explained that *ZEUS* had come to Alcmene disguised as her husband in order to father a mortal who would aid the gods in their forthcoming battle against the *GIANTS*.

So Alcmene became pregnant with twins: Heracles, the son of Zeus, and Iphicles, the son of Amphitryon. Zeus could not hide his satisfaction from his wife *HERA* who realized what had happened. She sent the goddess of childbirth,

Eileithyia, to frustrate the delivery, but a trick saved Alcmene and her two sons. Hera then put snakes into Heracles' cradle, but the infant hero strangled them.

Zeus never let Hera fatally injure Heracles, and always protected Alcmene. Once Amphitryon tried to burn her for infidelity, but was stopped by a sudden downpour. When Alcmene died naturally of old age, Zeus sent *HERMES* to bring her body to the Elysian Fields.

THE AMAZONS (opposite), *fierce and independent maiden warriors, fought with passion and skill. In early images, they appear in exotic Scythian leotards, bearing half-moon shields, but in later Greek art, they wore Dorian chitons, with one shoulder bare, as seen here.* (THE BATTLE OF THE AMAZONS BY PETER PAUL RUBENS, WOOD, 1600.)

THE AMAZONS were a tribe of female warriors, supposedly descended from *ARES*, the Greek war god, and the *NAIAD* Harmonia. Their home was situated beyond the Black Sea. It is thought that their name refers to their breastless condition, for Amazons voluntarily removed their right breasts in order that they might more easily draw a bow. The ancient Greeks believed these fierce warriors periodically mated with the men from another tribe, afterwards rearing their female children but discarding or maiming all the males.

During the Trojan War they fought against the Greeks. Although he killed the Amazon queen Penthesilea, *ACHILLES* never succeeded in shaking off the rumour that he had been in love with her. He even slew a comrade who mentioned it. Fascination with Amazon power affected other heroes besides Achilles. The adventures of both *HERACLES* and *THESEUS* involved battles with Amazons. One of Heracles' famous labours was the seizure of a girdle belonging to the Amazon queen Hippolyta, a theft that required considerable nerve.

AMULIUS, in Roman mythology, was a descendant of the Trojan hero *AENEAS*. He usurped the throne of Alba Longa from his younger brother Numitor and forced Numitor's daughter *RHEA SILVIA* to become a Vestal Virgin so as to deny her father an heir. When Rhea Silvia was raped by the war god *MARS*, Amulius imprisoned her and ordered that her twin sons, *REMUS AND ROMULUS*, be drowned in the Tiber. But the two boys escaped a watery death and grew up in the countryside. Once they realized their parentage, Romulus and Remus returned to Alba Longa and killed their uncle Amulius.

ANDROMACHE, the daughter of Eetion, a king of Mysia in Asia Minor, was the wife of *HECTOR*, the foremost Trojan warrior. Her entire family – parents, brothers, husband and son – was killed during the Trojan War. After the sack of Troy, Andromache was taken off into captivity by Neoptolemus, the son of the great Greek hero *ACHILLES*. Neoptolemus had shown the same violent and tempestuous temper as his father when he ruthlessly killed the Trojan king, *PRIAM*, at the altar of *ZEUS'* temple. Andromache bore Neoptolemus three sons, and in consequence suffered the hatred of his barren Greek wife. When Neoptolemus died, Andromache went on to marry Helenus who, like her, was a Trojan captive. Her final years were spent in Asia Minor at Pergamum, which was a new city founded by one of her sons.

ANDROMACHE, Hector's young wife, bows her head in captivity. One of the noblest but most ill-starred of heroines, she sees her husband, father and seven brothers killed by Achilles, and her son hurled from the city walls; while she falls as a prize of war to Achilles' son. (CAPTIVE ANDROMACHE BY LORD LEIGHTON, CANVAS, C. 1890.)

AMULIUS (left) *casts out his nephews, Romulus and Remus, the twin sons of Rhea Silvia and the war god Mars, ordering that they be drowned in the river Tiber. But they are eventually found by a she-wolf who suckles them until a shepherd, Faustulus, takes them home.* (ILLUSTRATION FROM STORIES FROM LIVY, 1885.)

ANTIGONE (above) *sprinkles earth on the body of her brother, Polynices, as a symbolic act of burial. For the Greeks, burial was a sacred duty, without which a soul could not rest; yet Creon, her uncle, had denied Polynices a burial, violating divine law.* (ILLUSTRATION BY NICK BEALE, 1995.)

ANDROMEDA (left), *chained to a rock as a sacrifice to a sea monster, can only pray, while high overhead, the hero Perseus is on his way. Swooping down on the winged horse, Pegasus, he cuts Andromeda free and slays the monster.* (PERSEUS RELEASES ANDROMEDA BY JOACHIM WIEWAEL, CANVAS, 1630.)

in an uprising against the new ruler *CREON*, and his body was condemned to rot unburied outside the city. Antigone refused to accept this impiety and sprinkled earth over the corpse as a token burial. For this she was walled up in a cave, where she hanged herself like her mother Jocasta. There are a number of different versions of the myth, but they all cast Antigone as the heroic victim of a family wrecked by a terrible deed.

ANTIOPE see *LOVERS OF ZEUS*

APHRODITE was the Greek goddess of love, beauty and fertility. Unlike her Roman counterpart *VENUS*, with whom she was identified, Aphrodite was not only a goddess of sexual love but also of the affection that sustains social life. The meaning of her name is uncertain, although the ancient Greeks came to believe it referred to foam. Quite possibly this belief arose from the story of Aphrodite's

ANDROMEDA was the daughter of Cassiope and Cepheus, king of the Ethiopians. When Cassiope boasted that Andromeda was more beautiful than the Nereids, the sea nymphs, they complained to the sea god *POSEIDON*. He avenged this insult by flooding the land and sending a sea monster to devastate Cepheus' kingdom. To avoid complete disaster it was decided to sacrifice Andromeda to the beast and she was chained to a rock at the foot of a cliff. There *PERSEUS* saw her as he flew past on winged sandals carrying the head of the Gorgon Medusa. He fell in love with Andromeda, and obtained both her and her father's consent to marriage if he defeated the monster. This Perseus did by using Medusa's head, the sight of which turned all living things to stone. After some time, Perseus and Andromeda settled in Tiryns, which Perseus ruled. The constellation of Andromeda lies close to that of Pegasus, and both Cepheus and Cassiope were also commemorated in the stars.

ANTIGONE was the daughter of *OEDIPUS*, king of Thebes, and his wife and mother Jocasta. On learning of their unwitting incest, Oedipus tore out his eyes while Jocasta hanged herself. The penitent Oedipus was then guided by Antigone in his wanderings round Greece. She was with him at the sanctuary of Colonus, near Athens, when her distraught father gained some kind of peace just before his death. She returned to Thebes, but her troubles were not over. Her brother Polynices had been killed

APHRODITE, goddess of love and beauty, was born from the foam of the sea; she rose from the waves on a seashell, stepping ashore on Cyprus. At her side, the west wind, Zephyrus, and Flora, the spring, blow her gently ashore in a shower of roses, her sacred flower. (THE BIRTH OF VENUS BY SANDRO BOTTICELLI, TEMPERA, C. 1482.)

birth. When the Titan *CRONOS* cut off the penis of his father Ouranos with a sharp sickle, he cast the immortal member into the sea, where it floated amid white foam. Inside the penis Aphrodite grew and was then washed up at Paphos on Cyprus. There were in fact sanctuaries dedicated to her on many islands, which suggests that she was a West Asian goddess who was brought to Greece by sea-traders.

Once she arrived, the ancient Greeks married her in their mythology to the crippled smith god *HEPHAISTOS*. But Aphrodite was not content to be a faithful wife and she bore children by several other gods, including *DIONYSUS* and *ARES*. When Hephaistos found out about Aphrodite's passion for the war god Ares, the outraged smith god made a mesh of gold and caught the lovers in bed together. He called the other gods from Mount Olympus to see the pair, but they only laughed at his shame, and *POSEIDON*, the god of the sea, persuaded Hephaistos to release Aphrodite and Ares.

Perhaps Aphrodite's greatest love was for the handsome youth Adonis, another West Asian deity. Killed by a wild boar, Adonis became the object of admiration for both Aphrodite and *PERSEPHONE*,

queen of the dead. Their bitter quarrel was only ended by *ZEUS*, who ruled that for a third of the year Adonis was to dwell with himself, for a third part with Persephone, and for a third part with Aphrodite. So it was that the ancient Greeks accommodated a West Asian mother goddess and her dying-and-rising husband. Indeed the Adonia, or annual festivals commemorating Adonis' death, were celebrated in many parts of the eastern Mediterranean.

Because of her unruly behaviour, Zeus caused Aphrodite to fall in love with Anchises, the father of *AENEAS*. In the Roman version of this myth Venus herself is deeply attracted to the Trojan, but warns him to keep the parentage of their son Aeneas a secret. This Anchises fails to do, and as a result suffers blindness or a disability of the limbs. While the Roman goddess provided, through the leadership of Aeneas, a means for some of the Trojans to escape and flourish anew in Italy, the Greek Aphrodite actually helped to cause the Trojan War. In order to ensure that he would name her as the most beautiful of the goddesses, Aphrodite promised *PARIS*, son of *PRIAM* the king of Troy, the hand of the most beautiful woman in the world. This fatefully turned out to be *HELEN*, wife of *MENELAUS*, king of Sparta.

APOLLO was the son of *ZEUS* and the Titaness *LETO*, and the twin brother of the goddess *ARTEMIS*, the virgin huntress. He was one of the most important deities of both the Greek and

Roman religions, and was the god of prophecy, archery and music. The origin of his name is uncertain but it is probably non-European.

A fight with the gigantic earth-serpent Python at Delphi gave Apollo the seat of his famous oracle. Python was an offspring of *GAIA*, mother earth, which issued revelations through a fissure in the rock so that a priestess, the Pythia, could give answers to any questions that might be asked. After he slew the earth-serpent, Apollo took its place, though he had to do penance in Thessaly for the killing. Indeed, Zeus twice forced Apollo to be the slave of a mortal man to pay for his crime.

Apollo's interest in healing suggests an ancient association with the plague and its control. His son *ASCLEPIUS* was also identified with healing and connected with sites in northern Greece. Indeed, so accomplished was Asclepius in medicine that Zeus slew him with a thunderbolt for daring to bring a man back to life. (See also *FORCES OF NATURE*)

ARES, the son of *ZEUS* and *HERA*, was the Greek god of war, and was later identified with the Roman war god *MARS*. Although Ares had no wife of his own, he had three children by *APHRODITE*, the goddess of love. The twins, Phobos, "panic", and Deimos, "fear", always accompanied him on the battlefield. In Greek mythology, Ares is depicted as an instigator of violence, a tempestuous and passionate lover and an unscrupulous friend. The Roman god Mars, however, has nothing of Ares' fickleness.

APOLLO (above), the sun god, urges the sun-chariot to rise in the sky. This unusual version of the myth has Apollo, rather than Helios, as rider, and lions, instead of horses, pull the chariot, recalling the link between Leo and the sun. (PHOEBUS APOLLO BY BRITON RIVIERE, CANVAS, C. 1870.)

ARES (below), in full armour, leads the gods into battle. However, in war, the gods were not impartial; Ares, Aphrodite (left), Poseidon and Apollo (centre) would often aid the Trojans, while Hera and Athena (right) supported the Greeks. (ILLUSTRATION FROM STORIES FROM HOMER, 1885.)

LOVERS OF ZEUS

A STRIKING ASPECT OF GREEK MYTHOLOGY is the marital conflict between the two chief deities, Hera, an earth goddess, and her husband, Zeus, supreme power on Olympus. One of the most amorous gods in mythology, Zeus loved countless women and he courted them in as many forms, sometimes as a bull, as a satyr, as a swan, sometimes as a mortal man, and even in the form of a golden shower. Hera was notoriously jealous and vengeful, pursuing without mercy his lovers and their offspring. The antagonism between the two could be viewed as a clash between different religious traditions or local cults, each cult recognizing a different lover who was often regarded as the ancestor of a ruling family.

*ANTIOPE (above), daughter of a river god, was loved by Zeus in the form of a satyr, a goat-like creature. She bore him twin sons, Amphion and Zethus. Here, Zeus, disguised as a youthful satyr, gently shades Antiope from the sun while she sleeps beside Eros, sweet god of love. (*ANTIOPE SHADED BY ZEUS DISGUISED AS A SATYR *BY* ANTONIO CORREGGIO, *CANVAS, 1523-25.)*

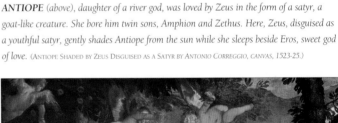

*CALLISTO (above), forest nymph and companion of Artemis in the chase, was loved by Zeus and bore him a son, Arcas. She was then changed into a bear either by Zeus, wishing to hide her from Hera, or by Hera herself. As a bear she was shot by Artemis in the forest and was placed among the stars as the She-Bear. Here, surrounded by the trophies of the chase, Artemis and her nymphs comfort Callisto possibly after her encounter with the overwhelming god, Zeus. (*DIANA AND CALLISTO *BY* PETER PAUL RUBENS, *CANVAS, 1636-40.)*

*EUROPA (right) was wooed by Zeus in the shape of a beautiful bull who emerged from the waves and carried her over the sea to Crete where she bore him three sons. The various stages of the drama are represented here: on the left, Europa mounts the bull encouraged by its tameness. On the right, she is borne sedately down to the sea, with many little Erotes (love spirits) hovering in the sky. Finally she floats happily away, waving to her maidens. (*THE RAPE OF EUROPA *BY* PAOLO VERONESE, *CANVAS, 1580.)*

DIONYSUS (above), Zeus' child by Semele, appears here hugging his mother, while Apollo stands by with a bay tree. Once he became a god, Dionysus raised his mother to heaven and placed her among the stars as Thyone. This Etruscan mirror is bordered with ivy, which was Dionysus' sacred plant. (ILLUSTRATION FROM DR SMITH'S CLASSICAL DICTIONARY, 1895.)

DANAE (below) was confined in a brazen tower by her father who feared an oracle predicting that he would be killed by a grandson. In her tower she was visited by Zeus in the form of a golden shower, and bore him a son, Perseus. When her father discovered the baby, he cast both of them out to sea in a wooden chest, but they floated ashore on the Isle of Seriphos where they were rescued by Dictys. (ILLUSTRATION BY GEORGE SOPER FROM TANGLEWOOD TALES, C. 1920.)

SEMELE (left), encouraged by Hera, persuaded Zeus to show himself in all his splendour. When he appeared before her as the radiant god of thunder and lightning, Semele was consumed by the flames and, dying, gave birth prematurely to Dionysus, whom Zeus saved from the fire. In this powerful Symbolist version of the myth, the great god radiates fiery, blood-red lightning. A winged child hiding from the light could be Dionysus, while the dark, horned god seems to be a fusion of Hades and Pan. (JUPITER AND SEMELE, BY GUSTAVE MOREAU, CANVAS, 1896.)

THE ARGONAUTS were very early explorers, most likely the first Greek voyagers to the Black Sea. They sailed from Thessaly, where their leader, *JASON*, was the rightful king of Iolcus. According to the myth, Jason's father, Aeson, was deposed by his half-brother Pelias, who was warned at the time how he would in turn be overthrown by a man wearing only one sandal. In order to protect Jason from Pelias, Aeson had secretly sent his son to *CHIRON* to educate the young man, like many other heroes. On reaching manhood, Jason determined to return to Iolcus and reclaim the throne. During the journey, however, he was tested by the goddess *HERA*, who was disguised as an old woman. She begged him to carry her safely across a swollen river,

THE ARGONAUTS (top) commissioned Argus to build the Argo, a ship with twenty oars. Here he carves out the stern, while Athena makes sails. Behind her, perched on a pillar, her sacred creature, the owl, symbolizes her wisdom. (ILLUSTRATION FROM DICTIONARY OF CLASSICAL ANTIQUITIES, 1891.)

JASON (above left), helps Hera, disguised as an old woman, across the stream. In the current he loses a sandal, fulfilling part of an oracle that a half-shod man would take Pelias' throne. The peacock beside Hera denotes her all-seeing vision. (ILLUSTRATION FROM TANGLEWOOD TALES, C. 1920.)

JASON (above), with Medea's help – she anoints him with a salve to protect him from fire and steel – ploughs the fields with the bulls of Aietes. He was the first hero to yoke the wild and fiery creatures. (ILLUSTRATION FROM TANGLEWOOD TALES, C. 1920.)

which Jason did at the cost of one of his sandals. Thus the prophecy was fulfilled: a man wearing only one sandal arrived at Iolcus to challenge Pelias. Because Jason made his intentions known at the time of a religious festival, Pelias could not kill his nephew without the risk of suffering divine disfavour. So the king told Jason that he could have the throne provided he obtained the Golden Fleece, which was an apparently impossible task. This miraculous fleece belonged to a ram which had flown to Colchis, a distant land identified with modern Georgia. It hung from a tree there, guarded by an enormous snake that never slept.

The *DELPHIC ORACLE* encouraged Jason to undertake the quest. Hera inspired a group of Thessalian

ARIADNE (above) hands the vital skein to Theseus, which allows him to track his way through the Labyrinth. After killing the bull-like beast, the Minotaur, in the Labyrinth, he sailed away with her, but then deserted her on Dia, possibly believing that she was destined to marry a god. (ILLUSTRATION FROM TANGLEWOOD TALES, C. 1920.)

warriors to join his expedition and they became known as the Argonauts, the crew of the ship *Argo*. Among their number were Castor and Polydeuces, *ORPHEUS* the poet, Calais and Zetes the sons of *BOREAS* and the hero *HERACLES*. Together they crossed a sea of marvels, visited strange lands and overcame many obstacles before reaching Colchis, where Hera used the goddess of love *APHRODITE* to make *MEDEA*, the second daughter

of King Aietes, fall in love with Jason. The king hated Greeks but he kept his feelings hidden from the Argonauts. He even consented to Jason's attempt to capture the Golden Fleece. But first Aietes set Jason a challenge that was intended to result in his death. The hero was required to yoke a team of fire-breathing bulls, plough and sow a field with dragon's teeth, and slay the armed men who would at once rise from the ground.

With the assistance of Medea's skills in the magic arts, Jason accomplished Aietes' task within a single day. But the king of Colchis was not prepared to give up the Golden Fleece so easily. He secretly planned to attack the Argonauts, who were warned by Medea, now Jason's lover. She employed her magic once again to deal with the unsleeping snake, and Jason seized the Golden Fleece. The Argonauts quickly rowed away from Colchis with the fleece and Medea, whom Jason had promised to marry once back in Thessaly.

The Colchian princess seems to have been associated with the rites of dismemberment as well as magic, for during the pursuit of the Argonauts across the Black Sea, Medea slowed the fleet of her father Aietes by killing and cutting up her own brother, Apsyrtus. Pieces of Apsyrtus' body were thrown over-board, forcing the Colchians to gather up the remains for a decent burial. Later, in Thessaly, Medea also persuaded the daughters of King Pelias to cut their father to pieces and boil him, so as to restore his youth. This they did, and in killing him avenged the disgrace of Jason's father Aeson.

Jason and Medea led an unsettled life in Greece. After a few years he deserted her for another woman, but Medea killed this rival and her own children by Jason. Jason died in Corinth as a result of a rotten piece of the *Argo* falling on his head. Afterwards the gods raised the ship to the sky and made it into a constellation. The Golden Fleece also appears in the heavens as the first constellation of the Zodiac, Aries the ram.

ARIADNE, in Greek mythology, was the daughter of *PASIPHAE* and King *MINOS*, the ruler of Knossos on the island of Crete. When the Athenian hero *THESEUS* came to Knossos to pay the annual tribute of seven young men and seven girls, Ariadne gave him a sword and a skein of thread that allowed him to escape from Daedalus' Labyrinth after a bloody struggle with the dreaded bull-headed man, the *MINOTAUR*. Theseus and Ariadne then fled from Crete, but for some unknown reason the hero abandoned the princess on the nearby island of Dia. The deserted princess may then have become the wife of *DIONYSUS*, the god of ecstasy and wine. Local legend would suggest such a connection, although the whole story of the Minotaur was probably no more than a garbled version of far older tales of the sport of bull-leaping, which dated from the pre-Greek era of Cretan history. Dionysus himself was known to the Greeks as "the roaring one", a "bull-horned god" who was full of power and fertility.

ARION see *VOYAGERS*

ARTEMIS was the daughter of the Titaness *LETO* and *ZEUS*, and the twin sister of *APOLLO*. She was in all likelihood a very ancient deity whom the Greeks adopted as goddess of the wild. Traces of human sacrifice could still be found in her worship. Most of all, Artemis liked to roam the mountains with a companion band of nymphs. Certainly the virgin goddess resented any kind of intrusion into her domain, or any harm done to her favourite animals. For killing a stag sacred to Artemis, the leader of the Greek expedition against Troy, King *AGAMEMNON* of Mycenae, found his fleet stranded by contrary winds

ARTEMIS, virgin goddess of the wild, always resisted the love or attentions of men. When the hunter Actaeon saw her in the nude, bathing with her nymphs, she indignantly turned him into a stag, which was set upon by his own hounds. (DIANA AND ACTAEON BY TITIAN, CANVAS, 1556-59.)

at Aulis. Only a promise to sacrifice his daughter *IPHIGENIA* was enough to appease the goddess, although there are differing accounts as to whether the girl was actually killed.

Another mortal punished by Artemis was *ACTAEON*. He had the misfortune while hunting to come upon the goddess as she was bathing. She changed him into a stag and he was chased and torn apart by his own hunting dogs. However, according to a different version, Actaeon actually tried to approach the naked goddess hidden beneath a stag's pelt.

To the Romans, Artemis was closely identified with their goddess Diana, who was also a goddess of light as well as of the wild.

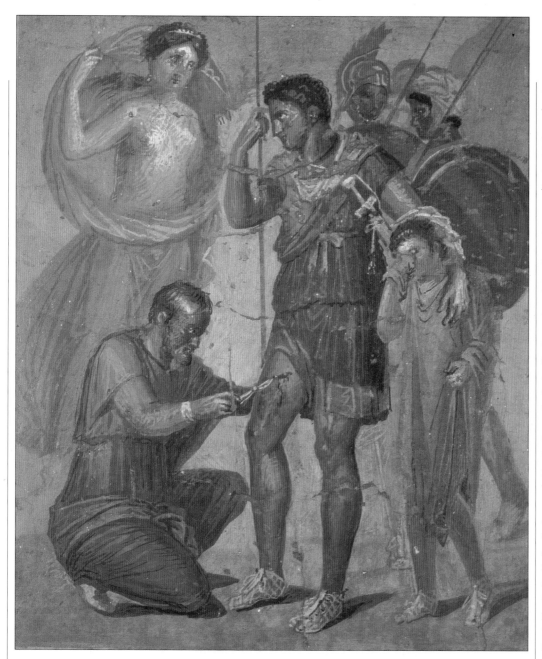

ASCANIUS was the son of *AENEAS* and Creusa. According to the Romans, he founded the city of Alba Longa thirty-three years after the arrival of the Trojan refugees in Italy. An alternative tradition makes Ascanius' mother Lavinia, a Latin princess whose marriage to Aeneas brought peace and unity to the Latin and Trojan peoples. It was in her honour that Aeneas founded Lavinium within three years of landing. This would mean that Ascanius was king of Lavinium following Aeneas' death, and before he left to take up residence in a new city at Alba Longa. Early rivalry between the two cities probably explains the removal myth.

The family of Julius Caesar, the Julii, claimed descent from Aeneas through Ascanius, who was also called Iulus Ilus ("made of Ilium"), Ilium being the old name for Troy.

ASCLEPIUS, the Greek god of healing, was the son of *APOLLO*, god of prophecy, and the lake nymph Coronis. In mythology he is a somewhat shadowy figure, which suggests his late arrival as a major deity. Asclepius would seem to have been a Thessalian healer whose skills became known throughout Greece: his cult eventually took over the sanctuary at Epidauros in the Peloponnese. Sacred snakes resident there were believed to embody the god's healing power. The ancient association between snakes and medicine is probably due to the snake's apparent ability to renew its youth each year by sloughing off its own skin.

Only the stories of Asclepius' birth and death were ever well known to the Greeks and Romans. When Coronis dared to take in secret a mortal as a second lover, an enraged Apollo sent his sister *ARTEMIS* to kill the lake nymph with a disease. However, as the flames of the funeral pyre burned Coronis, Apollo felt sorry for his unborn son and removed him from the corpse. Thus was Asclepius born. He was taught medicine by the Centaur *CHIRON*, whose knowledge was so great that *ZEUS* himself feared that Asclepius might learn a way of overcoming death. When he did succeed in resurrecting one of his patients, Zeus decided that Asclepius should be punished for threatening the gods' monopoly over immortality. Asclepius was slain by a thunder-bolt, but at Apollo's request the god of medicine was placed among the stars, as Ophiuchus, the serpent-bearer.

So impressed were the Romans with Asclepius' cult that during a time of plague they requested aid from Epidauros and a sacred snake was duly shipped to Rome.

ATALANTA, in Greek mythology, was the daughter of Iasus of Arcadia and was known as a famous huntress. As an unwanted daughter she was exposed and left to die on a mountainside, but was suckled by a bear and later brought up by hunters. This experience may have inclined her to manly pursuits. She even tried to enlist with the *ARGONAUTS*, but *JASON* refused her because the presence of one woman on the ship might cause jealousies amongst them.

Atalanta's most famous myth concerns the lengths to which she went to avoid marriage. She said that her husband must first beat her in a race and any man who lost would be put to death. Despite the awful consequence of losing, there were many who admired Atalanta's beauty and paid the price against her speed. None could catch her, although they ran naked while she was fully clothed. Finally, the love goddess *APHRODITE* took pity on a young man named Melanion and provided him with a way to delay

ASCLEPIUS, Greek god of healing, tends a man on his sickbed. A son of Apollo, the greatest healer, Asclepius was gifted with miraculous powers, once resurrecting a mortal from death. His attributes, staff and serpent, signify power and renewal of life. (ILLUSTRATION BY NICK BEALE, 1995.)

Atalanta. She gave him three golden apples, which he placed at different points on the course. Curiosity got the better of Atalanta, who stopped three times to pick up the apples. So Melanion won the race and Atalanta as a wife. But in his haste to make love to her, Melanion either forgot a vow to Aphrodite or consummated their union in a sacred place. To pay for the sacrilege both he and Atalanta were turned into lions.

ATALANTA, the gifted huntress and unusually athletic heroine, found her match in the equally resourceful and energetic Melanion. Here the heroic pair hunt and slay the monstrous wild boar which has been ravaging the plains of Calydon. (ILLUSTRATION FROM TANGLEWOOD TALES, C. 1920.)

ATHENA, sometimes Athene, the daughter of ZEUS and the Titaness Metis, was the Greek goddess of war and crafts. Although a fierce virgin like ARTEMIS, she did not shun men but on the contrary delighted in being a city-goddess, most notably at Athens. This city adopted her cult when an olive tree grew on its acropolis: the other divine rival for worship was the god POSEIDON, who produced only a spring of brackish water. Athena sprang into being fully grown and armed from the head of her father Zeus, after he had swallowed the pregnant Metis. The smith god HEPHAISTOS assisted the birth with a blow from his axe. Quite likely this intervention accounts for her title of Hephaistia, the companion of the smith god. Athena's symbol was the wise owl, which featured on Athenian coins. The Romans identified her with MINERVA, a goddess of wisdom and the arts.

An early myth relates how Hephaistos tried to rape Athena. To avoid losing her virginity, she miraculously disappeared so that the semen of the smith god fell to the ground, where it grew into the serpent Erichthonius. The three daughters of Cecrops, the semi-serpent who first ruled Athens, were given a box by Athena and told not to look inside it. Ignoring this command, two of them looked inside, found themselves gazing upon Erichthonius, and went insane. However, Athena continued to protect Athens. Although the city fell into enemy hands during the Persian invasion of Greece in 480–479 BC, the Athenians later went on to achieve mastery of the sea and found their own empire. It was during this period that the Parthenon was built on the Athenian acropolis.

Athena was always regarded by the Greeks as an active goddess, involved in the affairs of men. She helped several heroes such as BELLEROPHON, JASON, HERACLES and PERSEUS. Also, it was she who eventually got ODYSSEUS back to the island of Ithaca, following his epic voyage home from the Trojan War. Perhaps Athena's most significant aid was given to the matricide ORESTES. Not only did she offer him protection, but she also arranged for him to be tried and acquitted of his terrible crime by the ancient court of the Areopagus, in Athens. The verdict meant an end to the blood-feud, not least because for the first time even the FURIES accepted Orestes' deliverance from guilt.

ATLAS was a TITAN, the son of Iapetus and the Oceanid Clymene. He was thought by the ancient Greeks to hold up the sky, and his name means "he who carries". His most famous encounter was with the hero HERACLES, one of whose labours was to obtain the golden apples of the HESPERIDES, female guardians of the fruit that mother earth, GAIA, presented to HERA at her marriage to ZEUS. Atlas offered to fetch them for Heracles if the

ATHENA, goddess of wisdom and crafts, guided and helped her favourites. Here she visits the hero Bellerophon with a gift – the bridle with which to tame and mount the winged horse, Pegasus. (ILLUSTRATION FROM STORIES FROM GREECE AND ROME, 1930.)

hero took over his job of holding up the sky. When Atlas returned with the apples he suggested that he should deliver them himself, as Heracles was doing so well. The hero pretended to agree and then asked if Atlas would take the world for a moment so that he could adjust the weight on his shoulder, so tricking Atlas into resuming his lonely duty. (See also GIANTS)

ATLAS, the great Titan giant, was condemned to shoulder the heavens forever, as punishment for fighting the sky god Zeus. (ILLUSTRATION FROM DICTIONARY OF CLASSICAL ANTIQUITIES, 1891.)

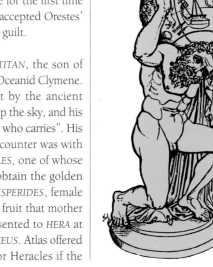

B

ATREUS was the son of *PELOPS*, an early king after whom the Peloponnese in southern Greece is named, and Hippodaemia. The house of Atreus was infamous for the hereditary curse laid upon it by the son of *HERMES*, the messenger god. A terrible cycle of murder and revenge was ended only by the trial in Athens of Atreus' grandson *ORESTES* on a charge of matricide.

Family misfortune stemmed from the action of Pelops, the father of Atreus. He seems either to have brought about the death of Hermes' son Myrtilus, or to have caused him great grief by refusing to make a promised gift. Friction between the sons of Pelops, Atreus, Thyestes and Chrysippus, arose about the ownership of a golden ram, a wondrous animal placed in Atreus' flock by Hermes. First, Chrysippus was murdered by Atreus and Thyestes, then Thyestes seduced Aerope, the wife of Atreus, in order to gain her help in seizing the golden ram. An enraged Atreus slew Aerope and exiled Thyestes.

At a banquet supposedly for reconciliation, Atreus served his brother Thyestes with the flesh of his children. When Thyestes had

ATREUS, son of Pelops, cherished a golden ram, a double-edged gift of the god Hermes. The god gave the coveted treasure to Atreus, hoping to sow strife and discord in the house of Pelops, in revenge for the murder of his son, Myrtilus.
(ILLUSTRATION BY NICK BEALE, 1995.)

BELLEROPHON swoops down for the kill on his winged horse, Pegasus, diving through the smoke and flames of the fire-breathing Chimaera, a monster with the forepart of a lion, the hindpart of a dragon and its middle formed from a goat.
(ILLUSTRATION FROM TANGLEWOOD TALES, C. 1920.)

finished eating, Atreus showed his brother the hands and feet of his dead sons and told him what he had consumed. In horror the sun halted in its course. Thyestes' only surviving son, Aegisthus, may have slain Atreus in revenge for this outrage. Certainly he became the lover of *CLYTEMNESTRA*, whose husband *AGAMEMNON* was the eldest son of Atreus and his successor as king of Mycenae, or Argos. Not until Clytemnestra and Aegisthus had murdered Agamemnon, and were themselves killed by Agamemnon's son *ORESTES*, did the curse of Myrtilus come to an end.

BELLEROPHON was a Greek hero from the city of Corinth and the son of Glaucus. He possessed a wonderful winged horse named *PEGASUS*, which had sprung out of the *GORGON* Medusa's blood when she was beheaded by *PERSEUS*. The goddess *ATHENA* gave Bellerophon a special bridle in order to help him tame Pegasus.

Bellerophon's problems began, as his own name indicates, with a murder. He evidently killed an important Corinthian because in exile he changed his name from Hipponous to Bellerophon ("killer of Bellerus"). Although he was given refuge in Argos by King Proteus, the passion of the local queen Sthenoboea for him caused further difficulties, and not least because he steadfastly rejected her advances. Sthenoboea accused him of attempted rape and the enraged

BOREAS, one of the four winds, blew from the north, whistling through his conch. He often helped sailors with a friendly breeze. Along with his brother winds, Eurus, Zephyrus and Notus, he was depicted in the Temple of Winds. (ILLUSTRATION FROM DR SMITH'S CLASSICAL DICTIONARY, 1895.)

Proteus dispatched Bellerophon to southern Asia Minor, where he was supposed to meet his end, but service in the local king's forces saved his life. Mounted on Pegasus, the hero was able to overcome the monstrous Chimaera, defeat neighbouring peoples, including the Amazons, and even become the champion of Lycia. A constellation was named after his fabulous winged horse.

Two tales cast a certain shadow over Bellerophon's character. In the first he is credited with a brutal revenge on the false Argive queen. By pretending that he really loved her, Bellerophon persuaded the queen to elope with him on Pegasus, only to push her off the winged horse's back in mid-air. The second tale almost ends in the hero's death when he attempted to fly to Mount Olympus, the home of the gods. *ZEUS* in anger caused Pegasus to unseat Bellerophon, who was lamed for life.

BOREAS, the north wind, was the son of *EOS*, the goddess of dawn, and the Titan Astraeus. His home was thought to be Thrace, which is situated to the north of the Aegean Sea. In contrast to Zephyrus, the

gentle west wind, Boreas was capable of great destruction. During the Persian invasion of Greece, he helped the Greek cause by damaging the Persian fleet at the battle of Artemisium in 480 BC.

Boreas abducted Orithyia, a daughter of King Erechtheus of Attica. Coming across Orithyia dancing near a stream, he then wrapped her up in a cloud and carried her off to Thrace. She bore Boreas twin sons, Calais and Zetes, who were known as the Boreades. At birth these boys were entirely human in appearance, but later they sprouted golden wings from their shoulders. They were killed by the great hero HERACLES.

Boreas was worshipped in the city of Athens, where an annual festival, known as the Boreasmi, was celebrated in his honour.

BRITOMARTIS fled from King Minos who pursued her for nine months, until at last, in despair, she leapt into the sea. Luckily, she became entangled in some fishing nets, and when Artemis changed her into a goddess she was known as Dictynna, which means "net".
(ILLUSTRATION BY NICK BEALE, 1995.)

BRITOMARTIS ("sweet maid") was said to be the daughter of ZEUS. She lived on the island of Crete, where she spent her time as a huntress. King MINOS of Knossos tried to make Britomartis his mistress. But she fled from him and in her desperation to preserve her virginity threw herself off a cliff into the sea. The king finally gave up the pursuit when the Cretan goddess sought sanctuary in the sacred grove of ARTEMIS, and became her close associate. The myth is almost certainly an account of the amalgamation of two ancient cults.

BRUTUS was said to be the son of Tarquinia, who was the sister of TARQUINIUS SUPERBUS. He was the founder of the Roman Republic. Like most Roman myths, the story of Lucius Junius Brutus lays emphasis on duty to the state, even though in this instance it involved the sacrifice of two sons. During the early part of his life Brutus was regarded as a simpleton, which his name implies. Indeed, he was something of a joke in the court of Tarquinius Superbus, the last Etruscan king to rule Rome. When a snake was found in the king's palace, two princes travelled to Delphi to ask the Oracle to explain this event and Brutus accompanied them almost in the role of a jester. The Oracle told the Romans that the first person in the delegation to kiss his mother would be the next ruler of Rome. The princes drew lots to decide who was to kiss their mother on their return home, but Brutus tripped and kissed the earth, much to their amusement.

BRUTUS, the first consul of the new republic of Rome, condemns his sons to death for rising against the government. Brutus, as his name implies, feigned idiocy but was no fool; wisely and dutifully, he led the trial against his rebel sons.
(ILLUSTRATION FROM STORIES FROM LIVY, 1885.)

Shortly after their return to Rome, the youngest prince raped LUCRETIA, a Roman matron. This act of violation was the last straw for the oppressed Roman aristocracy, especially when it was learned that Lucretia had stabbed herself to death. The outrage was cleverly used by Brutus as a means of overthrowing the monarchy and setting up a republic. The now eloquent Brutus was elected consul, one of the two highest offices of state. But this fulfilment of the Oracle was soon to cause him grief, when a conspiracy to restore Tarquinius Superbus to the throne was found to have the support of Titus and Tiberius, two of Brutus' own sons. As he was the chief magistrate, Brutus, with great dignity, oversaw their arrest, trial and execution. Thus, at the moment of the new Republic's triumph, the typically Roman idea of self-sacrifice appears as part of its foundation myth.

C

CACUS see GIANTS

CADMUS was the son of Agenor, king of Phoenicia, and Telephassa, and the brother of EUROPA. When Europa was forcibly taken to Crete by ZEUS, disguised as a bull, Cadmus and his four brothers were sent after her, with instructions not to return home without her. Although the five Phoenician princes failed in their task, they seem to have had an impact on the places where they eventually settled. Cadmus himself was told by the Oracle at Delphi to forget about Europa and instead find a cow with a moon-shaped mark on its flank. He was to follow the animal and build a city on the spot where it chose to lie down and rest. Having found the cow and followed it eastwards to Boeotia, where at last it sank in exhaustion, Cadmus then sent some of his men for water so that they might sacrifice the animal to ATHENA. But these men were attacked by a serpent sprung from the war god ARES. After Cadmus had killed the monster, the goddess Athena advised him to remove its teeth and sow half of them in the ground. Immediately, armed men arose, but wily Cadmus threw stones among them so that, suspecting each other, they fell upon themselves. It was later believed

CADMUS sows the teeth of a dragon he has slain, and instantly the soil bristles with armed warriors, who spring up to attack each other. Only five survived, to become ancestors of the Thebans, whose city Cadmus founded on the site. (ILLUSTRATION BY NICK BEALE, 1995.)

that the Theban aristocracy was descended from the five warriors who survived the mutual slaughter.

After a period of penance for killing Ares' serpent, Zeus gave Cadmus a wife – none other than Harmonia, the daughter of Ares and APHRODITE, goddess of love. Since he was marrying a goddess, the gods themselves attended the wedding and gave wonderful gifts. The unusual union of mortal and immortal was not blessed by particularly successful offspring, however. One of their descendants, Pentheus, suffered a horrible fate. Having insulted DIONYSUS, he was torn to pieces by the god's female worshippers when he spied on their secret rites. Among the frenzied worshippers was Pentheus' own mother, Agave, the daughter of Cadmus and Harmonia.

The ancient Greeks always acknowledged the importance of Cadmus' reign, hence, his divine wife. He was credited with the introduction from Phoenicia of an alphabet of sixteen letters. There

are in fact a number of ancient accounts of Phoenician activity in the Aegean Sea. For instance, on the island of Cythera, which lies off the southern Peloponnese, a shrine to Aphrodite is known to have been erected based on the goddess's chief temple in Phoenicia.

CALCHAS see ORACLES AND PROPHECIES

CALLISTO see LOVERS OF ZEUS

CASSANDRA was the daughter of PRIAM, king of Troy, and his wife Hecuba. Her beauty was as remarkable as her power of prophecy, which was said to have been a gift from APOLLO, who loved her, but because she refused his advances he condemned her to prophesy the truth but never to be believed.

Cassandra foretold the Trojan War, the true purpose of the Wooden Horse and the murder of

CASSANDRA, frenzied seer, flees through burning Troy, aghast at the sight of her own predictions. Gifted with prophecy, she clearly foresaw the Trojan War and the trickery of the Wooden Horse, but no one believed her for she was fated to be ignored. (ILLUSTRATION BY NICK BEALE, 1995.)

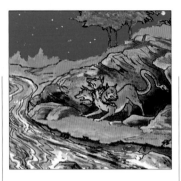

CERBERUS snarls and growls by the mouth of Hades. A three-headed hound with a snake for a tail, he allowed no shades to return from the dead, though a few slipped by with the help of the gods. His dark den opened onto the Styx along which Charon ferried the dead. (ILLUSTRATION BY GLENN STEWARD, 1995.)

AGAMEMNON, to whom she was awarded as part of his share of the spoils. But ultimately Cassandra had her revenge on the Greeks. When Troy fell, she had sought sanctuary in ATHENA's temple but was raped, and so the goddess punished this sacrilege by killing many of the Greeks during their voyage home. However, Cassandra met her own end at the hands of Agamemnon's wife CLYTEMNESTRA. (See also ORACLES AND PROPHECIES)

CECROPS see FOUNDERS

CENTAURS, according to Greek mythology, were said to be the descendants of IXION, son of ARES. These strange creatures had the head, arms and chest of a man but the legs and lower half of a horse. They lived in Thessaly, fed on meat and were given to riotous behaviour. They were usually depicted as drunken followers of DIONYSUS, except for wise CHIRON who was the tutor to several heroes, including ACHILLES. (See also MONSTERS AND FABULOUS BEASTS)

CERBERUS was a three-headed hound, the offspring of two monsters, TYPHON and Echidna. He was the watchdog of the Greek underworld and stopped anyone trying to return to the land of the living. One of HERACLES' labours was to fetch Cerberus, a challenge the god of the dead, HADES, allowed him to

CINCINNATUS was a Roman hero who was instrumental in saving the early Republic. In 458 BC, Rome was in danger of being destroyed by the Aequi, a neighbouring Italian tribe. To defeat this threat, the Senate voted to appoint Cincinnatus as dictator, a temporary office vested with unlimited powers. A deputation was sent to his small farm, which was the smallest landholding allowed to qualify for citizenship. The senators found Cincinnatus at work tending his crops. He was told of the Senate's decision and was saluted as dictator. However, the plebeians, the ordinary people, feared that Cincinnatus might abuse his position. Their fears proved groundless and, after the defeat of the Aequi, they voted Cincinnatus a golden wreath at the end of his sixty days of office. He then returned to his fields and was remembered as the perfect example of a virtuous and dutiful Roman citizen.

CINCINATTUS, one of the most modest of Roman heroes and a model of Roman integrity. After 60 days in office, he quietly returned to his farm. (ILLUSTRATION FROM STORIES FROM LIVY, 1885.)

undertake, but only on condition that he was unarmed. Like the *GORGONS*, Cerberus was so dreadful to behold that anyone who looked upon him was turned to stone. He was brother to the Hydra and the Chimaera.

CHIRON was the son of Philyra, daughter of *OCEANOS*, and the Titan *CRONOS*, who had adopted the form of a horse to hide from his wife *RHEA* his passion for Philyra, which is why Chiron had the appearance of a typical *CENTAUR*, with the body and legs of a horse, and the arms and head of a man.

His unusual parentage explains why Chiron was so wise, unlike other Centaurs, for he was learned in music, medicine, hunting and warfare. He was a friend of *APOLLO* and the tutor to several Greek heroes such as *ACHILLES, ASCLEPIUS* and *JASON*. He lived in a cave on Mount Pelion in Thessaly, and when he died *ZEUS* set him in the sky as the constellation Centaurus.

HEROES

THE MYTHS OF ALL CULTURES contain inspiring individuals who express ideal traits and talents, such as the courage of Achilles, might of Heracles, wit of Odysseus and endurance of Oedipus. A classic hero is a champion in every sense, overcoming trials, ridding the world of troublemakers, blazing trails and winning through despite all the odds. Yet he is neither invulnerable nor immortal, though often helped, and sometimes hindered, by the gods. Greek mythology is unusually rich in heroes and heroines of every kind. Some, such as Achilles and Hector, are wartime champions; others, such as Odysseus or Theseus, are heroes for peacetime; some are positive and outgoing, such as Heracles or Perseus; still others are heroes of attitude rather than action, such as Oedipus, Antigone, or Hector, who, at the end, remained steadfast in the face of hopeless defeat.

HERACLES (below) shoots his poisoned arrows at his old foe, the Centaur Nessus, who raced away with his wife, Deianira, while ferrying her across the river Evenus. The dying Centaur offered Deianira the gift of his blood as a salve for preserving the love of Heracles. The love philtre proved to be a fatal trick by which Heracles died many years later, tragically, by the hands of his insecure but loving wife, Deianira, who in her sorrow killed herself. (HERCULES AND NESSUS BY FRANZ VON STUCK, CANVAS 1863-1928.)

HERACLES (above), best known for his mighty labours, was all his life a helper of gods and men, setting the earth free of many monsters and rascals. Worshipped as a hero and deity, he was invoked as a saviour; as the hero of labour and struggle, he was patron deity of the gymnasium. In art he appears as the ideal of manly strength, with massive muscles and grave expression. This celebrated Greek sculpture shows the hero in repose leaning on his club, draped with the famous lion's skin. (THE FARNESE HERCULES BY GLYCON, C. 200 BC.)

ACHILLES (above), godlike hero and peerless warrior was, paradoxically, disguised as a girl in his youth. His divine mother, Thetis, wishing to save him from the Trojan War, hid him amongst the daughters of Lycomedes on Scyros. There Odysseus went, disguised as a merchant, and showed the girls jewels, dresses and arms. Only Achilles seized the arms eagerly, suddenly realizing his true sex and role in life. He then accompanied Odysseus to Troy. (ODYSSEUS RECOGNISING ACHILLES AFTER FRANS FRANCKEN THE YOUNGER, CANVAS, C. 1570.)

PERSEUS, guided and guarded by the gods, was able to slay the mortal Gorgon, Medusa, one of three frightful sisters who dwelt on the farthest shore of the ocean, and whose looks turned men to stone. By viewing Medusa in his shining shield, Perseus was able to cut off her head as she slept. Hidden by the invisible helmet of Hades he flew to safety on winged sandals given him by the nymphs. Medusa's head was placed on Athena's breastplate – a paralysing power in battle. (ILLUSTRATION FROM TANGLEWOOD TALES, C. 1920.)

CLOELIA (above), Roman heroine, was given as a hostage to the Etruscan, Lars Porsenna, during his campaign against Rome. But she escaped from his camp and swam across the Tiber to Rome. When the Romans sent her back to Porsenna, he was so taken by her gallantry, that he set her free with some other hostages and gave her a splendid horse. Here she rides triumphantly to freedom with her companions. (ILLUSTRATION FROM STORIES FROM LIVY, 1885.)

JASON (above), the celebrated captain of the Argonauts, embarked on a great adventure to bring back the Golden Fleece, which was suspended from a branch of an oak tree in the grove of Ares in Colchis. It was greatly cherished by Aietes, the king of Colchis. With the help of a potion from the sorceress Medea, daughter of the king of Colchis, Jason charmed to sleep the ever-watchful dragon that guarded the Golden Fleece. (ILLUSTRATION FROM TANGLEWOOD TALES, C.1920.)

HORATIUS (above), brave Roman hero, held the Sublician Bridge with two comrades against the Etruscan army. While he held off the Etruscans, the Romans hacked the bridge behind him until it collapsed. Having sent back his comrades, Horatius stood alone until the bridge fell, then he swam to safety across the raging Tiber, amid enemy arrows. The state erected a statue to his honour in the Comitium. (ILLUSTRATION FROM LAYS OF ANCIENT ROME, 1891.)

CIRCE (left), an enchanting nymph, invites Odysseus to drink from her magic cup, containing a potion which turns men into swine. But Odysseus has been forewarned and, immunized with the herb moly, he drinks without coming to harm.
(ILLUSTRATION FROM TANGLEWOOD TALES, C.1920.)

CLYTEMNESTRA (above), the estranged wife of Agamemnon, watches and waits for the ships from Troy, bringing her husband home. Yet no hero's welcome awaits the returning warrior, only betrayal and murder by his wife and her lover.
(ILLUSTRATION BY NICK BEALE, 1995.)

CIRCE, daughter of *HELIOS*, the sun god, was a powerful witch who had poisoned her husband, king of the Sarmatians, before going to the fabulous island of Aeaea. Her magical powers turned *ODYSSEUS*' men into swine when they landed on Aeaea on their way home from Troy. Aided by *HERMES*, the messenger god, Odysseus was immune to Circe's magic and restored his crew to human form, and also gained the witch's aid for the next part of his journey. For a year he stayed as her lover, before she told him how to navigate through the waters of the Sirens and between Scylla, a monster, and Charybdis, a whirlpool. Scylla had been a rival of Circe, who had turned her into a monster when one of her many lovers had shown an interest in the unfortunate girl. In some accounts, Circe eventually married Odysseus' son Telemachus.

CLOELIA see *HEROES*

CLYTEMNESTRA was the daughter of *LEDA* and Tyndareos, king of Sparta, and the estranged wife of *AGAMEMNON*. Sometimes she is portrayed as a weak woman, easily persuaded by her lover Aegisthus to assist in the murder of her husband on his return from the Trojan War. Otherwise it is Clytemnestra who is the strong character, the instigator of the murder, while Aegisthus is little more than a weakling. Even before the the Greek force departed for Troy, Clytemnestra already had good reason to hate her husband. In order to gain a fair wind to Troy, he agreed to sacrifice her favourite child *IPHIGENIA*. Even though the champion *ACHILLES* had promised to defend the girl against all threats, the Greek host had its way and Iphigenia was offered to the goddess *ARTEMIS*, either as sacrificial victim or as priestess.

Like her sister *HELEN*, whose elopement with *PARIS* caused the Trojan War, Clytemnestra felt no loyalty towards her husband. She openly conducted an affair with Aegisthus, Agamemnon's cousin, and ruled Mycenae with him. The end of the war required desperate measures. When he returned home Agamemnon was butchered by Aegisthus, using a two-headed axe, while Clytemnestra had him entangled in a net. For this terrible crime, Clytemnestra was herself killed by her son *ORESTES*.

CORIOLANUS was a legendary Roman traitor of the fifth century BC. Conscious above all of his noble birth, Coriolanus objected to the Senate's wish to distribute free bread to poorer citizens, who were starving because of Rome's endless wars. He said that unless the plebeians, the ordinary people, were willing to restore to the nobility its full ancient privileges they should expect no charity. Hounded from Rome for such an opinion, he joined the Volsci and eventually led a Volscian army against the city. All seemed lost until his mother Volumnia spoke to him, asking Coriolanus whether he saw her as his own mother or as a prisoner of war. As a result he quit the battlefield and went into exile.

CREON, in Greek mythology, was the brother of Jocasta and a reluctant ruler of Thebes. He was regent during the uncertain period after King *LAIUS*, Jocasta's husband, had been killed near the city. Creon offered the throne and the hand of Jocasta to any man who could solve the riddle of the *SPHINX* and thus rid Thebes of this bloodthirsty

CORIOLANUS, a Roman exile, marched against his old city with an army of Volscians, encamping just outside Rome. There, he ignored all entreaties for peace until visited by his mother (centre), his wife and the Roman matrons, whose tears softened his stern heart. (ILLUSTRATION FROM STORIES FROM LIVY, 1885.)

monster. OEDIPUS managed to achieve the apparently impossible task, then took over the kingdom, married Jocasta and raised a family. Not until a plague threatened Thebes and the Delphic Oracle was consulted about its cause, did it become known that Jocasta was Oedipus' mother and that he had killed Laius. Oedipus blinded himself, Jocasta committed suicide and Creon became regent once more.

A quarrel between Oedipus' sons, Eteocles and Polynices, caused another period of dismay, eventually leaving both of them dead and Creon on the throne. Whereas Eteocles was regarded by Creon as a patriot and properly buried, the body of the rebel Polynices was thrown outside the city walls and forbidden burial. Such a situation was unacceptable to ANTIGONE, Oedipus' daughter and companion during his wanderings around Greece, and on her return to Thebes she sprinkled Polynices' corpse with earth, so as to give her brother a token burial.

As a result of this act of defiance, Creon had Antigone walled up in a cave. The seer TIRESIAS told Creon to bury the dead and disinter the living, but he refused. The result was personal grief, when his own son committed suicide on learning of Antigone's death, and his own wife soon followed suit.

Although Creon was well known to the ancient Greeks, his own character seems less important in myth than his role as regent in the troubled city of Thebes.

CRONOS, in Greek mythology, was the son of Ouranos, the sky god, and GAIA, the earth mother. With the help of Gaia, Cronos emasculated Ouranos and seized control of the universe. He then married his sister RHEA and followed the example of Ouranos in disposing of his children by swallowing them, because he had been warned that he would be displaced by one of his sons. Rhea, however, gave him a stone wrapped in swaddling clothes instead of the infant ZEUS, his youngest son, who was taken secretly to Crete in order to grow up safely on the island. When Zeus came of age, he forced Cronos to vomit up his brothers and sisters – POSEIDON, HADES, HERA, HESTIA and DEMETER – and to release his uncles and aunts, especially the Titans, whom Cronos had chosen

CREON, reluctant king of Thebes, lost his son, wife and niece in a tragic cycle of suicides caused by his inflexible will. His crushing fate was to endure a life of solitary grief and remorse. (ILLUSTRATION BY NICK BEALE, 1995.)

to keep chained up. In gratitude, the Cyclopes, the single-eyed giants, fashioned for Zeus his famous lightning and thunderbolts.

In a subsequent struggle for power, Zeus and his brothers successfully dealt with all the might and power that Cronos could direct against them. After his defeat, Cronos was either banished to a distant paradise, or he simply slowly faded away as an unimportant deity. The Romans equated Cronos with their SATURN, who

was a corn god whom they associated with the Golden Age.

CUPID was the Roman god of love and son of the love goddess VENUS. He was depicted as a beautiful but wanton boy, armed with a quiver full of "arrowed desires". Some of his arrows, however, would turn people away from those who fell in love with them.

According to one myth, Venus was jealous of PSYCHE ("the soul") and told Cupid to make her love the ugliest man alive. But Cupid fell in love with Psyche and, invisible, visited her every night. He told her not to try to see him, but, overcome by curiosity, she did try and he left her. Psyche searched the world for him, until the sky god JUPITER granted her immortality so that she could be Cupid's constant companion. The couple's daughter was named Voluptas ("pleasure").

CUPID fishes playfully amongst the waves. He is usually portrayed as a cute, capricious child with wings and often with a quiver of arrows or a torch to inflame love in the hearts of gods and men. (CUPID FISHING BY GEORGE FREDERICK WATTS, SEPIA C. 1890.)

D

CURTIUS leaps into the chasm in the Roman forum. The seers declared that the chasm could only be filled by Rome's greatest treasure, and so Curtius jumped in, declaring that there was no greater treasure than a gallant Roman citizen. (ILLUSTRATION FROM STORIES FROM LIVY, 1885.)

CURTIUS

CURTIUS is the subject of a strange incident in Roman mythology. Around 362 BC a great chasm appeared in the Forum in Rome, which led straight down to the underworld. It had appeared because the Romans forgot to make an appropriate sacrifice to the dead. Marcus Curtius therefore plunged on horseback into the bottomless pit and was seen no more.

CYCLOPES see GIANTS

DAEDALUS, according to Greek mythology, was said by some to be the son of Alcippe, the daughter of the war god ARES, and by others to be the son of Merope. It is agreed, though, that he came from Athens. He was a gifted craftsman and was employed by King MINOS at his palace of Knossos in Crete. Daedalus designed and built the Labyrinth for the dreaded MINOTAUR. This was the offspring of PASIPHAE, Minos' wife, and a great bull. Daedalus had designed an artificial cow into which the queen could place herself and so be able to mate with the bull. Thus was the Minotaur conceived. Minos later imprisoned Daedalus for revealing the secret of the Labyrinth, but he managed to escape by constructing

DAPHNE, a river nymph, was loved by Apollo who pursued her until, on the banks of her father's river, she prayed for help and was at once changed into a laurel tree. Here, her father, the river god Peneius, weeps inconsolably, while Apollo strokes her leafy arms in wonder. (APOLLO AND DAPHNE BY NICOLAS POUSSIN, CANVAS, C.1627)

wings of wax and feathers for himself and his son Icarus. Despite his father's warning, Icarus flew too close to the sun, the wax of his wings melted and he fell into the sea and drowned. Daedalus managed to arrive safely in Sicily, where he amused the daughters of King Cocalos with his inventions. When Minos eventually caught up with the fugitive craftsman, a battle of wits ended in Daedalus' favour: Minos was killed by boiling water, or oil, which Daedalus persuaded Cocalos' daughters to pour down a pipe into the king's bath.

DANAE was the mother of the Greek hero PERSEUS and the daughter of Acrisius, king of Argos in the Peloponnese. It had been foretold that her son would cause the death of Acrisius, so he locked her in a bronze tower. But ZEUS visited her as a shower of golden rain and Perseus was conceived. The king banished the mother and her son, but after many adventures Perseus did accidentally kill Acrisius when throwing a discus. (See also LOVERS OF ZEUS)

DANAE (above) was imprisoned in a bronze tower by her father, because he feared a prophecy that he would be killed by his grandson. Yet even hidden away in her tower, she was still accessible to the god Zeus, who came to her as a golden shower. They had a son, Perseus. (DANAE AND THE GOLDEN RAIN BY TITIAN, CANVAS, 1554.)

DAPHNE, in Greek mythology, was the daughter of the river god Peneius. She was similar in many ways to the goddess ARTEMIS, in that she was also a virgin huntress who happily roamed the wilderness. One day, the love god EROS shot a flurry of arrows in response to taunts from APOLLO, the god of prophecy. The first of Eros' arrows

DAEDALUS (right) crafted wings of feathers, held together by wax, to escape from Crete, and taught his son, Icarus, how to fly, warning him that he must not fly too close to the sun. But Icarus was drawn to the light of the sun, so his wings melted and he fell into the sea, now named the Icarian. (DAEDALUS AND ICARUS BY CHARLES LANDON, 1799.)

was a gold-tipped shaft and when it struck Apollo it made him fall immediately in love with Daphne. The second one, however, had a lead tip and caused Daphne to become even more indifferent than she already had been to any lover. Apollo, however, pursued Daphne relentlessly until, in desperation, she turned herself into a laurel tree

HELEN

HELEN was the daughter of *LEDA* and *ZEUS*, the wife of the Spartan king *MENELAUS*, and the cause of the Trojan War. Her immortality as the daughter of the supreme Greek deity suggests that Helen was once a goddess and that her incorporation into myth as an unfaithful queen only occurred when her worship was largely forgotten.

Zeus mated with Leda, wife of the Spartan king Tyndareos, in the guise of a swan. Leda laid an egg, and when Helen hatched from it she brought her up as a member of the royal family. Helen's brothers were Castor and Polydeuces, the mysterious *DIOSCURI*, and her sister was King *AGAMEMNON*'s unfaithful wife *CLYTEMNESTRA*.

At the time of her marriage to Menelaus, the younger brother of Agamemnon, Helen was the most

HELEN (above) paces the walls of Troy. The most beautiful woman of the ancient world, she was also, according to Homer, a thoughtful heroine, given to self-mockery and ever aware of the misery caused by her beauty. (HELEN ON THE WALLS OF TROY BY LORD LEIGHTON, CANVAS, C. 1880.)

desirable bride in Greece. At first Menelaus and Helen were very happy, but then *PARIS*, the eldest son of King *PRIAM* of Troy, visited Sparta and, with the help of the love goddess *APHRODITE*, gained Helen's affection. They even eloped with a part of Menelaus' treasury. When the Trojans refused to return Helen and the stolen treasure, Agamemnon assembled a great army to help his brother Menelaus. For ten years the city of Troy was besieged and then only captured through the trick of the Wooden Horse. Throughout this long war the sympathies of Helen were mainly with the Greeks, although she was treated as the proper wife, and not merely the mistress, of Paris. After the fall of Troy, Helen and Menelaus were reconciled and they lived undisturbed at Sparta.

HELIOS

HELIOS was the Greek sun god and son of the *TITAN* Hyperion. To the Romans he was known as Sol. It was thought that Helios, after crossing the sky, sailed during the night around the earth in a golden bowl on the encircling waters of *OCEANOS*, and so arrived back in the east just before dawn. Both the Greeks and the Romans held that the inhabited world was a large

HELIOS, god of the sun, appears in works of art as a strong and beautiful youth with gleaming eyes, and a crown of flaming rays. Just as the sun's rays penetrate everywhere, so Helios saw everything, and was invoked as a witness of oaths. (ILLUSTRATION FROM DR SMITH'S CLASSICAL DICTIONARY, 1895.)

island surrounded by an ocean. Although Oceanos was sometimes described as a river, it stretched into the unimaginable distance and far from any shore.

One myth of Helios concerns the death of his son *PHAETHON*. Once this impetuous youth tried to steer his father's radiant chariot, but he quickly lost control. Only the timely action of *ZEUS* steadied its runaway horses and prevented the earth from catching fire. Phaethon fell from the vehicle and was drowned. However, Helios had many other children, among them Augeas, *CIRCE* and *PASIPHAE*. A gigantic statue of the sun god was erected at the harbour of Rhodes, an island sacred to him. This so-called Colossus was one of the seven wonders of the ancient world, but was toppled by an earthquake around 226 BC.

HEPHAISTOS

HEPHAISTOS was the son of *ZEUS* and *HERA*, and was the Greek smith god. His Roman equivalent was *VULCAN*, whose smithy lay beneath the crater of Mount Aetna in Sicily. Hephaistos was lame as a result of having interfered in a quarrel between his parents. So angry did Zeus become that he flung his son from the top of Mount Olympus and let him fall heavily on the volcanic island of Lemnos, in the northern part of the Aegean Sea. In another version, Hera tried to drown her imperfect child, only to be thwarted by sea nymphs who took him to a beach. A sequel to this tale has the smith god gain his revenge as a fully grown man by making a golden throne for his mother which was actually a trap. None of the gods could release Hera, so Hephaistos was invited to return permanently to Mount Olympus. There, under the influence of drink, he was persuaded by his friend *DIONYSUS* to unlock the cunning device and let his mother escape.

Hephaistos seems to have come originally from Asia Minor, where iron mines date from a very early period. His cult was strong in Caria and Lycia, along its south-western shore. His marriage to the love goddess *APHRODITE* may have something to do with this eastern connection, as she also came to Greece from West Asia. Their relationship was almost as tumultuous as that of Zeus and Hera. Once Hephaistos fashioned a trap to catch his unfaithful wife in bed with the war god *ARES*. The Olympian gods merely laughed at Hephaistos' situation; the sea god *POSEIDON* only

HEPHAISTOS, god of fire, fashions exquisite golden works in his fiery forge. Lame, he leans on one leg. By him stands Apollo, who reveals that his wife, Aphrodite, loves Ares, and Hephaistos resolves to trap the guilty pair. (THE FORGE OF VULCAN BY DIEGO VELASQUEZ, CANVAS, 1630.)

promised some remedy if he agreed to release Aphrodite and Ares.

A myth about ATHENA's birth recounts how Hephaistos split open Zeus' head with an axe in order to release the fully grown goddess. Apparently, Zeus had swallowed Athena's mother, Metis, once he realized she was pregnant with a powerful deity. Later, Hephaistos fell in love with Athena, but was rejected by her and his semen fell to earth where it gave birth to the serpent Erichthonius. (See also FORCES OF NATURE)

HERA means "lady" and was undoubtedly the title of a powerful mother goddess whom the Greeks inherited from the earlier inhabitants of Argos, which was a major city in the Peloponnese. It was claimed that she was the daughter of CRONOS and RHEA; however, her addition to the Greek pantheon was not an easy or straightforward matter, as the ceaseless conflicts between her and her husband ZEUS readily bear witness. Often her fits of jealousy and quarrelsomeness led to disaster for gods, heroes and men, when she relentlessly persecuted Zeus' mistresses and their children. For example, against the baby HERACLES, whom Zeus had fathered in order to help in the coming battle against the GIANTS, she sent two serpents to kill him, but the infant hero strangled them

HERA, queen of heaven, directs Helios across the sky. She is crowned with a diadem and veil, symbolizing her status as Zeus' bride. Her sceptre is tipped with a cuckoo, sacred to her as the messenger of spring, the season in which she married Zeus. (ILLUSTRATION FROM STORIES FROM LIVY, 1885.)

in his cradle. However, later in his life, Hera succeeded in driving Heracles temporarily mad.

There are a number of myths about Zeus' courtship of Hera. In one of them he disguised himself as a cuckoo and took shelter inside her clothes during a heavy downpour. Once out of the rain, Zeus resumed his normal shape and promised to marry Hera. Later she bore him the war god ARES, the goddess of birth Eileithyia, and Hebe, the cupbearer of the gods. Another child was the smith god HEPHAISTOS, who is said in some myths to have been the son of Zeus and Hera, but in others the offspring of Hera alone. Hera was worshipped with particular reverence in Crete and at Samos, where a great temple was said to have been built for her by the ARGONAUTS.

HERACLES wrestles with Antaeus, a giant who draws his strength from the earth. To weaken the giant's might, Heracles lifts him high above the earth, and crushes him in mid-air. This bronze expresses the classical ideal of heroic skill and might. (HERCULES AND ANTAEUS BY PIER ANTICO, BRONZE, 1460-1528.)

HERACLES, the son of ZEUS and ALCMENE, was the greatest of all the Greek heroes. To the Romans he was known as Hercules, and they added various encounters in Italy to his already large cycle of adventures. The name Heracles means "Hera's glory" – a circumstance that firmly ties the hero to Argos, the site of the goddess HERA's temple. It remains a mystery that Heracles should have been persecuted so much by Hera, even going mad at one point during his life.

Because Zeus needed a mortal champion in the forthcoming battle between the gods and the GIANTS, he fathered Heracles at the court of Thebes. The chosen mother was Alcmene, the Theban queen. Zeus intended Heracles to be ruler of Mycenae or Tiryns,

HERACLES slays the Hydra, while a crab, sent by the vengeful goddess Hera, nips at his heels. After burning away the Hydra's eight mortal heads, Heracles buried its ninth immortal head under a huge rock in the swamp. (HERCULES AND THE HYDRA, A F GORGUET, CANVAS, C. 1920.)

strongholds close to Argos, but Hera frustrated this plan so well that the hero became the slave of Eurystheus, king of Tiryns. She struck Heracles with a fit of madness, in the course of which he killed his wife and their three sons with arrows. To atone for this terrible deed he had to become Eurystheus' dependent and undertook his famous twelve labours.

These labours began with the killing of the Nemean lion, which could not be harmed by arrows.

Heracles had to fight it with his bare hands and a wooden club. After overcoming the lion, he cured the skin and wore it as a trophy. His next opponent, the Hydra, was a nine-headed serpent sacred to Hera. It lived in a swamp at Lerna, not far from Argos. The problem that the hero encountered when fighting with the Hydra was that for every head he cut off with his sword two new ones grew in its place. But with assistance from his nephew Iolaus he was able to triumph, for Iolaus burned the stumps of the necks as soon as Heracles severed each head. When he returned to Eurystheus, the king refused to count the exploit as a labour, because Heracles had received help from his nephew.

The next labour was not quite so bloody. Heracles had to capture the Ceryneian hind, which was a beast sacred to ARTEMIS, goddess of the wild. According to different accounts, he returned to Tiryns with either its golden antlers or the hind itself. Another labour required

him to capture the Erymanthian boar, which plagued the country-side of Arcadia. He trapped it with a net, and during the hunt Heracles encountered a band of CENTAURS, beast-like men who lived in woodlands. One of them, Nessus, was later to cause the hero's death.

The fifth labour was the cleansing of Augeas' stables. The son of the sun god, Augeas had vast herds of animals, which he pastured in the kingdom of Elis in the western Peloponnese. King Eurystheus told Heracles to remove the immense piles of dung from the stables, a feat he achieved by diverting the course of a nearby river. The last labour that the hero performed in the Peloponnese was the removal of the Stymphalian birds. Although they had steel-tipped feathers with which they killed both men and animals, these birds were frightened away by the noise of a rattle, which the goddess ATHENA had specially made for Heracles.

On the island of Crete the hero tracked down the bull that MINOS had failed to sacrifice to the sea god POSEIDON. The bull had mated with Minos' wife, PASIPHAE, who then gave birth to the MINOTAUR, the bull-headed man slain by the Athenian hero THESEUS. Heracles captured Poseidon's bull alive and brought it back to Tiryns, where he let it go free at the end of this seventh labour. The eighth labour was more gruesome. It took Heracles to Thrace in pursuit of the man-eating mares of Diomedes, which he subdued after feeding them on their master's flesh.

The last four labours were quite different in nature. First of all Eurystheus had Heracles fetch the girdle of Hippolyta, queen of the fierce AMAZONS. Then he captured the cattle of Geryon, a western king who had three heads, three bodies and six hands. After this labour Heracles brought back the golden apples of the HESPERIDES, female guardians of the fruit that the earth goddess GAIA gave to Hera on her

HERMAPHRODITOS, the beautiful son of Aphrodite and Hermes, inspired the love of the water nymph Salmacis. Here, the golden boy bathes in a shower of sunlight, unaware of his beautiful admirer on the river bank. (SALMACIS AND HERMAPHRODITOS BY BARTHOLOMEUS SPRANGER, CANVAS, C. 1581.)

wedding to Zeus. The last exploit of Heracles was the most testing, for it meant a descent into the underworld, the realm of the dead. From there the hero managed, with some help from PERSEPHONE, queen of the underworld, to bring briefly back to Tiryns the three-headed hound CERBERUS. As a result of this labour, hard-working Heracles attained immortality for himself. No other hero gained this honour.

Heracles' death on earth, an event that the Greeks expected to precede his translation to Mount Olympus as a god, was the work of the Centaur Nessus, who gave the hero's second wife a poisoned garment for him to wear. Realizing that his death was near, Heracles consulted the Delphic Oracle, which told him to build a funeral pyre in Thessaly. When the dying hero climbed on to it, there was a great flash of lightning and Zeus took his son to join the immortals.

Some of the labours of Heracles are reflected in the names of certain constellations, such as Leo, which represents the Nemean Lion, and Cancer, the crab that was allegedly sent by Hera to help the Hydra. (See also HEROES)

HERMAPHRODITOS

HERMAPHRODITOS was the bisexual offspring of the messenger god HERMES and APHRODITE, the goddess of love. According to one Greek myth, this handsome boy excited the passion of Salmacis, who was a nymph of a fountain near to the city of Halicarnassus in Asia Minor. When the young Hermaphroditos ignored her attentions, Salmacis prayed to the gods that she might be eternally united with him. The wish was granted when he bathed in some waters and she merged with him physically. The result was a female boy, hence the term hermaphrodite. But Hermaphroditos was not emasculated like Attis, the lover of the Phrygian mother goddess Cybele, for this West Asian god intentionally cut off his own manhood.

HERMES was the Greek messenger god, and the son of ZEUS and Maia. He enjoyed playing tricks and games. During the Trojan War, it was Hermes who was always sent to steal something that was otherwise unobtainable. Before the sea nymph THETIS persuaded her son ACHILLES to stop mutilating the corpse of HECTOR, the gods considered that the simplest solution might be to let Hermes steal the broken body. Hermes was the god who most easily crossed the line between the living and the dead, for the Greeks believed that he guided the dead to the realm of HADES, the underworld. This duty helps to explain the later identification of the Germanic god Odin with the Roman equivalent of Hermes, MERCURY. Odin was the champion of warriors and the father of the slain.

Hermes is usually depicted as a young man with a wide-brimmed hat and winged sandals, carrying a herald's staff crowned with two snakes. In ancient Greece this staff assured the messenger safe passage even during time of war. Hermes' greatest passion was for the love goddess APHRODITE.

The two sons that are attributed to them were both renowned for their unusual sexuality. HERMAPHRODITOS was the first female boy, while the gnome-like Priapus was famous for his enormous penis. Like that of Hermaphroditus, the cult of Priapus originated in Asia Minor, though some distance farther north at Lampascus, near the Black Sea.

HERMES leads Eurydice (centre) and Orpheus (right) through the underworld. As psychopomp, Hermes conducted souls from life on earth to death in Hades. (ILLUSTRATION FROM DICTIONARY OF CLASSICAL ANTIQUITIES, 1891.)

VOYAGERS

THE LURE OF THE UNKNOWN prompts all restless heroes to strike out on a new path in search of a fabulous treasure or shining dream, or for the sheer joy of discovery and adventure. Three intrepid explorers stand out in Classical mythology: Jason, Aeneas and Odysseus. Jason set sail with his fearless crew of Argonauts in search of the Golden Fleece; while Aeneas' seven-year voyage after the fall of Troy led him to the site of future Rome. Most famous and appealing, perhaps, was the fabled Odyssey of the shipwrecked wanderer, Odysseus. Tossed from shore to shore by the angry sea god, Poseidon, he found his way home after ten years' wandering through fabulous lands. The lure of the underworld, or a foray into a monster's den, attracts many heroes, too, such as Theseus who went into the Labyrinth to slay the Minotaur, and found his way out again. Aeneas and Odysseus both journeyed to the underworld in search of prophetic counsel.

*AENEAS' (above) seven-year voyage after the fall of Troy was described in Virgil's epic tale, the Aeneid, in part a Roman Odyssey. After fleeing with his father and son from burning Troy, Aeneas and his comrades sailed away by way of Thrace and Delos to Crete and onwards to Sicily and Carthage, before reaching Latium in Italy where he became the ancestral hero of the Romans. Here, Aeneas, arriving on Delos, is kindly welcomed by King Anius. (*AENEAS IN DELOS, MAIOLICA DISH, 1497.)

ORPHEUS (left) went down into Hades, the underworld, to bring back his wife, Eurydice. Charming the shades and even Persephone with his music, he was allowed to take Eurydice back to the upper world as long as he did not look back until clear of Hades. Just as they were about to step out into the light, Orpheus turned round only to see Eurydice slip back into the world of shades forever. Here, Orpheus bids farewell to Eurydice, while Hermes (left), waits to lead Eurydice back through the world of shades. (HERMES, EURYDICE AND ORPHEUS, MARBLE, C. 420 BC.)

ARION (right), a lyrical poet and cithara player, sailed to Sicily to take part in a magical contest which he won. On his way home in a Corinthian ship, he was robbed by the sailors, and forced to leap overboard where he was borne away to safety by song-loving dolphins. Here, Arion plays his cithara on the prow of the ship, invoking the gods of the sea, before leaping overboard. (ILLUSTRATION FROM TANGLEWOOD TALES, C.1920.)

ODYSSEUS (above), celebrated traveller, was renowned for his wits and silver tongue, for his cunning, craft and curiosity. On his way home from Troy, he beached at Sicily, home of the lawless race of one-eyed giants, the Cyclopes. Bold and inquisitive, Odysseus wandered into a Cyclops' den where he and his comrades became trapped by the hostile giant. To escape, they blinded the giant and slipped out, hidden under sheeps' bellies. Here, Odysseus and his comrades pierce the giant's single eye with a sharpened stake. (THE BLINDING OF POLYPHEMUS BY ALESSANDRO ALLORI, FRESCO, 1580.)

JASON (below) sailed across the seas on a perilous voyage in his famous ship, the Argo, accompanied by all the heroes of the age. They went in search of the Golden Fleece, guarded by a watchful dragon at Colchis. After snatching the treasure from under the dragon's eye, Jason and his Argonauts sailed away, finally arriving at Iolcus. Here, Jason steals past with his trophy, casting a furtive glance at a statue of Ares in the sacred grove of the god. (JASON AND THE GOLDEN FLEECE BY ERASMUS QUELLINUS, CANVAS, C. 1670.)

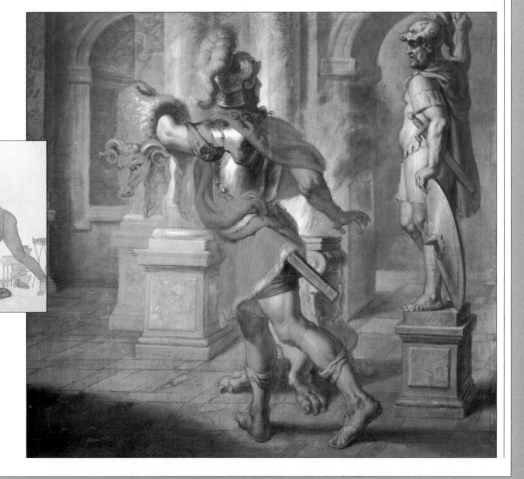

ODYSSEUS (above), fast asleep, is laid on his own coat by Phaeacian sailors. As predicted by the seer, Tiresias, Odysseus reached home alone on a foreign ship, only after many years' wandering. Once back on his island kingdom of Ithaca, he had another battle to fight – with the suitors of his wife – before he could regain his throne and settle down with Penelope. (ILLUSTRATION FROM STORIES FROM HOMER, 1885.)

H

HERO AND LEANDER were one of the great pairs of lovers in Greek mythology. Hero was a priestess of *APHRODITE* at Sestos in the Dardanelles, while Leander lived on the Asian side of the channel at Abydos. They met and fell in love, but because of her religious calling Hero was barred from marriage. In order to keep their affair secret, they arranged that Leander should swim across to Hero each night, guided by a light that she placed in her tower. Next morning he would swim back at dawn. One stormy night the light blew out,

Leander lost his sense of direction and he drowned in the cold waters. When his body was washed ashore at Sestos, Hero threw herself from her tower and died.

THE HESPERIDES were supposedly the daughters of Hesperus, the evening star. Their names were Hespera, Aegle and Erytheis, and they were the guardians of a tree of golden apples given by *GAIA*, mother earth, to the goddess *HERA* on her marriage to *ZEUS*, chief of the Greek gods. This tree stood in the Garden of the Hesperides on the

HERO (below) looks for her Leander, who usually swam to her across the Hellespont guided by a light in her tower. But her light blew out in a storm and Leander was drowned. (THE LAST WATCH OF HERO BY LORD LEIGHTON, CANVAS, 1880.)

THE HESPERIDES (right) guarded the golden apples in the garden of the gods. The serpent recalls the myth of the dragon Ladon who guarded the apples until he was slain by Heracles. (THE GARDEN OF THE HESPERIDES BY EDWARD BURNE-JONES, CANVAS, 1869-73.)

slopes of Mount Atlas in the far west. For one of his labours the hero *HERACLES* tricked the Titan *ATLAS* into getting him the golden apples, offering to hold up the heavens in his stead.

HORATIUS (below), a Roman hero, held the Sublician Bridge, with two of his comrades, against the Etruscan army. While other Romans hacked down the bridge, he held off the enemy until the last moment when he leapt into the stream and swam to safety. (ILLUSTRATION FROM STORIES FROM LIVY, 1885.)

HORATIUS was a Roman hero who saved the early Republic from the Etruscans, when they tried to restore *TARQUINIUS SUPERBUS* to the Roman throne by force of arms. The Etruscans mounted a surprise attack and attempted to capture Rome by crossing a poorly defended bridge over the River Tiber. With two comrades, Horatius held the enemy back until the Romans had destroyed the wooden bridge. As the final supports were sawn away, he ordered his comrades

INO rescues shipwrecked Odysseus by throwing him her veil which saves him from drowning. She was honoured along the Greek shores as a marine deity who aided sailors in distress and guided ships through storms. (ODYSSEUS AND THE GODDESS INO BY ALESSANDRO ALLORI, FRESCO, 1580.)

back to the Roman bank. They just made it, but Horatius was obliged to swim back in full armour. Only prayer saved the hero as he dodged the Etruscan arrows and struggled across the waters of the Tiber.

His full name was Horatius Cocles ("Horatius the one-eyed"). Whether he was wounded in the eye remains uncertain, though tradition says that an ancient statue of a lame, one-eyed man was erected near the bridge in his honour. He was also given as much land as he could drive a plough over in a day. (See also HEROES)

HYPNOS ("Sleep"), in Greek mythology, was the son of Nyx, the night goddess, and the brother of Thanatos ("Death"). Morpheus, the god of dreams, was his son. Hypnos lived in the underworld, the realm of HADES, and never saw the sun. On several occasions HERA asked Hypnos to lull her husband ZEUS to sleep so that she could attack his son HERACLES. Hypnos usually refused to anger Zeus, possibly because he had already come close to having a thunderbolt hurled at him. He was saved by taking refuge with Night, whose power Zeus always respected.

ILUS see FOUNDERS

INO was the daughter of CADMUS, the Phoenician king of Thebes, and Harmonia. In Greek mythology, she brought up DIONYSUS, the son of ZEUS and Semele, who was Ino's dead sister. Semele had been tricked by the goddess HERA, the jealous and vengeful wife of Zeus, who advised her to test the divinity of her lover by telling him to come to her in his true form. This Zeus was also tricked into doing, and the unfortunate result was that he appeared to Semele as lightning and thunderbolts, and she was

killed. The unborn Dionysus, however, was taken from her womb and placed in Zeus' own thigh until it was time for his birth. Then, at the suggestion of HERMES, the messenger god, Ino suckled the divine child and kept him safe from Hera. However, such a powerful goddess could not be thwarted without great personal cost. When she discovered the deception, Hera made Ino kill her own children. After she had done this Ino killed herself by jumping off a cliff into the sea. In another myth, she and her infant son Melicertes leapt into the sea and became marine deities.

IO was the daughter of the river god Inachus, and was one of the mortal women who bore children by ZEUS. Although Io was a virgin priestess of HERA, Zeus's wife, at her temple in Argos, this did not prevent Zeus from having her expelled from Argos so that he could make love to her without any difficulties. According to one version, he turned Io into a beautiful heifer, and would have mated with her at once had not Hera guessed his intentions and sent a gadfly to prevent the animal from standing still. It seems that Zeus eventually made love to Io on a cloud over Egypt, where she was returned to her human form. Surprisingly, she was forgiven by Hera. Because Io had been bovine in shape on her arrival, she became identified with the Egyptian cow goddess Hathor.

IO, "the wanderer", was loved by Zeus who changed her into a heifer in order to avoid his jealous wife Hera. Hera ordered all-seeing Argus to watch Io, but Zeus, in his turn, sent Hermes to lull Argus to sleep by the dreamy notes of his flute. (MERCURY AND ARGUS BY PETER PAUL RUBENS, CANVAS, C. 1635.)

J

IPHIGENIA was the eldest daughter of King *AGAMEMNON* and Queen *CLYTEMNESTRA* of Mycenae. When Agamemnon and the Greek fleet were about to sail for Troy, contrary winds caused by *ARTEMIS* kept the ships at Aulis. The goddess of the forest and wild animals had been offended, either by Agamemnon himself or by an action committed by his father *ATREUS*. In any event, Artemis demanded that Iphigenia should be sacrificed. To bring the sacrificial victim all the way from Mycenae to the port of Aulis in Boeotia, without his wife Clytemnestra's becoming suspicious, Agamemnon pretended that Iphigenia was to be married there to the Greek hero and champion *ACHILLES*. After she discovered his true intention, Clytemnestra never forgave her husband, and years later on his return from the Trojan War helped her lover Aegisthus to murder him.

IXION was a Thessalian king of Larissa and supposedly the son of Phlegyas, though some say his father was *ARES*, god of war. In order to avoid paying a bride-price to Eioneus for his beautiful daughter Dia, Ixion prepared a trap for his unsuspecting father-in-law – a pit filled with fire. Eioneus fell into it on a visit to Larissa and died, and Ixion thus became the first man to shed the blood of a kinsman.

IXION, chained to a rolling wheel, expiates his sins in Tartarus, a hell beneath Hades. Alongside him, fellow prisoners Sisyphus and Tantalus endure their own ordeals – Sisyphus condemned to endless toil and Tantalus to endless thirst. (ILLUSTRATION FROM DR SMITH'S CLASSICAL DICTIONARY, 1895.)

IPHIGENIA, the young daughter of Agamemnon and Clytemnestra, was offered as a "sacrificial lamb" to appease Artemis who was angry with Agamemnon. Here, while the high priest Calchas raises his arms in prayer, Agamemnon (right) bows his head sorrowfully. (ILLUSTRATION FROM STORIES FROM HOMER, 1885.)

Because he was polluted by this unprecedented act, the Thessalian king could not properly rule his land. Perhaps a secret passion for Dia prompted *ZEUS* himself to devise special rites of purification for Ixion. At first Ixion was grateful to the god, but it was not long before he took an interest in *HERA*, Zeus' wife. It was therefore Ixion's turn to be trapped, when Zeus made an exact copy of Hera from a cloud and enticed the unwary king to rape it. The punishment for such sacrilegious crime was to spend eternity in Tartarus, the prison beneath the underworld.

JANUS was a very old Italian god whom the Romans associated with beginnings. In Rome, his double-gated temple in the Forum was always kept open in time of war and closed in time of peace. The month of January – a time for people to look backwards and forwards – was sacred to Janus. There are few myths concerning him, although his extra eyes did on one occasion enable him to catch the nymph Carna, who liked to tease her lovers with sexual advances before suddenly running away. Their son became a king of the important city of Alba Longa.

JASON, the son of Aeson and Philyra, was a Greek hero and voyager, born in Iolcus, a town in Thessalian Magnesia. However, difficulties arose when Aeson, ruler of Iolcus, was deposed by his half-brother Pelias. Either because Philyra distrusted Pelias' intentions towards Jason, or simply because it would better for the boy if he were educated elsewhere, she placed him in the care of the wise Centaur *CHIRON*, who lived in the Thessalian woodlands. Chiron was skilled in many things, including medicine, and may have given the boy the name Jason ("healer").

The Delphic Oracle warned Pelias that he would be turned off the throne of Iolcus by a man wearing only one sandal. So the usurping king was amazed and frightened when a mature Jason arrived

JANUS, a dual-faced god, presided over all that is double-edged in life. His image was found on city gates, which look both inwards and outwards, and he was invoked at the start of each new day and year when people look both backwards and forwards in time. (ILLUSTRATION FROM DR SMITH'S CLASSICAL DICTIONARY, 1895.)

in the city with only one of his sandals. The hero had lost it while carrying what seemed to be an old lady across a swift stream; it was in fact the goddess *HERA* in disguise. Unable to harm the unwelcome guest because he had arrived at the time of a religious festival, Pelias decided to rid himself of the threat he represented by sending Jason on an impossible quest. He offered to name Jason as his successor provided he should bring home from Colchis the Golden Fleece belonging to a wonderful ram which had flown there from Iolcus.

Jason gathered together his companions, who became known as the *ARGONAUTS*, and crossed a sea of marvels, overcame difficult tasks, defeated a guardian serpent and returned with the magic fleece. Part of his success was due to the aid of the Colchian princess and witch, *MEDEA*, whom Jason made his wife with the assistance of the goddess *ATHENA*. On returning to Iolcus, the Argonauts found that Pelias had assumed that they had died in a shipwreck and murdered Jason's father Aeson. Two versions of the myth exist from this point onwards. In one of them Pelias is destroyed by means of Medea's magic. In another the Argonauts, seeing that Pelias will not honour his promise to Jason, sail off to Corinth after failing to capture Iolcus. Jason seems to have accepted exile in Corinth with Medea, where for some ten years they lived happily together and had three sons. Then the hero was offered the hand of a princess named Glauce. When he deserted Medea for her, Jason brought down on his own head the full fury and magical powers of the Colchian princess. For Medea not only killed Glauce but she also destroyed her sons by Jason. Alone and depressed, the hero lingered at Corinth until one day, as he sat in the shade of the *Argo*, his old ship, a piece of rotten timber fell and crushed his skull. (See also *HEROES; VOYAGERS*)

JASON (left), the celebrated hero of the Argonauts, was loved by the dark sorceress Medea, whose magic arts helped him slay the dragon guarding the Golden Fleece. With salves and invocations, she protected him from harm by fire, demon or sword. (JASON BY GUSTAVE MOREAU, CANVAS, 1865.)

JUNO was the Roman equivalent of *HERA*, the wife of *ZEUS*, the chief god of the Greeks. Juno was the queen of the sky and the wife of *JUPITER*. She was always associated with the Greek goddess of birth, Eileithyia, and was called by the Romans "the one who makes the child see the light of day". At the touch of a magical herb specially grown by Flora, the goddess of flowering and blossoming plants, Juno became pregnant with the war god *MARS*. Juno's own warlike aspect is apparent in her attire. She often appears armed and wearing a goatskin cloak, which was the garment favoured by Roman soldiers on campaign. In Rome she was worshipped on the Capitol hill along with Jupiter and *MINERVA*, goddess of wisdom and the arts. The festival of Matronalia was held in her honour on 1 March.

JUNO (below), the Roman queen of heaven and of womanhood, accompanied every woman through life from birth to death. She is here portrayed in classical style, with a regal diadem, severe hairstyle, and tranquil, majestic air. (JUNO WITH DIADEM, MARBLE, C. 200 BC.)

L

JUPITER *and Mercury, who is wearing his travelling hat, enjoy a wholesome meal with the kindly rustics, Philemon and Baucis, who alone among mortals welcomed the gods as they wandered in human form through Phrygia.* (JUPITER AND MERCURY WITH PHILEMON AND BAUCIS, BY PETER PAUL RUBENS, CANVAS, 1620-25.)

JUPITER was the Roman sky god, the equivalent of *ZEUS*. The cult of Jupiter Optimus Maximus ("the best and greatest") began under the Etruscan kings, who were expelled from Rome around 507 BC. At first, Jupiter was associated with the elements, especially storms, thunder and lightning, but he later became the protector of the Roman people and was their powerful ally in war. The games held in the circus in Rome were dedicated to him.

LAIUS, son of Labdacus, king of Thebes, was the father of *OEDIPUS* and one of the most tragic figures in Greek mythology. The fate that destroyed his family was due to a curse uttered by *PELOPS* in revenge for Laius carrying off Pelops' young son Chrysippus, who later hanged himself for shame.

In Thebes, Laius took Jocasta as his wife, but they had no children, which the Delphic Oracle told them was fortunate, because Laius was destined to be killed by his own son. For a time Laius and Jocasta did not share the marriage bed. Then one night, full of wine, Laius slept with her and Jocasta conceived a son. So as to overcome the prophecy, the baby was left to die on a distant mountainside, his feet having been cut through with a spike. This action may have been intended to hasten death, but it is not impossible that Laius was also concerned to prevent the child's ghost from walking freely. But the effect was quite the opposite. A shepherd heard the baby's screams and took him to Corinth, where the childless King Polybus adopted him and gave him the name of Oedipus ("swell-foot").

When Oedipus reached manhood he went to Delphi to ask about his parentage. He was told that he would be reunited with his parents in a terrible manner, for he was destined to kill his father and marry his mother. Concluding incorrectly that Corinth was his place of birth, Oedipus travelled towards the north and approached Thebes. On the road he encountered Laius, who was on his way to consult the Delphic Oracle about the *SPHINX*, a monster with the face and breasts of a woman, the body of a lion and wings, which was causing havoc in the Theban countryside. Oedipus refused to stand aside for the king, a fight ensued and Laius was killed. Thus was Laius' destiny, and the first part of his son's, fulfilled.

LAOCOON was a Trojan, said by some to be the brother of Anchises, and a priest of the sea god *POSEIDON*. Both the Greeks and the Romans remembered him as the man who warned the Trojans not to accept the so-called Greek gift of the Wooden Horse. He even drove a spear into its side to show his fellow countrymen that inside the hollow belly could lurk a terrible danger to Troy. However, like the prophetess *CASSANDRA*, Laocoon was ignored. Worse than the fate of Cassandra was that of Laocoon and his two sons, for no Trojan lifted a hand to help when two great sea-serpents suddenly arrived and crushed them to death.

There was no agreement, however, among the Greeks or the Romans about why Laocoon and his sons were killed by the sea-serpents. One opinion was that Laocoon's punishment was not connected with the Trojan War at all. The god of prophecy, *APOLLO*, was simply punishing the priest for disobeying a divine command. An alternative view was that the death of Laocoon and his sons was the work of *ATHENA* or Poseidon for causing damage to the dedicatory horse. A Greek named Sinon had informed the Trojans that it was an offering to the goddess Athena: if they destroyed it, then Troy would fall, but if they dragged it inside the city walls, then the Wooden Horse was a guarantee of Troy's safety. In the event the cunning plot worked for the benefit of the Greeks, as those warriors hidden within the horse began a slaughter that led to the eventual overthrow and destruction of the besieged city.

As for the two serpents, once they had crushed Laocoon and his sons to death, they hid themselves in either the temple of Apollo or the temple of Athena.

LAOCOON *and his sons were crushed to death by a pair of giant sea-serpents. The ancient poets differed as to the serpents' origin, whether they were sent by Athena or Apollo, and whether Laocoon was innocent or guilty and of what sin.* (ILLUSTRATION FROM DICTIONARY OF CLASSICAL ANTIQUITIES, 1891.)

LEDA *was loved by Zeus in the shape of a swan. From their union, Leda produced two eggs, one containing the twins, Castor and Polydeuces. As young men, the twins are often depicted with egg-shaped helmets, recalling their unusual parentage. LEDA AFTER LEONARDO DA VINCI, CANVAS, C. 1515-16.)*

LEDA *was loved by Zeus in the shape of a swan. From their union, Leda produced two eggs, one containing the twins, Castor and Polydeuces. As young men, the twins are often depicted with egg-shaped helmets, recalling their unusual parentage. LEDA AFTER LEONARDO DA VINCI, CANVAS, C. 1515-16.)*

LETO was the daughter of the *TITANS* Coeus and Phoebe, and she was one of the few Titanesses to be worshipped in ancient Greece. However, her cult was commonly associated with those of her more famous son and daughter *APOLLO* and *ARTEMIS*, whose father was the sky god *ZEUS*. Leto may have given birth to her divine children on the sacred island of Delos, which a helpful *POSEIDON* is said to have fastened permanently to the bottom of the sea with a huge pillar. Later, one of Apollo's most important temples was built on the island. Even the invading Persians respected this sanctuary, when in 490 BC their fleet passed by on its way to punish the Eretrians and Athenians for providing aid to the Greek rebels who were fighting Persia in Asia Minor.

LETO (below), clutching her tiny twins, children of Zeus, flees a giant serpent sent by the vengeful Hera who relentlessly plagued her husband's lovers. The boy, Apollo, plucks a cithara, his attribute as god of the arts, while Artemis clutches a tiny bow, symbol of her role as goddess of the wild. (ILLUSTRATION BY NICK BEALE, 1995.)

LEDA was the daughter of King Thestius of Aetolia, which was a state in north-western Greece. Her husband was King Tyndareos of Sparta. Two of Leda's children were *CLYTEMNESTRA*, the murderous wife of *AGAMEMNON*, and *HELEN*, who was the unfaithful wife of *MENELAUS*, Agamemnon's brother, and the cause of the Trojan War. Leda was also the mother of the *DIOSCURI*, the twin sons Castor and Polydeuces. Various accounts are given of the fathers of her children, for Leda was loved by *ZEUS* who came to her disguised as a swan. Some say that as a result of their union Leda produced two eggs, one contained Clytemnestra and Helen, and the other the Dioscuri, but that Helen's and Polydeuces' father was Zeus while Tyndareos was the father of the mortals Clytemnestra and Castor. In the case of Helen there is little doubt that the myth of the Trojan War turned a goddess into a Queen. She clearly has a connection with older Aegean goddesses who were associated with birds and eggs.

MONSTERS AND FABULOUS BEASTS

CLASSICAL MONSTERS come in all shapes and colours, sometimes hideous, but sometimes bewitchingly fair, sometimes half-human and sometimes entirely demonic. Monsters generally symbolize the dark and unresolved forces in life and in human nature. Greek mythology is full of composite creatures, such as the Chimaera, Sphinx and Scylla, symbolizing complex evil. Not all monsters were cruel, and some, such as Ladon, guarded a precious treasure, while the Sphinx guarded the pass to the city of Thebes. Other monsters ravaged the land, such as the Hydra and Chimaera. Still others were raised by a curse, as when Poseidon sent a sea monster in response to Theseus' rage. Savage beasts, such as satyrs and Centaurs, part human and part animal, represent man's unruly, instinctive nature. Although less awesome than demons, they still harassed and haunted humans.

PYTHON (above), a monstrous serpent, son of Gaia, haunted the caves of Parnassus until slain by Apollo with his first arrows. Apollo founded the Pythian games to commemorate his victory and was afterwards named Apollo Physius. The monster's defeat was celebrated every nine years at the festival of Stepteria at Delphi and involved an enactment of the whole event. (ILLUSTRATION BY GLENN STEWARD, 1995.)

SCYLLA (above), a six-headed sea monster, fished for dolphins, sea-dogs and sailors from her cavern in the Strait of Messina. According to one myth, she was originally a beautiful sea nymph, loved by Zeus and Poseidon in turn, until changed by the jealousy of Circe into a snapping, barking monster. Here, she snatches up the crew of Odysseus as his ship sails past her cavern. (ILLUSTRATION FROM STORIES FROM GREECE AND ROME, 1930.)

THE SIRENS (right) were beautiful sea nymphs who charmed sailors by their alluring songs. Although initially depicted as bird-maids, they later became fair temptresses. Here, Odysseus sails past with his crew; having advised his men to stop their ears with wax, he had himself bound to the mast so that he could hear the sirens' magic song without being lured away. (ODYSSEUS AND THE SIRENS BY FRANCESCO PRIMATICCIO, CANVAS, 1505-70.)

SATYRS (above), wild spirits of the forest, appeared as goat-like creatures with puck noses, bristling hair, budding horns and goat's ears, tails and sometimes hooves. Usually portrayed as wanton and crafty, they frolicked in the forest, chased after nymphs and played impish tricks on men. Here, Diana's forest nymphs are plagued by licentious old satyrs. (DIANA'S NYMPHS CHASED BY SATYRS BY PETER PAUL RUBENS, CANVAS, C. 1670.)

CENTAURS (below), apparently the offspring of Ixion and a cloud, were man-horse beasts who led a wild and savage life in Thessaly, and were fond of riotous revelries. They came to symbolize the dark, unruly forces of nature. The wise Centaur, Chiron, who instructed heroes, was a unique case. Here, the centaurs, writhing in a fierce battle, symbolize the blind and brute force of human nature. (BATTLE OF THE CENTAURS BY ARNOLD BOCKLIN, CANVAS, 1873.)

HARPIES (left), storm goddesses, were feared as robbers and spoilers who raged over battlefields and carried away the weak and wounded or stole children without warning. Originally they were imagined as winged goddesses with beautiful hair. Later on, they appear as awful monsters and spirits of mischief, half-birds, half-maids. (ILLUSTRATION BY GLENN STEWARD, 1995.)

M

LUCRETIA, after her suicide, returned to haunt Sextus Tarquinius, "false Sextus", the high-handed Etruscan who had raped her, incensing the whole of Rome. She appears as a pale, shrouded phantom who sings as she spins through the watches of the night. (ILLUSTRATION FROM LAYS OF ANCIENT

LUCRETIA was the wife of Tarquinius Collatinus and represented the ideal of Roman womanhood. When Sextus, youngest son of the Etruscan king *TARQUINIUS SUPERBUS*, raped her at dagger point around 507 BC, she made her father and her husband promise to avenge her honour before she stabbed herself to death. According to Roman legend, Lucretia's funeral roused the people and their anger was channelled by the inspiring eloquence of Lucius Junius *BRUTUS* into a desire for the overthrow of the monarchy.

MARS, the son of *JUNO* and a magical flower, was originally the Roman god of fertility and vegetation but later became associated with battle. As the god of spring, when his major festivals were held, he presided over agriculture in general. In his warlike aspect he was offered sacrifices before combat and was said to appear on the battlefield accompanied by Bellona, a warrior goddess variously identified as his wife, sister or daughter. Mars, unlike his Greek counterpart,

MARS, god of war, forces himself on gentle Pax and Abundanti, spirits of peace and plenty, while Minerva skilfully steers him away. The allegory dramatizes an age-old conflict, keenly felt in the warring Roman heart. (MINERVA DRIVING MARS BY JACOPO ROBUSTI TINTORETTO, CANVAS, C. 1576.)

ARES, was more widely worshipped than any of the other Roman gods, probably because his sons *REMUS AND ROMULUS* were said to have founded the city.

MEDEA was the daughter of Aietes, king of Colchis, a country adjoining the Black Sea, and the first wife of the voyager *JASON*. Medea means "the cunning one" – a suitable name for a princess skilled in the magic arts. In fact, to the Greeks she hovered somewhere between witch and goddess.

Medea fell in love with the Thessalian hero Jason as soon as he landed in Colchis with the *ARGONAUTS*, and she used magic to help him gain the Golden Fleece, the object of their expedition. On the hasty voyage back, when the Colchian fleet gave pursuit, Medea sacrificed her brother to slow the pursuers. On their return to Iolcus, Jason's birthplace, she managed to

rejuvenate an old ram by boiling him in a magic pot whereupon he turned into a lamb. She also disposed of Jason's enemy, King Pelias of Iolcus, by persuading his daughters to give him a similar course of beauty treatment, but which killed him. As a result, Jason and Medea were banished to Corinth.

The relations between Jason and Medea went badly wrong. Jason put his first wife aside in order to marry Glauce, a Theban princess. Medea, feeling very insulted, took a terrible revenge on Jason. Glauce was burned alive in a poisoned wedding dress, and Medea saw to it that her own children by Jason were also killed. She then escaped to Athens in a magic chariot, which was said to belong to her grandfather *HELIOS*, the sun god.

In Athens, Medea married its king, *AEGEUS*, and bore him a son named Medus. At this time Aegeus believed he was childless, although

he already had a son in the hero *THESEUS*. Through her wily skills, Medea prevailed upon Aegeus to reject Theseus when he came to Athens to claim his inheritance, and she may also have persuaded him to send Theseus to subdue the bull of Marathon. When Theseus succeeded in this dangerous task and at last Aegeus recognized him as his own successor, Medea fled with Medus to Colchis, where they avenged the recent overthrow and death of Aietes. Medus became a ruler of Colchis, but nothing else is known of Medea.

MENELAUS, king of Sparta, was the younger son of *ATREUS*. It was to recover Menelaus' wife *HELEN* that his older brother *AGAMEMNON*, king of Mycenae, led the Greek expedition against Troy. In spite of being warned, Menelaus not only entertained *PARIS*, the eldest son of King *PRIAM* of Troy, but he also

MERCURY (above), as the messenger god of the Romans, was closely identified with the Greek god Hermes. In works of art, he typically wears a winged helmet, or wide-brimmed traveller's hat, and carries a herald's staff, the emblem of peace. (MERCURY AND ARGUS BY PETER PAUL RUBENS, DETAIL, CANVAS, 1635.)

MEDEA, a ruthless sorceress, flees from Colchis with Jason and the Golden Fleece across the seas to Greece, with her father, Aietes, in pursuit. To slow him down, she cut up her brother and cast the parts into the sea, forcing Aietes to pick up the pieces for a pious burial. (THE GOLDEN FLEECE BY H J DRAPER, CANVAS, C. 1880.)

went off to Crete and left Helen alone at Sparta with the handsome visitor. Paris and Helen eloped, taking many of the treasures for which Menelaus was famous.

During the ten-year struggle against Troy, Menelaus played a secondary role to Agamemnon and the other Greek kings, although he was no coward. In single combat with Paris, Menelaus tried to settle the dispute between the Greeks and the Trojans. He won and was only prevented from killing his rival by the intervention of the love goddess APHRODITE. She was indebted to Paris for judging her more beautiful than the goddesses HERA and ATHENA; in gratitude she had given him the love of Helen, the most beautiful woman alive.

After the fall of Troy, Menelaus could not bring himself to kill Helen because of her outstanding beauty. Once again the goddess Aphrodite cast her spell and they were reconciled and returned to Sparta, where they lived happily for many years. When Menelaus died he went to live in the Elysian Fields with his immortal Helen.

MERCURY was the Roman messenger god, and was also the deity who watched over trade and commerce, as his name suggests. He was associated with peace and prosperity. He was apparently imported from Greece around the fifth century BC. Mercury is usually depicted in the same way as his Greek counterpart HERMES, with a winged hat and staff.

MIDAS was said to be the son of Gordius and Cybele, or to have been adopted by Gordius. He was the king of Phrygia and renowned for his wealth. According to the Greeks, his fabulous riches were the result of a kindness he showed to SILENUS, the old goat-like tutor of DIONYSUS, the god of vegetation, wine and ecstasy. So pleased was Dionysus with this behaviour that he offered Midas whatever he wished. The king asked for everything he touched to be turned into gold. At first Midas was overjoyed with the gift, but once he realized that even his food and drink were being transformed on touching his lips, he was horrified. Out of pity

Dionysus told him how to wash away his golden touch, which Midas did in the River Pactolus, thereafter famous for the gold dust to be found on its bed.

Another myth told about Midas concerns a musical competition between the gods APOLLO and PAN, the divine inventors of the lyre and pipes respectively. When the prize was awarded to Apollo, Midas incautiously expressed his surprise at the outcome and received from Apollo a set of ass's ears for his foolish presumption.

MIDAS, the fabled king of Phrygia, was fabulously rich, yet chose, when granted a wish by the gods, to become richer still, by asking for everything he touched to turn to gold. His wish was granted, but joy quickly turned to grief when he could neither eat nor drink. (ILLUSTRATION BY NICK BEALE, 1995.)

MENELAUS (left) was usually a gentle, even-tempered man, but here he fights fiercely over the fallen body of Patroclus who lies naked, for Apollo had struck off his helmet, splintered his ash spear and broken his corselet, stripping him bare so that he would be easily killed by Hector. (ILLUSTRATION FROM STORIES FROM HOMER, 1885.)

N

MINERVA (whose name may have originally meant "thought") was the Roman goddess of wisdom and the arts, the equivalent of the Greek goddess *ATHENA*. She was worshipped throughout Italy, though only in Rome did she take on a warlike character. Minerva is usually depicted wearing a coat of mail and a helmet, and carrying a spear. The Romans dedicated the spoils of war to her.

MINOS was the son of *ZEUS* and *EUROPA* and became the king of Crete, with his palace situated at Knossos. The Greeks regarded him both as a just lawgiver and as a cruel oppressor. To build his wonderful palace, Minos employed the Athenian craftsman *DAEDALUS*, whose creations were thought to be almost divine. So lifelike were his statues, for instance, that they had to be chained down in order to stop them running away. Minos was less pleased, however, with the hollow cow that Daedalus made for his queen, *PASIPHAE*, so that she might satisfy her desire for the white bull which *POSEIDON* had sent from the waves as a sign that Minos should ascend the Cretan throne. The *MINOTAUR*, a man with a bull's head, was the outcome of Pasiphae's unnatural union. This monstrous creature was housed in the Labyrinth, a special maze built by Daedalus at Minos' request.

Minos was known to the Greeks as an ancient ruler of the seas. His naval strength could well have owed something to Daedalus' inventiveness. Certainly he was not prepared for another ruler to enjoy the remarkable services of the craftsman. When Daedalus and his son Icarus left Crete without permission, Minos sailed to Sicily in hot pursuit. There, in the city of Kamikos, Minos met his death. Daedalus had arrived in Sicily as a refugee. He quickly went to ground and was hidden by King Cocalos of Kamikos. In order to find out where the craftsman was hiding,

MINERVA (above), the Roman goddess of wisdom, is depicted here taming a wild Centaur, who symbolizes the dark unruly side of human nature. His yearning expression suggests man's longing for divinity, despite himself. (MINERVA AND THE CENTAUR BY SANDRO BOTTICELLI, CANVAS, C. 1482.)

Minos carried a shell and promised to reward anyone who could pass a thread through it. Daedalus alone could solve the problem, which eventually he was unable to resist. When King Cocalos, on Daedalus' behalf, claimed the prize, Minos demanded that the craftsman be surrendered to him. But the daughters of Cocalos were unwilling to lose the inventive man who made them beautiful toys, and with his help they plotted Minos' death. When they took their royal guest to the bathroom, Daedalus led a pipe through the roof and boiling water, or oil, was poured down upon the

THE MINOTAUR (below) wrestles with Theseus in the Labyrinth, which is represented by the meander pattern at the sides. The bull-baiters above illustrate the sport of bull-leaping, part of the mysterious bull-cult of ancient Crete. (THE BULL-BAITERS BY JOHN DUNCAN, WATERCOLOUR, C. 1880.)

unsuspecting Cretan king. After his death Minos became a stern judge in the realm of *HADES*, the underworld, the land of the dead.

THE MINOTAUR was the monstrous son of a white bull, which was sent by the sea god *POSEIDON*, and *PASIPHAE*, the wife of King *MINOS* of Crete. When the child was born it had the head of a bull and the body of a man, and was given the name Minotaur ("Minos' bull").

The creature was fed on seven boys and seven girls sent annually as tribute by the Athenians. To free his countrymen of this terrible burden the hero *THESEUS* came to Knossos, entered the maze-like Labyrinth where the Minotaur lived and killed it. He was assisted by King Minos' daughter *ARIADNE*, who gave him a ball of thread, instructing him to unravel it on his way into the maze so that he could find his way out again. She also gave Theseus a sword.

In the strange story of the Minotaur the Greeks recalled in a garbled form the glories of the older inhabitants of Crete. It is now known that the bull games of the ancient Cretans involved young athletes leaping over bulls, even attempting somersaults holding the horns. Although some of them doubtless sustained serious injury, or may even have been killed, there is nothing to suggest that a man-eating creature was involved.

MOERAE see *FATES*

THE MUSES, from the Roman name, Musae, were the daughters of *ZEUS* and Mnemosyne, a *TITAN*, whose name means "memory". They used to dance and sing at parties held by the gods and heroes. For the Greeks, the Muses were the inspiration of poetry, music and dance. Later, other intellectual activities were added to their care. Although accounts of their number differ, it is generally accepted that

the echo of her voice. Narcissus was then condemned by Nemesis, goddess of retribution, to spend the rest of his days admiring his own reflection in a pool. At last he died and was turned into the flower that bears his name.

NEPTUNE was an ancient Italian water god whom the Romans identified with *POSEIDON*. Compared to Poseidon, however, Neptune plays a minor role in Roman mythology.

NOTUS see *FORCES OF NATURE*

OCEANOS was a *TITAN*, the son of Ouranos and *GAIA*, but never an enemy of *ZEUS*. On the contrary, he protected Zeus' wife *HERA* and mother *RHEA* when the gods fought the Titans. As ruler of the encircling sea, which the Greeks believed surrounded the world, Oceanos married his sister Tethys and they produced three thousand rivers.

THE MUSES, guiding spirits of the arts, inspired all gifted artists, though they resented any serious competition and deprived the Sirens of their feathers for daring to be better than them in song. The nine Muses appear here amid the aspiring artists of the Renaissance. (THE REALM OF THE MUSES BY LORENZO COSTA, CANVAS, C. 1506)

OCEANUS (left), father of the river gods, is depicted here with a typically tempestuous face, unruly locks and horned brow. Above him, Selene, the crescent moon, sheds a mild light; and on either side flash the stars, Phosphorus (left) and Hesperus (right). (ILLUSTRATION FROM DICTIONARY OF CLASSICAL ANTIQUITIES, 1891.)

there were nine Muses altogether – Clio, Euterpe, Thalia, Melpomene, Terpsichore, Erato, Polyhymnia, Urania and Calliope.

NAIADS see *FORCES OF NATURE*

NARCISSUS, according to Greek mythology, was the beautiful son of the River Cephissus in Boeotia and the nymph Liriope. Among the many who loved him, including immortals and mortals, was Echo, who slowly pined away, leaving just

NARCISSUS (right), a beautiful youth, was loved by the nymph Echo who, failing to attract him, died of grief. He, in his turn, fell in love with his own reflection and pined away until changed by the gods into the flower that bears his name. (ECHO AND NARCISSUS BY J W WATERHOUSE, CANVAS, 1880.)

ODYSSEUS alights on the island of Aeaea where he is warned by Hermes of the horrors of Circe's enchanting wine, which turns men into swine. This fate has already befallen one comrade and so Odysseus must keep his guard. (CIRCE WITH THE COMRADES OF ODYSSEUS BY ALESSANDRO ALLORI, FRESCO, 1580.)

ODYSSEUS, king of Ithaca, was one of the Greek leaders who took part in the Trojan War. He was celebrated for both his part in this conflict and his remarkable voyage home to his island kingdom in the Ionian Sea.

A brave and clever man, Odysseus was sometimes thought to have been the son of *SISYPHUS*, the trickster of Greek mythology. But his real father was probably Laertes, whom he succeeded as king of Ithaca. His mother was named Anticleia and his faithful wife Penelope was the sister of King Tyndareos of Sparta.

From the start of the campaign against Troy it is clear that King *AGAMEMNON*, the Greek leader, placed great store upon Odysseus' cunning. He was sent with Nestor, the aged king of Pylos, to discover where the great warrior *ACHILLES* was hidden. Again, at Aulis, where the Greek fleet was stranded by contrary winds, it was Odysseus who tricked Agamemnon's wife *CLYTEMNESTRA* into sending her daughter *IPHIGENIA* from Mycenae, supposedly to marry Achilles. Instead, however, Iphigenia was to be sacrificed to *ARTEMIS*, goddess of the wild, in order to obtain a fair wind to Troy. Throughout the ten-year struggle against the Trojans, Odysseus was important not so much as a fighter but as a counsellor and a schemer. His eloquence was renowned, and it was probably Odysseus who thought of the Wooden Horse, which gave the Greeks victory.

Odysseus deceived the Trojans with this horse built of wood whose hollow belly was filled with Greek warriors under his own command. The Trojans dragged the Wooden Horse inside their walls when they learned from a Greek, deliberately left behind when the rest put to sea, that the offering would bring their city a guarantee of divine protection. But during the night the Greeks emerged from it, and surprised the Trojans. Hence, the ancient saying "Never trust the Greeks bearing gifts".

Although Troy fell, the wildness of the looting and the slaughter deeply offended the gods. In particular, the goddess *ATHENA* was enraged at the rape of *CASSANDRA* within the sanctuary of her own temple. Odysseus tried to appease Athena, and he escaped drowning in the great storm which the angry goddess sent to shatter the victorious Greek fleet on its homeward journey. But he could not entirely avoid blame, and *POSEIDON* saw to it that he was the last Greek leader to reach home, after a voyage lasting some ten years.

The long period of wandering that Odysseus suffered was a favourite story of both the Greeks and the Romans, who knew the voyager by the name of Ulysses. The exact route that he followed remains a mystery, not least because his travels took him beyond known territory and into strange and dangerous lands. From Troy Odysseus sailed first to

ODYSSEUS raises his great bow and, with effortless might, stretches the bowstring which the suitors had struggled in vain to bend. He then slays the suitors who have devoured his wealth and plagued his wife during his long voyage home. (ILLUSTRATION FROM STORIES FROM HOMER, 1885.)

ODYSSEUS, *on his way through the ghostly underworld, consults the shade of Tiresias, who warns him that if he offends Helios he will return home alone on a foreign ship only after many years' wandering.* (TIRESIAS COUNSELS ODYSSEUS BY ALESSANDRO ALLORI, FRESCO, 1580.)

Thrace, where he lost many of his men in battle. After this bloody incident the places he touched upon are less easy to identify. Storms drove him to the land of the Lotophagi ("the lotus-eaters"), whose diet made visitors forget their homelands and wish to stay on forever. Then he encountered in Sicily, it was later believed, the Cyclops POLYPHEMUS, whose father was Poseidon. By putting out Polyphemus' single eye when the gigantic man was befuddled with wine, Odysseus and his companions managed to escape becoming his dinner. They then arrived on the floating island of Aeolus, who was the ruler of the winds. There Odysseus received a rare present, a sack full of winds. The idea appears in many different mythologies, but according to the Greeks, it was of little use on the voyage because the curiosity of Odysseus' men got the better of them and they opened the sack and the winds no longer blew in a helpful direction.

A tragedy overcame the squadron of ships that Odysseus led among the Laestrygones, a race of giant cannibals. Only his own ship survived the attack and reached Aeaea, the island of the enchantress CIRCE, later considered to be situated off Italy. Odysseus resisted her spells, with the aid of the messenger god HERMES, and made the enchantress restore to human shape his men who had been turned to swine. Afterwards, on Circe's advice, he sailed to the western edge of the encircling sea, the realm of OCEANOS, where ghosts came from the underworld realm of HADES to meet him. The shade of the blind seer TIRESIAS gave Odysseus a special warning about his homeward journey to Ithaca. He told him that if the cattle of the sun god HELIOS on the isle of Thrinacia were harmed by him he would never reach his home. The ghost of Odysseus' mother also spoke of the difficulties being faced by Penelope in Ithaca at the time. The ghost of Agamemnon, his old comrade-in-arms, also warned him about his homecoming; when he returned home he had been murdered by his wife and lover in the bathroom.

Turning eastwards, Odysseus sailed back towards Greece and was the only man who dared to listen to the alluring song of the Sirens, bird-women of storm. He filled his men's ears with wax and had himself bound with strong cords to the mast. Odysseus then passed through the straits between Sicily and Italy, where six of his crew were seized by the six-headed monster Scylla. On the island of Thrinacia, as Tiresias had foretold, the voyagers were tempted by hunger to slay some of Helios' cattle. Despite his warning, the desperate men killed and cooked several cows when Odysseus was asleep. Later they deserted him, but were drowned in a storm sent by ZEUS at Helios' request.

Alone, Odysseus was almost swallowed by the great whirlpool Charybdis. In an exhausted state he drifted to the wondrous island of the sea nymph Calypso, who cared for him and eventually proposed marriage. But not even immortality would tempt him, and after seven years the gods forced Calypso to let Odysseus set off again. Shipwrecked once more in the land of the Phaeacians, he was welcomed as an honoured guest and offered a passage back to Ithaca. So it was that he was secretly landed near his own palace, which he entered disguised with Athena's aid as a beggar.

Penelope had been patiently awaiting Odysseus' return from the war. Although pressed to marry one of her many noble suitors, she had put them off for a while by pretending that she could not marry until she had finished weaving a shroud for Laertes, her father in law. But Penelope unravelled it each night, until one of her maids betrayed the trick. Finally, after ten years, Penelope agreed to marry the suitor who could bend and string Odysseus' great bow. This challenge was proposed on the advice of the goddess Athena. The only suitor who succeeded at the challenge was a beggar, who then threw off his disguise and revealed himself as Odysseus.

Assisted by his son Telemachus and two loyal retainers, Odysseus dispatched the suitors and hanged the treacherous maids. Reunited with his family at last, including his father Laertes, Odysseus then defeated an attack by the relations of the suitors and returned Ithaca to peace. Zeus himself threw down a thunderbolt to signal an end to the fighting. (See also VOYAGERS)

ODYSSEUS *the wanderer returns home after twenty years and embraces Penelope at last. She had refused to acknowledge her husband until he had reminded her of the secret of their bed, which was carved out of a great olive tree grown in the courtyard.* (ILLUSTRATION FROM STORIES FROM HOMER, 1885.)

FORCES OF NATURE

THE WONDERS AND MYSTERIES OF NATURE are explained in mythology through the will and actions of the gods. Sunrise and sunset, storms and tidal waves, summer and winter unfold as part of a divine drama. For the ancient Greeks, the sun rose and set because Phoebus Apollo drove the glittering sun-chariot on a fiery course across the sky, preceded by Eos who sprinkled morning dew from her vase. Springtime came when Persephone, who symbolized the seed-corn, rose from the underworld to live in the light of day with her mother, Demeter, goddess of corn. The tempestuous sea god, Poseidon, could stir up sea-storms, or soothe the waves; while mighty Zeus could strike from afar with a bolt of lightning or brighten the sky with rainbows. In addition to the great gods of sky, land and sea, nature spirits or nymphs infused the forests, fields and rivers.

APOLLO (above), god of light, symbolized not only sunlight – for originally Helios (the sun) radiated daylight and was only later identified with Apollo – but also the bright, life giving, pure, healing light of divinity. Apollo's light underlies his other roles as god of healing, god of prophecy and god of the arts. He withdrew in winter to sunny Lycius and returned in spring to dispel winter. Here, he drives the sun-chariot on its course across the heavens. (ILLUSTRATION FROM STORIES FROM LIVY, 1885.)

POSEIDON (above), the turbulent god of the seas, symbolized the might of the sea-storm. He dwelt in a golden palace in the depths of the ocean, and rode the waves in his sea-chariot, drawn by sea-horses, speeding so fast that he passed from Samothrace to Aegae in three great strides. Beside him basks his wife, the sea nymph Amphitrite, while a school of tritons (part men, part fish) frisk around his chariot blowing their conches, which they used to raise or calm the waves. (POSEIDON AND HIS CHARIOT BY MIRABELLO CAVALORI, C. 1497.)

ZEUS (left), the chief deity, governed the winds and clouds, rain, thunder and lightning. By striking his aegis he caused storms and tempests to rage, but equally, he could calm the elements and brighten the sky. As the father of the hours, he governed the changing seasons. An awesome but benign god, he is seen here resplendent in fiery light, bearing his aegis, symbol of his sovereign power over all forces of nature and all other gods. (JUPITER AND SEMELE BY GUSTAVE MOREAU, CANVAS, DETAIL, 1896.)

FLORA (right), blooming Roman goddess of spring, was honoured every year at the time of the Floralia, a theatrical festival when the people decked themselves in flowers and enjoyed a great feast lasting for six days. Flora, serene and benign, is here honoured in a lavish parade. Poussin's atmospheric scene vividly revives the pagan splendour of the early Greek pastoral festivals. (THE TRIUMPH OF FLORA BY NICOLAS POUSSIN, CANVAS, C. 1627.)

HEPHAISTOS (below), the smith god, is typically depicted as a grave, intense man wearing a workman's cap and immersed in his fiery craft. He had forges beneath volcanoes but also on Olympus where 20 bellows worked at his bidding. Famed for his artistry, he crafted works of wonder, such as Achilles' shield, embossed with a dramatic scene of life and death, joy and grief, peace and war. (APOLLO IN THE FORGE OF HEPHAISTOS BY DIEGO VELASQUEZ, CANVAS, DETAIL, 1630.)

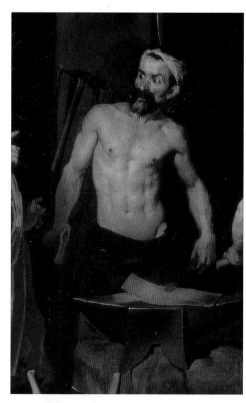

THE NAIADS (above), or water nymphs, dwelt beside running water. Like their cousins, the Nereids and Oceanids of the oceans, the Oreads of the hills and the Dryads of forests and trees, they were usually sweet, benign spirits. Naiads, especially, were helpful and healing, nurturing fruits, flowers and mortals. Yet the youth Hylas who went to draw water from a pool was lured by the nymphs into the water and never seen again. (HYLAS AND THE WATER NYMPHS BY J W WATERHOUSE, CANVAS, C. 1890.)

NOTUS (below), the south wind, brought with it fog and rain. Here, as a winged deity, Notus pours rain from a vase, much as his mother, Eos, goddess of dawn, sprinkles dew from a vase before the sun-chariot in the early morning. (ILLUSTRATION FROM DR SMITH'S CLASSICAL DICTIONARY, 1891.)

ZEPHYRUS (below), the west wind, dwelt with his brother wind, Boreas, in a palace in Thrace. He was father of the immortal horses, Xanthus and Balius, Achilles' battle steeds who galloped with the speed of wind. (ILLUSTRATION FROM DR SMITH'S CLASSICAL DICTIONARY, 1891.)

P

PAN (above) plays his pipes at dusk. As a spirit of the dark forest, he often startled solitary travellers, arousing sudden awe and panic. He is usually depicted with shaggy head, goat's horns and hooves, dancing or playing a syrinx. (ILLUSTRATION FROM TANGLEWOOD TALES, C. 1920.)

PAN was the son of the messenger god *HERMES*. As the Greek god of the mountainside, the pastures of sheep and goats, he was himself goat-horned and goat-legged. Pan was especially associated with Arcadia, the mountainous state in central Peloponnese. He was playful and energetic, but very irritable, especially if disturbed during his afternoon nap. He liked to play on a pipe, which was known as a syrinx after a nymph of that name who turned herself into a reed-bed to avoid his advances. For Pan could also be a frightening god when he blew on his conch. Our

PANDORA (below), "all-gifts", was the first woman to appear on earth, created by the gods to work mischief for men. Irrepressibly curious, she could not resist opening a sealed jar, containing the horrors of life: strife and sickness, sorrow and grief. (ILLUSTRATION BY NICK BEALE, 1995.)

word "panic" derives from this aspect of his divinity. His worship spread from Arcadia to Athens immediately after the Athenian and Plataean victory over the Persians at Marathon in 480 BC, because he made the Persians flee in panic. He rendered a similar service for *ZEUS* during the battle against *CRONOS* and the *TITANS*. His conch deeply worried Zeus' opponents.

PANDORA was the Greek Eve, the bringer of all sorrows for mankind. She was the first woman and was created by *HEPHAISTOS*, the smith god, on *ZEUS'* orders in

order to upset *PROMETHEUS*, the Greek god of fire and friend of men. When she went to live among men, she was given a gift from the gods which was a sealed jar that contained all the misfortunes of existence. But soon Pandora's great curiosity overcame a natural fear of what might be inside, and she broke the seal, releasing sorrow, disease and conflict. As a result, the men who originally comprised the human race gained a mortal, female companion, but also untold woes. Appropriately, the name Pandora means "all gifts" – the bad as well as the good.

PARIS (above), the judge of a divine beauty contest, chose Aphrodite as the winner because she offered him the world's fairest woman. Behind her, wise Athena had promised him fame, while queenly Hera had offered him power. (THE JUDGEMENT OF PARIS BY JEAN REGNAULT, CANVAS, 1820.)

PARIS was one of the fifty sons of King *PRIAM* of Troy. According to the Greeks, he was responsible for causing the Trojan War. Paris was a very handsome young man and wooed *HELEN* so well that she left her husband *MENELAUS*, king of Sparta, and fled with her lover to Troy. His unusual attractiveness was believed to have been a gift from *APHRODITE*, the goddess of love. In return for choosing her as the fairest of goddesses, Aphrodite offered Paris the most beautiful woman in the world, Helen.

During the long siege of Troy Paris cut a poor figure as a warrior. His single combat with Menelaus, Helen's husband, was supposed to have settled the outcome of the whole war. Instead it revealed Paris as a coward, who only escaped with his life through the intervention of Aphrodite. As a result, the Trojan champion *HECTOR*, his eldest brother, treated him very badly. It was an irony of fate that a poisoned arrow shot from Paris' bow should have found the one vulnerable spot on the mighty Greek champion *ACHILLES*, his heel. Paris himself was killed by an arrow, prior to the fall of Troy.

PASIPHAE, in Greek mythology, was the daughter of *HELIOS*, the sun god, and wife of *MINOS*, king of Crete. The sea god *POSEIDON* sent a white bull as a sign of Minos' right to rule the island, but the king refused to sacrifice the animal when it emerged from the waves, and Poseidon pronounced a curse in anger at the lack of respect

PASIPHAE, queen of Crete, was drawn irresistibly to a mysterious white bull which emerged from the waves. She developed a strange passion for the bull, and from her union with the creature she bore a dreadful bull-man, the Minotaur, who was kept hidden in an underground maze.
(ILLUSTRATION BY NICK BEALE, 1995.)

PEGASUS, a magnificent winged horse, dips and dives through the flames of the fire-breathing monster, the Chimaera. On his back, Bellerophon urges him on. The hero had successfully tamed Pegasus with a golden bridle given to him by Athena.
(ILLUSTRATION FROM TANGLEWOOD TALES, C. 1920.)

shown to himself. Pasiphae was to be stricken with a passionate desire for the bull. In order to gratify her lust, the great craftsman *DAEDALUS* made a cow, into which Pasiphae fitted and so could mate with the bull. Later, she gave birth to the *MINOTAUR* ("Minos' Bull"), which was kept in the Labyrinth.

PEGASUS, in Greek mythology, was the flying horse belonging to the Corinthian hero *BELLEROPHON*. The winged steed was born from blood which spilled from the severed head of the *GORGON* Medusa, who was already pregnant by the sea god *POSEIDON* (a deity always associated with bulls and horses). Bellerophon was given a magic bridle by *ATHENA* to help him tame Pegasus. When the hero tried to fly to Mount Olympus, Pegasus threw him on the instruction of *ZEUS*.

PELOPS was the son of King *TANTALUS*, the ruler of a kingdom in Asia Minor. Pelops' name is still recalled in the Peloponnese ("the isle of Pelops"), which is the large peninsula of southern Greece.

The sea god *POSEIDON* so loved Pelops that he seized the youth and carried him off to Mount Olympus. Possibly because of this divine favour shown to his son, Tantalus was honoured by the gods as no other mortal. He was allowed to eat nectar and ambrosia, the immortal food served to the deities on their mountain home. But Tantalus fell from divine favour and suffered eternal torment as a result.

According to one version of the myth, Tantalus cut up, boiled and served his own son Pelops to the gods in order to test their omniscience. Only *DEMETER*, the goddess of vegetation, partook of the feast, inadvertently eating a piece of Pelops' shoulder. Later, when the gods returned the youth to life, the missing piece of his body was replaced by ivory.

By favour of Poseidon the restored Pelops became famous as a champion charioteer, which was an accomplishment that the ancient Greeks regarded as one of the greatest. So when Oenomaus, king of Elis, offered his daughter Hippodameia in marriage and also his lands to anyone who could defeat him in a chariot race, Pelops accepted the challenge. But he had to agree that Oenomaus could shoot an arrow at him if he caught up with his chariot. Thirteen contestants had already perished.

It was said that Pelops bribed a certain Myrtilus, the king's charioteer, to remove the linchpins from his master's chariot, but when he won Pelops refused to acknowledge this assistance. In different versions of the story, he either threw Myrtilus into the sea, or he spurned him. As a consequence, the father of Myrtilus, who was the messenger god *HERMES*, saw that a curse afflicted the descendants of Pelops. The consequences of this curse on the house of *ATREUS*, Pelops' eldest son and the father of *AGAMEMNON*, is the basis for that family's tragic story.

PELOPS, in the winning chariot, races along the Greek track, fast outstripping his rival Oenomaus, whose chariot swerves and crashes. Pelops' white shoulder was made of ivory, fashioned by the gods after he had been partly eaten by Demeter. (ILLUSTRATION BY GLENN STEWARD, 1995.)

PENELOPE was the daughter of Icarius, king of Sparta, and a nymph Peribaea. As the faithful wife of *ODYSSEUS*, the ruler of Ithaca, she was celebrated for her patience in waiting almost twenty years for his return from Troy. Beset by suitors, Penelope kept them at bay for a long time by pretending to weave a shroud for her father-in-law Laertes. Each night she would secretly unravel the day's work. Eventually, the return of Odysseus saved her from an enforced second marriage, but she remained cold towards her saviour until she was absolutely certain of his identity. Penelope refused to be convinced that the new arrival really was Odysseus until he described their bed, carved in part from a tree trunk still rooted in the ground.

PERSEPHONE was the daughter of *ZEUS* and *DEMETER*, the earth goddess, and became queen of the underworld as the abducted wife of *HADES*. According to the Greeks, Zeus promised his beautiful daughter to Hades without consulting her mother. When Hades rose from the underworld and took his bride by force, Demeter was beside herself with grief. The goddess wandered the earth searching for her daughter, two burning torches in her hands. As a result the land was no longer fertile. Plants wilted, animals

PENELOPE (right), patient wife of Odysseus, shared her husband's cleverness. During his long absence, she kept her many suitors at bay by refusing to marry until she had completed a shroud which she secretly unravelled each night, until the suitors discovered her ploy. (ILLUSTRATION FROM STORIES FROM HOMER, 1885.)

PERSEPHONE (far right), goddess of death, spent the winter in the underworld, rising each spring to live with her mother, the goddess of corn. She symbolizes the seed-corn that is buried, rises and falls again in a cycle of constant renewal – a theme central to the Eleusian mysteries. (PERSEPHONE, MARBLE, DETAIL, C. 490 BC.)

PERSEUS and Andromeda (above) peer gingerly at the face of Medusa, reflected in the water. Burne-Jones' Medusa recalls the tranquil air and death-like beauty of the Greek Medusas carved on amulets and charms, which remind us that she was once beautiful. (THE BALEFUL HEAD BY EDMUND BURNE-JONES, CANVAS, 1887.)

bore no offspring and death stalked mankind. In the end, Zeus was obliged to intervene and ruled that Persephone should spend time each year with both her husband and her mother. Persephone could never return entirely to the living world because she had eaten in Hades' realm: a very old idea that strictly divided the food of the dead from that of the living.

The story of Persephone's abduction, disappearance and return parallels the fertility myths of West Asia. She may well have been a pre-Greek goddess, a deity worshipped by earlier settlers of the country who was later incorporated into Greek religion. Her association with the dead may have a similar origin. The Athenians, who were originally a non-Greek speaking people, referred to the dead as "Demeter's people".

PERSEUS was the son of ZEUS and DANAE, daughter of Acrisius, king of Argos. Danae had been shut up in a bronze tower in order to thwart a prophecy that if she had a son he would kill Acrisius. But Zeus visited her as a golden shower and Perseus was born. A terrified Acrisius placed mother and son in a wooden chest and cast it on the sea. The protection of Zeus, however, was enough to bring them safely to the shores of the island of Seriphos, where Perseus grew up among fishermen.

On reaching manhood Perseus was sent by the local ruler, Polydectes, to fetch the head of the GORGON Medusa, a very dangerous task. Luckily for the hero the goddess ATHENA hated Medusa and instructed him how to proceed.

PHAEDRA, seen here with her sister Ariadne and husband Theseus, was the unfortunate daughter of King Minos and Queen Pasiphae of Crete. She fell in love with her stepson Hippolytus which eventually proved to be her downfall.
(THESEUS WITH ARIADNE AND PHAEDRA BY BENEDETTO GENNARI THE YOUNGER, CANVAS, 1702.)

First he visited the Graiae, three old hags who shared a single eye. Perseus seized the eye and obliged the Graiae to tell him about the nature of the Gorgons, their three dreadful sisters.

Most important of all, they informed him how a direct glance from Medusa's eyes would turn him to stone. He also received three useful gifts from some friendly nymphs: a cap of invisibility, winged shoes and a bag for Medusa's head. Ready for the exploit at last, Perseus put on the shoes and flew to the Gorgon's cave in the far west. Careful not to look at Medusa directly, he approached by watching her reflection in his shield. Having cut off Medusa's head and stowed it in his bag, Perseus flew away unseen by her two sisters.

The chilling powers of the head were used to good purpose by Perseus on his way home. Having

saved the beautiful ANDROMEDA from a sea monster, he married her, but several people had to be turned to stone before he and his bride returned safely to Danae. Having returned his magical equipment to HERMES, the messenger god, Perseus visited Argos only to find that Acrisius had already fled to Larissa on hearing of his grandson's arrival. The prophecy was fulfilled, nevertheless, when Perseus was invited to compete in the games at Larissa and his discus hit the old man on the head.

Because of the accident the hero chose to be king of Tiryns rather than Argos. On hearing of their deaths Athena placed both Perseus and Andromeda in the sky as constellations. (See also HEROES)

PHAEDRA was the daughter of King MINOS and Queen PASIPHAE of Crete. According to the Greeks, the Athenian hero THESEUS made

her his second wife. He seems to have abandoned her sister ARIADNE not long after she helped him kill the MINOTAUR, the bull-headed creature kept in the Labyrinth at Knossos. Like her mother Pasiphae, who gave birth to the Minotaur, Phaedra was soon overcome by an illicit desire. It was not for an animal this time, but for her stepson, Hippolytus, the son of Theseus' earlier marriage to the queen of the AMAZONS, Hippolyta. When she saw how Hippolytus was horrified by her passion for him, Phaedra hanged herself and left a message to Theseus saying that his son had tried to rape her. Theseus exiled his son, who was later killed in a chariot accident. In another version, Theseus cursed his son and asked POSEIDON to destroy Hippolytus, which he did by sending a seamonster. Phaedra, filled with sorrow, then killed herself.

PHAETHON was the son of the sun god HELIOS and Clymene, daughter of OCEANOS. He drove his father's four-horse chariot so fast that he lost control and threatened the world with a terrible heat. ZEUS stopped him with a thunderbolt, which sent Phaethon crashing to the earth. The great god may have also flooded the earth in an attempt to reduce the temperature. It was believed that Phaethon's mad exploit could be traced in the shape of the Milky Way, while he was reflected in the constellation of Auriga, the charioteer.

THE PLEIADES were the seven daughters of the Titan ATLAS, and were named Maia, Electra, Taygete, Celeno, Merope, Asterope and Alcyone. They may have become stars, or doves, in order to escape from the passionate intentions of Orion, the giant hunter. Their appearance in the night sky in May coincides with the beginning of summer, and the constellation of Orion then appears to be in perpetual pursuit of them.

POLYPHEMUS, a one-eyed giant, was in love with the nymph Galatea, but she scorned him, loving instead the handsome Acis. In a jealous rage, the giant crushed Acis with a rock; but Galatea turned her beloved into a Sicilian river bearing his name. (POLYPHEMUS AND THE NYMPH GALATEA BY ANNIBALE CARRACCI, FRESCO, C. 1595.)

POLYPHEMUS was the son of *POSEIDON* and the sea nymph Thoosa. He was a Cyclops, a one-eyed giant, and was thought to have lived on the island of Sicily. *ODYSSEUS*, during his long journey home, came to the island and asked for hospitality, but called himself Nobody. Polyphemus indeed proved to be a dangerous host and treated the Greeks as part of his flock, shutting them up in his cave and eating them one by one for his evening meal. Odysseus dared not kill the Cyclops during the night because his men lacked the strength to move the boulder blocking the entrance to the cave. So Odysseus thought of a cunning plan to enable their escape. He got Polyphemus drunk on wine and then put out his single eye with a stake. The injured giant roared with

pain, but in response to the other Cyclopes' questions he cried out that he was being attacked by Nobody, so they went away, considering him drunk or mad. In the morning Polyphemus opened the entrance to the cave to let out his flock and felt the back of each animal as it passed to ensure no men escaped. But Odysseus and his men tied themselves to the undersides of the sheep and managed to leave undetected. For this crime against his son, Poseidon promised revenge on Odysseus.

POSEIDON was the son of *CRONOS* and *RHEA*. He was the Greek god of the sea, and the equivalent of the Roman *NEPTUNE*. He was particularly associated with horses and bulls. After the overthrow of Cronos, his three sons divided the world between them:

POSEIDON, god of the oceans, rode the waves in a chariot drawn by golden seahorses. With his three-pronged trident, symbol of his power, he shattered the rocks, called forth storms and shook the earth. (NEPTUNE AND HIS HORSES BY E K BIRCE, CANVAS, C. 1880.)

ZEUS took the sky, *HADES* the underworld and Poseidon the sea, while the land was ruled by all three. It was agreed that Zeus was the senior deity, though Poseidon frequently asserted his independence. Once he even chained up Zeus, with the aid of *HERA*, Zeus' wife, and his daughter *ATHENA*. Possibly because his element was the tempestuous sea, Poseidon was thought of as an unruly god. Earthquakes were attributed to his anger, and Hades was often afraid that the roof of the underworld would cave in because of the shaking Poseidon gave the earth.

Poseidon was pictured riding the deep in a chariot pulled by golden seahorses. In his hands was a mighty trident, a weapon capable of stirring the waters to fury, like the sudden violence of an Aegean storm. His wife was Amphitrite, a sea nymph whose name recalls that of the sea monster Triton. This fearful pre-Greek creature was turned by the Greeks into the merman. One of Poseidon's children by Amphitrite bore this name. However, the sea god had many other offspring by other partners. He even mated with the *GORGON* Medusa, much to the annoyance of the goddess Athena. From the severed head of Medusa sprang the winged horse *PEGASUS*, surely a favourite of Poseidon. Worship of the sea god was widespread among

PRIAM, the king of Troy, savours a moment of rare peace with Helen on the city walls, as she describes the kings and chieftains of the Greek host, who circle the city on the plains below. (ILLUSTRATION FROM STORIES OF GREECE AND ROME, 1930.)

the Greeks, although the maritime state of Athens did not always enjoy the best relations with him.

Because the Athenians chose Athena as the deity of their city, Poseidon flooded the countryside until Zeus brought about an understanding. The temple of Athena stood on the acropolis in Athens and Poseidon's own sanctuary was conspicuously sited on Cape Sunium, which majestically juts out into the Aegean Sea.

Another naval power that offended Poseidon was Crete. When its ruler, King *MINOS*, asked

the sea god for a sign, a white bull emerged from the waves. Religious custom required Minos to sacrifice the animal, but he chose not to do so, with the result that his own wife *PASIPHAE* became the bull's lover. Their strange union produced the *MINOTAUR*, the bull-headed man slain by Athenian hero *THESEUS*. (See also *FORCES OF NATURE*)

PRIAM was the son of Laomedon and the nymph Strymo, daughter of the River Scamander. By the time of the Trojan War Priam, the king of Troy, was already an old man, father of fifty sons, some by his queen Hecuba, the rest by other women. Although he disapproved of the conflict with the Greeks and its cause, Priam was always kind to *HELEN* throughout the long siege. She had eloped to Troy with his son *PARIS*. Priam was killed in the courtyard of his palace when the Greeks sacked Troy.

PROMETHEUS was a son of the *TITAN* Iapetus and one of the older Greek gods who sided with *ZEUS* in his fight against his father *CRONOS*. His fame was due to his affection for mankind, to whom he gave fire. Zeus, the leader of the new and stronger gods, had hidden fire away, but Prometheus stole it and brought it to earth with him. But this drew Prometheus into conflict with Zeus, who chained the rebellious Titan to a rock and sent an eagle to eat his liver. As this organ was immortal, it grew at night as fast as the bird could consume it by day. Prometheus was only released when he gave Zeus the information that the sea nymph *THETIS*, whom both Zeus and *POSEIDON* were pursuing, would give birth to a son

mightier than his father. By making sure that Thetis married a mortal ruler, the newly victorious gods protected themselves because her son turned out to be the warrior *ACHILLES*, an invincible but not immortal fighter.

Zeus' anger with mankind was on occasion explained by poor sacrifices. But Prometheus himself was not a straightforward helper either. He gave fire, an essential of civilized

life, but other gifts were perhaps less helpful. Out of the flaming forge came weapons of war, plus all the miseries that follow the disruption of a simple way of life.

PSYCHE in Greek religious belief was the "soul", but in mythology she was represented as a princess so beautiful that people adored her instead of *APHRODITE*. To put an end to this sacrilege, Aphrodite

sent her son *EROS* to make Psyche fall in love with the ugliest creature he could find. But when Eros saw her he fell in love and forgot his mother's command. They became lovers, though Eros forbade Psyche ever to look upon him. When at last she did, he fled in fear of what Aphrodite would do to him now the secret was out. In the end, however, *ZEUS* agreed that the lovers could be united for eternity.

GIANTS

GIANTS SYMBOLIZE IMMENSE PRIMAL forces, neither good nor bad, but larger than life. While Greek giants could be "gentle" guardians, such as Talos, the gigantic bronze man who defended the island of Crete, others, such as Geryon, were predators, preying on unwary travellers. Equally, the Cyclopes were orginally creative beings, making armour and ornaments in the forge of Hephaistos, and building the massive city walls of Tiryns. Later on they were also portrayed as moody, rebellious shepherds who ignored divine laws and preyed on mortals. The gods themselves are gigantic, especially the older gods, reflecting their primal nature, such as the Titans, and the Giants, who were beings with mighty torsos and snake-like legs. The Titans overthrew their father Ouranos, replacing him with Cronos, who was in his turn dethroned by his son Zeus. Such a cosmic struggle between older primal gods and a younger generation is a common feature in world mythology.

ATLAS (right), the "bearer" or "endurer", bore the heavens on his shoulders, as punishment for having fought against Zeus with the o divine Titans. The myth probably arose from the impression that gr mountains bear the heavens. In another story, Atlas, because he ref Perseus shelter, was turned to a stony mountain, named after him. Here, the heavens are depicted as a celestial globe showing the constellations. (THE FARNESE ATLAS, MARBLE, C. AD 200.)

THE CYCLOPES (left), fabulous race of one-eyed giants, were initially regarded as creative craftsmen who helped Hephaistos in his volcanic forge, crafting special armour, such as Hades' invisible helmet, Zeus' thunderbolt and Poseidon's trident. Yet they were also portrayed as lawless, man-eating shepherds. One such, Polyphemus, here looms over Odysseus and his comrades who have rashly strayed into his den. (ILLUSTRATION FROM STORIES FROM HOMER, 1885.)

ORION (above left), who was one of Poseidon's unruly sons, was a gigantic and handsome hunter, who could walk through the oceans with his feet on the seabed and his head above the waves. Like his giant brother, the one-eyed Polyphemus, Orion was blinded in a quarrel, but his eyes were healed by the radiance of the sun god Helios. There are many differing stories concerning his death, but according to one myth, the love that Eos, the goddess of the dawn, felt for Orion was such that it caused divine jealousy until Artemis was persuaded to shoot him with an arrow on behalf of the gods. He was then raised to the stars to form a constellation. (ILLUSTRATION BY NICK BEALE, 1995.)

CACUS (above), son of Hephaistos, and a goat-like giant, preyed on human beings who strayed by his cave near Rome. Cacus stole Geryon's red cattle from Heracles while he slept, and hid them in his cave. However, the cattle began to bellow and Heracles came and slayed Cacus, retrieving the cattle that he had originally stolen from Geryon. (HERACLES SLAYS THE GIANT CACUS BY GIAMBATTISTA LANGETTI, C. 1670.)

R

PYGMALION was a king of Cyprus. According to the Greeks, he commissioned an ivory statue of his ideal woman, since no real one measured up to his expectations. Not surprisingly, Pygmalion fell hopelessly in love with the statue, an even more unsatisfactory fate than he had previously suffered. Because of his obviously genuine disappointment, the love goddess *APHRODITE* brought the statue to life and made it love him. Some traditions tell how the couple had a daughter named Paphos, who gave her name to the town.

PYTHON see *MONSTERS AND FABULOUS BEASTS*

REMUS AND ROMULUS were the twin sons of *RHEA SILVIA* and *MARS*, and the two founders of Rome. Rhea Silvia had been the only child of King Numitor of Alba Longa. When Numitor's brother *AMULIUS* deposed him, he also forced Rhea Silvia to become a Vestal Virgin, thereby ensuring that there would be no other claimant to the throne. But the war god Mars raped her in his sacred grove, and Rhea Silvia gave birth to Romulus and Remus.

Amulius ordered his servants to kill the new-born twins, but instead they cast them on the Tiber. Their cradle was carried swiftly away and eventually came to rest on a mudbank. To look after his children Mars sent his sacred animal, the wolf. Later Romulus and Remus were discovered in the wolf's lair by a shepherd named Faustulus, who took the foundlings home. So they were raised as shepherds, although the ability of the brothers to lead others, and to fight, eventually became widely known. One day Numitor met Remus and guessed who he was and so the lost grand-children were reunited with him, but they were not content to live quietly in Alba Longa. Instead, they went off and founded a city of their own – Rome. A quarrel, however,

REMUS AND ROMULUS (above) were set adrift on the Tiber by Amulius, but the cradle came ashore and was found by a she-wolf. The twins (left) march triumphantly from Alba Longa. On the left, Romulus bears aloft the head of their treacherous uncle, Amulius. On the right, Remus carries the wild head of Camers, a priest who counselled the king to drown the twins. (ILLUSTRATIONS FROM LAYS OF ANCIENT ROME, 1881.)

RHEA SILVIA (below), a vestal virgin, was loved by Mars, and bore him twin sons, Romulus and Remus. For violating the laws of her holy order, she was thrown into the Tiber, but the god of the river, Tibernus, saved and married her. (MARS WITH RHEA SILVIA BY FRANCESCO DEL COSSA, FRESCO, 1476.)

ensued and Romulus killed Remus, possibly with a blow from a spade. Though he showed remorse at the funeral, Romulus ruled Rome with a strong hand and the city flourished. It was a haven for runaway slaves and other fugitives, but suffered from a shortage of women, which Romulus overcame by arranging for the capture of Sabine women at a nearby festival. After a reign of forty years he disappeared to become, some of his subjects believed, the war god Quirinus.

The Romulus and Remus myth was as popular as that of *AENEAS*. From the beginning of republican times, around 507 BC, the she-wolf became the symbol of Roman nationhood. (See also *FOUNDERS*)

RHADAMANTHYS was the son of *EUROPA* and *ZEUS*, and the brother of *MINOS* and *SARPEDON*. According to one tradition he married *ALCMENE* after the death of her husband Amphitryon. Others say that he was one of the three Judges of the Dead and lived in the paradise of Elysium, in the far west.

RHEA was the daughter of Ouranos and *GAIA*. As the wife of *CRONOS*, she bore six children, the hearth goddess Hestia, the goddess of vegetation *DEMETER*, the earth goddess *HERA*, the underworld god *HADES*, the sea god *POSEIDON* and *ZEUS*, the sky god. Cronos, having learned that one of his children would depose him, swallowed all of them, except for Zeus, as they were born. Rhea substituted the baby Zeus with a stone wrapped in swaddling clothes. He was then taken to the island of Crete, where the worship of Rhea was notable, and was secretly raised.

RHEA SILVIA was the mother of *REMUS AND ROMULUS*. She was the only child of Numitor, the king of Alba Longa. When he was deposed by his younger brother *AMULIUS*, the new king forced Rhea Silvia to become a Vestal Virgin. However, Amulius could not guarantee Rhea Silvia's protection from the attentions of the gods and she was raped by *MARS* in his sacred grove. Her twin sons were then cast into the swollen Tiber, where she may have been drowned.

ROMULUS see *REMUS*

SARPEDON was the son of *ZEUS* and *EUROPA*. He was adopted by Asterius, king of Crete. Sarpedon quarrelled with one of his brothers, *MINOS*, over the throne of Crete and fled to Asia Minor, where he founded the Greek city of Miletus. It is said that Zeus allowed him to live to a great age.

SATURN was an ancient Italian corn god, the Roman equivalent of the Greek god *CRONOS*, though he had more in common with the goddess *DEMETER*. He was believed to have ruled the earth during a lost Golden Age. His festival, the Saturnalia, was celebrated in Rome over seven days and was held at the end of December.

THE SATYRS were the wild spirits of Greek and Roman woodlands. Their bestial nature was shown in their horse-like or goat-like appearance. They were mainly associated with *DIONYSUS*, the Greek god of vegetation, wine and ecstasy, and played a crucial role in his festivals. (See also *MONSTERS AND FABULOUS BEASTS*)

S

SCYLLA see *MONSTERS AND FABULOUS BEASTS*

SEMELE see *LOVERS OF ZEUS*

SIBYL, in Roman mythology, was the prophetess who dwelt near Cumae, in southern Italy. One tale explains how she became immortal but still grew old. She refused the favours of *APOLLO*, the god of prophecy, so he condemned her to an endless old age. She was already ancient when *AENEAS* consulted her about his visit to the underworld. Another story concerns the famous Sibylline Books, which were a collection of oracles that detailed Rome's destiny. These were offered for sale to Rome during the rule of the Etruscan kings.

SIBYL, the gifted seer, foretold the destiny of Rome as predicted in the Sibylline Books, which became a vital source of religious inspiration and guidance. (SIBYL AND THE RUINS OF ROME BY GIOVANNI PANNINI, CANVAS, 1750.)

SISYPHUS, the slyest and craftiest of men, was punished for his sins by being condemned forever to push a marble block up a hill only to see it roll down again. (ILLUSTRATION BY NICK BEALE, 1995.)

When the offer was refused, Sibyl burned three books and offered the other six at the same price, but the offer was still refused, so three more were burnt and then she offered the last three at the original price. In haste the Romans closed the deal before all the irreplaceable oracles were totally destroyed.

SILENUS was a jovial satyr, much given to sleep and drink. Bald but hairy, and as fat and round as his wine-bag, he was more often drunk than sober, but when drunk or asleep, he became an inspired and much sought-after prophet. (ILLUSTRATION FROM DICTIONARY OF CLASSICAL ANTIQUITIES, 1891.)

SILENUS was variously described as the son either of the Greek messenger god *HERMES*, or of *PAN*, the goat-like god of the pastures. He was usually portrayed as the elderly companion of *DIONYSUS*, the Greek god of vegetation, wine and ecstasy. In appearance Silenus was a fat, bald man with the tail and ears of a horse. Because of the kindness shown to Silenus by King *MIDAS* of Phrygia, Dionysus granted the king his famous and short-sighted wish for a golden touch.

SIRENS see *MONSTERS AND FABULOUS BEASTS*

SISYPHUS was the son of King Aelus of Thessaly and Enarete. He was known to the Greeks as the craftiest of men, and suffered for his trickery by endless labour in Tartarus, a place of punishment beneath the underworld. Sisyphus is credited with the foundation of Corinth. According to one tradition, he angered *ZEUS* by revealing that the god had abducted the daughter of a river god. Zeus therefore sent Thanatos, god of death, to take Sisyphus to the underworld. Somehow the ingenious king temporarily made Thanatos his own prisoner. When the gods again claimed him, Sisyphus tricked *HADES* into letting him return to earth. Having told his wife to do

nothing if he died, Sisyphus said that his body was unburied and the customary offerings to the dead had not been made. He must therefore see to the arrangements himself before he could be said to be truly dead. Finally, Zeus lost patience and condemned Sisyphus to Tartarus to pay for his lifelong impiety. For the rest of eternity he had to roll a block of stone to the top of a hill only to see it roll back again as it reached the crest.

THE SPHINX, according to Greek mythology, was the daughter of Echidna, either by *TYPHON* or by Orthus. A monster with the face and breasts of a woman, the body of a lion and the wings of a bird, she was sent as a curse on the city of Thebes by the goddess *HERA*. The Sphinx guarded a pass to the city and asked all who wished to pass a riddle. Those who failed to give the correct answer were eaten. The riddle was: "What thing walks on four legs in the morning, on three in the evening, and is weakest when it walks on four?" The correct answer was Man, because he walks on four as a baby and leans on a stick in old age. When *OEDIPUS* gave the correct answer, the Sphinx hurled herself over a cliff and died. As a reward for destroying the monster, he was made king of Thebes and married

THE SPHINX, or throttler, perched on a rock at a pass to the city of Thebes and challenged all travellers with a riddle, devouring all who failed the test. In Moreau's chilling scene, the queenly, feline Sphinx paws her victims. (THE TRIUMPHANT SPHINX BY GUSTAVE MOREAU, WATERCOLOUR, 1888.)

the widowed queen Jocasta, and so fulfilled his tragic destiny because the queen was his mother.

The Greek Sphinx should not be confused with the Egyptian Sphinx. The Great Sphinx at Giza was the protector of the pyramids and scourge of the sun god Ra.

TARPEIA was a Roman heroine, the daughter of Spurius Tarpeius, the commander of the Capitoline fortress at Rome. She may have played a role in saving the city. A war between Romans and Sabines, a people of central Italy, had been provoked by *ROMULUS*' abduction of Sabine women to provide wives for Rome's men. One tradition says that Tarpeia let the Sabines into her father's fortress after making them promise to give her what they wore on their left arms, their shields. Another mentions only their bracelets. In the first version the Sabines realized that they had been tricked and threw their shields at her and killed her. The Romans could not agree how Tarpeia died but, whatever her motive was, real traitors were always thrown from the Tarpeian Rock.

TARPEIA, a Roman heroine, was crushed to death by the shields of the Sabines as they stormed through the gates of the Capitoline fortress. According to one legend, she had lured the Sabines inside, to trap them, so giving her life for Rome. (ILLUSTRATION FROM STORIES FROM LIVY, 1885.)

TARQUINIUS SUPERBUS

was the seventh and last Etruscan king of Rome, who reigned in the sixth century BC. His youngest son, Tarquinius Sextus, caused the end of the monarchy by raping the Roman matron *LUCRETIA*, which caused *BRUTUS* to lead a rebellion. Tarquinius was defeated and the Roman republic was established.

TARQUINIUS SEXTUS, as he fled the battlefield of Lake Regillus, was struck from behind. His inglorious death was recounted in Macaulay's lays: "And in the back false Sextus felt the Roman steel./ And wriggling in the dust he died, like a worm beneath the wheel." (ILLUSTRATION FROM LAYS OF ANCIENT ROME, 1881.)

THESEUS

was the son either of *POSEIDON* or *AEGEUS* the king of Athens. His mother was Aethra. The childless Aegeus consulted the Delphic Oracle and was told not to untie his wine skin until he returned home. He did not understand what the oracle meant and so visited his friend King Pittheus of Troezen. Realizing that Aegeus was going to beget a powerful son immediately after the celebration feast for his safe return to Athens, Pittheus made his guest drunk and put him to bed with his daughter Aethra, and so Theseus was conceived. Before he left for home, Aegeus took the pregnant Aethra to a great boulder underneath which he placed his sword and sandals. He told her that, should she have a son, she must wait until he was strong enough to raise the boulder before she sent him to his father's court. After Aegeus' departure the wily Pittheus said his daughter's lover was really Poseidon.

When Theseus came of age, Aethra explained that he was heir to the Athenian throne and he retrieved the sword and sandals. On his journey to Athens he slew several desperate bandits, a fearsome son of *HEPHAISTOS*, and a dreadful sow, the daughter of the monster *TYPHON*. At Eleusis, then a kingdom separate from Athens, Theseus was forced to accept the challenge of a wrestling match with its king, Cercyon. The aggressive ruler died as a result of the contest, so Theseus became king of Eleusis, which he later added to the Athenian kingdom.

On his arrival in Athens, Theseus learned that his father Aegeus was hardly able to hold on to the throne. Not only was the apparently heirless king challenged by the fifty sons of his half-brother Pallas, but, worse still, Aegeus had fallen under the spell of *MEDEA*, the former wife of *JASON* and a powerful witch. She hoped that her own son Medus would succeed Aegeus. Although Theseus hid his true identity, Medea knew who he was and persuaded Aegeus to let her poison the mighty stranger at a banquet. Theseus was saved when

TARQUINIUS SUPERBUS, a cruel and tyrannical king, sired a no less cruel and ignoble son, Tarquinius Sextus, who raped the Roman matron, Lucretia. She, in shame, killed herself. The outrage provoked an uprising and Tarquinius was overthrown. (THE RAPE OF LUCRETIA BY PALO IL GIOVANO, CANVAS, C. 1570.)

the king recognized his sword as the hero carved the meat. The plot was revealed, Medea fled from Athens with her son, and Aegeus named Theseus as his successor.

The next cycle of Theseus' exploits was designed to secure the safety of Athens. First, he dealt with Pallas' sons. Then he killed a wild bull that was ravaging Marathon, to the north-east of the city. He also overcame the *MINOTAUR*, the strange offspring of *PASIPHAE*, the wife of King *MINOS* of Crete. An annual tribute of young Athenians was fed to the Minotaur, which lived in the Labyrinth that had been designed by *DAEDALUS*. No one had ever managed to find their way through this maze, so when Theseus volunteered to confront

the Minotaur his father despaired. It was agreed that if Theseus should, by some miracle, survive, he was to change the sail of the tribute ship from black to white on the homeward voyage.

At Minos' palace in Knossos the goddess *APHRODITE* gave Theseus an invaluable ally in *ARIADNE*, a daughter of the Cretan king who fell in love with the hero. Princess Ariadne knew that the Labyrinth was so complex that the only way out was to follow back a thread fastened to the entrance. After Theseus had promised to marry her, Ariadne gave him a ball of thread and a sword. The hero entered the Labyrinth, slew the Minotaur and then set sail for Athens with Ariadne and the rest of the Athenian party. He then left the princess on the nearby island of Dia. It is thought that he was in love with another woman, but whatever the reason he was soon repaid for his heartlessness. As the ship approached Athens, Theseus forgot to change the sail to indicate to his father that he was alive. Aegeus saw a black sail and, thinking his son dead, threw himself off the Athenian acropolis.

The suicide meant that Theseus was now king of Athens, and he joined all the communities of Attica into one state. Apart from enlarging Athens' territory, Theseus also undertook a number of heroic exploits. On one expedition he captured Hippolyta, the queen of the *AMAZONS*, who bore him a son, Hippolytus, but she died shortly afterwards. Theseus gave the accursed *OEDIPUS* and his daughter *ANTIGONE* sanctuary at Colonus,

near Athens. But discord entered his own house when his second wife *PHAEDRA*, another daughter of Minos, came to desire her stepson Hippolytus, to the young man's horror. Although he promised to keep her passion a secret, Phaedra

was so humiliated by his rejection that she hanged herself and left Theseus a letter in which she accused Hippolytus of attempted rape. He was exiled and died in a chariot accident before his father discovered the truth. In another

version, Hippolytus was killed by a sea monster that was raised by Theseus' anger, and Phaedra, filled with remorse, killed herself.

Theseus later seized the twelve-year-old *HELEN*, daughter of *ZEUS*, as a future wife. He claimed that only she was worthy enough to be his wife, possibly because of her divine father. But she had powerful kinsmen, and her two brothers, the *DIOSCURI*, defeated the Athenians and drove Theseus abroad. He died on the island of Scyros, when its king, fearing the presence of such a man, pushed him over a cliff as he admired the view. It was believed that in the fifth century BC, the Athenian admiral Cimon went to Scyros and brought the hero's bones back to Athens, where they were kept in a shrine.

FOUNDERS

THE ANCIENTS BELIEVED that many of their fabulous cities were founded by the pioneering heroes and heroines of legend, such as Cadmus of Thebes and Dido of Carthage. In Classical mythology, the heroic ethic combined with the Greek ideal of *polis*, or city-state, to create a variety of dynamic founders who built such celebrated cities as Athens, Mycenae, Sparta and Thebes. The Greek *polis* was an autonomous, independent community of citizens, slaves and foreigners who gathered within and around a fortified city. Each city honoured its own hero who was also often its legendary founder, such as Perseus of Mycenae and Lacedaemon of Sparta. Mythic founders were innovative, godlike heroes, guided by destiny and deity to create a fresh, vibrant culture. Apart from leading a tribe to a bright new land, and building a strong citadel, founders often developed helpful new ways and customs: Cecrops of Athens, for instance, encouraged religious worship, while Cadmus of Thebes introduced an alphabet of 16 Phoenician letters. A city or tribe sometimes honoured its founder hero by sharing his name, such as Ilium, named after Ilus, the Trojans after Tros, and Rome after Romulus.

CECROPS (above), one of the mythic founders of Athens, and the first king of Attica, is depicted with a serpent's tail, recalling his origin as an aborigine of Attica. He divided the natives into twelve communities and founded the Acropolis, the stronghold of Athens, which was also named Cecropia after him. An innovator, Cecrops abolished blood sacrifice, encouraged the worship of Zeus and Athena and introduced basic laws of property, politics and marriage.

(ILLUSTRATION FROM DICTIONARY OF CLASSICAL ANTIQUITIES, 1891.)

ATHENS (right), the splendid capital of Attica, owed its origin both to Cecrops, who founded the ancient Acropolis, and to Theseus who united Attica's twelve states into one, and made Athens their capital. The city divided into the upper town, or Acropolis, and the lower walled town, as well as three harbour towns. The Acropolis, seen here, rises on a steep rock, its summit once crowned with sparkling temples. Most famous of all was the Parthenon, built of Pentelic marble in pure Doric style and adorned within and without with gilded and painted sculpture. North of the Parthenon rose a great statute of the city's goddess, Athena, whose helmet and spear were seen from the sea. Athens, the artistic centre of the ancient world, reached its greatest splendour in the time of Pericles (460-429 BC).

(THE ACROPOLIS BY CARL HAAG, CANVAS, C. 1890.)

ROME (above), the world-ruling capital of Italy, situated on the River Tiber, was founded in c. AD 753 by the mythic hero, Romulus. The Colosseum, seen here, was one of the greatest monuments of the ancient city, initiated by the Emperor Vespasian and inaugurated by his son, Titus, in 80 AD. The gigantic amphitheatre was designed to accommodate 87,000 spectators around circular tiers, overlooking a central arena. In front of the amphitheatre rises the triumphal Arch of Titus, erected in AD 81, to celebrate Titus' victorious campaign in Judaea. (VIEW OF THE COLOSSEUM BY LIPOT KERPEL, CANVAS, 1846.)

ROMULUS (above), the mythic founder of Rome, was suckled at birth by a she-wolf, with his twin brother, Remus. The twins had been cast into the River Tiber by their great-uncle Amulius who coveted the throne of Alba Longa, but their divine father, Mars, sent his sacred animal, the wolf, to save his sons. Later the twins were rescued by the good shepherd Faustulus who raised them as his own. Once grown, they left Alba Longa to found Rome, but the belligerent brothers bickered over the site and name of the future city, and Romulus slew Remus, setting the warlike tone of the future city. (ILLUSTRATION BY PAUL WOODROFFE, C.1920.)

DIDO (above), legendary founder of Carthage, supervises a team of architects and masons on the left bank of the bay. Dido had fled to Africa from Tyre in Phoenicia where her husband, Sychaeus, had been murdered by her brother, Pygmalion, who coveted the throne of Tyre. On the coast of North Africa, the local king, Iarbus, sold Dido as much land as she might contain in a bull's hide. By artfully cutting the hide into narrow strips, Dido managed to secure enough land to build a citadel, named Byrsa, or "hide". Around this fort, the fabulous city of Carthage flourished from 853 BC. On the right bank, the still, calm tomb of Sychaeus rises beside a new sapling, symbolizing the growth of Carthage. The girls and boys playing on the bank represent the future power and generations of Carthage; while the rising sun, likewise, symbolizes the rising power of the bright new city. (DIDO BUILDING CARTHAGE BY J W TURNER, CANVAS, 1815.)

TROY (above) or Ilium arose on the grassy plain of Troas by the foot of Mount Ida. Founded by the mythic hero, Ilus, son of Tros, the ancient city was named Ilium and Troja after both father and son. The famous walls of Troy were built by the gods, Poseidon and Apollo, in the reign of Ilus' son, Laomedon. The next king, Priam, ruled during the tragic Trojan War, provoked by Paris' abduction of Helen, wife of the Greek chieftain, Menelaus. At a critical stage in the ten-year siege, the Greeks dreamt up the Trojan Horse, a massive wooden model hiding within its hollow belly an army of Greeks. (THE TROJAN HORSE BY NICCOLO DELL' ABBATE, TEMPERA, C. 1560.)

V

THETIS was a sea nymph and the daughter of Nereus and Doris. She was the mother of ACHILLES, the great Greek hero. Because it was known that she was fated to bear a son mightier than his father, both ZEUS and POSEIDON gave up all thoughts of possessing Thetis, who was much admired on Mount Olympus, the home of the gods. Instead, Zeus ensured that she became the wife of a mortal king, Peleus of Phthia. Thetis bore him seven sons, but she was dissatisfied with the mortality of her children. She tested them with fire and boiling water, but none could withstand such treatment, not even the youngest boy Achilles until Thetis dipped him in the Styx, the river of the dead. Even then, she forgot to wet the heel she held him by, with the result that he was not totally immortal. About this time Thetis left Peleus and returned to the sea, although she continued to assist Achilles as far as she could during his eventful life.

TIRESIAS, in Greek mythology, was the son of a nymph, Chariclo, and Everes, descendant of one of CADMUS' own men. The blind seer of Thebes, he was so wise that even his ghost had kept its wits, and not been overcome by forgetfulness like the other inhabitants of the underworld. At the edge of the world Tiresias advised ODYSSEUS that he would never return home to Ithaca if he harmed the cattle of HELIOS, the sun god.

During his lifetime Tiresias played a part in several myths. For instance, he warned King Pentheus in vain about the identity of DIONYSUS, when that powerful god

THETIS, although an immortal sea nymph, loved her mortal son, Achilles, with all the care and tenderness of a human mother. She shared his sorrows, and rushed to his aid, ever conscious of his mortality. Here she brings him some splendid armour as he mourns Patroclus' death. (ILLUSTRATION FROM STORIES FROM HOMER, 1885.)

came in disguise to Thebes. As a result of Pentheus' refusal to listen to the seer, he gravely offended Dionysus and was torn to pieces by the god's frenzied worshippers, the maenads. Tiresias also confirmed the pronouncement of the Delphic Oracle that it was indeed King OEDIPUS who was personally responsible for the plague which troubled the Thebans.

The blindness of Tiresias was explained by two tales. One account states that the affliction was a punishment for seeing the goddess ATHENA bathing. The other story is a somewhat less traditional explanation. Tiresias one day saw snakes mating and struck them with a staff, whereupon he turned into a woman. After living as a woman for a period of time,

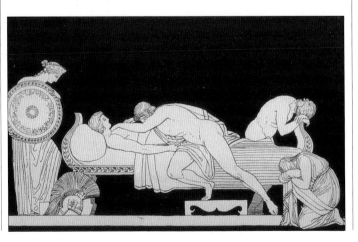

TIRESIAS, the legendary blind seer, advised many heroes. Some listened to him, but others, to their cost, ignored him, such as hard-headed Creon, or short-sighted Pentheus. His golden staff was a gift from Athena and enabled him to find his way like a sighted man. (ILLUSTRATION FROM DICTIONARY OF CLASSICAL ANTIQUITIES, 1891.)

the seer witnessed the same sight and became a man again. His unique experience led to Tiresias being asked by ZEUS and HERA, the chief Greek deities, to settle a dispute between them as to which sex got most pleasure out of love. When he said that it was the female, Hera blinded him, but Zeus awarded him a long life and the power of prophecy.

THE TITANS and Titanesses, according to Greek mythology, were the children of Ouranos, the sky, and GAIA, the earth. These gigantic beings were the older gods who ruled before the Olympian gods, who were the brothers, sisters and children of ZEUS. The Titans included CRONOS, RHEA, Coeus, Metis, Mnemosyne and Hyperion.

They came to power after Cronos emasculated his father Ouranos with a sickle provided by Gaia, his long-suffering mother. The eventual battle between the older generation of gods, the Titans led by Cronos, and the younger generation, the Olympians led by his son Zeus, lasted ten years and shook the universe like no other conflict. Afterwards Zeus threw those deities who had opposed him down to Tartarus, which was a land beneath the underworld.

The battle against the Titans should not be confused with the Olympian gods' later struggle with the GIANTS. In order to win this terrible confrontation, Zeus knew that he would require the help of a mighty, mortal champion, and so he fathered by ALCMENE the greatest of the Greek heroes HERACLES.

supreme deity, but the recently victorious *ZEUS* destroyed him with a mighty thunderbolt. The volcanic activity of Mount Aetna in Sicily was believed to be caused by Typhon's imprisonment beneath the crater. The struggle between Typhon and Zeus was an evenly balanced fight, however. At one point Zeus was left helpless in a cave, weaponless and without his sinews. Fortunately the messenger god *HERMES* came to his aid on this occasion. Before his final defeat, Typhon sired the Chimaera, the huge sea monster killed by the hero *PERSEUS*.

VENUS was the Roman equivalent of *APHRODITE*, the Greek love goddess. Venus was originally a goddess connected with agriculture, but when she was identified with Aphrodite she took on a more active and different role in mythology. One of her most crucial actions was to return *AENEAS'* spear after it had stuck in a tree stump during his fight with the Italian champion Turnus. Indeed, in some versions Aeneas is her son.

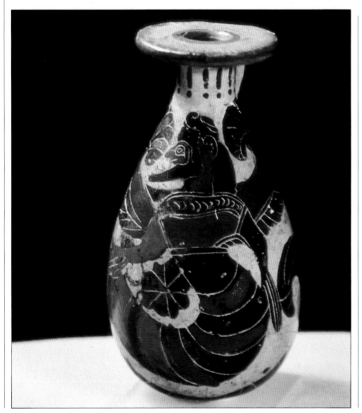

TYPHON (left), *a fire-breathing serpent, was imprisoned beneath the crater when the volcano at Mount Aetna erupted. Symbolizing the dark forces of earth, he sired monsters as hideous as himself: the flaming Chimaera and snarling Cerberus.* (GREEK VASE, C. 600 BC.)

TYPHON was a terrible, serpent-like monster whose eyes shot out flames. He was conceived by *GAIA*, mother earth, when she was banished to Tartarus along with the other defeated *TITANS*.

According to the Greeks, Typhon endeavoured to establish himself as the ruler of the world, the

VENUS, the Roman goddess of love, is rarely portrayed without her capricious and cherubic son, Cupid. This graceful portrait of her by the French artist Boucher, full of light and charm, owes much to Venus of Arles. (ILLUSTRATION FROM DICTIONARY OF CLASSICAL ANTIQUITIES, 1891.)

VESTA was the Roman equivalent of the Greek goddess Hestia, who was the goddess of the hearth. Vesta, however, was worshipped both as the guardian of the domestic hearth and also as the personification of the ceremonial flame. Ceremonies in her honour were conducted by the Vestal Virgins, who were young girls from noble families who took vows of chastity for the thirty years during which they served her. Vesta's chief festival, the Vestalia, was held on 7 June.

VIRGINIA was the daughter of a Roman centurion named Virginius and, as with LUCRETIA, she was a Roman connected with a major constitutional change. Whereas Lucretia's rape and suicide led to

VIRGINIA (above) dies in the arms of her father who killed her to release her from bondage to the corrupt Appius Claudius. He then cursed the Claudian line, who were overthrown by the outraged Romans. (ILLUSTRATION FROM STORIES FROM LIVY, 1885.)

VULCAN (below), Roman god of fire, presents Venus with glorious arms for her son, Aeneas. The golden sword was described in the Aeneid as loaded with doom. (VENUS IN THE FORGE OF VULCAN BY FRANCOIS BOUCHER, CANVAS, 1757.)

the dethronement and exile of the Etruscan monarchy, the death of Virginia was a major factor in the ending of an aristocratic tyranny in 449 BC.

The lust of a corrupt official, Appius Claudius, for Virginia knew no bounds. He even dared to claim that the girl was his slave and used the law to have her handed over to him. At the last moment her father stabbed Virginia through the heart, declaring that her death was less painful to suffer than her dishonour. The Roman army rose to support him, along with the poorer citizens not then bearing arms, and checks were placed thereafter on magistrates' powers.

VULCAN was the Roman smith god and the equivalent of the Greek HEPHAISTOS. He was widely associated with Maia and VESTA, who were both goddesses of the hearth. His smithy was believed to be situated underneath Mount Aetna in Sicily. At the Vulcanalia festival, which was held on 23 August, fish and small animals were thrown into a fire.

XANTHUS was said to be the offspring of the HARPY Podarge and ZEPHYRUS, the west wind. He was one of two immortal horses belonging to the great Greek champion ACHILLES and had the power of human speech. Achilles inherited the horses from his father, King Peleus of Phthia, who had received them as a present from the gods on his wedding to the sea nymph THETIS. Achilles took Xanthus and Balius, the other wonderful steed, to Troy with him. They performed extremely well on the battlefield, although they seemed unnerved by the slaughter. When Achilles questioned them, Xanthus warned the champion that his own death was near, at which point the horse was struck dumb by the FURIES.

ZEPHYRUS see FORCES OF NATURE

ZEUS, *all-powerful father of the gods, enthroned on Olympus, is begged by Thetis to help her son, Achilles; she tugs his beard and clasps his knee in her affectionate way, as described in the* Iliad, *and the great god nods his assent.* (ZEUS AND THETIS BY JEAN-AUGUSTE INGRES, CANVAS, 1811.)

After the overthrow of Cronos, Zeus divided up the world between himself and his two brothers, *HADES* and *POSEIDON*. Zeus chose to rule the sky, Hades the underworld, and Poseidon the sea: the earth and Mount Olympus, which was the home of the gods, were regarded as common territory. A rare visitor to either of them was Hades, who preferred to be among the dead. Zeus' influence, however, was felt everywhere, although he had no control over destiny itself. Rather he was the god who saw that fate took its proper course.

The many lovers taken by Zeus, both mortal and immortal, form the very stuff of mythology. It is highly likely that they describe the coming together of several religious traditions, as Zeus incorporated the attributes of rival deities and gained credit for all important events. The continual antagonism between Zeus and his wife *HERA*, who was definitely an ancient, pre-Greek mother-goddess in origin, often broke out into major conflict. So jealous was Hera that she spent most of her time persecuting Zeus' lovers and their children. Once Zeus became so angry about Hera's cruelty to the hero *HERACLES*, his greatest son by a mortal woman, that he suspended the goddess from a pinnacle by her wrists and hung weights on her ankles. (See also *FORCES OF NATURE*)

XANTHUS AND BALIUS, *immortal horses and children of the west wind, "tore with the speed of wind". They were Achilles' battle steeds during the Trojan War, and wept for fallen heroes on the field. Here, Zeus leads them as a gift of the gods to Peleus on his wedding day.* (ILLUSTRATION BY GLENN STEWARD, 1995.)

ZEUS was the supreme deity in Greek mythology and the son of the Titans *CRONOS* and *RHEA*. The Romans identified Zeus with their *JUPITER*, an all-powerful sky god. The tyrannical Cronos insisted on swallowing all Zeus' older brothers and sisters as soon as they were born, but Zeus escaped this fate when his mother Rhea offered Cronos a stone wrapped up in swaddling clothes to swallow instead. In secrecy, Zeus was raised on the island of Crete. He grew to manhood determined to topple his father. The wise Metis, an early love and daughter of *OCEANOS*, gave Zeus the idea of a potion that would make his father vomit up all the children he had swallowed.

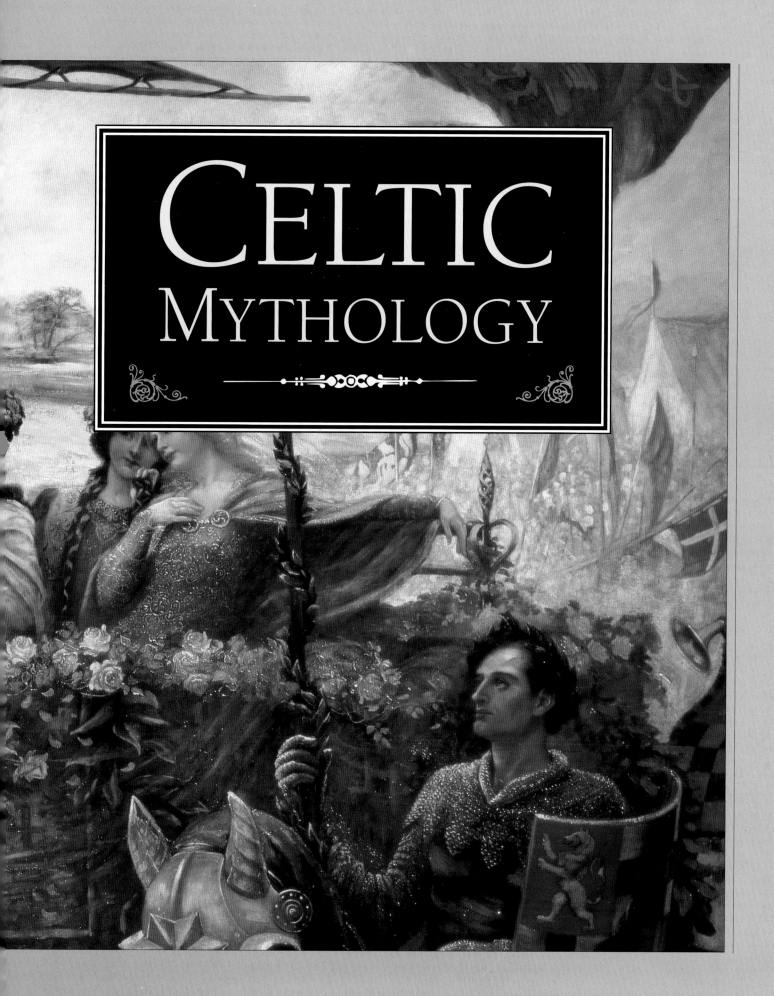

CELTIC
MYTHOLOGY

INTRODUCTION

TODAY PEOPLE OF CELTIC DESCENT IN Europe are concentrated on its western shores. They live chiefly in Brittany, Cornwall, Wales, Scotland, the Isle of Man and Ireland. At one time, however, the Celts were spread over a large part of the Continent, and in 278 BC one roving band even penetrated as far east as Asia Minor, where they gave their name to Galatia. Until the rise of Roman power, the Celts were a force to be reckoned with. Rome itself had been sacked by them in 385 BC, a historical fact not forgotten by the legionaries who gave Julius Caesar victory between 59 and 49 BC over the Celtic tribes living in Gaul, present-day France. Although largely incorporated into the Roman Empire, the Celts continued to worship their own gods and goddesses right up to the time of the official adoption by the Romans of the Christian faith. Then their religion and mythology waned in importance, except where people remembered tales about the Celtic gods and heroes of the past. Even in distant Ireland, an island that was never under Roman control, the influence of Christianity was soon felt. But here conversion did not mean the wholesale destruction of the Celtic heritage, for monks took great care from the fifth century onwards to write down the ancient sagas.

To this remarkable effort of preservation we owe almost our entire knowledge of Celtic mythology. For except in Wales, where a small group of stories was recorded, nothing else was ever committed to writing. The Celts always distrusted script and preferred to rely on speech and properly trained memories.

In Ireland the poet was held in particular esteem. Possibly because there was a clear distinction there between druid and poet in pre-Christian times. The newly-founded monasteries could therefore undertake the work of recording the ancient texts without any fear of paganism. It seems that poets went on reciting the sagas long after St Patrick converted the Irish and cleared the country of snakes, because these tales were seen as entertainment. Irish folklore insists, however, that they kept something of their magic, since the Devil could never enter a house where the exploits of the heroes were being sung.

BRANWEN was a classic Celtic heroine who remained calm and dignified under pressure. A falsely slandered wife, she was forced to suffer unjustly, until rescued by her brother, Bran the Blessed. (BRANWEN BY G SHERRINGHAM, CANVAS, C. 1920.)

Irish myths nearly always include fighting, though the combat is undertaken more often by heroes than by gods. The fearless warrior Cuchulainn, the lone defender of Ulster during the invasion of forces raised by Queen Medb of Connacht, is very much the ideal. He was chosen as the Irish champion after a beheading contest with the water giant Uath. No other man had courage enough to receive the giant's return blow. Yet Cuchalainn, "the Hound of Culann", enjoyed but a brief life; his refusal to return the affections of Morrigan, the goddess of slaughter, sealed his fate. Not even the intervention of his father Lugh, the sun god, could save him.

The apparently endless conflict appears less terrible when it is recalled how the Celts believed in reincarnation. Their otherworld, unlike the Greek or Roman underworld, was not a dismal abode of the dead. Rather it was a paradise in which souls rested prior to their rebirth in the world. The warrior-poet Oisin, son of the Fenian leader Finn MacCool, spent three hundred years there before returning to Ireland. Oisin was warned that he would never be able to go back to the underworld if he dismounted from a magic steed. When the saddle slipped and he fell to the ground, Oisin was immediately changed from a handsome youth into a blind, grey-haired, withered old man. Only St Patrick is said to have bothered to listen to his fantastic story as it was being written down.

The interest of St Patrick in the adventures of Oisin and, indeed in the exploits of many other heroes of old, is obviously a later embellishment, but it does indicate a degree of tolerance not readily found elsewhere in Christian Europe. Yet saints in Ireland could curse as well as anyone else when the occasion demanded. For instance, the troublesome King Suibhne Geilt was cursed by St Ronan for his violence towards the faith, and

CELTIC EUROPE

HEROIC combat was a feature of Celtic culture and myth. Champions, such as Cuchulainn, fought to the death, often defending their clan alone. The warriors here wear helmets with boar and raven motifs; symbols of ferocity and death. (GUNDESTRUP CAULDRON, GILDED SILVER, C. 100 BC.)

spent the rest of his life with the characteristics of a bird, leaping from tree to tree and eating at nights nothing but watercress.

In late Celtic mythology, especially the Arthurian myths, Christianity has become a central element. The quest for the Grail is the most obvious example. Although similar to a Celtic magic cauldron, this holy vessel was the cup used at the Last Supper and, at the Crucifixion, the one that received the blood which flowed from the spear thrust in Christ's side. It was brought to Britain by Joseph of Arimathea, but was later lost and its quest preoccupied King Arthur's knights. Only Sir Galahad was pure enough to be granted a full vision of the Grail, which he took as "Our Lord's body between his hands".

Whether or not Arthur was a historical

MERLIN AND NIMUE represent opposite poles of the Celtic otherworld. Merlin, in the tradition of Celtic druids, guided his king, Arthur, with wisdom and foresight; while Nimue, his enchantress, symbolized the threatening powers of the otherworld. (THE BEGUILING OF MERLIN BY E BURNE JONES, CANVAS, C. 1870–74.)

figure is still uncertain. It is quite likely that he may have been a successful warlord in the confused and violent period following the withdrawal of the Roman legions from Britain around 410 AD. That his myth blames the ultimate victory won by the Anglo-Saxon invaders on civil strife perhaps reflects a kernel of truth. The Celtic peoples were notorious for only rarely combining against an external, common foe, so deep-rooted were their own bitter quarrels. Thus British chivalry came to an end with King Arthur's disastrous battle against his nephew Modred near Salisbury. Hardly a knight survived and the King himself was badly wounded. His departure to Avalon, accompanied by three mysterious ladies, gave rise to the idea of his undeath. In an otherworld, it was believed, King Arthur lingered, awaiting reincarnation as a national saviour.

ARTHUR and his Christian Fellowship of Knights probably derived from the earlier Welsh warlord Arthur, who journeyed to the otherworld with his warband in search of a wondrous cauldron. Here, the Knights of the Round Table experience the Grail vision for the first time, amid divine light and splendour. (MANUSCRIPT ILLUSTRATION, C. 1470.)

A

ABARTA, which probably means "doer of deeds", was, in Irish mythology, a mischievous god. He was one of the *TUATHA DE DANANN*, who ruled Ireland until they were overcome by the Milesians, war-like invaders from Spain. Driven underground, Abarta and his kin appear in the Irish sagas more like heroic mortals than gods, although in the tale of his trick on the Fenian warriors there remains a strong trace of his original divinity.

Abarta offered himself as a servant to *FINN MACCOOL*, one of the foremost Irish heroes, and hereditary leader of the *FIANNA*. Abarta tried to serve Finn MacCool shortly after the hero had succeeded his father as leader of the band. As a gesture of goodwill, tricky Abarta presented the Fianna with a wild, grey horse. Only after great effort did the warriors manage to get a bridle on the animal, and then it refused to move even one hoof when mounted. It was not until fourteen warriors had climbed on its powerful back that it would stir at all. Once Abarta had mounted behind them, it broke immediately into a gallop, even pulling along a fifteenth warrior who was unable to let go of the horse's tail. Abarta took them to the otherworld, for that was the reason for his appearance on earth. This wonderful land was thought by the Celts to be the home of the gods and goddesses, and the place where souls briefly rested before rebirth. The rest of the Fianna, or Fenians, acquired a magic ship to give chase to Abarta's steed. The best tracker among them was Finn MacCool's assistant Foltor. He succeeded in navigating a course to the otherworld for the rescue expedition. There Abarta was compelled to release the prisoners as well as to run back to Ireland himself holding on to the horse's tail. Honour being satisfied, the Fenians agreed to a peace with Abarta.

AILILL, who was the brother of Eochaidh, a High King of Ireland,

AINE, Irish goddess of love and fertility, was worshipped on Midsummer Eve by the local people who lit up her hill with torches. When some girls stayed late one night, Aine appeared among them and revealed the hill to be alive with fairies, which were only visible through her magic ring. (ILLUSTRATION BY NICK BEALE, 1995.)

fell in love with his brother's wife, *ETAIN*, who was actually a goddess, one of the *TUATHA DE DANANN*. Etain had been the second wife of the proud and handsome god *MIDIR*, who lived under a mound in the middle of Ireland. She had been reborn as a human as punishment for her great jealousy of Midir's first wife, Fuamnach. When High King Eochaidh was looking for a bride himself, he heard reports that described Etain as the fairest maiden in Ireland. So he brought the beautiful former goddess back to his palace at Tara, the capital. There Eochaidh and Etain enjoyed a happy married life. Ailill, however, gradually succumbed to a terrible wasting disease because of his unrequited passion for the new queen.

Etain was steadfast in her love for Eochaidh, but she also

AMAETHON, though the fruitful rustic god of agriculture, was not always helpful. It was Amaethon that robbed Arawn, thereby provoking the Battle of Trees, and who refused to help hard-pressed Culhwch to plough, sow and reap a hill in a day – a task in his quest to win Olwen. (ILLUSTRATION BY NICK BEALE, 1995.)

felt sorry for ailing Ailill and eventually promised to satisfy his desire as the only means of saving his life. It was arranged that they should meet secretly in a house outside Tara. However, Ailill never came because he fell into an enchanted sleep.

AILILL MAC MATA, according to some versions of the myth, was the king of Connacht and husband of the warrior-queen *MEDB*. He is generally portrayed as a rather weak character who was entirely under the influence of Medb. It was due to her taunting that he agreed to go to war with Ulster over the Brown Bull of Cuailgne. Ailill finally met his death at the hands of *CONALL*, who killed him in revenge for the death of *FERGUS MAC ROTH*.

AINE was the Irish goddess of love and fertility. She was the daughter of Eogabail, who was the foster son of the Manx sea god *MANANNAN MAC LIR*. Her main responsibilty was to encourage human love, although one mortal lover of hers, King Aillil Olom of Munster, paid for his passionate audacity with his life. When he

attempted to force himself upon Aine and rape her, she slew him with her magic.

Aine's worship was always associated in Ireland with agriculture, because, as a goddess of fertility, she had command over crops and animals. Even as late as the last century, celebrations were still held in her honour on Midsummer Eve at Knockainy, or "Aine's hill", in County Kerry.

AMAETHON (whose name means "labourer" or "ploughman") was the god of agriculture and the son of the Welsh goddess DON. Amaethon was said to have stolen from ARAWN, the lord of the otherworld ANNWN, a hound, a deer and a bird, and as a result caused the Cad Goddeu or Battle of Trees. It was in this battle that Amaethon's brother, GWYDION,

magically transformed trees into warriors to fight in the battle.

AMAIRGEN, sometimes known as Amergin, was one of the first Irish druids, the ancient priests in Celtic lands. He came to Ireland with the Milesians. These children of MILESIUS, or Mil, who was a leader of the Celts who lived in Spain, were believed to be the ancestors of the present-day Irish. Having defeated the divine rulers of Ireland, the TUATHA DE DANANN, the Milesians could not agree on which of their leaders should be king. Two sons of Mil, Eremon and EBER, contested the throne and for the sake of peace the island was divided into two kingdoms, one in the north, the other in the south. However, peace was not to survive for long, and renewed fighting between the followers of the two

AMAIRGEN (above) was one of the first druids in Ireland. He possessed both spiritual and political authority, and pronounced the first judgement in the land, deciding who would be the first king. An inspired shaman and seer, he is credited with a mystical poem in the Book of Invasions. *(ILLUSTRATION ANON.)*

brothers plunged the country once again into dreadful strife. The fighting came to an end only with the death of Eber. Amairgen then installed Eremon as High King of Ireland at Tara. Even then conflicts still occurred because of the ceaseless rivalries between lesser rulers.

AMFORTAS see *PELLES*.

ANNWN was a Welsh otherworld that was an idyllic land of peace and plenty. In Annwn there was a fountain of sweet wine and a cauldron of rebirth, which, it would seem, was the basis of the medieval Grail myth. In one Welsh tradition, ARTHUR lost most of his warriors in a disastrous attempt to seize this magic cauldron.

The lord of Annwn was the grey-clad ARAWN, with whom the Dyfed chieftain PWYLL agreed to exchange shapes and responsibilities for a year. Arawn had a pack of hounds, the Celtic "hounds of hell", which were believed to fly at night in pursuit of human souls. (See also *CELTIC OTHERWORLDS; WONDROUS CAULDRONS*)

ANNWN (below), a Welsh otherworld, was a land of fruitfulness and rest, filled with the song of birds. Annwn's magical cauldron, guarded by nine maidens, healed the sick and restored the dead to life. A recurrent motif in Celtic myth, magic cauldrons feature in the tales of Bran and Dagda. (ILLUSTRATION BY NICK BEALE, 1995.)

ANU, a great earth goddess and mother of all the heroes, was known as the "lasting one" and also as Dana, mother of the Tuatha De Danann. In Munster there are two hills known as the Paps of Anu because they symbolized her breasts. (ILLUSTRATION BY GLENN STEWARD, 1995.)

ANU, sometimes called Danu or Dana, was the mother goddess of Irish mythology. The *TUATHA DE DANANN* ("the people of the goddess Dana") were her divine children and the gods and goddesses who ruled Ireland prior to the arrival of the Milesians. It is quite possible that the monks who wrote down the Irish sagas from the fifth century onwards underplayed the original role of goddesses in their compilations. Certainly, the stories they recorded show us a man's world, a place where warriors seem most at home. The cult of Anu was especially associated with Munster, and two hills in County Kerry are still known as Da Chich Anann ("The Paps of Anu").

AOIFA, sometimes known as Aoife, was the daughter of Ard-Greimne and an Irish warrior-princess in the Land of Shadows, an otherworld kingdom. Her sister *SCATHACH* instructed the Ulster hero *CUCHULAINN* in the arts of war. But when the sisters went to war Scathach was frightened to take the hero with her into battle in case Aoifa killed him. Undeterred by Aoifa's reputation as a fighter, Cuchulainn challenged her to single combat. Before the fight took place, Cuchulainn asked Scathach

what Aoifa loved best and Scathach told him that above all else she treasured her chariot. At first the combat went as expected in Aoifa's favour, but Cuchulainn distracted her attention at a critical moment by calling out that her chariot horse was in trouble. Afterwards, Aoifa became Cuchulainn's lover and bore him a son named *CONLAI*. It was, however, the boy's fate to be killed by his own father.

AONGHUS was the Irish love god. His father was *DAGDA*, the father of the gods and the protector of druids, and his mother was the water goddess *BOANN*. Rather like Zeus, Dagda deceived Boann's husband and lay with her. The monks

who wrote down the Irish sagas tried to legitimize the birth by making Boann the wife of Dagda, but it is obvious that Aonghus was a divine love-child.

Aonghus was handsome and four birds always hovered above his head which were said to represent kisses. Birds also feature in his courtship of *CAER*, a girl of divine descent who came from Connacht and lived as a swan. Her father, Ethal, was one of the *TUATHA DE DANANN*. He seems to have been reluctant about the marriage until Aonghus' father, Dagda, made Ethal his prisoner. It was finally agreed that Aonghus could marry Caer provided he could identify her and she was willing to be his bride. On the feast of Samhain, Aonghus found Caer swimming on a lake with a hundred and fifty other swans. He instantly recognized her and she agreed to marry him.

An interesting tale that has attached itself to Aonghus concerns his foster-son *DIARMUID UA DUIBHNE*, or "Diarmuid of the Love Spot". This attractive young man received a magic love spot on his forehead from a mysterious girl one

ARAWN, king of Annwn, strides through his enchanted forest accompanied by his flying hounds, the Celtic "hounds of hell", one of whose duties was to escort souls on their journey to the otherworld. Like some other fairy creatures, they appear white with red ears, a token of the otherworld. (ILLUSTRATION BY JAMES ALEXANDER, 1995.)

night during a hunt. From then on, no woman could ever see Diarmuid without loving him. This included *GRAINNE*, the princess who had been promised by the High King of Ireland to his Fenian commander *FINN MACCOOL*. Aonghus saved the lovers from the great warrior's wrath, but he could not protect Diarmuid from the fate given to him at birth by the gods, that he should be killed by a magic boar. Nevertheless, Aonghus brought Diarmuid's body back to his own palace at New Grange, on the banks of the River Boyne, where he breathed a new soul into it so that he could talk to his foster-son.

ARAWN was the ruler of the Welsh otherworld *ANNWN*, which was a paradise of peace and plenty. The Dyfed chieftain *PWYLL* became friends with Arawn and was allowed to claim in his title some authority over the otherworld. The two rulers met by chance. While out hunting, Pwyll encountered a strange pack of hounds chasing a stag, so he drove them off and set

AOIFA, a warrior-princess from the Land of Shadows, spars with her young son, Conlai, instructing him in the martial arts. The tradition of warrior-women was strong in Celtic society, where women bore arms as late as AD 700, and where the fiercest gods were often women. (ILLUSTRATION BY JAMES ALEXANDER, 1995.)

AONGHUS (left), an engaging god of love and courtesy, a Celtic equivalent of Eros, appears in this fanciful portrayal as a charming, if somewhat whimsical character, who calms the foamy sea with his fairy magic. (AONGHUS, GOD OF LOVE AND COURTESY, PUTTING A SPELL OF SUMMER CALM ON THE SEA BY JOHN DUNCAN, CANVAS, DETAIL, 1908.)

ART (above) confronts an army of savage and venomous giant toads on his perilous journey through the Land of Wonder, in search of Delbchaem. A taboo laid on the young hero by the jealous goddess Becuma, forced him to find and win the lovely girl imprisoned by her wicked parents. (ILLUSTRATION BY ARTHUR RACKHAM, C. 1900.)

than she gave birth to *DYLAN* and *LLEU*. *GWYDION*, Arianrhod's brother, immediately took charge of Lleu and brought him up, but this did not prevent Arianrhod placing a series of taboos upon him, including the stricture that he was to have no wife in the human race.

ART, in Irish mythology, was the son of Conn of the Hundred Battles. In one myth, Conn's jealous mistress, the goddess Becuma Cneisgel, contrived to send Art off on a perilous journey through the Land of Wonder in search of Delbchaem ("Fair Shape"). After facing untold dangers, he managed to find and rescue Delbchaem. Art's son by another woman was *CORMAC MAC ART*. Art was killed by the rebel Lugaide Mac Con in the battle of Moy Muchruinne.

his own hounds on to the prey. Just as the stag was about to fall, a grey-clad figure appeared and rebuked Pwyll for this discourtesy in the field. It was Arawn. In order to placate Arawn and to gain his friendship, Pwyll accepted a proposal that he should exchange forms with him for a year and then slay Arawn's enemy, Havgan. It was also agreed that Pwyll would share the bed of Arawn's queen for the

same period of time, but without making love to her.

Arawn warned Pwyll that he must kill Havgan by a single blow, for if struck a second time he instantly revived. When Pwyll and Havgan fought, the Welsh chieftain dealt him a fatal blow and ignored Havgan's plea to finish him off with another strike. As a result of this service, Arawn and Pwyll became close allies and Dyfed prospered.

ARIANRHOD was the daughter of the Welsh goddess *DON* and niece of *MATH*, king of Gwynedd. Math could sleep only if his feet were held in a virgin's lap, and when Goewin, the virgin who usually acted this part for him was raped by his nephew Gilvaethwy, it was suggested that Arianrhod should take her place. To test her purity Arianrhod had to step over Math's wand. No sooner had she done so

ARTHUR is undoubtedly the best known of the Celtic heroes. He was most popular during the Middle Ages, when the exploits of his followers, the Knights of the Round Table, impressed the greater part of western Europe. It was with some misgivings that the Church permitted a Christianized version of these Celtic myths to occupy such an important place in the medieval imagination. It was never quite at ease with the story of the Grail, or SANGREAL, which JOSEPH OF ARIMATHEA was believed to have brought to Britain, since its miraculous properties were clearly derived from the Celtic cauldron, a vessel of plenty as well as of rebirth. The strength of popular feeling for the Arthurian myth can be appreciated by a riot that occurred in 1113 at the town of Bodmin in Cornwall because the French servants of visiting nobility denied Arthur's undeath.

Although some of the earliest stories concerning Arthur are found in Welsh poems of the seventh century, there can be little doubt that the warlike king belongs to the heroic traditions of both Ireland and Wales. He appears in several

ARTHUR, prompted by Merlin, asks the Lady of the Lake for the sword, Excalibur. The young king marvelled at the shining sword but Merlin insisted that the scabbard was worth ten of the swords because it prevented loss of blood in battle. (ILLUSTRATION BY AUBREY BEARDSLEY, C. 1870.)

ARTHUR, a child of destiny, was guarded and guided by spiritual forces from birth. Smuggled out of Tintagel Castle by Merlin, the mage, he was fostered in safety and secrecy, unaware of his destiny until his rightful time to draw the sword from the stone, thus proving his birthright. (MERLIN AND ARTHUR BY W HATHERELL, CANVAS, C. 1910.)

Irish sagas, one of which describes how he stole the hounds of the Fenian leader FINN MACCOOL on one of his daring raids. Indeed, as a warrior, hunter of magic boars, killer of giants, witches and monsters, and as leader of a band of heroes whose adventures led them into untold mysteries and marvels, Arthur had much in common with Finn MacCool. But according to the ninth-century monk Nennius, Arthur was a historical leader who rallied the people of Britain against Anglo-Saxon invaders after the Roman legions had gone. Nennius credits Arthur with twelve victories, but does not mention the account of his death recorded slightly later in a history of Wales, which states that Arthur and his sworn enemy MODRED both fell in 537 at the battle of Camluan.

Arthur was the son of the British king UTHER PENDRAGON and Igraine, wife of the Cornish duke Gorlois. He was conceived out of wedlock and brought up away from his parents by the wizard MERLIN. The resourceful Merlin had already designed for Uther Pendragon a wonderful stronghold and placed in it the famous Round Table, at which one hundred and fifty knights could be seated. This unusual piece of furniture may

have a connection with Joseph of Arimathea, not least because it had a special place reserved for the Grail. While Joseph of Arimathea was imprisoned in Palestine, the Grail is said to have kept him alive. Later he brought it to Britain, where it disappeared due to people's sinfulness. Thus the recovery of the Grail became the great quest of Arthur's knights.

When Uther Pendragon died, the Knights of the Round Table were at a loss to know who should be the next king. They decided that Merlin should guide them. The wizard told them that they would know who Uther's successor was when he drew a magic sword from a stone, which had mysteriously appeared in London. Many knights tried to pull the sword from the stone, but none could move it.

After a number of years Arthur journeyed to London to watch his first tournament. A knight who had been appointed by Merlin to act as the boy's guardian was taking part, but finding he was without a sword, he sent Arthur to get one. Without realizing the significance of the sword in the stone, Arthur pulled it out and gave it to the amazed knight. Thus was the heir of Uther Pendragon revealed.

Even then, there were knights who would not accept Arthur as

ARTHUR, at rest in an enchanted forest, gazes in wonder at the amazing Questing Beast at the well. It was a ferlie or bewitching otherworldly wonder, which defied capture. Sir Pellinore and later Sir Palomides spent years in futile pursuit of the tantalizing chimaera.

(ILLUSTRATION BY AUBREY BEARDSLEY, C. 1870.)

king. Only with Merlin's aid was the young ruler able to defeat his opponents and bring peace to Britain. How much he depended on magic became obvious to Arthur early in his reign. Having drawn his own sword without cause against one of his knights, Arthur was dismayed to see the blade shatter. Merlin saved him by putting the knight to sleep, for Arthur was otherwise unarmed. In despair the king wandered along the shore of a lake when, to his amazement, he saw a hand and arm rise out of the water, holding another magic sword. This was the famous Excalibur, his sure support, according to the Lady of the Lake, who handed it to him.

Rearmed and reassured, Arthur went on to be a great king. He defeated the Anglo-Saxons, aided King Leodegraunce of Scotland in his wars against the Irish and even campaigned as far away from his kingdom as Rome. In return for the aid given to Leodegraunce, Arthur was betrothed to his daughter GUINEVERE. At first Merlin objected to the match, since he knew of Guinevere's love for Sir *LANCELOT*, the most handsome of the Knights of the Round Table. But he later blessed the married couple and, according to one version of the myth, gave Arthur the Round Table as a wedding gift. Nevertheless, the queen and Lancelot were soon lovers, and when Arthur found out about his wife's unfaithfulness Lancelot fled to Brittany.

Arthur pursued Sir Lancelot and besieged him in his Breton stronghold. The siege had to be lifted, however, because news reached the king that his nephew Sir Modred had seized Camelot and even forced Guinevere to consent to marriage, after spreading stories of the king's death on campaign. Returning to Britain, Arthur summoned his knights to do battle with the rebels. Prior to the conflict, it was agreed that the king and his nephew would meet between the two armies to discuss the possibility of peace. Because neither one trusted the other, each ordered his forces to attack if they saw anyone draw a sword. When a knight unsheathed his weapon to kill a snake, a terrible battle was fought, in which the flower of British chivalry fell.

Only two of Arthur's knights were left alive on a battlefield that was covered by the dead and dying. Although he had won, King Arthur had to be carried away by these knights, such was the severity of his wound. Knowing his own end was near, he had Excalibur thrown into a lake, where a hand swiftly seized it. Then Arthur boarded a magic boat and disappeared. His last words were that he was going to *AVALON* to be cured of his wounds so that he might return one day to lead his people once more.

The inscription on Arthur's tomb at Glastonbury picks up this Celtic idea of reincarnation. It reads: "Here lies Arthur, king that was, king that shall be." Such an undeath was not enough to save his weakened kingdom from the Anglo-Saxons, however. The whole of the Arthurian myth turns on the disintegration of the chivalric unity that was established by the Round Table, but which was finally destroyed by the implacable hatred between Arthur and Modred. (See also *MAGIC AND ENCHANTMENT; HEROIC QUESTS*)

B

AVALON was another name for the Welsh otherworld, *ANNWN*, and its name suggests that it was an island of apples. The mortally wounded *ARTHUR* was ferried there by three mysterious women in a black boat, following the terrible battle against Sir *MODRED*'s army. The undead king was expected to return from Avalon and lead the oppressed Celtic population of Britain to victory over their Anglo-Saxon and, later, Norman conquerors. According to one version of the myth, Excalibur was forged there. Traditionally, Avalon has been identified with Glastonbury, the supposed site of Arthur's tomb. (See also *CELTIC OTHERWORLDS*)

BADB (meaning "crow") was an Irish goddess of battle. She was one of a group of war deities who could influence the outcome of conflict by inspiring the combatants with fear or courage. The others were known as *MORRIGAN*, *NEMAIN* and *MACHA*. Myth connects Badb with the historical battle of Clontarf in 1014, when the High King Brian defeated the Viking invaders and Badb was said to have appeared over the warriors' heads.

BALOR, a formidable one-eyed god of death, led the misshapen Fomorii against the younger Tuatha De Danann. Here his grandson, Lugh, casts a fatal stone into Balor's deadly eye, forcing it back through his head where its lethal gaze destroys his warriors marching behind him. (ILLUSTRATION BY MIRANDA GRAY, 1995.)

BALOR was the Irish Cyclops. This one-eyed god of death was the most formidable of the *FOMORII*, the violent and monstrous sea gods who ruled Ireland before the arrival of the *TUATHA DE DANANN*. So dreadful was his one eye that he destroyed whoever he looked upon and his eyelid had to be levered up by four servants. It was prophesied that he would be slain by his own grandson. To avoid this fate he locked his only daughter *ETHLINN* in a crystal tower on Tory Island, off the north-west coast of Ireland. Even so, Balor was killed in battle with a sling-shot by the sun god *LUGH*, Ethlinn's son and the champion of the Tuatha De Danann.

Lugh's father was Cian, a lesser member of the Tuatha De Danann. With the assistance of a female druid, Cian had entered the crystal tower and slept with Ethlinn. When Balor learned that his daughter had given birth to three sons, he ordered that they be drowned in a whirlpool near Tory Island. Balor's servants duly rolled them up in a sheet, but on the way to the whirlpool one of the boys fell out unnoticed. Either the druid then handed the fortunate baby to the smith god *GOIBHNIU*, or alternatively *MANANNAN MAC LIR*, the god of the sea, decided to foster him. In either event, Lugh was saved and set on the road to his destiny as the slayer of Balor.

The fateful meeting between Lugh and Balor occurred at the second battle of Magh Tuireadh, a fierce contest between the Fomorii and the Tuatha De Danann. Nobody could stand Balor's lethal gaze, not even the Tuatha De Danann leader *NUADA*, the owner of a sword which previously none could escape. The battle was just turning into a Tuatha De Danann rout, when Lugh noticed that the

BANSHEE, or bean sidhe, women of the fairies, lived underground in sparkling sidhe – fairy heavens hidden beneath grassy mounds on Irish hillsides. Legend has it that a banshee attaches itself to a family and warns of impending death with an eerie wail. (ILLUSTRATION BY H J FORD, 1902.)

AVALON, Arthur's last resting place, was an otherworldly retreat of wonder, mystery and peace. Its nine guardian queens recall an actual, historical order of nine nuns who lived off the coast of Roman Brittany, as well as the nine mythical maidens guarding Annwn's magic cauldron. (KING ARTHUR IN AVALON BY E BURNE-JONES, CANVAS, 1894.)

single eyelid of Balor was slowly closing through weariness. Lugh crept near to him with a magic sling-shot in hand. The moment the eyelid opened again, he hurled the stone so hard that it forced the eyeball backward through Balor's head, with the result that it was the Fomorii who now suffered from the destructive effect of its paralysing stare. The Tuatha De Danann were able to defeat the Fomorii, who were driven from Ireland for ever. (See also *CELTIC OTHERWORLDS*)

BANSHEE is the modern name for the *bean sidhe* ("woman of the fairies"), the traditional fairy of the Irish countryside. After the arrival of the Milesians from what is now Spain (the ancestors of the present-day Irish) the gods and goddesses known as the *TUATHA DE DANANN* disappeared underground and dwelt in mounds, and over the centuries they were slowly transformed in the popular imagination into fairies. It was believed that the wailing of a banshee foretold the approach of a human death.

BEDIVERE see *BEDWYR*

BEDWYR, according to Welsh mythology, was a one-handed warrior who, together with his friend and companion *KAI*, played an important part in helping *CULHWCH* to procure the prizes he required to win the hand of *OLWEN*. They were both members of King *ARTHUR*'s court. In later Arthurian romance Bedwyr became Sir Bedivere, the faithful knight who remained with King Arthur after he was mortally wounded, threw the sword Excalibur into the lake on the king's instructions and bore his body to the boat which carried him to *AVALON*.

BEL see *BELENUS*

BELENUS, also known as Bel, was a Celtic sun god known to the Romans. Julius Caesar compared Belenus to Apollo, the god of prophecy. He appears in various forms across the Celtic world, as Beli to the Welsh, Bile to the Irish and Belenus to the Gauls. Beltaine,

one of the important festivals of the Celtic calendar, was celebrated on the first of May in his honour, and his name survives in a number of place names such as Billingsgate, "Bile's gate" (formerly a fish market in London). Although his worship was clearly widespread, little else is known about him.

BEN DIGEIDFRAN see *BRAN THE BLESSED*

BILE see *BELENUS*

BLATHNAT was the wife of King *CU ROI* of Munster. She fell in love with *CUCHULAINN*, the great Ulster hero and enemy of Cu Roi, and betrayed her husband's people by showing the hero how he could enter her husband's apparently impregnable fortress. A stream flowed through the fort and when Blathnat poured milk into the

water, Cuchulainn was able to follow its course. In the fierce battle that followed Cu Roi was killed and Cuchulainn was able to ride off with Blathnat. He also took with him Cu Roi's bard, Fer Cherdne. When the party halted on a cliff top, however, Fer Cherdne took the opportunity to avenge his former master's death by grabbing hold of Blathnat and jumping over the edge with her in his arms.

BELENUS, a Celtic sun god, was honoured on the eve of Beltaine when Celts lit bonfires, the "fires of Bel", symbolizing the rays of the sun and the promise of summer fruitfulness. Here, the fairies, once Celtic gods, ride out from their hollow hills to celebrate Beltaine. (THE RIDERS OF THE SIDHE BY JOHN DUNCAN, CANVAS, 1911.)

BEDWYR guarded Arthur at the end of his life, as they waited by a lake for the ship that would ferry the king to Avalon. This evocative scene blends photographic realism with a ghostly backdrop to create an effective and convincing representation of an otherworldly realm. (MORT D'ARTHUR BY JOHN GARRICK, CANVAS, 1862.)

CATHBAD (above), the inspired druid and seer, predicted Deirdre's tragic destiny at her birth. Druids, both male and female, held high rank in Celtic society. They were counsellors, judges, teachers and ambassadors. Even a high king could not speak at an assembly before his druid. (ILLUSTRATION BY NICK BEALE, 1995.)

CATHBAD, in Irish mythology, was a seer and druid, and advisor to *CONCHOBAR MAC NESSA*, the king of Ulster. Cathbad prophesied that though *DEIRDRE* would have great beauty she would bring destruction to Ulster. He also foretold that the hero *CUCHULAINN* would have a glorious but short life. When King Conchobar Mac Nessa became cruel towards the end of his reign, Cathbad cursed the king and his stronghold at Emain Macha. Cathbad had three children, *DECHTIRE*, the mother of Cuchulainn, Elbha, the mother of *NAOISE*, and Findchaem, mother of *CONALL* Cearnach.

CERIDWEN was a Welsh goddess of fertility and the mother of Afagddu, reputedly the ugliest man in the world. To compensate for his looks Ceridwen boiled a cauldron of knowledge for a year and a day so that Afagddu could become wise and respected, and she set Gwion Bach, the second son, to watch over the pot. But Afagddu was denied the prophetic gift when a drop fell on Gwion Bach's finger and he unthinkingly sucked it. In fury, Ceridwen chased and ate Gwion Bach, only later to reincarnate him as *TALIESIN*, who was the greatest of all the Welsh bards. Ceridwen had another equally ugly son, Morfan, who was also a fearsome warrior. He fought with King

CERIDWEN boils a magical brew hoping to endow her ill-favoured son with wisdom. At the end of a year, the broth would yield just three precious drops of inspiration; but these splashed on to the hand of Gwion Bach, who became all-knowing. (ILLUSTRATION BY JAMES ALEXANDER, 1995.)

ARTHUR in his last battle, at Camlan. At first none of Sir *MODRED*'s men would fight Morfan because they thought he was ugly enough to be a devil.

CERNUNNOS was a Celtic god worshipped in both France and Britain. He is usually depicted sitting cross-legged and wearing a sleeveless tunic and bead necklace. He has an impressive pair of antlers, and the name Cernunnos means "the Horned One", which suggests that he was a god of wild animals and the forest, although he has also been seen as a god of plenty. The Romans identified him with their god Mercury, the messenger god and the guide of the dead to the underworld. In medieval Ireland the antlers of Cernunnos were transferred to the Devil.

CESAIR was the daughter of Bith, son of Noah and one of the earliest arrivals in Ireland. In her myth, Celtic and Hebrew traditions were brought somewhat uncomfortably together by the monks who wrote down the sagas and who suggested that the first settlers had reached Ireland before the Flood. Although Bith was denied a place in the Ark, he was fortunate to be advised by a god to build his own boat. Cesair appears to have guided him to this decision as well. They sailed for seven years and eventually reached

CESAIR, granddaughter of Noah, set sail with her father, Bith, to escape the Flood. After a seven-year voyage, they reached the shores of Ireland. Yet neither Cesair nor her father survived the Flood when it engulfed the land, although her husband, Fintan, escaped by changing into a salmon. (ILLUSTRATION BY JAMES ALEXANDER, 1995.)

CERNUNNOS, a Celtic hunter god of beasts, is typically depicted in a lotus position. The "horned one" was a lord of animals and is here surrounded by wild creatures such as the stag, boar and lion. In one hand he clasps a warrior's torc, in the other a serpent, demonstrating his power. (GUNDESTRUP CAULDRON, GILDED SILVER, C. 100 BC.)

Ireland, where Cesair was married to *FINTAN*. When the rising waters of the Flood engulfed the land, Fintan saved himself by changing into a salmon, but the rest of Bith's family drowned. This myth is known as the first invasion of Ireland. Subsequent invasions were by the *PARTHOLON* and Nemed, the *FOMORII* and *TUATHA DE DANANN*, who were all more or less supernatural in nature. The final invasion of Ireland was by the sons of *MILESIUS*, who came from Spain and brought human rule to the island.

CLIODHNA, in Irish mythology, was an otherworld goddess of beauty. It was said that her three magical birds could sing the sick to sleep and cure them. Cliodhna was passionately in love with a mortal named Ciabhan, a youth with wonderful curling locks. One day on the shore near Cork, while Ciabhan went hunting inland, Cliodhna was put into a magic sleep by the sea god *MANANNAN MAC LIR*, who then sent a wave to pull her back to the Land of Promise.

CONAIRE MOR was a High King of Ireland. He was the son of a cowherd's foster-daughter named Mess Buachalla and the bird god *NEMGLAN*. His mother was actually

the daughter of Etain Oig and *CORMAC* king of Ulster. However, Cormac was so disappointed not to have a son that he ordered Mess Buachalla to be thrown into a pit. According to the myth, the baby girl was saved by two kind-hearted servants, who could not bring themselves to carry out the king's order. Instead they gave Mess Buachalla to a cowherd. When she grew up, her beauty was so remarkable that Eterscel, the High King of Ireland, decided to marry her. He was also persuaded by a prophecy which said that an obscure woman would bear him a famous son. But on the night before the wedding, Mess Buachalla slept with the god Nemglan, who had magnificent plumage. From this union was born Conaire Mor, whom Mess Buachalla passed off as the son of Eterscel. The one instruction that Nemglan told Mess Buachalla to give to their child was that he was never to kill a bird.

When Conaire Mor was a young man, Eterscel died and the right of succession was raised in Tara, the Irish capital. It was agreed to follow the ancient custom of the dream. After a feast, one of the court would have a spell of truth sung over him as he slept. The man the courtier dreamed about would then be the next High King. In the succession dream a naked man was revealed, walking along the road to Tara with a sling in his hand.

At this time Conaire Mor was some distance from Tara. As he headed back to the palace in his chariot, a flock of birds descended upon him. They had such wonderful plumage that Conaire Mor forgot the taboo about killing birds and got out his sling. The birds shed their feathers and attacked the charioteer as warriors. But one of the birdlike fighters, who was more handsome than the rest, protected Conaire Mor. He introduced himself as his father Nemglan and reminded the young man that he must never cast stones at birds for they were his own kin. As a penance, Nemglan told his son to walk naked along the road to Tara, carrying only his sling. If he did this, and promised to rule Ireland in peace, Conaire Mor would be made High King.

So it was that Conaire Mor was received at Tara as the High King. Peace and prosperity at first marked his reign, although the lure of plunder gradually drew the Irish back to their old habit of cattle-raiding. Since Conaire Mor was reluctant to punish severely those who took

CLIODHNA fled to Glandore to live with her mortal lover, Ciabhan, but the sea god, Manannan Mac Lir, sent a great wave to scoop her up and bring her home. Here, lulled to sleep by fairy music, she drifts back to fairyland. The Wave of Cliodhna is still one of the three great waves of Ireland. (ILLUSTRATION BY JAMES ALEXANDER, 1995.)

CONAIRE MOR was burdened by more geis (taboos) than any other Irish warlord. Violation of geis led to misfortune or death and marked a tragic turning-point in the hero's life. Despite his wisdom, Conaire Mor was lured by his enemies into breaking his geis one by one. (ILLUSTRATION BY STEPHEN REID, 1910.)

part in the growing disorder, the country soon slid back into clan warfare. Eventually, the High King had to forgo the ways of peace and break his promise to his father. Conaire Mor soon realized that this would bring about his own downfall. While on campaign, he came to a roadside hostel where he was greeted by three strange horsemen, whose clothes, weapons, bodies and horses were all red. A hideous old woman told Conaire Mor that during his stay in the hostel "neither skin nor flesh of you will escape from the place to which you have come, save what the birds will take in their claws." The same night a rebel force surrounded the hostel and attacked. Three times the building caught fire and three times the flames were brought under control, but all the water had now been used. When a druid accompanying the rebels laid a spell of thirst on the High King, he sent one of his companions to fetch some water. On returning, the warrior saw that the fight was over and Conaire Mor's severed head lay on the floor. So he poured the water into the king's head, at which Conaire Mor's decapitated head praised him for his sense of duty.

SAGES AND SEERS

THE SPIRITUAL SEERS and shamans of Celtic myth were endowed with extraordinary gifts of prophecy, wisdom and healing. They enjoyed a profound rapport with natural and supernatural forces, and acted as intermediaries between the realms of the living and the dead, between the visible world of men and the invisible otherworld, a realm of wondrous spirits. Most famous of all was Arthur's wise counsellor, Merlin; but other inspired druids – Amairgen, Taliesin and Cathbad – feature in Celtic myths as prophetic bards and counsellors to clan chiefs and kings. Some lived as hermits in the wilderness, while remaining powerful in Celtic society. Although on the whole helpful to mortals, some dark sorceresses, such as Morgan, Nimue or the Calatins, used their supernatural gifts to bewitch and manipulate mortals for their own ends.

MORGAN LE FAY (above right), Queen of Avalon, the otherworldly Isle of Apples, bears an apple bough, the Celtic symbol of peace and plenty. A gifted sorceress, she is often portrayed as a dark soul, thwarting Arthur and manipulating heroes. At a deeper level, she is a winter goddess of darkness and death, opposing Arthur, the Lord of Summer. She reveals the redeeming aspect of her character in her role as sovereign healer of Avalon and guardian of Arthur's body in death. (ILLUSTRATION BY STUART LITTLEJOHN, 1994.)

MERLIN (right) is best remembered as the fatherly and spiritual guardian of Arthur. A wise seer, Merlin counselled the young king, sometimes sternly and sometimes gently, but always with wisdom. Merlin was also a peerless sage, credited with the design of the Round Table, the plan for Camelot and the stone ring at Stonehenge. He learnt his craft from a master, Bleise, portrayed here as an historian recording the deeds of Arthur's reign, as reported by Merlin. (MANUSCRIPT ILLUSTRATION, C. 1300.)

HELLAWES (below) was a sorceress in the Arthurian myths who had set her heart on the noble knight Sir Lancelot, whom she had loved from afar for some seven years. Eventually, she managed to lure him into her Chapel Perilous and there she tried all the methods she knew to inspire his love for her. But it was to no avail because the steadfast and loyal knight loved one woman only, Arthur's queen, the fair Guinevere, and he had come to the chapel with but one mission in mind, which was to collect healing talismans for the wounded knight Sir Meliot. When Lancelot left with the talismans, he was completely untouched by Hellawes' love and even her magical craft. The sorceress finally realized that he would never love her and she died of a broken heart. (ILLUSTRATION BY AUBREY BEARDSLEY, C. 1870.)

DRUIDS (above) held both political and spiritual power in Celtic society and were gifted not only as shamans and seers but also as legal and moral advisors. Druids underwent a long apprenticeship of at least twenty years, learning the mysteries and laws by heart. Here, druids on a snowy hill celebrate the winter solstice by gathering a bough of mistletoe, cut with the sacred golden sickle borne by the foremost druid. (THE DRUIDS BRINGING IN THE MISTLETOE BY G HENRY AND E A HORNED, CANVAS, 1890.)

TALIESIN (left), a prophetic poet and shamanistic seer, was gifted with all-seeing wisdom after consuming a "greal" of inspiration from Ceridwen's cauldron. Wales's greatest bard, he foretold the coming of the Saxons and the oppression of the Cymry as well as his own death. He appears here as an eagle, the bird often chosen by shamans on their spirit-flights or trance journeys to the otherworld. The eagle's gold nimbus symbolizes Taliesin's radiant brow. (ILLUSTRATION BY STUART LITTLEJOHN, 1994.)

SIR. LAVNCELOT. AND. THE. WITCH. HELLAWES.

CONALL, in Irish mythology, was the foster-brother of the Ulster hero *CUCHULAINN*. As children, they swore that if either was killed first the other would avenge him. When Queen *MEDB* of Connacht invaded Ulster, Cuchulainn faced her army single-handed, but he was doomed because he had offended the war goddess *MORRIGAN*. After Cuchulainn had been killed, and his head and sword-hand cut off by the enemy, the warriors of Ulster were stirred by Conall to wreak bloody revenge. They caught up with Queen Medb's army and Conall slew those who had killed his foster-brother. Later, Conall went on to ravage the whole of Ireland as he punished Queen Medb's allies one by one. In doing so he earned his title, Caernach ("of the Victories").

CONCHOBHAR MAC NESSA,

in Irish mythology, was an Ulster king. He was the son of Fachtna Fathach and *NESSA*, a local beauty who, according to one tradition, conceived Conchobhar on the eve

CONALL of the Victories, a veteran warlord, avenged Cuchulainn's death by slaying his killers one by one. From the brain of one of his victims, Mac Da Tho, he made a magic brain ball, a lethal weapon. Conall here is welcomed by his Ulstermen at a feast in Mac Da Tho's dun.
(ILLUSTRATION BY STEPHEN REID, 1910.)

of her royal marriage through a secret affair with a druid. When her husband died shortly after the wedding, Nessa was courted by his half-brother and successor, *FERGUS MAC ROTH*. But she would only agree to become his wife on the condition that he would first let her son Conchobhar rule as king of Ulster for a year. An ambitious and determined woman, Nessa instructed her son how to be a great ruler so that when the time arrived for Fergus Mac Roth to return to the throne, the people of Ulster simply refused to let Conchobhar step down.

Although he was married, King Conchobhar fell deeply in love with *DEIRDRE*, who was sometimes called Derdriu ("of the Sorrows"). She was the daughter of an Ulster chieftain, and at her birth the druid *CATHBAD* had warned that, though Deirdre would be the most beautiful woman in Ireland and would marry a king, she would be the cause of death and destruction throughout the land. By the time Deirdre grew up, Conchobhar was an old man, and she in disgust

refused his advances and eloped with a handsome young warrior named *NAOISE*. But the king never gave up his passion, and so eventually he had Naoise killed and was married to Deirdre. She found her situation so intolerable that she committed suicide by throwing herself from a speeding chariot. Fergus Mac Roth, appalled by Conchobhar's behaviour, offered his services to Ulster's enemies and a long war ensued. Conchobhar was himself killed by a magic sling-shot. It was the famous "brain ball" made by Conall out of the brains of a slain Leinster king. The ball lodged in the king's skull, and his doctors advised him to avoid any strenuous exercise and excitement. Some years later Conchobhar Mac Nessa got into a rage and the "brain ball" caused his death.

CONLAI, sometimes known as Connla, was the doomed son of the great Ulster hero *CUCHULAINN*. According to one Irish tradition, Cuchulainn had visited the Land of Shadows in order to challenge the warrior woman *AOIFA* to single combat. After the fight, which the

hero just managed to win by the use of cunning, they became lovers and Conlai was conceived. When he left, Cuchulainn gave Aoifa a gold ring. Years later Conlai wore this ring on a visit to Ulster, where he challenged the local heroes to combat. Just like his father, Conlai was quick to anger and soon overcame *CONALL*, Cuchulainn's foster-brother. Despite the misgivings of his wife *EMER*, Cuchulainn could not resist fighting the young stranger himself. Too proud to announce his own identity when challenged by Cuchulainn, Conlai accepted the possibility of death and drew his sword. Although Cuchulainn was impressed by sword-play that matched his own, he lost his temper the moment Conlai cut off one of his locks of hair. The terrible combat only

CONLAI, the ill-starred son of Aoifa and Cuchulainn, grew up in Skye, a stranger to his father. When he went to Ulster to challenge the local heroes, he met Cuchulainn in single combat and was killed. Recognizing his son too late, Cuchulainn was overwhelmed with grief.
(ILLUSTRATION BY JAMES ALEXANDER, 1995.)

CONCHOBHAR MAC NESSA, a high king of Ireland, granted arms to the young Cuchulainn, but when the boy grasped his spears, they splintered in his hand; next, a chariot shattered beneath his stamp. No weapons withstood the hero's mighty grasp until he was given the king's own arms.
(ILLUSTRATION BY STEPHEN REID, 1910.)

ended when Cuchulainn drove his spear through Conlai's stomach. Only then did Cuchulainn notice on his young opponent's finger the gold ring he had given to Aoifa. Cuchulainn, overwhelmed with remorse and grief, carried the dying Conlai to his house and afterwards buried his forgotten son.

CORMAC was the son of the Ulster king *CONCHOBHAR MAC NESSA*. An Irish myth tells of his distaste at his father's treachery in killing *NAOISE*, the husband of *DEIRDRE*, and of his going into voluntary exile with the deposed Ulster ruler *FERGUS MAC ROTH*. Not until he received an invitation from his father Conchobhar, when the dying king had nominated Cormac as his successor, did he consider returning home. However, a druidess had warned Cormac that if he went back to Ulster he would be killed, but he set out anyway and on the journey he fell into a deep magic sleep and was slain by a group of warriors. The attack was said to have been arranged by a jealous husband, whose wife had fallen in love with Cormac.

CORMAC (below), returning home after his long, voluntary exile, stopped by a roadside hostel where he was lulled to sleep by the soft notes of a harp. Defenceless in his enchanted sleep, he was slain by assassins, sent by the harpist, Craiftine, in revenge for Cormac's affair with his wife. (ILLUSTRATION BY NICK BEALE, 1995.)

CORMAC MAC ART'S (above) reign was distinguished by peace and plenty. A wise and good man, he was favoured by the Tuatha De Danann who invited him to their hidden world, and gave him a curative apple branch. In tune with Christian kindness, he warmly welcomed St Patrick at his court. (ILLUSTRATION BY JAMES ALEXANDER 1995.)

CORMAC MAC ART was the High King of Ireland during the period that *FINN MACCOOL* led the Fenian warrior band. He was the most famous of the early rulers of Ireland, his reign being tentatively dated from 227 to 266. Cormac Mac Art was the Irish Solomon, a wise and powerful king, who was well served by the brave exploits of Finn MacCool. His wisdom seems to have impressed the *TUATHA DE DANANN*. These gods and goddesses invited Cormac Mac Art to their home in the otherworld, where they gave him wonderful presents. One of these was a silver branch that bore golden apples, and when shaken produced music that could cure the sick and wounded. On his own death Cormac Mac Art had to hand back this incredible talisman. One of Cormac's sons, Cellach, raped the niece of Aonghus of the Terrible Spear. In the ensuing fight, Cellach was slain and Cormac lost an eye. As a High King could have no imperfection Cormac had to step down and his son Cairbe took his place. The reputation of the High King remained so strong that later the Irish Christians also adopted him. It was claimed that Cormac Mac Art learned of the Christian faith before it was actually preached in Ireland by St Patrick, with the result that he ordered that he should not be buried at the royal cemetery by the River Boyne because of its pagan associations.

CREIDHNE was the goldsmith of the *TUATHA DE DANANN* and the brother of *GOIBHNIU*, the smith god, and Luchtar, the carpenter. During the second battle of Magh Tuireadh, when the De Danann finally defeated the *FOMORII*, the three brothers could be seen on the battlefield making and repairing spears with magical speed. As Goibhniu fashioned a blade with three blows of his hammer, Luchtar carved a handle in a flash, and Creidhne crafted rivets that flew into place and bonded at once.

CUCHULAINN as a youngster lived at the court of the High King, where he trained with other sons of chieftains, whom he soon outstripped in arms and might. Although small, he glowed with an inner divine light and warmth, which he inherited from his father the sun god Lugh.

(ILLUSTRATION BY STEPHEN REID, 1912.)

CUCHULAINN, in Irish mythology, was the champion warrior of Ulster. His name means "the Hound of Culann", although he was usually called the Hound of Ulster. Cuchulainn was the Irish Achilles, a larger-than-life fighter whose bouts of temper often caused grief to himself and others. Anger certainly made him slay his son CONLAI, when the young man travelled from the Land of Shadows to visit Ulster. The fifteen-year-old warrior was Cuchulainn's son by the warrior-princess AOIFA. Neither father nor son would identify themselves, so a tragic fight ensued. A gold ring on Conlai's finger revealed too late that he was Cuchulainn's own offspring.

Cuchulainn's mother was DECHTIRE, the daughter of the druid CATHBAD, an advisor to the King CONCHOBHAR MAC NESSA. It was Cathbad who foretold that Cuchulainn would become a great warrior but die young. Shortly after her marriage to SUALTAM MAC ROTH, who was the brother of the deposed Ulster ruler FERGUS MAC

ROTH, Dechtire along with fifty of her kinswomen flew to the otherworld in the form of a flock of birds. During the wedding feast she had swallowed a fly and dreamed as a result of the sun god LUGH, who told her to make this journey. Cathbad reassured his son-in-law by saying that Dechtire had merely gone to visit her otherworld relations, for her mother was a daughter of the god AONGHUS. In fact, Lugh kept Dechtire there for his own pleasure for three years.

When Dechtire and her women returned to Emain Macha, the stronghold of the Ulster kings, in the form of brightly coloured birds, Dechtire was expecting Lugh's son, Setanta. Sualtam Mac Roth was so pleased to have his wife home again that when the boy was born he accepted him as his own child.

As a youth, Setanta quickly learned the ways of the warrior, but it was not obvious to everyone just how strong and brave he was until he killed an enormous hound with his bare hands. One day, arriving late at the gate of a house where King Cochobhar Mac Nessa was being entertained by the Ulster smith CULANN, the young hero was attacked by the ferocious guard dog and only saved himself by dashing out its brains on one of the gate's pillars. Their host had now lost a faithful guardian, so Setanta offered to take the hound's place while a replacement was found. When Culann thanked the young warrior but declined his offer, it was decided that henceforth Setanta would be known as Cuchulainn ("the Hound of Culann").

Even though Cathbad warned that anyone going to battle for the first time on a certain day was destined for a short life, Cuchulainn could not wait to deal with Ulster's enemies and he soon took up arms against three semi-divine warriors named Foill, Fannell and Tuachell, as well as their numerous followers, all of whom he killed. In this combat Cuchulainn displayed for the first time the dreadful shape of his battle-frenzy. His body trembled violently; his heels and calves appeared in front; one eye receded into his head, the other stood out huge and red on his cheek; a man's head could fit into his jaw; his hair bristled like hawthorn, with a drop of blood at the end of each single hair; and from the top of his head arose a thick column of dark blood like the mast of a ship. Returning to Emain Macha in his chariot, "graced with the bleeding heads of his enemies", and with the battle-frenzy still upon him, Cuchulainn was only stopped from circling the defences and screaming for a fight through a ploy of the Ulster queen Mughain. She led out of Emain Macha some hundred and fifty naked women carrying three vats of cold water. An embarrassed or amazed Cuchulainn was swiftly womanhandled into the vats. The first one burst its sides. The second boiled furiously, but the last vat became only very hot. Thus was the young hero tamed after his first taste of blood.

In his calm, everyday state of mind Cuchulainn was a favourite of womenfolk. But he fell in love with EMER, the daughter of Fogall, a wily chieftain whose castle was close to Dublin. Cuchulainn asked for Emer's hand but Fogall, who was against the match, pointed out that Cuchulainn had yet to establish his reputation as a warrior and suggested that he should go and learn

CUCHULAINN, the Irish Achilles, performed many mighty deeds in his brief years. The hero's dreamy eyes reflect his idealism, which is expressed in the inscription beneath this portrait, "I care not though I last but a day if my name and my fame are a power forever."

(CUCHULAINN BY JOHN DUNCAN, CANVAS, 1913.)

CUCHULAINN, mortally wounded in his final combat but determined to fight to the end, lashed himself to a pillar and died on his feet. At the end a crow settled on his shoulder, signifying death. This memorial symbolizes all those who fought for Irish independence. (THE DEATH OF CUCHULAINN BY O SHEPPARD, BRONZE, 1916.)

For a year and a day Cuchulainn was taught by Scathach, and became the lover of her daughter *UATHACH*. Scathach seems to have feared for the safety of Cuchulainn, and she warned him without success not to challenge her sister Aoifa. But Cuchulainn beat Aoifa by cunning, and afterwards she became his mistress, conceiving the unfortunate Conlai. Cuchulainn finally returned to Fogall's stronghold and claimed Emer, but only after a heated battle with Fogall and his warriors, during which Fogall leapt to his death escaping the hero.

Acclaimed as the champion of Ireland in a beheading contest, Cuchulainn was soon unbeatable in combat, a skill he was to need dearly in his last campaign, which was a single-handed defence of Ulster against the invading army of Queen *MEDB* of Connacht. The main reason for this large-scale cattle raid was a famous brown bull which was kept in Cuailgne. But the tyrannical ruler of Ulster, King Conchobhar Mac Nessa, also played a part in gathering rebellious Ulstermen and others from many parts of Ireland to Queen Medb's side. One prophecy told the queen that there would be "crimson and red" upon her forces because of Cuchulainn's prowess, but she was determined to invade and she also had three advantages. First, the great hero had made bitter enemies of the *CALATIN* family, whose daughters were witches. Just prior to his last stand along with his faithful charioteer *LAEG*, they cast a spell on Cuchulainn which withered a shoulder and a hand. Second, Medb attacked when Ulster's heroes were laid low by *MACHA*'s curse, and were unable to fight for five days and nights. Finally, Cuchulainn had lost the support of the goddess *MORRIGAN*, because he had rejected her passionate advances. Yet he still managed to conduct a successful single-handed defence and was able to slow the advance of Queen

from the Scottish champion Domhall. Domhall told Cuchulainn that his best trainer in arms would be *SCATHACH*, a warrior-princess in the Land of Shadows. So he travelled to this mysterious land and served Scathach. She taught the young hero his famous battle leap.

CUCHULAINN journeyed to the Isle of Skye to train in the martial arts. On the Isle he met a man who gave him a flaming wheel to guide him through the deadly quagmire. The guide was his father, the sun god, Lugh. (ILLUSTRATION BY STEPHEN REID, 1912.)

Medb's forces by the use of clever tactics and lightning attacks, until the effects of Macha's curse had almost worn off, and the dazed warriors were able to respond to Sualtam Mac Roth's call to arms. But their help came too late for Cuchulainn. Pressed on all sides by his enemies, the Ulster champion was overcome in spite of aid from his divine father, the sun god Lugh. His only companion, Laeg, was laid low with a spear, then Cuchulainn himself suffered a terrible stomach wound that even Lugh could not heal. Finally, Cuchulainn tied himself to an upright stone in order to fight till his last breath. As soon as he died Morrigan, in the form of a crow, settled on his shoulder and his enemies cut off his head and right hand, leaving his body for the carrion birds. Conall, his foster-brother, managed to recover the missing parts, but Ulster wept for the loss of their champion. Indeed, so widespread was Cuchulainn's fame that his exploits influenced the development of the Arthurian myths in Britain and France. (See also *MAGIC AND ENCHANTMENT; CELTIC ROMANCE*)

119

C

CULANN, in Irish mythology, was an Ulster smith who was thought to be a reincarnation of the sea god *MANANNAN MAC LIR*. It was his enormous guardian dog that young Setanta killed with his bare hands. Culann was angry about this so Setanta offered to become his hound until a new one was trained. Thereafter the young man was known as *CUCHULAINN*, "the Hound of Culann".

CULHWCH, in Welsh mythology, was the son of Cildydd, one of King *ARTHUR*'s knights. His stepmother hated Culhwch so much that she placed a curse on him that he could marry only *OLWEN*, the daughter of the giant Yspaddaden. This fate, however, seemed less dreadful once Culhwch found Olwen, a task which took over a year, for they fell deeply in love. Culhwch's next problem was how to persuade her giant father to agree to the match. Like the Irish Cyclops *BALOR*, Yspaddaden's eyelids needed to be levered up with supports in order for him to see

CULANN (below), the Ulster smith, and the High King Conchobhar gaze in amazement at the young Cuchulainn who slew Culann's fierce hound outright when the great guard dog had attacked the hero at the gate. To compensate for killing his hound, Cuchulainn offered to take its place. (ILLUSTRATION BY STEPHEN REID, 1912.)

CU ROI and his comrade, Cuchulainn, on one wild escapade, raided Inis Ter Falga, carrying off the king's booty and beautiful daughter, Blathnat. When the heroes fell out over the girl, Cuchulainn was at one point beaten and buried up to his arms while Cu Roi galloped off with Blathnat. (ILLUSTRATION BY JAMES ALEXANDER, 1995.)

Culhwch. Also like Balor, the Welsh giant did not favour the idea of his daughter marrying a man. At interviews held on successive days Yspaddaden threw a poisoned spear at Culhwch and his companions, but they managed on each occasion to catch it and throw it back. When Culhwch finally put out one of the giant's eyes with a return throw, Yspaddaden agreed to the marriage on condition that Culhwch perform a whole series of difficult tasks. With the assistance of King Arthur's men and a couple of divine allies, Culhwch successfully completed these trials, then killed Yspaddaden and married Olwen. (See also *HEROIC QUESTS*)

CUMAL (whose name means "sky") was the father of the Fenian hero Finn Mac Cumal, more commonly known as *FINN MACCOOL*, who was born after his father's death. Cumal was also a renowned leader of the *FIANNA* and chief of the Clan Bascna. He was killed by Jadhg, a druid, who had been enraged when Cumal eloped with his daughter.

CU ROI (whose name means "hound of Roi") was a Munster king. It was King Cu Roi who transformed himself into *UATH*, the dreadful giant, in order to choose the champion of Ireland. The three

CULHWCH (right), on his quest for Olwen, arrives at Arthur's court, seeking help and counsel. This Victorian painting evokes a medieval mood, portraying the hero as a courtly hunter from the Age of Chivalry. The surly steward could be Arthur's brusque seneschal, Kay. (KILHWYCH, THE KING'S SON BY ARTHUR GASKIN, WOOD, c. 1900.)

contenders for the championship – Laoghaire, Cuchulainn's foster-brother *CONALL*, and *CUCHULAINN* himself – were invited by Cu Roi to a beheading contest, which only Cuchulainn had enough courage to go through with. Later, Cu Roi and Cuchulainn carried off *BLATHNAT*, a beautiful woman. Although she expressed her love for Cuchulainn, Cu Roi took her to his castle in Munster. When Cuchulainn laid siege to the stronghold, Blathnat betrayed Cu Roi by showing how the place could be entered.

CYNON, according to a late Arthurian myth, was a knight who encountered a black man with one foot and one eye, and bearing a large wooden club. This Fomorii-like fighter, doubtless a cousin of the violent and misshapen Irish sea gods, ordered Cynon to go to a fountain and fill with water a silver bowl that he would find there , and then to throw the water against a marble slab. Sir Cynon did as he was instructed and a Black Knight appeared to the sound of thunder and the singing of magic birds. Sir

CYNON, an Arthurian hero, battles with the Black Knight, a mysterious warrior who appeared by magic. Although defeated, Cynon returned home on foot to tell the tale, and thus inspired Owain to set out on his memorable quest. Years later Cynon retraced his steps in search of Owain. (ILLUSTRATION BY H THEAKER, 1920.)

Cynon then fought his mysterious opponent but was defeated.

DAGDA means "the good god". He was in fact the great god of Irish mythology, and was usually depicted as a man in rustic clothes dragging an enormous club on wheels. With one end of this weapon he could slay his enemies and with the other he could restore the dead to life. Dagda was believed to be wise, full of knowledge and well versed in the magic arts. He was a chief of the *TUATHA DE DANANN*.

Dagda was a great fighter and the lover of *MORRIGAN*, the war goddess. The bones of his enemies were described as "hailstones under horses' hooves" when he wielded his mighty club. Like an all-powerful chieftain, Dagda led the Tuatha De Danann on the battlefield, slaying all those who dared to confront him. Yet he was also associated with abundance, being able to satisfy the hunger of everybody by means of an inexhaustible cauldron. That Dagda took great pleasure in eating was apparent, when just before the second battle of Magh Tuireadh he visited the camp of the *FOMORII*, his bitter enemies, during a truce at the time of the New Year festival. There they made for him a porridge of milk, flour, fat, pigs and goats, enough for fifty men.

On pain of death Dagda was ordered by the Fomorii to consume this massive meal, which he readily did with a huge wooden ladle "so big that a man and a woman could have slept together in it". This test turned Dagda temporarily into a gross old man, but it did not prevent him from making love to a Fomorii girl, who promised to use her magic on behalf of the Tuatha De Danann. The story may recall, in a distorted form, a holy marriage between a chieftain and a maiden at the beginning of each year; similar to

DANA, the great mother goddess, gave her name to the Tuatha De Danann, a race of wonderful, beautiful but often vulnerable gods who lived in the sparkling otherworld. Here, they gather to hear the poignant song of Lir's children, ill-starred gods who were turned into swans. (ILLUSTRATION BY STEPHEN REID, 1912.)

DAGDA, father of the gods, owned a wondrous cauldron of plenty and a double-edged magic club, carried on wheels. This bronze relief of a powerful Celtic deity, with a wheel, is regarded by some to be Dagda, with the wheel symbolizing his treasures. (GUNDESTRUP CAULDRON, GILDED SILVER, C. 100 BC.)

the sacred rite that was performed by a Sumerian ruler and a priestess in Mesopotamia. This union was meant to ensure prosperity, strength and peace.

Although the eventual defeat of the Fomorii at the second battle of Magh Tuireadh was really due to the sun god *LUGH*, it was Dagda who was held in the greatest respect, even after the Tuatha De Danann were in their turn overthrown by the sons of *MILESIUS*, the ancestors of the present-day Irish.

To Dagda fell the important task of settling the defeated Tuatha De Danann underground. Just as the Fomorii had retreated beneath the waves, so the vanquished De Danann disappeared underground. Over the centuries these powerful deities were gradually transformed into fairies – the *bean sidhe* or *BANSHEES* of Irish folklore. (See also *WONDROUS CAULDRONS*)

DANA, another name for *ANU*, was the goddess after whom the *TUATHA DE DANANN* were named – "the people of the goddess Dana".

DECHTIRE, in Irish mythology, was the mother of *CUCHULAINN*. She was a daughter of Maga, the child of the love god *AONGHUS* and of the druid *CATHBAD*, advisor to King *CONCHOBHAR MAC NESSA* of Ulster. When Dechtire married *SUALTAM MAC ROTH*, a fly flew into her cup during the wedding feast and she swallowed it. She fell into a deep sleep and dreamed that the sun god *LUGH* insisted that she and fifty of her kinswomen follow him to the otherworld as a flock of birds. Three years later a flock of brightly coloured birds reappeared at Emain Macha, the capital of Ulster. The Ulstermen went after them with slings, but were unable to hit any of them. It was decided, therefore, to surprise·the birds at night as they rested. So it was that the warriors came upon Dechtire, her women and Lugh sleeping in a hut on a site renowned for its magical properties. When Conchobar was told of of this he sent for Dechtire at once, but she told her captors that she was too ill to be able to travel for another day. The next morning she showed them her new-born son, a gift to Ulster.

DECHTIRE, who had disappeared mysteriously on her wedding day, returned three years later with the shining sun god, Lugh. Dechtire brought with her a gift from the otherworld – her child, Setanta, who became Ulster's greatest hero, Cuchulainn. (ILLUSTRATION BY G DENHAM, C. 1900.)

DEIRDRE was the cause of Ulster's sorrows, according to Irish mythology. The druid *CATHBAD* foretold this before she was born, as well as telling of how beautiful she would become. When she grew up, King *CONCHOBHAR MAC NESSA* wished to marry her, even though he was already advanced in years, but Deirdre would have none of this. She persuaded *NAOISE* and his brothers to run away with her to Alba. After living for many years in their voluntary exile, they were tricked into returning to Ulster on the understanding that they would come to no harm. But Conchobhar arranged to have Naoise killed and then forced Deirdre to agree to marry him. Once married, however, Deirdre remained sad and kept her distance from the king, with the result that he handed her over to the killer of Naoise. Rather than sleep with this man, she threw herself from his speeding chariot and smashed her brains out on a rock. From each of the graves of Naoise and Deirdre grew a pine, which eventually intertwined and grew as a single tree.

DERBFORGAILLE was the daughter of a ruler of Lochlann. When her father left her on the shore as a tribute for the *FOMORII*, she was rescued by the Ulster hero *CUCHULAINN* and fell in love with him. In order to follow him, she turned herself into a swan. However, unaware of the bird's true identity, Cuchulainn brought her down with a sling-shot. She returned to human form and he sucked the stone out of the wound, but now they were linked by blood and so he could not marry her.

DIAN CECHT was the Irish god of healing. It was said that with his daughter Airmid, he had charge of a spring whose waters restored the dying gods to life. After *NUADA*, the leader of the *TUATHA DE DANANN*, lost his hand fighting the *FIRBOLG* at the first battle of Magh Tuireadh, Dian Cecht gave him a silver hand, thus earning him the title Nuada "of the Silver Hand". Impressed though the Tuatha De Danann were by Dian Cecht's handiwork, Nuada was felt to be no longer fit to be a war leader and *BRES*, who was half *FOMORII*, took his place. But Bres was a tyrant and became very unpopular, so Nuada was restored to the leadership, once Dian Cecht's son Miach had made him a new hand of flesh and blood. Apparently the god of healing grew jealous of his son's medical skills and so killed him.

DIARMUID UA DUIBHNE, or Diarmuid "of the Love Spot", was the foster-son of the Irish love god *AONGHUS*. His mortal father gave him to the god as a child, a gift that was returned when Diarmuid received the famous love spot as a young Fenian warrior. One night, when out hunting, Diarmuid and three companions took shelter in a small hut in a wood. There a beautiful young woman received them but chose to sleep only with Diarmuid. She told him that she was Youth, and that the love spot she put on his forehead would make him irresistible to women. As a consequence, Diarmuid's life was almost continuously troubled by desperate women, the worst being *GRAINNE*, the passionate daughter of High King *CORMAC MAC ART*. Grainne was betrothed to *FINN MACCOOL*, the Fenian commander, but she wanted Diarmuid and forced him to elope with her. For sixteen years the Fenians pursued them until, at the request of the king and the love god, a peace was grudgingly made.

It seemed that Diarmuid and Grainne would settle down to a contented family life and they had several children. But Diarmuid's own destiny was about to catch up with him. His mortal father had killed his brother at birth because

he believed that Aonghus' steward, Roc, was responsible for the pregnancy. However, Roc revived the infant as a magic boar and told it to bring Diarmuid to his death. When hunting one day with Cormac Mac Art and Finn MacCool, Diarmuid came face to face with this creature. His hounds fled in terror, his slingshot had no impact on the charging boar's head and his sword broke in two, so the irresistible Diarmuid was left bleeding to death on the ground. Finn MacCool refused to fetch the dying Diarmuid a drink of water, and by the time the other hunters arrived on the scene, he was too near to death to be saved. Grainne was devastated by the loss, although she was moved by the way that Aonghus took care of Diarmuid's corpse. He took the body to his own palace by the River Boyne, where he breathed a new soul into Diarmuid so that they could converse each day. This was how the young man came to live with the *TUATHA DE DANANN*, who had by this time left the upper world and lived beneath the soil of Ireland.

DIARMUID, gored by a wild boar, was denied healing water by Finn, still smarting over Diarmuid's love affair with Grainne. A Celtic Adonis, the hero was loved by women often against his will, and, like Adonis, was killed by a boar, but enjoyed some form of immortality. (ILLUSTRATION BY H J FORD, 1912.)

DON was the Welsh equivalent of the Irish mother goddess *DANA* and was the daughter of Mathonwy, sister of *MATH*, and the wife of Beli, the god of death. She had many children, including *AMAETHON*, *ARIANRHOD*, Govannon, *GWYDION*, Gilvaethwy and *NUDD*.

DIAN CECHT (above), god of healing, guards the sacred spring of health with his daughter, Airmid. Its miracle waters cured the sick and restored the dead to life. Known as the father of medicine, Dian Cecht is credited with a remarkable sixth-century Brehon Law tract on the practice of medicine. (ILLUSTRATION BY NICK BEALE, 1995.)

DON (below), the Welsh mother goddess, was as popular as her Irish counterpart, Dana. This female figure, surrounded by birds and children, is widely assumed to be a Celtic mother goddess. She is one of several Celtic deities embossed on the gilded panels of the Gundestrup Cauldron. (GILDED SILVER, C. 100 BC.)

DIARMUID (below), a gifted Fenian warrior, was lured underground by the De Danann who often recruited champions to fight in their otherworldly battles. To test his skill, they sent a mysterious warrior to challenge him as he drank from their forest well. (ILLUSTRATION BY STEPHEN REID, 1912.)

MAGIC AND ENCHANTMENT

ENCHANTMENT PERMEATES Celtic myth, shrouding the tales in a haunting, dreamlike quality. The all-pervasive otherworld lies behind much of the mystery and magic, penetrating the forests and lakes, and crafting charmed rings and weapons. Yet spells and magic also arose in the visible world where bards, druids and some privileged heroes, such as Finn MacCool, possessed magical powers. Bards could weaken the enemy with satire or enchanted sleep, while druids bewitched the host with magical illusions. Off the battlefield, love and romance were also subject to spells, love philtres or magical trickery, as in the romances of Sadb, Rhiannon and Iseult. On the brighter side, many heroes enjoyed the gifts of the otherworld, such as Arthur's sword, Excalibur, or Fergus Mac Roth's *sidhe* sword; while Fergus Mac Leda's water-shoes afforded underwater adventures; and countless heroes were nourished or reborn from magical cauldrons.

FERGUS MAC LEDA, (above), a high king of Ulster, owned a pair of water-shoes with which he enjoyed underwater travel. He never tired of exploring the depths of the lakes and rivers of Ireland until he encountered a fierce river-horse in Loch Rury. The incident so terrified Fergus that his face became permanently distorted with fear. As only an unblemished king could rule Ireland, Fergus returned to the loch to slay the monster before going down himself, but with a face at last restored and serene. (ILLUSTRATION BY STEPHEN REID, 1912.)

THE ENCHANTED FOREST (left) of Arthurian legend, was alive with beguiling fairy maidens, who often taunted errant knights. One such, La Belle Dame Sans Merci, described by the poet Keats, was a banshee who attracted mortal lovers for her own amusement, inspiring them with a hopeless infatuation and then leaving them bereft of will or purpose until they withered on the lake, "alone and palely loitering". As the languishing knight here sleeps, he dreams of the pale kings and warriors whom La Belle Dame holds in thrall. (LA BELLE DAME SANS MERCI BY H M RHEAM, CANVAS. 1897.)

EXCALIBUR (above), Arthur's enchanted sword, shone with the light of thirty torches and dazzled his enemies. The precious scabbard prevented the loss of blood in battle, but Arthur rather rashly handed this talisman over to his half-sister Morgan Le Fay for safekeeping; she instantly made a duplicate for Arthur, passing the original on to her lover, Accolon. Here, Arthur marvels at the sword rising from a white-clad arm in the enchanted lake. (ILLUSTRATION BY AUBREY BEARDSLEY, C. 1870.)

PWYLL'S (above) family wander in an enchanted wilderness after their country, Dyfed, had been spirited away in a peal of thunder. The baffling enchantment was part of a lingering curse placed on Pwyll to avenge Gwawl, a rival suitor for the hand of Rhiannon. Even after Pwyll's death, the spell blighted his family, until Rhiannon's new husband, Manawydan, struck a deal with the enchanter, who at last restored Dyfed to its former beauty. (ILLUSTRATION BY ALAN LEE, 1984)

MERLIN (right), wise and thoughtful though he was, was enchanted by the ravishing Lady of the Lake, Nimue, and despite his foresight, he allowed himself to be lured deep beneath a stone and bound there by his own magic spells. In another legend, Nimue put Merlin into a trance beneath a thorn tree and then trailed her veil around him, creating an invisible tower of air in which he was trapped forever. It is said that his voice can still be heard in the plaintive rustling of leaves. (ILLUSTRATION BY ALAN LEE, 1984.)

E

DONN ("the Dark One") was the Irish god of the dead. He is sometimes confused with *EBER* Donn, one of the leaders of the sons of *MILESIUS*, who insulted *ERIU*, one of the *TUATHA DE DANANN*, and was drowned off the south-west coast of Ireland. Donn's home, the House of Donn, was thought to be an assembly point on the journey to the otherworld.

DRUIDS see *SAGES AND SEERS*

DUBH was a druidess. According to one Irish tradition, her anger at her husband Enna's passion for another woman ultimately led to the name of Dublin. Dubh used magic to drown her rival, but her husband in turn drowned her in what became known as Dubhlinn ("Dubh's pool").

DYLAN ("Son of the Wave") was a Welsh sea god whose parents were *ARIANRHOD* and her brother *GWYDION*. As soon as he was born

DYLAN, a Welsh sea deity, leapt from his mother's arms at birth and plunged straight into the sea and swam as well as any fish. Beloved by the sea, all the waves wept when he was killed, and his death-groan can still be heard in the roar of the incoming tide. (THE BAPTISM OF DYLAN, SON OF THE WAVE BY GEORGE SHERRINGHAM, CANVAS, C. 1900.)

DONN, god of the dead, gathers souls around him as they assemble on his stormy island before setting out on their journey to the otherworld. Inevitably, he became associated in popular folklore with shipwrecks and sea storms, and was often confused with Eber Donn, who died at sea. (ILLUSTRATION BY JAMES ALEXANDER, 1995.)

he headed straight to the sea, where he immediately swam as well as a fish. When his uncle, the smith god Govannon, killed him, all the waves of Britain and Ireland lamented his death.

EBER was the name of two of the three leaders who led the Milesians in their conquest of Ireland. They were Eber Donn, or Eber "the Brown", and Eber Finn, or Eber "the Fair". The third was named Eremon. Eber Donn failed to reach the Irish coast because his ship foundered in a storm caused by, it was said, his bloody war cry. The

druid *AMAIRGEN* had only just succeeded in casting a spell over the turbulent waves, when Eber Donn was seized by a battle-frenzy and the charm was broken by his wild cries. After the defeat of the *TUATHA DE DANANN*, the advice of Amairgen was ignored by Eber Finn, who refused to acknowledge the right of his older brother Eremon to be king of the whole island. So it was that Ireland was partitioned into two kingdoms, with Eremon ruling the north and Eber Finn the south. But Eber Finn invaded Eremon's territory and laid waste to his lands until he fell in battle. Eremon then became the first High King of all Ireland.

EFNISIEN, in Welsh mythology, was the troublesome half-brother of *BRAN THE BLESSED* who caused the rift between Bran and King *MATHOLWCH*. Because Efnisien had not been consulted by Bran over the marriage of his half-sister *BRANWEN* to the Irish king, he proceeded to cut off the lips, ears and tails of Matholwch's horses during the wedding feast. To compensate for this act, Bran gave Matholwch a magic cauldron that was capable of restoring dead warriors to life, but with one small imperfection – they came back to life without the power of speech. However, the

Irish did not consider this gift a sufficient redress for Efnisien's act of mutilation, and some time after her arrival in Ireland Branwen was demoted from being queen to just a lowly cook in the palace kitchens. Efnisien accompanied the army that was sent against Matholwch to avenge this insult. It was fortunate for Bran that his half-brother did come, because Efnisien foiled a cunning trap that had been laid for the Britons by Matholwch in his hall. He had placed behind each of Bran's strongest warriors a sack hung from the wall containing an armed Irishman, and at a signal they were to fall upon the Britons during what was supposed to be a feast of welcome. When Efnisien inspected the hall beforehand, he asked what was in one of the bags. On being told it was corn, Efnisien laid hold of the sack and felt about till his fingers closed on the head of the warrior within it, then he squeezed and cracked his skull. One by one Efnisien asked about the contents of the sacks and each time repeated his squeezing.

The feast took place therefore not as Matholwch had planned. An even more unexpected turn of events occurred when Efnisien threw Matholwch's three-year-old son by Branwen on to the fire. Branwen would have leapt after her

ELATHA (above), a Fomorii king, lived beneath the waves with his violent and misshapen people. Unlike the other Fomorii, Elatha was a godlike being with long golden hair. Emerging from the sea one day in his silver ship, he met the lovely goddess, Eri, who fell immediately in love with him. Soon after, they had a handsome but troublesome son, Bres. (ILLUSTRATION BY NICK BEALE, 1995.)

EBER DONN (above) and the Milesian chiefs drift in the fairy sea mists off the Irish coast. On board Eber's ship, the druid Amairgen charmed the sea with magic of his own, but Eber let out his great war cry which broke the druid's spell and stirred up a storm in which he was drowned. (ILLUSTRATION BY JAMES ALEXANDER, 1995.)

EFNISIEN (below) inspects sacks in Matholwch's hall. In each sack he felt a warrior's head, which he crushed between his fingers. The moody trickster went on to provoke a deadly contest, but then, in remorse, sacrificed himself to save his comrades. (ILLUSTRATION BY STEPHEN REID, 1910.)

son, but Bran held her back. In the fight that took place afterwards the Britons were almost defeated by the magic cauldron that Bran had given Matholwch, because at night it restored to life the Irish warriors who had been slain during the day. The Britons were in a desperate predicament and so Efnisien, at the cost of his life, destroyed the magic cauldron. He hid among the Irish dead and was thrown into the boiling cauldron, where he stretched and burst its sides, but the great effort involved killed him.

ELATHA, in Irish mythology, was the son of Delbaeth, the leader of the *FOMORII* and father of *BRES*, who was briefly the leader of the *TUATHA DE DANANN*. Unlike the other Fomorii, who were described as being hideous and deformed, Elatha was fair and had golden hair. He met the goddess Eri on the sea shore and there they conceived their child Bres. When Bres was removed from the leadership of the De Danann, he and his mother went to Elatha to ask for help, but the Fomorii were defeated at the second battle of Magh Tuireadh and driven from Ireland.

EMER, in Irish mythology, was the daughter of Fogall and the wife of *CUCHULAINN*, who first saw her when he was at the court of the High King of Ireland at Tara. She appeared "dark-haired almost as himself, and her skin white as mare's milk, and her eyes wide and proud and brilliant like the eyes of Fedelma, his favourite falcon". Emer's father was a chieftain from Meath and was against the match. He told Cuchulainn to travel to improve his fighting skills and only then would he consider him as a son-in-law. Cuchulainn survived and returned to claim his bride. Indeed, Cuchulainn was forced to attack the reluctant Fogall's fortress before the wedding could take place. Although Emer was totally enraptured by her handsome husband, their marriage was not without its troubles, not least because many other women also found the Ulster hero attractive. Just before his final battle, when he fought the army of Queen *MEDB* alone, Emer tried to persuade him to remain in the fortress of Emain Macha, the seat of King *CONCHOBHAR MAC NESSA*. However, he got on his chariot when it was brought

around to the front of his house. Even then, he thought of Emer's request, but his enemies the witches of *CALATIN* cast a spell to harden his resolve to fight single-handed.

ENID see *CELTIC ROMANCE*

EMER, a peerless Irish maiden, inspired the love of Ulster's great hero, Cuchulainn. She was blessed with the six gifts of womanhood: beauty, chastity, wisdom, sweet speech, song and needlecraft. When the hero courted her, she smiled at his youth, and said that he had "deeds to do". (ILLUSTRATION BY STEPHEN REID, 1912.)

ETAIN (right), one of the High Queens of Ireland, appears with her peers in power and beauty: from left to right, Etain, Greek Helen, Medb and Fand, the fairy queen. The jewelled cup of plenty recalls Etain's links with the otherworld. (ETAIN, HELEN, MEDB AND FAND BY HARRY CLARKE, GLASS, C. 1900.)

EPONA, the Celtic horse goddess, won the favour of the Roman army and was depicted in monuments set up at its cavalry barracks as a woman riding a fast steed, her cloak billowing with air behind her. She was even given her own festival in Rome on December 18. Originally, Epona was almost certainly seen by the Celts as a mare, possibly like the great white horse carved in the chalk downs near Wantage, in southern England. The fact that she is often depicted riding a horse with a foal suggests that she was also a goddess of fertility. In the Welsh myth of *PWYLL* there is a connection between Epona and his wife *RHIANNON*, who is made to carry visitors into her husband's palace.

ERIU, or Erinn, was the wife of Ma Greine, son of *OGMA*, and herself one of the *TUATHA DE DANANN*. When the Milesians invaded, she and her two sisters, Banba and

EPONA (below), the Celtic horse goddess, was adopted by the Roman cavalry who spread her cult across Europe. Her effigy, often placed in stables, portrayed her riding side-saddle, sometimes with a foal, which reflected her role as a fertility goddess, symbolized here by the wheat and birds.

(ILLUSTRATION BY MIRANDA GRAY, 1995.)

ETHNE, a gentle Tuatha De Danann maiden, was lost to the otherworld when she mislaid her Veil of Invisibility, key to the Realm of Fairy. She was rescued by monks and, according to a later legend, became a nun, but she was disturbed by "voices", the cries of her fairy folk, seeking her in vain. (ILLUSTRATION BY STEPHEN REID, 1910.)

Fotla, went to greet them. All three asked that the newcomers would name the island after her. AMAIRGEN, druid and advisor to the sons of MILESIUS, promised that Ireland would be named after Eriu.

ETAIN, in Irish mythology, was one of the TUATHA DE DANANN and was reincarnated several times. She was the second wife of the god MIDIR. His first wife was jealous of Etain and by a druid's spell Etain was reborn as a mortal, the daughter of the Ulster warrior Etar. To hinder Midir's search for her, Etain was turned first into a pool of water, then a worm and finally a fly. When Etar's wife accidentally swallowed the fly she became pregnant with Etain. Unaware of her previous existence, Etain was loved both by the High King Eochaidh, whom she married, and by his brother AILILL. This potentially difficult situation was solved by her sudden discovery that she was already married to Midir, who had awakened her memories. High King Eochaidh lost Etain to the god at a game of chess, but although she lived once again with Midir for a period of time, Etain decided in the end to return to Tara and finish her mortal life as Eochaidh's queen.

ETHLINN, sometimes Ethnea, was the only daughter of BALOR, the one-eyed giant of Irish myth. Balor imprisoned Ethlinn in a crystal tower on Tory Island, off the north-western coast of Ireland, because of a prophecy that said he would be killed by his own grandson. However, a certain Cian, brother of the smith god GOIBHNIU, managed to reach Ethlinn, and so the sun god LUGH was conceived. Despite Balor's attempts to have the baby killed, he survived to be brought up either by Goibhniu or, according to another version of the myth, by the sea god MANANNAN MAC LIR, and so fulfilled his destiny by killing Balor at the second battle of Magh Tuireadh.

ETHNE was the daughter of Roc, steward of the love god AONGHUS, and acted as maid to the daughter of MANANNAN MAC LIR. After a chieftain of the TUATHA DE DANANN tried to rape her, she refused to eat or drink. Aonghus and Manannan searched for a remedy and found two magic cows whose milk never ran dry and she lived on their milk.

ETHNEA see ETHLINN

EXCALIBUR see MAGIC AND ENCHANTMENT

FAND, in Irish mythology, was the wife of MANANNAN MAC LIR. One day she quarrelled with her husband and he left her. When she was attacked by the FOMORII, Fand sent for CUCHULAINN, who came to her island and defeated her enemies, and remained for one month as her lover. Before he returned home, they arranged to meet again in Ireland. But Cuchulainn's wife, EMER, found out about this secret meeting and took fifty of her maidens armed with sharp knives to kill Fand. A confused argument then took place between Fand, Emer, Cuchulainn and Manannan Mac Lir, who had also learned of the arrangement. But in the end, Fand

FAND's maidens appeared to Cuchulainn in a vision, beating him with rods, which left him sore for a year. Having gained his attention, they explained that the goddess, Fand, needed his help to fight the Fomorii. After defeating her attackers, Cuchulainn stayed on Fand's island for a month. (ILLUSTRATION BY STEPHEN REID, 1912.)

decided to stay with her husband and forget Cuchulainn. Manannan Mac Lir then shook his magic cloak between Fand and Cuchulainn so they would never see each other again, and druids gave Cuchulainn and Emer drinks of forgetfulness. (See also CELTIC ROMANCE)

FEDLIMID the story-teller was the father of DEIRDRE. One day, when CONCHOBHAR MAC NESSA and some fellow Ulstermen were drinking at his house, the unborn Deirdre cried out from her mother's womb. The druid CATHBAD then foretold that the child would cause nothing but doom and destruction.

FERDIA son of Daman the FIRBOLG, was a friend and comrade of CUCHULAINN. As young men, they were both taught to fight by SCATHACH. During the war of the brown bull of Cuailgne, Ferdia fought on the side of Queen MEDB and against Cuchulainn and the men of Ulster. Ferdia did his best to avoid coming up against his friend, but eventually Medb taunted him into fighting the great hero in single combat and he was killed.

FERGUS MAC LEDA see MAGIC AND ENCHANTMENT

FERGUS MAC ROTH, a king of Ulster, according to one myth fell in love with his predecessor's widow, NESSA. She would only marry him if her son, CONCHOBHAR MAC NESSA, was allowed to rule for a year. Conchobhar, with help from his mother, proved to be a popular king and the people refused to let him stand down. At first Fergus accepted this but, later, when Conchobhar lost the support of several leading Ulstermen, he led them in revolt. Conchobhar's love for DEIRDRE was the cause of his unpopularity, especially after he had her lover NAOISE killed in order to marry her. Fergus with three hundred Ulster warriors joined Queen MEDB in her invasion of Ulster. The great CUCHULAINN lost his life in this war, but not at the hands of Fergus. They had been friends before the war and had sworn not to fight each other. During the final battle, Fergus pretended to retreat and the next time they met Cuchulainn would do the same. It was due to Fergus' retreat that CONALL, Cuchulainn's foster-brother, was able to defeat Medb's army and rally the Ulstermen after the death of Cuchulainn.

FERDIA is borne from the battlefield by his lifelong friend, Cuchulainn. The two were goaded into single combat by Medb and fought grimly to the death. At Ferdia's death, Cuchulainn fell exhausted, lamenting, "Why should I rise again now he that lies here has fallen by my hand?" (ILLUSTRATION BY E WALLCOUSINS, 1912.)

THE FIANNA was the famous band of warriors responsible for the safety of the High King of Ireland. Popularly called the Fenians, their greatest leader was *FINN MACCOOL* and the majority of their members came from one of two clans, the Bascna and the Morna. Many of the adventures of the Knights of the Round Table recall the exploits of the Fenians. To join, "no man was taken till in the ground a hole had been made, such as would reach the waist, and he put into it with his shield and a forearm's length of a hazel stick. Then must nine warriors, having nine spears, with a ten furrows' width between them and him, assail him and let fly at him. If he sustained injury, he was not received into the band."

FINEGAS, in Irish mythology, was a druid. Hoping to become supremely wise, he caught the Salmon of Knowledge, but unfortunately for his own ambitions he gave it to the young *FINN MACCOOL* to cook. Finn burnt his thumb on the flesh of the fish and sucked the burn. Realizing that his pupil Finn was the one destined to gain the wisdom, Finegas generously let the boy eat the whole fish.

FINN MACCOOL, sometimes called Finn Mac Cumaill or Fionn MacCumal, was the leader of the *FIANNA*, or Fenians, the select band of warriors which guarded the High King of Ireland. His father, *CUMAL*, a previous leader of the Fenians, was killed by Goll, a Fenian warrior. Cumal had eloped with a girl named Hurna and her father urged Goll to avenge this dishonour. Goll slew Cumal, but later Cumal's son Finn was born and brought up secretly. One of his tutors was the druid *FINEGAS*, who lived beside the River Boyne and caught the Salmon of Knowledge. He gave the fish to his pupil to cook, but Finn burnt his thumb on the flesh and in sucking it obtained wisdom.

So great was Finn MacCool's prowess as a warrior that he was soon appointed over the head of Goll to lead the Fenians, as his father had done. Goll accepted this decision with good grace, a gesture that may explain why Finn MacCool did not challenge Goll over his father's death. Indeed, Goll eventually married one of Finn MacCool's daughters, though he also slew his son. This last act of violence was too much and the Fenians pursued him. Trapped, Goll chose to starve to death rather than surrender. Finn MacCool used to quote a saying of Goll: "A man lives after his life but not after his dishonour."

Under Finn MacCool's leadership, the Fenians reached the high point of their fame as a warrior band. The pursuit of *DIARMUID UA DIUBHNE*, the foster-son of the love god *AONGHUS*, alone took sixteen years. He had taken *GRAINNE*, the daughter of High King *CORMAC MAC ART*, but she was betrothed to Finn MacCool at the time. The Fenians were relentless in the chase, but a peace of sorts was begrudgingly agreed. However, Finn never forgave Diarmuid for

the elopement, and he exulted over his rival's mortal wound, which he had received when hunting.

The account of Finn MacCool's own death is unclear. Some sagas tell how he fell attempting to quell an uprising among the Fenians

themselves, while others refer to an *ARTHUR*-like undeath in a cave. There he was supposed to remain in a deep sleep until such time as Ireland needed his aid.

FINTAN was the husband of Noah's granddaughter *CESAIR*. It is likely that the monks who first recorded the Irish sagas altered the original myth in order to link it with Noah's descendants, because of the deluge that only Fintan managed to survive by becoming a salmon. The monks wanted to tidy up the Irish myth of Fintan's mysterious transformation. The same name was also given to the Salmon of Knowledge, which was so called because it had eaten the nuts of a hazel tree that grew over the waters of *NECHTAN*'s well.

THE FIRBOLG, or bag-men, arrived in Ireland after escaping a life of slavery in Thrace, where they had been forced to cultivate the land by heaving heavy bags of fertile earth up rocky hills. In revolt, they turned their bags into boats and sailed to Ireland. (ILLUSTRATION BY NICK BEALE, 1995.)

THE FIRBOLG, or "bag men", in Irish mythology were said to have acquired their name from a time when they were enslaved in Thrace and made to carry bags of earth. They lived in Ireland just before the arrival of the *TUATHA DE DANANN*. But they were already being hard pressed by the *FOMORII*, the sea gods whom the Tuatha De Danann eventually overcame. At the first battle of Magh Tuireadh the Tuatha De Danann defeated the Firbolg, though the De Danann leader, *NUADA*, lost a hand. In the second battle of Magh Tuireadh the Fomorii were thoroughly beaten, due mainly to the bravery of the sun god *LUGH*, and were driven from Ireland for ever.

THE FOMORII were sea gods in Irish mythology. Violent and misshapen, the Fomorii emerged from the waves to challenge two rulers of Ireland: the *FIRBOLG* and the *TUATHA DE DANANN*. The Tuatha De Danann were younger gods, and they seized control of Ireland from the Firbolgs at the first battle of Magh Tuireadh, only to have to defeat the Fomorii at a second battle there in order to secure their conquest. Often the Fomorii were described as having only a single hand, foot or eye.

FORBAI was the son of the Ulster king *CONCHOBHAR MAC NESSA*. According to one myth, Queen *MEDB* of Connacht fell back before the fury of the Ulster warriors after her invasion of the kingdom. In Galway, however, Forbai caught up with her as she was bathing in a lake. A shot from his sling fatally struck the old warrior-queen in the centre of her forehead.

FRAOCH ("wrath" or "fury"), in Irish mythology, was a warrior who defeated a fearsome water monster in order to marry Findbhair, who was the daughter of Queen *MEDB* of Connacht. The terrible struggle with the monster left Fraoch very badly wounded and he recovered fully only after a timely visit to the

otherworld. His mother Be Find (who was a goddess and sister of the river goddess *BOANN*) nursed him back to health so that he could claim the hand of Findbhair. The account of Fraoch and the water monster is thought to have had some influence on the Danish legend of Beowulf's battle with Grendel, a monster invulnerable to weapons who lived in an underwater cavern.

FINN MACCOOL stands guard on the ramparts of Tara awaiting a fiery goblin whose magic music usually disarms his foes. Armed with a fairy spear, Finn breaks the spell and slays the unsuspecting demon. For his valour he was made captain of the Fianna. (ILLUSTRATION BY STEPHEN REID, 1910.)

WONDROUS CAULDRONS

MIRACULOUS CAULDRONS feature as a recurrent motif in Celtic myth. Some overflow with plenty, others restore the dead to life, while still others contain a special brew of wisdom. Dagda's gigantic Cauldron of Plenty overflowed with abundant, delicious meats; no hero left his bowl hungry, though cowards never had their fill. From Bran's massive Cauldron of Rebirth warriors emerged alive but dumb; another Cauldron of Rebirth in Annwn was guarded by nine maidens. Cauldrons of Inspiration provided "greals" or brews of wisdom. The most famous belonged to the goddess Ceridwen, whose magical broth endowed Taliesin with all-knowing insight. Some cauldrons, such as Dagda's, combined the magical properties of both plenty and rebirth. Similar mystery bowls or cups feature in Greek and eastern myths as holy vessels of spiritual insight. Ultimately, the early Celtic cauldrons find expression in the Arthurian Grail, which overflows with spiritual sustenance and leads the hero from death to immortality.

CAULDRONS OF PLENTY (left) glittered in bronze, copper, silver or gold, embossed with exquisite craftsmanship. The gilded Gundestrup Cauldron, here, found in a bog in Denmark, is a magnificent surviving example of a Celtic cauldron. Embossed in silver gilt, it is beautifully decorated in the La Tene style with Celtic deities and ritual activities, such as hunting or fighting. (GUNDESTRUP CAULDRON, GILDED SILVER, 100 BC.)

BRAN'S (above) Cauldron of Rebirth restored warriors to life, but without the power of speech. Bran received his wondrous cauldron from two martial giants, in gratitude for his kindness. Here, the great and gloomy giants brood over their bubbling cauldron, flanked by armed warriors on either side, for the warlike giants produced a grown warrior every six weeks. (ILLUSTRATION BY ALAN LEE, 1984.)

THE GRAIL, or Sangreal, (above) appeared to the knights of the Round Table amid dazzling light in which they saw each other more wisely and generously than ever before. The vision rendered them speechless, much like the Celtic warriors who emerged from their Cauldron of Rebirth alive but dumb. The Grail itself, shrouded in white samite, appears in the form of a Chalice of the Mass, recalling the Cup of the Last Supper. The chalice filled the hall with spicy odours and the knights ate and drank as never before, which all recalls the earlier Celtic Cauldrons of Plenty. (MANUSCRIPT ILLUSTRATION C. 1400.)

CAULDRONS OF REBIRTH (below), such as Annwn's or Bran's, must have been as large as tubs to contain the bodies of fallen warriors. In this section, a towering god appears to be dipping warriors into a mighty bucket or bowl, probably a cauldron of rebirth. Foot soldiers march in procession towards the cauldron, while a line of mounted infantry gallop off at the top, after their renovating dip. (CELTIC CAULDRON, GILDED SILVER, 100 BC.)

CELTIC CAULDRONS (below right) varied greatly in size, but such legendary cauldrons as Dagda's were so huge that they had to be conveyed on wheels or by chariot; while Bran's mighty cauldron was carried on the back of the giant Llaser. This cult wagon depicts just such a monumental cauldron. Mounted heroes in their peaked helmets, possibly hunters, travel triumphantly either to or from the hunt. The two stags, plus the hunters, suggest that the deity bearing the cauldron of plenty could well be the hunter god Cernunnos. (CULT WAGON, BRONZE, 100 BC.)

G

GALAHAD (left), the pure and peerless knight, stands resplendent in a blaze of holy light, armed as a Christian Crusader. His snow-white shield, marked with the blood of Joseph of Arimathea, was designed in Sarras for Galahad alone. (GALAHAD BY W HATHERELL, GLASS, C. 1910.)

GALAHAD (right), robed in red, entered Arthur's court escorted by a hermit, and took his place at the Round Table, filling the Siege Perilous. Completing the circle of knights, his arrival sparked off the Grail Quest. (GALAHAD ENTERS ARTHUR'S COURT BY W HATHERELL, CANVAS, C. 1910.)

GALAHAD was unique at the court of King *ARTHUR*, for he alone saw the entire Grail, or *SANGREAL*. He may even have handled the sacred vessel, as one version of the Arthurian myth states that Sir Galahad took "Our Lord's body between his hands" and then died. The quest for the Grail was an important preoccupation of the Knights of the Round Table. One of the seats was always left vacant as it was the place reserved for the knight who would find the Grail. Until Sir Galahad sat there, no knight had earned the right to occupy the place without being instantly swallowed by the earth.

The worthy young Sir Galahad was the son of Sir *LANCELOT*, the secret lover of Queen *GUINEVERE*, Arthur's wife. From the beginning of Galahad's manhood, however, it is made clear that he is without blemish. Twelve nuns, who had raised Galahad, told his father that he should "make him a knight, for there is no man alive more deserving of the order of knighthood". As soon as Sir Galahad had taken his rightful place at the Round Table, the presence of the Grail was felt in

Camelot. A mysterious lady then announced how the sacred vessel would come and feed all the knights. This happened, although none at the wonderful meal saw or touched the Grail. When Sir Gawain vowed to find its home in order to see the Grail for himself, most of the Knights of the Round Table followed suit, despite the efforts of King Arthur to dissuade them from undertaking what might prove to be their final quest. Although they set off in different directions, Sir Galahad was in the company of Sir *PERCIVAL* and Sir

Bors when he encountered the Grail. Together they had received the sacrament from the long-dead *JOSEPH OF ARIMATHEA*, who told Sir Galahad to take a bleeding spear to the castle of the "Maimed King" and rub it on this crippled ruler's body and limbs. Once this task was carried out, and the strange king restored to health, Sir Galahad saw the Grail in a vision. When he prayed that "he might leave the world", a voice told him how his soul would live in the next life with Christ the moment his request could be granted.

After this, various miracles took place and Sir Galahad was even obliged to become a king for a time while he waited patiently for his request to be fulfilled. When Joseph of Arimathea eventually returned, Galahad was at last granted his wish to leave the world. Joseph first allowed the pure and humble knight to hold the Grail for a few moments, then, as Sir Galahad knelt down to pray for his deliverance, his soul was suddenly released from his body and "a great multitude of angels bore it up to heaven".

GALAHAD receives spiritual nourishment from the Grail, followed by Percival and Bors. The idea of an all-sustaining and all-inspiring "greal" or brew is rooted in Celtic myth. (HOW SIR GALAHAD, SIR BORS AND SIR PERCIVAL WERE FED WITH THE SANC GRAEL BY DANTE ROSSETTI, CANVAS, 1864.)

GAWAIN, in Welsh Gwalchmai, was the most courteous knight at *ARTHUR*'s court. He was a strict upholder of chivalry and the enemy of Sir *LANCELOT*. Sir Gawain's most extraordinary adventure concerned the Green Knight. Rather like the hazard faced by the Ulster hero *CUCHULAINN*, when a water giant came to test the courage of Irish warriors, the gigantic Green Knight strode into King Arthur's hall at Camelot one New Year's Eve and challenged the Knights of the Round Table to a beheading contest. Sir Gawain accepted and cut off the stranger's head in a single blow. As the severed head rolled around the hall, the royal court relaxed and thought the challenge over. But to the amazement of all

present, the giant behaved as if nothing had happened. Calmly stooping, he picked up his head and mounted his green charger. Then, from the saddle, the Green Knight pointed his severed head in Sir Gawain's direction and told him to be at a lonely chapel a year from that day in order to take a turn at receiving a blow from an axe. On the journey to this dangerous appointment Sir Gawain stayed with Sir Bercilak de Hautdesert who had a beautiful wife. He was sorely tempted by Sir Bercilak's wife but managed to resist her advances for two days. However, on the third day Sir Gawain accepted from her a green sash, which was the usual token worn by a knight to show his love for a lady.

At the meeting between Sir Gawain and his fearful opponent, the Green Knight turned out to be none other than Sir Bercilak himself. Three times the axe was swung at Sir Gawain's neck. Twice it was deflected because he had not abused his host's hospitality by making love to his wife. The third time it made a slight cut, at which Sir Gawain flinched. It did not cut off his head because Sir Gawain had only accepted the green sash out of good manners. Yet Sir Gawain realized that courtesy was no equal to moral purity, and thereafter he always wore the green sash as a reminder of his lapse.

This late British version of the Celtic beheading contest was quite clearly influenced by Christianity.

GAWAIN, an active and restless knight, lost interest in the Grail Quest quite early on. Although one of the first to set forth, inspiring the rest of the Knights, he lost heart, lacking the necessary discipline, patience and humility. (THE FAILURE OF SIR GAWAIN BY W MORRIS, TAPESTRY, 1895–96.)

Unlike Sir Gawain, Cuchulainn had no hesitation in slipping away from the battlefield in order to keep a secret meeting with a lover, even during Queen *MEDB*'s invasion of Ulster. The magical transformation of Sir Bercilak de Hautdesert into the Green Knight was explained as the work of the witch *MORGAN LE FAY*, King Arthur's half-sister.

GERAINT see *CELTIC ROMANCE; SINGLE COMBAT*

H

GOIBHNIU was the Irish smith god and one of the *TUATHA DE DANANN*. He could make a perfect sword or spear with three blows of his magic hammer. Just before the second battle of Magh Tuireadh, a *FOMORII* spy came to see how Goibhniu made such impressive weapons, and even wounded the god. Goibhniu was said to preside over an otherworld feast called *Fled Goibnenn*, for which he brewed the ale. His Welsh counterpart was named Govannon.

THE GRAIL see *SANGREAL*; see also *WONDROUS CAULDRONS*; *HEROIC QUESTS*.

GRAINNE, in Irish mythology, was the daughter of *CORMAC MAC ART*, the High King of Ireland. She was promised to *FINN MACCOOL*, leader of the *FIANNA*, the body-guard of the High King. Although still powerful, Finn MacCool was quite old and Grainne preferred *DIARMUID UA DUIBHNE*, who was

GOIBHNIU, the Irish smith god, was an outstanding craftsman and armourer. Along with his gifted brothers, Creidhne the goldsmith, and Luchtar, the carpenter, he repaired the Tuatha De Danann armour with miraculous speed on the battlefield. (ILLUSTRATION ANON.)

the foster-son of the love god *AONGHUS*. By using magic, Grainne managed to escape from Tara, the Irish capital, with a rather reluctant Diarmuid. Gradually, however, he came to love Grainne, although for sixteen years they had to keep moving in order to avoid capture

by the Fenians. But Diarmuid was killed by a magic boar in a hunting accident after Cormac Mac Art and Finn MacCool had finally accepted his marriage to Grainne. Although Grainne blamed Finn MacCool for Diarmuid's death and swore to obtain vengeance through her four sons, the wily Finn wooed her until she agreed to marry him.

GUINEVERE, whose Welsh name, Gwenhwyfar, probably means "white spirit", was the wife of *ARTHUR* and the secret lover of Sir *LANCELOT*. In the stories about the Knights of the Round Table, Guinevere is always compared with Helen of Troy, the famous beauty of Greek mythology. Such a comparison is not unjustified, for both these women brought disaster to those who loved them. In Guinevere's case the love affair with Sir Lancelot weakened the unity of the Round Table. It was her beauty that also attracted Arthur's nephew Sir *MODRED*, who seized Camelot

GRAINNE (above), a passionate and wilful maiden, fell for the irresistible Diarmuid. As she was betrothed to Finn MacCool, Diarmuid politely refused her advances. But she persisted until he agreed to elope, with the Fianna in hot pursuit. Here, the guilty pair hide in a magic tree. (ILLUSTRATION ANON.)

GUINEVERE (below), in her original role as Flower Bride, is crowned May Queen in a bower of petals. On May Morning, Arthur and his knights celebrated with sports and contests. Lancelot, her champion, always excelled. (LANCELOT AND GUINEVERE BY HERBERT DRAPER, CANVAS, 1900.)

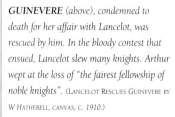

GUINEVERE (above), condemned to death for her affair with Lancelot, was rescued by him. In the bloody contest that ensued, Lancelot slew many knights. Arthur wept at the loss of "the fairest fellowship of noble knights". (LANCELOT RESCUES GUINEVERE BY W HATHERELL, CANVAS, C. 1910.)

and forced Guinevere to consent to marry him during the king's absence abroad. The confrontation between Arthur and Modred at the battle of Camlan brought to a bloody end the golden age of British chivalry, as hardly a knight was left alive. Arthur, mortally wounded, was taken to *AVALON*, while Guinevere became a nun at Amesbury, where she later died. It is believed by some that her body was buried at Glastonbury, not far from Arthur's tomb. (See also *CELTIC ROMANCE*)

GWERN, according to Welsh mythology, was the son of the Irish king *MATHOLWCH* and the Welsh princess *BRANWEN*. A dispute between the two royal families led to Branwen becoming a cook, which caused her brother, *BRAN THE BLESSED*, to sail to Ireland to avenge the insult. Matholwch suggested a compromise to settle the

quarrel. He proposed that Gwern, though only three, should be placed on the Irish throne. But Branwen's half-brother *EFNISIEN* would not agree and threw the child on to a fire.

GWYDION was the nephew of *MATH*, lord of the Welsh kingdom of Gwynedd. In order to help his brother, Gilvaethwy, sleep with Gowein, the young woman who was Math's footholder, Gwydion stirred up a quarrel between Math and *PRYDERI*, which meant that the king went away to war. When Math returned and discovered the deception, he turned his nephews into a stag and a hind for one year, into a boar and a sow for the next, and into a pair of wolves for the third. Later, Gwydion took charge of his sister *ARIANRHOD*'s son *LLEU*.

GWION BACH see *TALIESIN*.

GWYN AP NUDD, in Welsh mythology, was an otherworld king who crossed swords with King *ARTHUR*. Gwyn abducted Griddylad, the daughter of Lludd Llaw Ereint, on her wedding day. According to one late myth, Lludd Llaw Ereint was the son of the death god Beli

and the builder of London. King Arthur set out after Griddylad and demanded that Gwyn ap Nudd return her to her rightful husband, his loyal follower Gwythyr. The siege of the otherworld king's castle proved to be long and difficult, so a strange compromise was agreed by both sides. Gwyn ap Nudd and Gwythyr agreed to meet in combat each May Day until the end of time; whoever was the winner on doomsday could have Griddylad.

HELLAWES see *SAGES AND SEERS*.

IRNAN, in Irish mythology, was a witch who once spun a magic web to catch some members of the *FIANNA*, or Fenians, the bodyguard of the High King of Ireland. When this plan failed, Irnan changed herself into a monster and challenged any one of the Fenians to single combat. *FINN MACCOOL*, the leader of the Fenians, stepped forward but was persuaded that it would not be heroic enough for a warrior of his stature to fight a hag, even if she was in the form of a monster. So another Fenian, Goll, slew Irnan and as a reward Finn allowed him to marry his daughter.

GWYDION (above) and Gilvaethwy flee from Pryderi's castle with his precious swine. The daring theft was part of an ingenious plan to help Gilvaethwy win Gowein. A resourceful magician, Gwydion had tricked Pryderi into exchanging his swine for some illusory horses. (ILLUSTRATION BY ALAN LEE, 1984.)

IRNAN (below) was one of three sister witches. She spun a magic web to snare the Fenian warriors. The warriors were rescued by Goll who slew two of the sisters, but spared Irnan when she begged for mercy. However, Irnan instantly changed into a monster and Goll killed her. (ILLUSTRATION BY STEPHEN REID, 1910.)

ISEULT, sometimes Isolde, was an Irish princess, and the story of her love for *TRISTAN* was extremely popular in medieval times. The Celtic myth of Tristan and Iseult originated in Brittany and was retold in almost every European country. It became attached to the Arthurian stories by the later addition of *ARTHUR* to the myth.

Iseult, a beautiful woman with wonderful golden hair, cured the orphan Tristan of a wound in the side; a lingering ailment similar to the one afflicting the "Maimed King" in the story of the Grail. On Tristan's arrival in Cornwall, his uncle King *MARK* wanted to name the young man his successor, but the nobles objected to this arrangement, so the king said that he would marry only the girl to whom belonged the golden hair a swallow had just dropped. Sir Tristan, recognizing the hair as belonging to Iseult, suggested to his uncle that he should go on his behalf to ask for her hand.

Disguised as a Cornish trader, Sir Tristan arrived in Ireland to find the country terrorized by a dragon,

ISEULT and Tristan unwittingly drank a love philtre which heightened their already awakened passion, forging an unbreakable and finally tragic bond. Duncan's strongly Celtic portrayal captures the intense and undying nature of their love. (TRISTAN AND ISOLDE BY JOHN DUNCAN, CANVAS, 1912.)

ISEULT (below), an Irish beauty, was also a gifted healer, and cured the Cornish knight Tristan of a lingering wound. While nursing him to health, they fell in love, but their bliss was shortlived as Tristan was forced to leave the Irish court for political reasons. (ILLUSTRATION BY EVELYN PAUL, C. 1900.)

an enormous "crested serpent". Realizing that the best way to advance King Mark's suit would be to slay this monster, Sir Tristan sought out its lair and fought it. Although he just managed to overcome the dragon, its poisonous breath weakened him temporarily and an imposter claimed to have won the contest. Iseult and her mother, however, suspected trickery and discovered the injured young knight. While they were nursing Sir Tristan back to health, Iseult noticed that his sword had a piece missing exactly like the fragment of metal found in the head of *MORHOLT*, the Irish champion. Sir Tristan had mortally wounded him on the last occasion the Irish tried to collect tribute from Cornwall.

Iseult wanted to kill Sir Tristan in revenge, but she found that her heart would not let her wield the sword against him. It came as a shock then, on his recovery, that Sir Tristan asked for Iseult on behalf of King Mark. When her own father readily agreed to the marriage as a means of restoring good relations between Ireland and Cornwall, Iseult was deeply upset. But her mother gave Iseult's maid *BRANGAINE* a love potion which, if drunk on their wedding night, would make the couple love each other forever. All would have been well had not Tristan accidentally drunk the potion and given some to Iseult on the journey to King Mark's court. Although Iseult did marry the Cornish king, on the wedding night, under the cover of darkness, Brangaine took her place in the royal bed so that he would suspect nothing. For a time the lovers managed to meet in secret, but, like the love of *GUINEVERE* and *LANCELOT*, they were eventually discovered. It happened one day

that King Mark found them asleep with Sir Tristan's sword between them, but he decided not to slay them there and then. Instead he exchanged Sir Tristan's sword for his own and left them sleeping. Overcome by the mercy shown by his uncle, Tristan persuaded Iseult to return to her husband and he left for voluntary exile in Brittany.

In Brittany Sir Tristan married but without happiness. On several occasions he returned to Cornwall in disguise and secretly met Iseult again, but war took up most of his energies. A serious wound forced Sir Tristan to send for Iseult. It was agreed that Iseult should indicate her imminent arrival with a white sail. Jealous of the reunion of the lovers, Sir Tristan's Breton wife said a ship with a black sail had been sighted. Tristan lost the will to live and threw himself on his sword before Iseult could land and reach his bedside. Iseult followed him into death shortly afterwards.

Stories of elopements, courtships and ill-fated lovers were always popular with the Celts, for whom this late story of frustrated passion held great appeal. (See also CELTIC ROMANCE)

ITH was said to have dwelt in a great tower in Spain, from which he was able to see Ireland and so decided to go there. He landed with ninety followers just after the TUATHA DE DANANN had defeated the FOMORII at the second battle of Magh Tuireadh. The Tuatha De Danann suspected Ith of harbouring invasion plans and so killed him. When his body was returned to Spain, his sons swore to conquer the island. The leader of this

IUBDAN (below), one of the Wee Folk, was inclined to brag of his greatness, inciting his bard to cut him down to size by insisting that far greater men lived in Ulster, a veritable race of giants. To prove his valour, Iubdan ventured off to the dun of the "giant", Fergus Mac Leda. (ILLUSTRATION BY STEPHEN REID, 1910.)

JOSEPH OF ARIMATHEA (above), the man who interred Christ's body in his own tomb, is believed to have brought the Grail to Glastonbury. After building a church for it where Glastonbury Abbey now stands, he founded a family of Grail Guardians. (MANUSCRIPT ILLUSTRATION C. 1450.)

invasion of Ireland, the last to be recorded in Irish mythology, was Ith's uncle Mil, or MILESIUS.

IUBDAN was a ruler of tiny people. According to Irish mythology, King Iubdan liked to boast a lot; to put a stop to this annoying habit his court poet told him that Ulster was a land of giants. He even made King Iubdan and his wife, Queen Bebo, travel there in secret and try the porridge of the king of Ulster, Fergus Mac Leda. Unfortunately, Iubdan fell into the porridge and, along with his wife, was taken prisoner by Fergus. No ransom offer proved acceptable to the king of Ulster, although the tiny people offered him an abundant crop of corn. So they went on to the offensive: milk became scarce, rivers and wells were made foul and polluted, mills burned and during the nights the hair of

men and women was entirely cut off. After a year and a day of this harassment Fergus Mac Leda eventually agreed to release Iubdan and Bebo, but only on the condition that in return he was given the king's most valuable and treasured possession, a pair of magic shoes. Whoever wore these shoes was able to travel across the surface of water as if walking on dry land, and when Fergus Mac Leda put them on they grew to fit his feet exactly. Echoes of the tiny people in this Irish myth can be found in Jonathan Swift's novel, *Gulliver's Travels*.

KAI (above), Arthur's steward, was a knight of legendary might and prowess. Endowed with unusual skills, he could go for nine days underwater and could grow as tall as a forest tree at will. He was very gruff, thwarting both Peredur and Culhwch at the gate. (MANUSCRIPT ILLUSTRATION C. 1450.)

JOSEPH OF ARIMATHEA was a biblical figure who was included in Arthurian mythology because of the Grail story. Joseph allowed Christ's body to be placed in his own tomb. His own long life was said to have been due to the Grail. Either Joseph, or his brother-in-law Bron with his son Alan, brought the Grail to Glastonbury. Later, it disappeared and its recovery was the greatest quest for the Knights of the Round Table. Only GALAHAD was granted a complete vision of the Grail. It was handed to him by Joseph of Arimathea, a "bishop already dead for more than three hundred years"; this "good man took Our Lord's body between his hands, and offered it to Sir Galahad, who received it with humble joy".

KAI, in Welsh mythology, was one of the senior warriors of ARTHUR's court. In medieval romance, he became the steward Sir Kay. In one tradition, he is a Cornishman and Arthur's foster-brother. He was said to have magical powers: he could go nine days and nine nights without sleep and breathe for nine days and nine nights under water.

KAY see KAI

CELTIC ROMANCE

THE LIVELY AND COMPELLING character of Celtic romance stems from the theated rivalries and passions of the lovers. Most, if not all, tales involve a love triangle with two men contesting one desirable woman. Sometimes one of the rivals is young and handsome, while the other is an oppressive guardian, as in the tale of Naoise and Conchobhar; elsewhere, the two suitors are simply rival admirers, one loved and the other despised, as in the case of Pwyll and Gwawl. This recurrent rivalry probably symbolizes a seasonal battle between a Lord of Summer and a Lord of Winter for the Spring Maiden. Celtic love triangles create tension, drama and colourful characters of timeless appeal. The attractive young heroes, such as raven-haired Naoise, or Diarmuid of the Love-Spot, are quite as irresistible as the ravishing Celtic beauties, Deirdre and Fand. While all the characters are portrayed with touching flaws, the heroines emerge as strong and independent women, expressing warmth and wisdom.

LANCELOT (above) and Guinevere's abiding love for each other wounded Arthur, shook his court and split the Fellowship of Knights. Yet both lovers are portrayed by Mallory as essentially good but tragic characters. Even Arthur realized that Guinevere had been true to him in her way as a generous and faithful consort, and he was never lessened by their love. Here, the couple kiss at their first meeting, contrived by Galleot in an embroidered medieval setting. Although their love grew out of the courtly tradition, it went far beyond what the courtly code would have allowed. (MANUSCRIPT ILLUSTRATION C. 1400.)

TRISTAN (above) and Iseult snatch a tense moment together in their clandestine romance. They had grown obsessively attached to one another after accidentally drinking a love philtre intended for Iseult and her betrothed, King Mark of Cornwall. The doomed lovers embarked on a desperate and tragic romance, fraught with guilt and unrequited longings. (TRISTAN AND ISOLDE BY A W TURNBALL, CANVAS, 1904.)

THE LADY OF THE FOUNTAIN (right), a shining vision in gold, appeared to young Owain as the fairest, wisest, noblest, most chaste, most generous woman in the world. But, as Owain had just slain her husband, the Black Knight, he had to press his suit with care. The Lady's faithful handmaiden, Luned, helped Owain woo her mistress by reminding her that the realm required a strong guardian. Luned here escorts Owain to her Lady's chamber. (ILLUSTRATION BY ALAN LEE, 1984.)

FAND (above), a breathtaking beauty from the otherworld, set her heart on the Ulster hero, Cuchulainn, and lured him to her realm to fight a Fomorii giant. After a month in her delightful company, the two arranged a tryst where the hero's wife, Emer, joined them, lamenting, "What's new is sweet, what's well-known is sour…" Her heartfelt plea inspired the generous Fand to give up her beloved Cuchulainn, realizing that he had a worthy mate in Emer. (ETAIN, HELEN, MAEV AND FAND BY HARRY CLARKE, GLASS, DETAIL, C. 1900.)

GERAINT (right), suspecting his wife of infidelity, forced her to accompany him on a gruelling journey of errands, and so tested her love and obedience every step of the way. Like other strong-minded Celtic heroines, Enid endured her ordeal calmly, remaining loyal and loving throughout. Geraint, for his part, finally felt "two sorrows" of remorse for having mistrusted and mistreated her so. At one stage in their journey, the pair passed through a wonderful walled tower, as seen here. (ILLUSTRATION BY ALAN LEE, 1984.)

L

LAEG, chariot of Cuchulainn, drove the hero on all his adventures, acted as scout and comrade and finally cast himself in front of a spear meant for his master. War chariots played a key role in Celtic battle, with driver and warrior acting as a single unit. (ILLUSTRATION BY J LEYENDECKER, 1916.)

LANCELOT, most handsome and gifted of Arthur's knights, attracted both mortal and immortal queens. Four fairy queens here kidnap the sleeping knight and hold him in their castle, demanding that he choose one of them to be his mistress. (HOW FOUR FAIRY QUEENS FOUND LANCELOT SLEEPING BY W F CALDERON, CANVAS, C. 1900.)

LAEG was *CUCHULAINN*'s charioteer. The Celts were renowned in the ancient world for their skill in handling chariots on the battlefield, and Laeg's skill was crucial to many of Cuchulainn's victories. He was also a great friend and companion. When *FAND* invited Cuchulainn to the Land of Promise, he sent Laeg before him to survey the place. During Cuchulainn's final and mortal combat, Laeg threw himself in front of a spear aimed at his master. Id, Laeg's brother, was charioteer to *CONALL* Caernach.

LANCELOT was one of the greatest and noblest knights in the Arthurian tales. He was known as Lancelot of the Lake because the Lady of the Lake had plunged him into a magic pool when he was a child. Sir Lancelot, described as "the flower of knights", was very attractive to women, not unlike the handsome Irish warrior *DIARMUID UA DUIBHNE*. Once King *ARTHUR*'s half-sister and enemy *MORGAN LE FAY* cast a spell over the sleeping knight and shut him in a dungeon. There she demanded that he must choose among four enchantresses who would be his "paramour", or mistress. When he turned them all down, including Morgan Le Fay, the knight admitted his love for *GUINEVERE*. All of Sir Lancelot's great adventures and exploits were indeed informed by this secret love. For a time Queen Guinevere would not allow Sir Lancelot to come to her, but they eventually became lovers. Sir Meliagaunt, however, was suspicious and confronted Sir Lancelot in the presence of King Arthur and Queen Guinevere. A tournament was held to discover the truth. "With such great force Sir Lancelot smote Sir Meliagaunt on the helmet that the stroke carved the head into two parts."

LANCELOT, after much fasting and praying, came at last to Carbonek, the Grail Castle. Being tainted with sin, he could not enter but was granted a vision. When he stepped too close he was struck by fire and left dazed for 24 days. (LANCELOT REFUSED THE GRAIL BY E BURNE-JONES, CANVAS, 1870.)

Honour seemed satisfied and the reputation of Arthur's queen also appeared unblemished, but there were other Knights of the Round Table who could not accept this judgement by arms. So Sir Agravain and Sir *MODRED* led twelve knights to Guinevere's chamber and surprised the lovers. Although Sir Lancelot managed to make a fighting exit and several days later saved Queen Guinevere from being burnt to death, his actions effectively split the Round Table and weakened the strength of King Arthur's realm. First, Arthur conducted an unsuccessful siege of Sir Lancelot's castle in Brittany. Then a second and more deadly challenge to the king's authority came from Sir Modred, his nephew. In the subsequent battle at Camlan, near Salisbury, most of the Knights of the Round Table were slain. King Arthur was mortally wounded and taken by a magic boat to *AVALON*. Queen Guinevere retreated from the world and became a nun at Amesbury, where she died. Sir Lancelot and Guinevere met only once more before the knight renounced the ways of war to lead the life of a hermit. (See also *CELTIC ROMANCE*)

LLEU (right) had to turn into an eagle to escape his murderous wife, Blodeuedd. He hid in the forest, wounded and starving, until Gwydion lured him down and restored him to health. Blodeuedd was turned into an owl. (ILLUSTRATION BY ALAN LEE, 1984.)

LIR, or Llyr in Welsh, was the father of *MANANNAN MAC LIR*, the Manx sea god, magician and god of healing. Although Lir was also a sea god he is hardly mentioned in mythology, despite giving his name to many places, including Leicester in England. Shakespeare probably had the Welsh Llyr in mind when he wrote his tragedy *King Lear*.

LLEU, named Lleu of the Skilful Hand, in Welsh mythology was the son of *ARIANRHOD*. His mother laid a series of curses upon him, including the promise that he was to have no name unless she gave him one, no weapons unless she provided them and no wife of the human race. With the help of his uncle *GWYDION*, who raised him, Lleu overcame all these taboos, though the wife conjured by Gwydion and the magician *MATH* was nearly his undoing. For this woman, *BLODEUEDD*, fell in love with

LIR'S four lovely children were turned into swans by their jealous stepmother. For 900 years they endured cold and hunger in icy waters, charming listeners with their poignant song. When at last restored to human form, they were bent and bony. (LIR'S CHILDREN BY JOHN DUNCAN, CANVAS, 1912.)

another man and plotted Lleu's death. When the guilty lovers struck him, Lleu rose into the air in the shape of an eagle. After a long search, Gwydion found him, restored him to human form and healed his wounds.

LLUD see *NUDD*

LUGH was the Irish name for the Celtic sun god, who was known as Lleu in Wales and as Lugos in France. He was always described as a young and handsome warrior.

Lugh was himself part *FOMORII*, since his grandfather was the Irish one-eyed god *BALOR*, the Fomorii champion. The Fomorii were sea gods who challenged the *TUATHA DE DANANN* for control of Ireland; they were sometimes described as having only a single hand, foot or eye. Lugh's mother was *ETHLINN*, the only daughter of Balor. Because a prophecy had said that Balor would be killed by his own grandson, he locked Ethlinn in a crystal tower on Tory Island, off the northwestern coast of Ireland. But Cian, son of the Tuatha De Danann healing god *DIAN CECHT*, succeeded in reaching Ethlinn and she bore Lugh as a result. Either the sea god *MANANNAN MAC LIR* or the smith

god *GOIBHNIU*, Cian's brother, saved Lugh from Balor's wrath and raised him to manhood.

Well before the final battle between the Tuatha De Danann and the Fomorii, Lugh's prowess as a warrior had been recognized. The De Danann leader *NUADA* stepped down in his favour, and at the second battle of Magh Tuireadh Lugh fulfilled the prophecy of Balor's death when he killed him with a sling-shot. Before delivering this decisive blow Lugh had circled the enemy host on one foot and with one eye closed, a magic circuit that copied the single-leggedness of the Fomorii in general and one-eyed Balor in particular. It would seem that, like the Ulster hero *CUCHULAINN* and the berserkers of Germanic mythology, the battle-frenzy gripped Lugh in such a way that one eye disappeared into his head while the other expanded into a hideous, paralysing stare. Balor's own single eyelid had to be raised by four servants, and Lugh sent his shot smashing into the eye the moment it was opened. Balor's eye was forced back through his head, with the result that its terrible gaze fell upon the Fomorii ranks behind. Thus Balor died and the Fomorii scattered. Lugh became known as

Lamfhada ("of the Long Arm"). Quite possibly this great victory represented the rise of younger gods amongst the Tuatha De Danann themselves, for the youthful Lugh felled Balor with a more modern weapon than *DAGDA*'s ancient club. Indeed, an alternative name for Lugh was Samildanach ("the many-skilled"). This ingenuity may account for Lugh's introduction as the father of Cuchulainn in the more historical sagas. The sun god was believed to have fought alongside his hard-pressed son during Queen *MEDB* of Connacht's invasion of Ulster. After Cuchulainn's death his foster-brother *CONALL* claimed to have received help from Lugh when he chased Cuchulainn's killers. On one occasion the sun god appeared in a magic mist.

Lugh's final claim to fame is that his name became part of the term used to describe the fairy in Irish folklore, because over time "Little stooping Lugh", or Luchorpain, turned into the leprechaun, the tiny guardian of hidden treasure and the expert cobbler.

LUGH, the resplendent Celtic sun god, led the Tuatha De Danann against the Fomorii led by his grandfather, Balor, whom he slew with his magic sling-shot. As god of arts and crafts, he invented the popular board game of fidchell, in which he excelled. (ILLUSTRATION BY E WALLCOUSINS, 1912.)

143

M

LUGUS was the name used in Britain and France for a god very similar to the Irish *LUGH* and the Welsh *LLEU*. His importance can be judged from the old name for Lyon, Lugdunum ("the fortress of Lug"). The Roman emperor Augustus made it the capital of the provinces of Gaul, and ordered the inhabitants to celebrate this choice each August, the month in which the feast of the Celtic sun god Lugus occurred. The god's name was used for many other place names, possibly even London: the Roman Londinium may have derived from Lugdunum.

MABON, son of the Welsh divine mother Modron, was said to have been abducted when only three nights old and imprisoned in Gloucester. However, since only he was able to control the hound which *CULHWCH* needed to win the hand of *OLWEN*, an expedition was mounted to release Mabon. Once free, he duly helped to capture the wild boar *TWRCH TRWYTH* with the aid of the hound and to take from between the boar's ears the razor

MACHA cursed the Ulstermen to suffer the pain of childbirth for five days, at the time of Ulster's greatest need. The bitter curse stemmed from her ill-treatment by the Ulstermen when, though near her term, she was forced to race on foot to prove a bet. (ILLUSTRATION BY STEPHEN REID, 1910.)

MABON, or Maponos, was the youthful Welsh love god. A gifted musician, he was also equated with the classical god Apollo. Although forgotten as a god, Maponos survived in Welsh myth as Mabon, a skilled hunter among Arthur's champions. (ILLUSTRATION BY MIRANDA GRAY, 1994.)

that Olwen's father had demanded. Apart from adventures like this, the actions of Mabon are uncertain, suggesting that he may have been a former god, possibly Maponos, a Celtic god of youth, who was incorporated in Welsh mythology as a warrior once his worship was all but forgotten. The Romans knew of Maponos, whom they equated with Apollo, the god of prophecy.

MAC CECHT was the Irish god of eloquence and the son of *OGMA*. After *NUADA* had been killed at the second battle of Magh Tuireadh, Mac Cecht and his brothers could not decide whether to divide Ireland between them and so they consulted a stranger named *ITH*. Suspecting from his response that he had designs on conquering the island himself, they killed him, thus provoking the invasion of the sons of *MILESIUS*.

MAC DA THO was king of Leinster at the time that *MEDB* was queen of Connacht. He owned a fine hound and a huge boar, and many of his neighbours coveted these animals, including Medb and *CONCHOBHAR MAC NESSA*, king of

Ulster. Mac Da Tho promised both these rulers that they could have the hound, and slaughtered the boar to provide a feast, to which he invited them. Fighting broke out between the Ulster king and the men of Connacht, but the latter soon retreated. When the hound, over which they had been quarrelling, ran after the king's chariot his charioteer cut off its head.

MACHA was one of the Irish war goddesses, often identified with *BADB*, *MORRIGAN* and *NEMAIN*. She first married Nemed, a Scythian ruler who defeated the *FOMORII*, the sea gods who slew her second husband *NUADA* and herself at the second battle of Magh Tuireadh. A later Macha laid a curse on Ulster after her boastful husband said that, though heavy with child, she could outrun all the king's horses and chariots. When the king of

Ulster threatened to execute her husband if she did not race, Macha cursed all Ulstermen to suffer the pain of childbirth for five days and five nights whenever the kingdom was in danger. Macha won the race and gave birth to twins, which is said to be the reason for calling the fortress of the Ulster kings Emain Macha ("Macha's Twins").

MAELDUN, or Mael Duin, was one of the great Irish voyagers. The late saga that describes his voyage is a mixture of Christian and pre-Christian ideas, in contrast to the fundamentally pre-Christian mythical voyage of the earlier *BRAN*.

Maeldun's father was a chieftain of the Aran Islands who attacked the Irish mainland, looted a church and raped a nun. He was killed shortly afterwards by raiders from overseas, in all likelihood Vikings. The nun gave birth to Maeldun and the child was fostered by the local ruler's wife, who was the sister of the unfortunate nun. It was only when children taunted Maeldun that he was not really well born that his foster-mother took him to see his true mother and his parentage was revealed. He then set out with three of his foster-brothers to find his father, only to learn that he had been murdered.

Determined to avenge his father's death, Maeldun was advised by a druid as to which were the favourable days for him to build, launch and sail a three-skinned coracle. Then, still accompanied by his foster-brothers and also a crew of seventeen warriors, he sailed on his long and strange voyage of revenge.

The first island Maeldun came to was inhabited by murderers, but apparently not the killers of his father. Next they landed upon an isle of enormous ants; as large as horses, the ants almost devoured the crew and the boat. Large birds living on another island were found to pose no threat, however. They even provided the voyagers with

on top of a pedestal; the offer of eternal youth on one island which was inhabited by a queen and her daughters; intoxicating fruits; contagious laughter; revolving fire; and a hermit who lived on salmon that was given by an otter and half a loaf provided each day by angels.

Eventually, Maeldun caught up with his father's killers, but they pleaded for mercy and a peace was agreed. Thus ended the voyage that was said to contain "the sum of the wisdom of Ireland". (See also FABULOUS VOYAGES)

MAEVE see MEDB.

MAELDUN (below) and his sailors found a wondrous silver column rising straight from the sea. Its summit, lost in the sky, was draped with a silver net, flung far out to sea. As they sailed through the mesh, Diuran hacked off a piece as proof of the tale. (ILLUSTRATION BY DANUTA MEYER, 1994.)

MAELDUN, on his epic voyage, stopped by the bleak island of the mill (above) where lived a gloomy miller grimly grinding mounds of corn. He observed dourly that the corn symbolized all that men begrudged each other. The voyagers, aghast, sailed away. (ILLUSTRATION BY ALAN LEE, 1984.)

meat. Two subsequent islands of monstrous, gigantic horses proved to be even more dangerous, so it was with some relief that Maeldun and his companions landed on the Island of the House of the Salmon. There they discovered an uninhabited house with food and drink, as well as comfortable beds, awaiting them. A regular supply of fresh salmon was provided by a device that periodically threw fish into the house from the sea. Similar luxury was encountered on the next isle, which was covered with orchards of delicious apples.

Danger was soon encountered again, however, on islands that were populated by revolving beasts, fighting horses, a mysterious cat and fiery swine. The ground on one

of them was hot like a volcano. Among other strange creatures and encounters on the voyage were gigantic swine and calves so huge that they could not be cooked whole; sheep that changed the colour of their wool apparently at will; a sombre miller who ground everything that was begrudged in the world; a population of mourners; an island divided into four kingdoms by fences made of gold, silver, brass and crystal; a castle with a glass bridge where there lived a beautiful girl who rejected Maeldun's advances; crying birds; a solitary pilgrim on a tiny island that was enlarged every year by divine providence; a wonderful fountain that gushed milk, beer and wine; giant smiths; a sea of glass; a sea of clouds in which castles, forests, animals and a fearsome monster suddenly appeared; an underwater island of prophecy; an amazing water-arch; a gigantic silver column and net, from which the voyagers cut off a small piece as a souvenir; an inaccessible island

MANANNAN MAC LIR, son of the Irish sea god *LIR*, took his name from the Isle of Man, which is situated in the Irish Sea about halfway between Ireland and Britain. Manannan was a sea god, magician and healer, and the ruler of the Land of Promise, where he lived in Emhain ("of the Apple Trees"). His home was imagined to be sited off the western coast of Ireland, somewhere in the Atlantic Ocean. His wife was the renowned beauty *FAND*, who fell in love with the Ulster hero *CUCHULAINN* but finally chose to stay with her sea god husband. Manannan therefore shook a magic cloak between Fand and Cuchulainn in order to make sure they would never meet again.

Manannan Mac Lir was a noble and handsome warrior, who drove a chariot as easily over the waves as over a plain and was said to have a ship that sailed itself. He had both divine and mortal children, and one of his mortal sons, *MONGAN*, was conceived by way of a deception similar to the ruse used for *ARTHUR*'s conception. Manannan slept with an Ulster queen when disguised as her husband. Mongan did, however, inherit supernatural gifts, including the ability to shape-change, and he went on to become a great king and mighty warrior.

MANANNAN, (below), the Irish sea god, rode the waves in a self-propelled boat called "Wave Sweeper". As a sea god, Manannan could stir up or soothe the sea, and help or hinder ships. He often appeared to voyagers, such as Bran, at the outset of their trip. (ILLUSTRATION BY MIRANDA GRAY, 1994.)

MANAWYDAN (above) tried to grow wheat after a mysterious blight had devastated his land. One field was ripe for harvest when overnight it was stripped to the stalks by mice. In despair, he planned to hang one of the mice, until dissuaded by a stranger. (ILLUSTRATION BY ALAN LEE, 1984.)

MARK (below) watches sadly as his wife, Iseult, kneels before a drawn sword, beside herself with grief at Tristan's death. Mark, who was often portrayed as a merciful man, gathered her up and bore her off to a tower where she was restored to health. (ILLUSTRATION BY RUSSELL FLINT, C. 1900.)

MANAWYDAN, son of Llyr, was the Welsh equivalent of the Irish sea god *MANANNAN*, though his links with the sea were far less well defined. The brother of *BRAN THE BLESSED* and *BRANWEN*, he married *RHIANNON* on the death of her husband *PWYLL*. One day he and Rhiannon, along with Rhiannon's son *PRYDERI* and his wife Cigfa, were enveloped in a magical mist. When it cleared, their palace was deserted and the land around it desolate, so they travelled to England, where Manawydan and Pryderi made a living as leatherworkers. So successful were they that the local craftsmen forced them to leave. On their return to Wales, both Pryderi and Rhiannon disappeared by magic, leaving Cigfa and Manawydan alone. He then tried to support them by growing a crop of wheat, but his fields were stripped by mice. He caught one of the mice and would have hanged it, but a passing stranger offered him whatever he wanted in return for the mouse's life. Manawydan asked for the return of Rhiannon and Pryderi. The stranger agreed and revealed himself to be Llwyd, a magician and friend of Gwawl, the suitor whom Rhiannon had refused in order to marry Pwyll. (See also *MAGIC AND ENCHANTMENT*)

MAPONOS see *MABON*.

MARK was the king of Cornwall in the Breton myth of *TRISTAN* and *ISEULT*. He was the guardian of his orphaned nephew Tristan and the husband of Iseult, an Irish princess. Although jealous of Tristan and Iseult, he was not entirely unsympathetic, and even when he came upon the lovers sleeping together with Tristan's sword between them he did not kill them. He exchanged the sword for his own and left without waking them. Shamed by this act of mercy, the lovers knew that they must part. Tristan solemnly returned Iseult to his uncle and went into exile in Brittany.

MATHOLWCH'S (left) convoy of ships glides up to the ragged Welsh shore in the prelude to a doomed marriage between himself and Branwen, the beautiful sister of Bran the Blessed. The ships had ensigns of brocaded silk and an uptilted shield as a sign of peace. (ILLUSTRATION BY ALAN LEE, 1984.)

MEDB (above), the magnificent but malevolent queen of Connacht, was a warrior who fought as fiercely as Morrigan. A wild and wilful woman, she precipitated and perpetuated the bloody war with Ulster in which Cuchulainn and other heroes lost their lives. (ILLUSTRATION BY J LEYENDECKER, 1916.)

MATH was the brother of the Welsh mother goddess DON and a great magician. At the time that PRYDERI ruled over Dyfed in the southern part of Wales, Math was the lord of Gwynedd in the north. Except during war, Math could only live if his feet were held in the lap of a virgin. When Gilvaethwy, one of his nephews, fell in love with the young woman who held Math's feet in her lap, his brother, GWYDION, tricked Math into going to war with Pryderi so that the girl might be left behind. On discovering that he had been deceived, however, the furious Math turned his nephews into animals.

MATHOLWCH, in Welsh mythology, was the Irish king married to BRANWEN, the sister of BRAN THE BLESSED and half-sister of EFNISIEN. Efnisien, because he claimed that he had not been consulted over Branwen's wedding, "cut off the lips of Matholwch's horses at their teeth, their ears to their heads, and their tails to their bodies". Later, when Bran took his army to Ireland to avenge the insult of Branwen being made a cook, Efnisien tossed Matholwch's three-year-old son GWERN into a fire. In the battle that followed, nearly all the Britons were killed and all of the Irish except for five pregnant women.

MAXEN see FABULOUS VOYAGES

MEDB, also known as Maeve, was the warrior-queen of Connacht. According to Irish mythology, no king could reign in Connacht unless he was married to Medb, who was believed to hold the kingdom's sovereignty in her person. It was also said that she "never was without one man in the shadow of another". Medb's most famous action was the invasion of Ulster, when her forces captured the great brown bull of Cuailgne and killed the Ulster hero CUCHULAINN. She was herself slain by Forbai, the son of King CONCHOBHAR MAC NESSA, while she was bathing in a pool. Forbai had discovered that Queen Medb was in the habit of regularly taking her bath in a Galway pool. He very carefully measured the exact distance between the spot where she bathed and the shore, then he returned to the Ulster stronghold of Emain Macha and practised with a sling-shot until he was able to knock an apple from the top of a pole over the same distance. Satisfied at last that his aim was perfect, he stealthily made his way back to the pool and hit Queen Medb in the centre of her forehead using his sling-shot. Thus was Ulster revenged.

SINGLE COMBAT

IN WAR, THE ANCIENT CELTS relied on heroic single combat, rather than all-out warfare, as a means of settling disputes. Shortage of manpower forbade multiple pitched battles. Instead, chosen champions, such as Cuchulainn or Morholt, duelled to the death. Even in a large-scale epic war, like the campaign of Cuailgne, the Ulster champion fought in single combat every day with a different warrior. In the Arthurian legends, single combat continued in the form of knightly jousts. While the Celtic heroes wore scant armour, Arthur's mounted knights encased themselves in glittering iron. In addition to the basic weapons of spear, sword, sling and shield, the hero of legend had recourse to magical skills and a range of enchanted weapons, such as Arthur's Excalibur or Fergus Mac Roth's Caladcholg, the original Excalibur.

CUCHULAINN (left), the Irish champion, enjoys a short respite between battles. Exhausted by continual combat, he suffered from chronic lack of sleep, snatching cat-naps between duels. Once, his father Lugh, pitying him, cast the hero into a magical sleep for three days and nights, during which he healed all his wounds. When Cuchulainn defended Ulster alone against the forces of Medb, he confronted chosen champions one by one. Between duels, the restless hero harassed the army with his sling. (ILLUSTRATION BY YVONNE GILBERT, 1994.)

CELTIC CAVALRY (right) ride their battle horses to war, armed with spears and crested helmets. Their comrades on foot wear breeches and caps, and bear spears and long bossed shields, while trumpeters bring up the rear. The Celts were heavily reliant on their long shields, which were usually made of wood and sometimes covered with decorative bronze work. Other sharp-rimmed shields could also be used as missile weapons. (GUNDESTRUP CAULDRON, GILDED SILVER, C. 100 BC.)

GERAINT (left) and the Knight of the Kestrel engage in single combat with such ferocity that they shatter each other's armour. Ostensibly, the duel was over the kestrel, but really Geraint was intent on avenging an insult to Guinevere's handmaiden, made by the knight's dwarf. Goaded on by their seconds, both champions fought tirelessly, until Geraint's rage gave him the edge and he overcame, but spared, the knight. (ILLUSTRATION BY ALAN LEE, 1984.)

OWAIN'S (below) kindness to a lion earned him a faithful friend who proved to be a valiant comrade-in-arms. In this unequal match, the giant was winning until Owain's lion leapt to Owain's defence. When the giant complained that he could handle Owain well enough if it were not for his lion, Owain pushed his pet back into the fortress, but the irrepressible creature leapt over the fortress walls and mauled the giant to death. (ILLUSTRATION BY ALAN LEE, 1984.)

MORGAN LE FAY (above) charmed the unsuspecting Tristram into accepting a beautiful gold shield decorated with a strange motif. The shield's design portrayed a knight, Lancelot, enslaving a royal couple, Arthur and his wife. Innocent of the shield's true motif or motive, Tristram rode to Arthur's court and jousted in the royal tournament. When he duelled with Arthur, the king's spear shattered on the enchanted shield. Such enchanted weapons could help or hinder the best of heroes. (ILLUSTRATION BY AUBREY BEARDSLEY, C. 1870.)

149

MERLIN, sometimes Myrddin, was the famous wizard of Arthurian mythology. So powerful was his magic that one medieval tradition credits him with the magical construction of Stonehenge, the outstanding British monument that has survived from ancient times. Another of his works was supposed to be King *ARTHUR*'s famous Round Table, a late copy of which can still be seen at Winchester today.

Merlin's birth was the subject of a strange story. Apparently, the Britons were told that a great fortress they had built on Salisbury plain, possibly near Stonehenge, would never be safe until the ground there had been soaked by the blood of a child who had no

MERLIN (below), for all his wisdom, was bewitched by the Lady of the Lake who turned his love to her own ends. She sapped his power and plundered his store of secret knowledge, and when done, she bound him in stone by his own spells. (MERLIN AND NIMUE BY E BURNE-JONES, CANVAS, C. 1870.)

mortal father. Such a half-human sacrifice seemed impossible to achieve, until it was learned that a beautiful girl was with child by a demon. The child turned out to be Merlin, who, though baptized as a Christian, still possessed fabulous powers inherited from his demon father. Somehow the boy did not need to be sacrificed for the sake of the fortress because it is likely that Merlin was able to deal with the

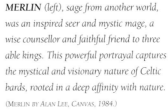

MERLIN (left), sage from another world, was an inspired seer and mystic mage, a wise counsellor and faithful friend to three able kings. This powerful portrayal captures the mystical and visionary nature of Celtic bards, rooted in a deep affinity with nature. (MERLIN BY ALAN LEE, CANVAS, 1984.)

MIDIR (right), one of the Tuatha De Danann, appeared at the palace of Tara to carry off Etain, the Ulster woman he loved, long since lost to him by enchantment. The pair drifted upwards and disappeared through a palace window, and flew to an otherworld. (ILLUSTRATION BY STEPHEN REID, 1910.)

problem by means of magic. Two dragons were, in fact, responsible for the problem.

This mixture of pre-Christian and Christian ideas sits strangely with Merlin's later assistance to King Arthur, whose father *UTHER PENDRAGON* was said to have successfully invaded Britain about this time. Merlin sided with Uther and employed his powers to enable him to sleep with Igraine, the wife of a Cornish nobleman, by disguising him as her husband. Due to this deception Arthur was conceived. Once he ascended the throne, King Arthur had Merlin as his trusted advisor and often used the wizard as a messenger because, as with many of the Celtic gods and goddesses, he could assume any shape he pleased.

There are various accounts of Merlin's death. One tells how the wizard forgot about the seat at the Round Table that only *GALAHAD* could use, being the only knight worthy enough to see the *GRAIL*. Merlin sat down and was at once swallowed up by the earth, like other sinful men who had tried it before him. Another story blames the wizard's death on his passion for women. Either Viviane, possibly the Lady of the Lake, or Nimue, the daughter of a Sicilian siren, imprisoned him in an enchanted wood after Merlin had explained all about the secrets of his own magic. As Merlin told Sir *GAWAIN*, who once

passed by: "I am also the greatest fool. I love another more than I love myself, and I taught my beloved how to bind me to herself, and now no one can set me free." (See also *SAGES AND SEERS; MAGIC AND ENCHANTMENT*)

MIDIR, in Irish mythology, was the proud son of *DAGDA*, father of the gods. Unlike his father, who is usually portrayed as a rough, coarse figure, Midir always appeared as a splendidly dressed young man. Midir's first wife was Fuamnach, the daughter of Beothach. She became furious with jealousy when Midir married a second wife, *ETAIN*, from Ulster. With a druid's aid, Fuamnach turned Etain first into a pool, then into a worm and finally into a fly in order to keep her away from Midir. As a fly Etain was swallowed by the wife of Etar, an Ulster warrior, and reborn as the wife of the High King of Ireland. Although Midir recovered Etain, he had to accept in the end that she was the High King's consort and leave her alone. Midir also had some difficulty in accepting his father's successors as leaders of the *TUATHA DE DANANN*. The conflict that he started seems to have had a dangerously weakening effect on this generation of gods just before the invasion of the Milesians, who then went on to defeat the gods.

MIL OR MILE see *MILESIUS*

MILESIUS sails for Ireland to avenge the death of his nephew, Ith, who was slain by the Tuatha De Danann, rulers of Ireland. Although Milesius did not reach shore himself, his family succeeded, defeating the De Danann who retreated into an invisible otherworld. (ILLUSTRATION BY STEPHEN REID, 1910.)

MILESIUS

MILESIUS, sometimes Mil or Mile, was the name given to a Spanish soldier whose sons were said to have organized the final invasion of Ireland. The murder there of their kinsman *ITH* caused the Milesians to take revenge by conquering the island. This they achieved by defeating the *TUATHA DE DANANN*, "the people of the goddess Dana", the existing rulers. Following the final decisive battle between the two forces, which the Milesians won, the Tuatha De Danann retired to an otherworld beneath the soil of Ireland.

MODRED

MODRED was the treacherous nephew of King *ARTHUR*. While he was away waging war in Brittany, Arthur had appointed Modred his regent, but his scheming nephew tried instead to take the throne and force *GUINEVERE* to marry him. On the king's return, a terrible battle was fought near Salisbury and most of the Knights of the Round Table were killed, including Modred. Arthur, who had been mortally wounded during the battle, was then taken to *AVALON* in a black boat by three mysterious women.

MONGAN

MONGAN was the son of the Manx sea god *MANANNAN MAC LIR*. According to Irish mythology, his conception had been made possible by the use of a deception akin to the one used by *MERLIN* so that *UTHER* could sleep with Igraine and so conceive *ARTHUR*. Manannan Mac Lir had assumed the shape of an Ulster king in order to sleep with his beautiful queen. When Mongan was three days old, his father took him to one of his otherworld realms, the Land of Promise, where the boy remained until he had grown to manhood. It is claimed by some traditions that Mongan then returned to Ireland reincarnated as *FIN MACCOOL*, the famous leader of the *FIANNA*, but in other accounts he retained his own identity. The stories about Mongan describe how he used his shape-changing ability to get his own way, and mention in particular the recovery of his wife Dubh Lacha. He had inherited the divine ability of metamorphosis from his father.

MORGAN LE FAY

MORGAN LE FAY was King *ARTHUR*'s half-sister and in some versions of the story she is said to have been the mistress of Sir Accolon of Gaul. Throughout all the British myths that tell of Arthur's incredible reign Morgan Le Fay is always depicted as the king's implacable enemy, often plotting his downfall. According to one story she is supposed to have stolen the magic sword Excalibur and sent it to Accolon, who then challenged Arthur to single combat. When Accolon dropped the sword Arthur recognized it and the other knight admitted his guilt and surrendered. However, after the bloody battle against Arthur's rebellious nephew Sir *MODRED*, Morgan le Fay was one of the three women who took the grievously wounded king in a black boat to *AVALON*. The other two were "the Queen of Northgales and the Queen of Wastelands". (See also *SAGES AND SEERS; SINGLE COMBAT*)

MORGAN LE FAY'S (below) paradoxical nature is reflected in her dual role as both healer and dark magician, as Arthur's thorn in life, yet also her guardian in death. Although educated at a convent, she managed to emerge as a gifted magician. (MORGAN LE FAY BY A SANDYS, WOOD, 1864.)

MODRED (above), Arthur's treacherous nephew, abused his role of regent and usurped the throne, forcing Arthur to quash the rebel forces. Both perished in the final battle that ended the war and so came to an end the Arthurian golden age. (ARTHUR AND MODRED BY W HATHERELL, CANVAS, C.1910.)

N

MORHOLT was the gigantic brother of the king of Ireland, to whom King Mark and Cornwall were expected to pay an annual tribute. Mark's nephew *TRISTAN* was determined to put an end to this practice. He therefore sailed to Ireland and succeeded in killing Morholt, but not before he had been wounded by the giant's great poisoned sword. Before he died, Morholt told Tristan that only his sister *ISEULT* would be able to cure his poisoned wound.

MORRIGAN, sometimes known as Morrigu, was an Irish goddess of death on the battlefield who helped the *TUATHA DE DANANN* at both battles of Magh Tuireadh. She was associated with the other war deities *MACHA*, *BADB* and *NEMAIN*. Her favourite form was the crow, and as such she settled in triumph on the shoulder of the Ulster hero *CUCHULAINN* when he was finally killed in the war against Queen *MEDB*'s forces. Cuchulainn had not only refused Morrigan's love, but in anger he had even wounded her. For such a deed his fate was sealed.

MORRIGAN, the terrible goddess of war, appeared sometimes as a warrior in a battle, siding with her favourites. Most often she soared overhead as a raven or crow, shrieking and flapping her wings to scare the host, or to signify imminent death, as here. (ILLUSTRATION BY STEPHEN REID, 1910.)

MORHOLT, the Irish champion, confronts Tristan, the Cornish newcomer, in a duel over Irish taxes. Despite Morholt's greater power and skill, the young Tristan fought like a mighty lion and dealt the older knight a mortal blow to his helm, lodging a piece of sword in his brain. (ILLUSTRATION BY EVELYN PAUL, C. 1900.)

NAOISE was the eldest son of Usna and his wife Elbha, daughter of *CATHBAD*. When *DEIRDRE* persuaded him to run away with her so that she could avoid marriage to the Ulster king *CONCHOBHAR MAC NESSA*, Naoise and his two brothers fled with her to Alba. Conchobhar sent *FERGUS MAC ROTH* to bring them all home. Suspicious of Conchobhar, but trusting Fergus' promise that no harm would come to them, Naoise agreed. In the event, Conchobhar had Naoise killed, and so enraged was Fergus Mac Roth that he joined the forces of Conchobhar's great enemy, Queen *MEDB* of Connacht.

NECHTAN was an Irish water god and, according to some versions, the husband of *BOANN*. On Nechtan's hill there was a holy well that was the source of all knowledge, to which only Nechtan and his three cup-bearers had access. When Boann found her way to the well, the waters rose from the ground and chased after her, becoming the River Boyne.

NEMAIN (whose name means "dreadful" or "venomous"), in Irish mythology, was a goddess of war. Along with *BABD*, *MORRIGAN* and *MACHA*, she formed one of a group

of war deities who sometimes appeared as beautiful young women and sometimes as crows, screeching over the battlefield. Nemain was said to have been the wife of *NUADA*, the leader of the *TUATHA DE DANANN*.

NEMGLAN, an Irish bird god, fell in love with Mess Buachalla, the betrothed of Eterscel, High King of Ireland. On the eve of the wedding, Nemglan came to her in a bird skin and seduced her, and this was how she conceived *CONAIRE MOR*. The child was passed off as High King Eterscel's son, but Mess Buachalla was careful to warn the boy that he must never, whatever the circumstances might be, kill a bird. When Conaire Mor was a young man, Eterscel died and the question of the succession was raised in Tara, the Irish capital. Unknown to Conaire, there was a prophecy to the effect that Eterscel's successor would be a naked man walking along the road to Tara with a sling in his hand. It happened one day that Conaire was driving his char-

NAOISE elopes with the great Irish beauty, Deirdre. They fled across the sea to Scotland, pursued by Fergus Mac Roth. By Loch Ness, they found refuge and hunted deer and salmon, living in pastoral bliss until they were lured back to a deadly trap in Ireland by an unsuspecting Fergus Mac Roth. (ILLUSTRATION ANON.)

NEMAIN, one of the dreadful goddesses of war, appeared sometimes as a washer at the ford, presaging doom. Before his last combat, Cuchulainn saw a washer weeping and wailing as she rinsed a heap of bloody raiment belonging to the great hero. (ILLUSTRATION BY STEPHEN REID, 1910.)

iot down this very road when a flock of birds with beautiful plumage descended upon him. Forgetting his mother's instruction never to harm any bird, he loaded his sling, at which point the birds immediately turned into armed warriors. The leader of these incredible warriors, however, introduced himself to Conaire as his real father Nemglan. To make up for his misconduct towards the birds, Conaire was told to undress and return home to Tara on foot, carrying only his sling. He thus became the next High King of Ireland.

NESSA, in Irish mythology, was the mother of *CONCHOBHAR MAC NESSA*, the Ulster ruler during the lifetime of the hero *CUCHULAINN*. Nessa's husband was King Fachtna of Ulster and when the king died his half-brother, *FERGUS MAC ROTH*, succeeded to the throne and proposed marriage to Nessa.

However, she would agree to the match only on the condition that her son should be allowed to rule Ulster for one year. Fergus Mac Roth was so in love with her that he readily agreed, but at the end of the year the people of Ulster refused to let Conchobhar step down from the throne, so excellent was his rule.

NEMGLAN, a bird god from an other-world, came to Mess Buachalla before her wedding to the High King. As he flew in, his plumage moulted to reveal a beautiful youth. Like Leda and Danae before her, she loved the god and bore him a son, Conaire Mor. (ILLUSTRATION BY NICK BEALE, 1995.)

NIAMH

NIAMH was the wife of *CONALL* Caernach. While *CUCHULAINN* was recovering from wounds sustained during the war against the men of Connacht, Niamh nursed him and became his mistress. She then tried to prevent him returning to battle. But the witch *BADB*, one of the daughters of *CALATIN*, cast a spell on Niamh so that she wandered away into the countryside. Badb then assumed the form of Niamh and told Cuchulainn that he must return to the war and fight.

NIAM OF THE GOLDEN HAIR

NIAM OF THE GOLDEN HAIR was a daughter of the sea god *MANANNAN MAC LIR*. She fell in love with the poet *OISIN* and they lived happily together in the Land of Promise, which was one of the otherworld realms. Niam bore the poet a daughter, Plur nam Ban ("Flower of Woman").

NODENS

NODENS was a British god of healing, whose magic hounds were also believed to be able to cure the sick. Nodens was worshipped during the Roman occupation; the ruins of a great temple have been found on the banks of the River Severn. In Ireland, he became *NUADA* of the Silver Hand and in Wales *NUDD* of the Silver Hand, also known as Llud to the Britons.

NUADA

NUADA, also known as Nuada Airgetlamh ("Nuada of the Silver Hand"), because of a temporary replacement for a hand he lost at the first battle of Magh Tuireadh, was an important Irish god and leader of the *TUATHA DE DANANN*. He was married to *NEMAIN*. The De Danann were a younger generation of gods than the *FOMORII*, the sea gods who were soon to challenge them at the second battle of Magh Tuireadh. For a while between the two battles, Nuada appointed *BRES* as leader because of the loss of his hand. The silver replacement was made by *DIAN CECHT*. But Nuada was dissatisfied with it and turned to Dian Cecht's son Miach, who made him a new hand of flesh and blood. Dian Cecht slew Miach out of jealousy. Nuada's restoration as leader caused the second battle of Magh Tuireadh, because the half-Fomorii Bres complained to his kinsmen about his treatment.

At the second battle the lethal eye of *BALOR* killed both Nuada and Nemain before the sun god *LUGH* destroyed it with a sling-shot. Their victory saved the Tuatha De Danann, but later they in turn were defeated by the sons of *MILESIUS*. That Nuada was the great De Danann leader, there is no doubt. He is described as sitting on his throne "with a white light about him as it had been a fleece of silver, and round his head a wheel of light pulsed and beat with changing colours". Nuada is cognate with the Welsh *NUDD*.

NUDD

NUDD, known as Llud to the British, is the Welsh equivalent of *NUADA*. He also had a silver hand, and in one tale was known as Llud Llawereint ("silver-handed").

NUDD, or Llud, ruled Britain at a time when it was plagued by a strange May Eve scream. It transpired that two subterranean dragons caused the scream during an annual battle. They were soothed by sinking mead into a pit dug through the centre of the earth. (ILLUSTRATION BY ALAN LEE, 1984.)

O

OGMA was the Irish god of eloquence and the inventor of Ogham, the earliest system of writing used in Ireland. Ogham is made up of a series of vertical or sloping lines inscribed on a base line. The sagas tell of vast libraries of Ogham writing, though only inscriptions in stone carvings have survived, and the sagas themselves were later recorded by monks using the Roman alphabet.

Ogma was a son of *DAGDA*, who was a god described as the "Lord of Knowledge". Besides having a truly remarkable skill as a poet, Ogma was a fighter like other Irish gods and also, like the the Greek god Hermes or the Roman Mercury, he was responsible for conveying souls to the otherworld. Whereas for the Greek and Roman messenger gods this was a sad duty, not least because the kingdom of Hades was not an inviting place, Ogma's task was a happier one since the Celtic otherworld was a delightful and peaceful resting-place for the soul prior to its next rebirth in the world. It is thought that Greek colonists in the western end of the

OGMA, god of eloquence, invented the Ogham script, consisting of vertical lines crossing a lateral baseline. Ogham messages were carved on stone and inscribed on barks and wands of hazel or aspen. Over 400 ancient messages have survived. (ILLUSTRATION BY NICK BEALE, 1995.)

OISIN and the fairy maiden, Niamh, flew away on a snow-white steed through golden mist to the Land of Promise, which was a delightful otherworld beyond all dreams, filled with birdsong and scented flowers, with overflowing mead and wondrous creatures. (ILLUSTRATION BY STEPHEN REID, 1910.)

Mediterranean first encountered the idea of the transmigration of souls from their Celtic neighbours. In the sixth century BC the famous and unusual Greek philosopher Pythagoras left the Aegean island of Samos and went to live in the city of Croton in southern Italy. He became extremely interested in the theory of reincarnation. His followers, who believed that the soul was immortal, accepted transmigration through animals and plants as well, and as a result proposed the kinship of all living things.

In some Irish myths Ogma is said to have married *ETAIN*, who was the daughter of the god of healing *DIAN CECHT*. At the second and final battle of Magh Tuireadh Ogma slew Indech, son of the *FOMORII* goddess Domnu. Indech was one of the leaders of the Fomorii, who were the older sea gods who had challenged the *TUATHA DE DANANN*, the younger generation of gods of which Ogma was one. After the terrible battle was over and the De Danann were victorious, Ogma claimed as his prize a magic Fomorii sword that was capable of recounting all the deeds it had performed.

OISIN, sometimes Ossian, was the son of the Fenian, or *FIANNA*, leader *FINN MACCOOL*. According to Irish mythology, Oisin was the greatest poet in Ireland, perhaps not a surprising achievement considering how as a young man his father had eaten the Salmon of Knowledge. Oisin's mother was none other than the goddess *SADB*, the granddaughter of *DAGDA*. This made *OGMA*, the god of eloquence, Oisin's uncle.

One day, as Finn MacCool with his companions and dogs was returning homewards, a beautiful deer started up on their path and the ensuing chase took them towards Tara, the Irish capital and the base of the Fenians. At last the exhausted animal stopped and crouched down on the ground, but instead of attacking their quarry the hounds began to play round her, and even to lick her head and limbs. So Finn MacCool ordered that no harm should be done to the deer, which followed them on the way home until sunset.

That same night Finn MacCool awoke to find the most beautiful woman he had ever seen standing next to his bed. It was Sadb. She

explained how a spell had been placed upon her, but that she had learned that if Finn MacCool came to love her, then all the enchantments would cease to have power and she could resume her normal shape. So it came to pass that Sadb lived with Finn MacCool as his mistress, and for months neither of them stirred from their dwelling. Then news arrived of invaders in ships off Dublin, most likely a Viking raid, and the Fenians were called to arms. For only one week Finn MacCool was absent dealing with the Vikings. On his return, however, he discovered that Sadb had been lured away by someone disguised as himself (a common trick among shape-changers in Irish mythology). Realizing that it must be the enchanter whom Sadb had rejected, Finn MacCool organized a search of every remote hill, valley and forest in the country, but without success. Eventually he gave up all hope of finding his mistress and returned to his pleasure of hunting. It happened, by chance, that his dogs tracked down a very strange quarry and Finn MacCool came upon them surrounding a naked boy with long hair. His two best hounds were, in fact, keeping the pack from seizing the child.

Having driven off the dogs, Finn MacCool and the other huntsmen regarded the boy with curiosity. He told them that he did not know the identity of his father, but that his mother was a gentle hind, with whom he lived in a quiet valley safely shut in by steep cliffs. To their home a tall, dark stranger came every now and again to see his mother, but she always shrank away in fear and the man left in anger. When the stranger finally

OISIN returned from the otherworld after his time and found himself an old man, alone and bereft, the sole survivor of a magical age. With his lyre he sang of the heroes and gods of his era, conjuring up the magical phantoms of that bygone age.
(OSSIAN BY FRANCOIS GERARD, CANVAS, 1800.)

His famous adventure concerns *NIAMH*, the daughter of the sea god *MANANNAN MAC LIR*. Oisin met her while on a hunt by the shores of a lake. She suddenly appeared riding a horse with silver hooves and a golden mane. When Niamh told Oisin how she had travelled a great distance to invite him to her father's otherworld realm, the Land of Promise, he readily mounted the magic steed and was never seen by his father again. In the otherworld kingdom he fought against a *FOMORII* giant in an undersea combat worthy of his father. But after a number of other exploits Oisin began to miss his own land of Ireland. Niamh gave him her magic horse so that he could visit his home, but told him not to dismount otherwise he would never be allowed to return. Ireland appeared to Oisin almost a strange land, for everyone he knew had died long before. The people seemed far sadder and more careworn than the heroes he had grown up with. By chance he came upon a ragged group of men attempting to move a boulder, which he easily lifted for them while still seated on his mount. However, his saddle slipped and he fell to the ground. In an instant the magic horse vanished and the valiant young warrior was turned into a blind and frail old man.

A Christian addition to the end of this myth includes St Patrick. Because everyone took Oisin to be mad he cried out: "If your god has slain Finn MacCool, then I would say that he is a strong man." So he was taken to the saint, who recorded his strange tale and explained the changes to Ireland since the arrival of Christianity.

struck her with a magic hazel wand, the hind was forced to follow him, although she tried to comfort her son as she left.

As soon as the boy finished this account, Finn MacCool embraced him as his own son by Sadb, and immediately named him Oisin ("Little Fawn"). He was trained as a Fenian warrior, which involved one of the most difficult courses of training imaginable, and became a skilled fighter like his father, but he also inherited the gentler ability of eloquence from his mother, and his songs and poetry were admired throughout Ireland.

***OISIN**, on his return from the otherworld, found Ireland bleak and cold, the people sad and small, and himself a weary and withered old man. After passing on the magic legends, he quietly slipped away, his end as strange as his beginning.*
(ILLUSTRATION BY STEPHEN REID, 1910.)

HEROIC QUESTS

T HE THRILLING PURSUIT of a real or visionary goal forms the plot of many compelling tales of adventure. The goal is not always the most tantalizing part of the venture and might seem like a tedious or even trivial task, but serves to spur the traveller on his way. Other goals, such as the Grail, seem barely attainable, but serve as shining symbols of aspiration. The impetus is sometimes romantic, as when Culhwch set out to find fair Olwen; or retributory, as when Geraint went forth to avenge a wrong; while Peredur, Owain and the Grail Knights were inspired by otherworldly visions and ideals. Whatever the goal, the quest usually takes on a magic of its own, leading the hero down unexpected bypaths of adventure and discovery. *En route* he meets new friends and travelling companions, learns much-needed lessons and catches sight of even more tantalizing quests ahead.

OWAIN (above), inspired by the tale of Cynon, set off in search of the Castle of the Fountain, which was guarded by the Black Knight. He passed through the fairest vale until he saw a shining castle on the hill. After entering its otherworldly domain Culhwch defeated the Black Knight, and went on to woo his widow. After a rather difficult beginning, he overcame her resentment, and guarded her realm until his yen for adventure lured him off again. (ILLUSTRATION BY ALAN LEE, 1984.)

CAMELOT (left), Arthur's shining city-castle, drew knights from far and wide to join the Fellowship of the Round Table, inspired by ideals of courage, honour and vision. From Camelot, the questing knight set forth on journeys of adventure and discovery, to seek honour, to avenge wrongs and to win ladies and renown. The figure of the questing knight became a symbol of aspiration. (ILLUSTRATION BY ALAN LEE, 1984.)

THE GRAIL QUEST (right) proved to be the hardest, highest and greatest of all quests. Many knights set forth but few returned. When Arthur's warriors resolved to undertake the Grail Quest, Arthur wept, lamenting that the fairest fellowship of noble knights would never meet again around the table at Camelot. He was right, for few of his company were fitted for the quest and many perished. (THE ARMING AND DEPARTURE OF THE KNIGHTS BY E BURNE-JONES AND W MORRIS, TAPESTRY, 1895–96.)

CULHWCH'S (left) quest for the fair Olwen involved thirty-nine impossible tasks, the longest series of tasks in Celtic mythology. En route the hero enlisted the help of Arthur's war-band who assisted Culhwch in one of his hardest tasks, which was the retrieval of a comb, razor and scissors from between the ears of the terrible, enchanted boar, Twrch Trwyth. (ILLUSTRATION BY ALAN LEE, 1984.)

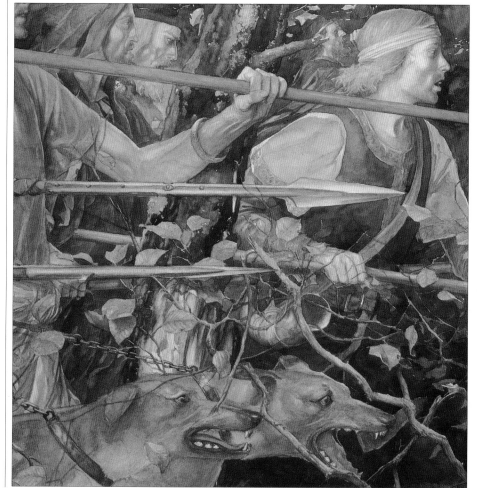

PEREDUR'S (above) quest for adventure led him through many wondrous lands. At one point he passed through a lovely river valley, filled with colourful pavilions and a wondrous multitude of windmills and water-mills. He lodged with the head miller and jousted in the tournament, defeating countless warriors with such skill and might that he impressed the local empress. After fighting her battles, he ruled with her for fourteen years before continuing his search for new adventures. (ILLUSTRATION BY ALAN LEE, 1984.)

OLWEN, in Welsh mythology, was the daughter of the giant Yspaddaden and her suitor was *CULHWCH*, one of King *ARTHUR*'s warriors. Culhwch's stepmother hated him so much that she cursed him to marry only Olwen, a girl whom the warrior came to love dearly. Yspaddaden was so upset by the obvious affection between Olwen and Culhwch that he set his daughter's lover a series of tasks in order to prevent the marriage. Among other things, Culhwch had to uproot a forest, burn the wood for fertilizer and plough the cleared land in one day; force *AMAETHON*, the god of agriculture, to nourish its crops; make the smith god Govannon forge tools for the work; bring four strong oxen to help; obtain magic seed; provide honey nine times sweeter than that of a virgin swarm; get a magic cup and a hamper of delicious meat; borrow the drinking-horn of the under-water king Gwyddbwyll and the magic harp belonging to Teirtu (an instrument that played itself); capture the birds of *RHIANNON*, whose song could wake the dead and lull the living to sleep; provide a magic cauldron; a boar's tusk for the giant to shave with and shaving cream made from a witch's blood;

OWAIN and Arthur (below) appear in a warrior's dream, playing gwyddbwyll. During the game, Arthur's knights battle with Owain's ravens, but the players simply play on, until Arthur smashes the pieces. The game symbolizes a battle, possibly for sovereignty. (ILLUSTRATION BY ALAN LEE, 1984.)

steal a magic dog, leash and collar; hire as a huntsman *MABON*, son of Modron, who had first to be released from prison; find a wonderful steed and swift hounds; steal a comb, scissors and a razor from between the ears of a fierce boar; and persuade a number of unlikely guests to come to Yspaddaden's stronghold. Undaunted by the

OLWEN (left), in flaming red, wanders through the otherworld, depicted here as a vibrant, brooding wooded idyll. Olwen was loved by Culhwch, a warrior of King Arthur's court, who had to go to great lengths to secure his bride.
(ILLUSTRATION BY ALAN LEE, 1984.)

sheer size and complexity of the challenges, Culhwch said that "King Arthur will provide horses and men to help him win Olwen". He also informed the giant that he would return to slay him. Culhwch succeeded and married Olwen "and she was his only wife as long as he lived". The giant was killed by one of Culhwch's fellow knights.

OWAIN (below) peers through the tangled branches of the wildwood, like a shy, wild creature. Overcome with shame after wronging his wife, he fled into the wilderness and lived as a wild man, wasting away until rescued by a noblewoman.
(ILLUSTRATION BY ALAN LEE, 1984.)

PARTHOLON (above) found a lush, primal country when he first landed in Ireland. The forests and plains were alive with strange, shy and beautiful creatures. Partholon cleared the land for cultivation and in his time three new lakes appeared, one of which was named after his son.
(ILLUSTRATION BY ARTHUR RACKHAM, C. 1910.)

OSCAR, in Irish mythology, was the son of *OISIN* and the grandson of *FINN MACCOOL*. His name means "deer lover" and recalls his grandmother, the goddess *SADB*, whom Finn MacCool first encountered while he was hunting. Sadb had been changed into a hind by a spell, which Finn MacCool briefly lifted. Oscar's mother was Eibhir, who was said to be "a yellow-haired maiden from a warm country".

Oscar was a mighty fighter, one of the best of all the *FIANNA*, or Fenians, the warriors who acted as a bodyguard to the High King of Ireland. But he lived during a time when the ruler, Cairbe, felt that the Fenians had too much power, and

a bloody struggle ensued. High King Cairbe refused to pay the Fenians for their services and raised another band of fighters to replace them. In a battle fought at Gabhra, near present-day Dublin, Oscar killed Cairbe in single combat but was himself mortally wounded. According to one version of the myth, Finn MacCool returned briefly from the otherworld to mourn Oscar's death.

OWAIN, in Welsh mythology, was the son of *URIEN* and one of King *ARTHUR*'s warriors. When a fellow warrior named *CYNON* was defeated by a mysterious Black Knight, Owain set out to find this stranger. He severely wounded the Black Knight but did not unseat him, and when the knight galloped off to a nearby castle, he gave chase only to find himself almost a prisoner once he entered its walls. Owain was saved by a lady named Luned, who gave him a ring of invisibility. Soon the lord of the

castle, the Black Knight, died of the wound Owain had inflicted on him. Not deterred by her grief, Owain persuaded Luned to plead his cause with such success that his widow consented to marry him. Thus he became master of the Castle of the Fountain, as the Black Knight's stronghold was called. But the long absence of Owain worried King Arthur a great deal, so he sent out a party of knights to find him. Owain returned with them to King Arthur's court, and he gradually forgot about his wife.

When a very angry lady arrived at court to accuse Owain of deceit, treachery and unfaithfulness, he was overcome with shame. A remorseful Owain fled to the forest and pursued the solitary life of a hermit. There he would have died but for a well-born lady who used a magic potion to restore his health. Sir Owain took up his arms, slew a dragon and befriended a lion. The knight and the lion had numerous adventures, which included saving Luned from death by burning and slaying a giant. Owain returned to the Castle of the Fountain, where he was reconciled with his wife. They seem to have spent the rest of their lives together in King Arthur's court. (See also *CELTIC ROMANCE; SINGLE COMBAT; HEROIC QUESTS*)

PARSIFAL see *PERCIVAL*

PARTHOLON, son of Sera, was believed to have led one of the early invasions of Ireland. Together with twenty-four men and their wives, he is said to have come out of the west after the waters of the Flood had receded and cleared the island of trees ready for cultivation. According to the myth, after living in Ireland for some five thousand years, the race of Partholon were stricken by disease and they all died within the space of a week.

PELLES was one of the names given to the "Maimed King" of the *GRAIL* story in whose castle of Carbonek the holy vessel was kept. In other versions of the tale he is known as Amfortas. Pelles was said to have been the father of Elaine, who fell in love with Sir *LANCELOT* and bore him the pure knight Sir *GALAHAD*, who was the only one of *ARTHUR*'s knights granted a vision of the Grail and allowed to hold it.

PELLES, the Grail King, guarded the Grail in Carbonek, the Grail Castle. Maimed by an incurable wound, symbolizing some spiritual imperfection, he lived in a twilight state, while his country wasted, awaiting the coming of Galahad, the redeeming knight. (ILLUSTRATION BY ALAN LEE, 1984.)

PERCIVAL, the Perfect Fool, attained a glimpse of the Grail through his innocence. Returning from Sarras, he became Grail King, heading the Order of Grail Knights, sometimes known as Parsifal, sometimes as Templeisen, after the Knights Templar.
(PARZIVAL BY MARTIN WIEGAND, CANVAS, 1934.)

PERCIVAL, who was also sometimes called Perceval or Parsifal in different traditions, was in later Arthurian mythology something of an outsider. He was brought up in a forest far from the court of Camelot and was completely ignorant of courtly manners. However, he travelled to King *ARTHUR*'s court and was duly made a knight, and then set off in quest of the Grail, the holy vessel that was used at the Last Supper and which received the blood that flowed from the spear thrust in Christ's side at the time of the Crucifixion. The Grail had been brought to Britain by *JOSEPH OF ARIMATHEA*, the rich man who had allowed Christ's body to be placed in his tomb. However, the Grail was later lost and its recovery became the great quest for the Knights of the Round Table.

The purity of Sir Percival may have meant that he was permitted a brief glimpse of the Grail, but he was denied the complete vision and heavenly release that was eventually granted to Sir *GALAHAD*, Sir *LANCELOT*'s son. Only Galahad was allowed to touch the Grail, "Our Lord's body between his hands", and then to die in the company of angels. The mysterious Queen of the Wastelands, one of the three ladies who took the dying King Arthur to *AVALON* after he had been wounded in the battle against *MODRED*, was Sir Percival's aunt. On his personal quest for the Grail, Sir Percival unfortunately fell somewhat short of the high standard of conduct required for recovering the Grail. One day on his journey he encountered a wondrous and mysterious ship and at once fell in love with its beautiful owner. Indeed, he was on the point of entering her bed when, "by chance and grace, Sir Percival saw his unsheathed sword lying on the ground, and on its pommel was a red cross, the sign of the Crucifixion, which reminded him of his knightly duty to behave as a good man. So he made the sign of the cross on his forehead, at which the boat was upended, then changed into a cloud of black smoke." So annoyed and filled with remorse was Percival by this moral lapse that he felt obliged to inflict a punishment on the weakness of his own flesh by wounding himself in the thigh. Meanwhile, the enchantress who had attempted to waylay him and divert him from his quest "set off with the wind roaring and yelling, that it seemed all the water was burned after her".

PEREDUR, in Welsh mythology, was the seventh son of Evrawg and the only surviving male. His father and brothers were killed before his own coming of age. This did not prevent Peredur from becoming one of *ARTHUR*'s warriors and his many adventures formed the basis for the later stories about *PERCIVAL*. Possibly because of his position as a seventh son, always a significant

PEREDUR, raised in rustic secrecy, grew up strong and agile but devoid of courtly manners. When he saw three shining knights, he was entranced. Devising a saddle of twigs, and armed with a sharpened stake, he set forth for Arthur's court. (ILLUSTRATION BY ALAN LEE, 1984.)

number, Peredur was particularly adept at defeating witches, who in Wales took to the field like knights attired in full armour. Indeed, his myth as it is told in the *Mabinogion* ends with a terrible duel between him and a leading witch. "For the third time the hag slew a man of Arthur's before Peredur's eyes, and Peredur drew his sword and smote the witch on the crest of her helmet so that the helmet and all the armour were split into two. And she raised a shout, and ordered the rest of the witches to flee, and said it was Peredur who was destined to slay all the witches of Caer Loyw." (See also HEROIC QUESTS)

PRYDERI, in Welsh mythology, was the son of *PWYLL*, a notable chieftain of Dyfed in south Wales, and of *RHIANNON*. Pryderi was snatched from his cot by one of

Rhiannon's rejected suitors and brought up by *TEIRNON*, a chieftain who discovered the infant in his stable. The chieftain's wife named the child Gwri, or "Golden Hair", but when, after seven years, he was finally returned home, Rhiannon renamed him Pryderi, "Care", because during the child's absence her life had been very careworn. She had been falsely accused of killing her son and was made to do penance by sitting at the gate of Pwyll's fortress and telling strangers of her crime, then offering to carry them on her back into his hall.

When Pwyll died, Pryderi succeeded him as lord of Dyfed and gave his mother in marriage to *MANAWYDAN*, son of the Welsh sea god Llyr, although in Pryderi's myth Manawydan appears as a mortal warrior rather than a god. At their wedding banquet there was a peal of thunder and a mist fell. "No one could see the other, although the great hall was filled with light." When the mist cleared, the land was desolate. People, animals and crops were gone. Pryderi, his wife Cigfa, Manawydan and Rhiannon were the only people left. After two

years eking out an existence on wild honey, fish and game, they finally decided to travel across the border to Lloegyr, present-day England. But the skill of Manawydan and Pryderi as craftsmen made them many enemies and they returned to Wales. In a ruined castle, Pryderi came across a golden bowl fastened by four chains on a marble slab. Pryderi went to pick it up, but his hands stuck to the bowl and he found that he could not move or let it go. He was also struck dumb. When his mother tried to save him, Rhiannon and Pryderi disappeared in another mist.

It later emerged that all the strange events had been caused by a spell laid on the household by an enemy of Pwyll, Pryderi's father. Manawydan discovered the truth as he was about to hang a mouse for eating their corn. The creature turned out to be the wife of Llwyd, the old enemy of Pwyll. Other mice helping to devour the crops were his warriors transformed by magic. During their temporary disappearance, Pryderi and his mother had been forced to work as donkeys.

PEREDUR aroused the rage of the Pride of the Clearing when he supped with his wife. The arrogant knight assumed his wife's guilt and punished her until Peredur finally challenged and overthrew him. Here, splendid as a peacock, the proud one rides out to joust with Peredur. (ILLUSTRATION BY ALAN LEE, 1984.)

PRYDERI, lord of Dyfed, marched into Gwynedd to avenge the theft of his swine by the resourceful magician, Gwydion. The dispute was to be decided by single combat, but the match was unequal as Gwydion bewitched Pryderi with magical illusions. (ILLUSTRATION BY ALAN LEE, 1984.)

R

PWYLL was a chieftain of Dyfed whose authority even reached into ANNWN, the Welsh otherworld. Indeed, he boasted the title Pen Annwn ("Lord of Beyond"). One day Pwyll was hunting in the forest when he saw an unusual pack of hounds running down a stag. These hounds were snow-white in colour and had red ears. Pwyll drove them off and was setting his own pack on the cornered stag when a grey-clad horseman rode up and accused him of discourtesy for chasing away his hounds. Pwyll accepted the charge and promised to make amends, at which the stranger revealed himself to be ARAWN, the ruler of Annwn. Arawn told Pwyll that he was being harried by a rival named Havgan, who could be slain only by a single blow, since a second one immediately revived him. Pwyll agreed to change places and shapes with Arawn for a

PWYLL (above), disguised as a beggar, lies in wait with 100 horsemen to trick Gwawl, a rival suitor for the hand of Rhiannon. Once overpowered, Gwawl agreed to leave the two in peace, but his bitter curse blighted their marriage with strange misfortunes. (ILLUSTRATION BY ALAN LEE, 1984.)

year, and to slay Havgan. During the period of exchange it was understood that Pwyll would not make love to Arawn's wife, even though he would share her bed.

Pwyll, having successfully killed Havgan and fulfilled his promise to Arawn, returned home. He then wooed and won RHIANNON for his wife, although a rival suitor never forgave him and laid a curse upon his household, both before and after Pwyll's death. For years no child was born and, angered at her barrenness, Pwyll treated Rhiannon unkindly. His attitude became worse after she gave birth to a son

at last, because when the baby was stolen her maids were so afraid of Pwyll that they blamed Rhiannon. They laid bones next to their sleeping mistress and smeared her face and hands with blood. When Rhiannon awoke in amazement, the maids told Pwyll how she had devoured the baby in the night.

Pwyll imposed a humiliating penance upon her. Every day she had to sit by his gate, tell her tale to every stranger who came and offer to carry them on her back to the great hall. Not until the eventual return of her son, whom she called PRYDERI ("Care"), was Rhiannon excused from her penance. (See also CELTIC OTHERWORLDS; MAGIC AND ENCHANTMENT)

RHIANNON, in Welsh mythology, was the daughter of Hereydd, and the long-suffering wife of PWYLL, a chieftan of Dyfed. All of Rhiannon's troubles stemmed from her rejection of Gwawl, the man to whom she had been promised, and as a result his enraged father had laid a spell on Pwyll's household.

Because of this curse, Rhiannon suffered years of barrenness and, after the birth of a son, she was unjustly accused of eating the baby. Even after the boy, whom she named PRYDERI, which meant "Care", had been restored and grown up, the spell continued to dog Rhiannon. At one stage she and Pryderi were changed into donkeys. Rhiannon herself had her own magical aspect, however, for the singing of her birds was said to be able to wake the dead and send the living to sleep.

Rhiannon is a singular figure in Welsh mythology. She bore her suffering and injustice with a patience that still seems remarkable. But her real nature was in all likelihood originally connected

RHIANNON (below), as first seen by Pwyll, was a vision in white and gold, riding a pearly steed, and clad in brocaded silk. The two seemed made for each other, but a curse clouded their love and marriage. As patient as she was beautiful, Rhiannon endured her lot without complaint. (ILLUSTRATION BY ALAN LEE, 1984.)

RHIANNON'S singing birds were heralds of the otherworld. Their beautiful and enchanting song was said to be able to wake the dead and to lull the living into a deep sleep. Celtic art and myth are alive with birds of every kind. While some, such as ravens, presage doom, swans and singing birds heal with their magical song. (ILLUSTRATION ANON.)

RUADH, an intrepid voyager, discovered a secret island beneath the waves, on which lived nine beautiful women who slept on nine bronze beds. Their eyes shone with rainbow light, bewitching Ruadh for nine blissful nights before he grew restless again. (ILLUSTRATION BY NICK BEALE, 1995.)

with horses. When Pwyll first set eyes on her, Rhiannon was riding "a big fine pale white horse, covered with a garment of shining gold brocaded silk". Also, Rhiannon's stolen son was found in a stable and her punishment for losing him was to act as a beast of burden to visitors who came to her husband's palace. It is tempting to link her with the horse goddess *EPONA*, one of the few Celtic gods or goddesses to be worshipped by the Romans.

RONAN, king of Leinster, was, in the tangled relations of his second marriage, the Irish equivalent of the great Greek hero Theseus. Just like Theseus' second wife Phaedra, the king's second wife Eochaid loved Ronan's son more than her husband. When the stepson showed his horror of her passion, Eochaid told her husband that the young man had attempted to rape her. Ronan ordered his son's execution and died of remorse when he later learned the truth. Eochaid ended her own life with poison.

RUADAN, in Irish mythology, was the son of the goddess *BRIGID* and of *BRES*, the half-*FOMORII* ruler

SADB, a gentle goddess, was compelled by an evil druid to live much of her life as a deer. However, she bore Finn MacCool a lovely son, from whose tiny forehead grew a tuft of deer hair where she had licked the boy, giving rise to his name, "Little Fawn". (ILLUSTRATION BY ARTHUR RACKHAM, C. 1910.)

of the *TUATHA DE DANANN*. At the second battle of Magh Tuireadh Ruadan was sent to spy on the Tuatha De Danann smith god *GOIBHNIU* who was busily making spears. Ruadan seized one of these weapons and thrust it into the god, but Goibhniu merely pulled it out again and drove it into Ruadan, mortally wounding him. When the goddess Brigid came to the battlefield to bewail her son, her weeping was said to have been the first keening in Ireland.

RUADH was a voyager whose ship became becalmed off the north coast of Ireland. According to Irish mythology, when he swam away to find help for his dying crew, he chanced upon a magical underwater island. On the island there lived nine beautiful women, and for nine wonderful nights Ruadh slept with all of them. The women then informed him that together they would bear him a son. Although Ruadh promised faithfully to return at the end of his voyage, he unfortunately forgot about his underwater lovers, and they, in their fury, pursued him, kicking the severed head of his son before them like a football.

SADB, in Irish mythology, was the mistress of *FINN MACCOOL*, the great leader of the *FIANNA*, popularly known as the Fenians, the bodyguard of the High King. She first appeared to the hero while he was out hunting, but although a goddess herself, Sadb had been placed under a powerful spell by a wizard and was compelled to take the form of a deer. That night, however, Sadb came to Finn as a woman and for a time they lived happily together. Then, when Finn was away from home, the wizard returned and turned Sadb into a deer again. Finn searched the whole of Ireland for his lost mistress, but the only trace he found of her was a naked boy who had been raised in the wild. The hero recognized him as his own son by Sadb, so he called him *OISIN*, meaning "Little Fawn". Oisin grew up to become one of the most famous of all Irish poets.

FABULOUS VOYAGES

THE EPIC VOYAGES of Celtic myth are fabulous tours of the otherworld, usually through an archipelago of wonder isles. The yen to travel itself was often inspired by tales of the otherworld, and the epic trips of both Bran and Brendan were sparked off by otherworldly visions. Like another intrepid voyager, Maeldun, they sailed across the oceans, exploring a myriad of dreamlike isles, some of timeless delights and some of deadly perils. Like time travellers, Celtic voyagers experienced a time warp, either returning home long after their time or condemned to wander on a journey without end. Another feature of the restless Celtic voyager was his eventual disenchantment with otherworldly delights, and a yearning for the changing seasons of his homeland.

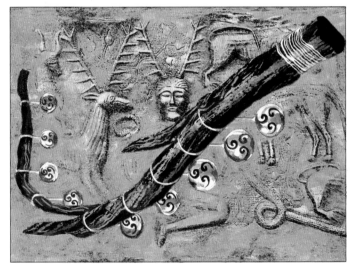

MAELDUN (left) set sail to avenge his father's murder and, en route, passed through a fabulous archipelago. In one striking episode, he reached an island surmounted by a fortress with a brazen door and a glass drawbridge which threw the travellers backwards – a telling sign of the otherworld. When they struck the bronze door, a soporific sound sent them to sleep until they awoke to the welcoming voice of the castle's enchantress. When Maeldun tried to woo her, the whole castle dissolved, and the sailors found themselves at sea again. (ILLUSTRATION BY ALAN LEE, 1984.)

BRAN'S (above) voyage was sparked off by a blossoming and scented silver fairy bough, left beside him as he slept. Later a beautiful woman clad in otherworldly robes came to reclaim the bough; she sang a lay about her lovely home across the sea which inspired Bran and his kinsmen to set sail. Far out to sea, they reached her wondrous isle of blossoming trees, just one of 50 such delightful heavens where people lived in timeless joy and plenty. Yet all too soon, Bran's crew craved the changing seasons of their homeland. (ILLUSTRATION BY DANUTA MEYER, 1994.)

A **DREAM** (below) of a fabulous voyage inspired the Roman ruler, Maxen, to set off on an epic voyage from Rome to Britain, in search of the lovely isle and even lovelier woman of his dream. He passed through river valleys and scaled mountains with their summits lost in heaven. Beyond, he reached a great harbour filled with beautiful ships. Picking the loveliest, crafted in silver, gold and ivory, he sailed across the wide sea until he reached the sparkling shores of Cornwall. Within a jewelled fortress, he found the lovely woman of his dream. (ILLUSTRATION BY ALAN LEE, 1984.)

BRIAN (above) and his brothers set off on a perilous mission to find eight objects deposited around the world. They voyaged in "Wave Sweeper", the self-propelled boat of Manannan, across the oceans to Greece and Persia. One task was to find an inexhaustible cooking spit, which was kept by sea nymphs on the sunken isle of Finchory. Brian, in a magical water suit, sank down among 150 maidens and seized the golden spit from the hearth of their underwater castle. (ILLUSTRATION BY STEPHEN REID, 1912.)

BRENDAN (above), an intrepid Irish monk inspired by tales of the Land of Promise, set sail on an epic voyage. Like Maeldun, he reached an island of bird-like spirits, possibly the Land of Promise, and crossed a translucent sea. Unlike Maeldun, he landed on an island which moved when he lit a fire and turned out to be the giant whale, Jasconius. Here, the dauntless saint tames a siren or merman of the sea. (ILLUSTRATION FROM THE MARVELLOUS ADVENTURES OF ST BRENDAN, 1499)

SANGREAL, or Grail, was the holy vessel of Arthurian mythology during the Middle Ages. It was said to be the cup that Christ drank out of at the Last Supper. It was also believed to have received the blood which flowed from the spear thrust in Christ's side at the Crucifixion. Brought to Britain by JOSEPH OF ARIMATHEA, the rich man who buried Christ, or by his brother-in-law Bron and his son Alan, the Grail was always associated with the early Christian settlement at Glastonbury. Another miraculous object connected with the Grail was a bleeding lance or spear. Sir GALAHAD used its magic power to cure a mysterious ruler, the "Maimed King", who lay between life and death in his castle. It seems, however, that Sir PERCIVAL was originally the knight who saw the Grail, and that it was only in later versions that Galahad took his place as the only knight worthy of such a vision.

The Grail was lost, but it was thought not to have left Britain, rather that it was hidden somewhere in the country because of the

SANGREAL (below) was guarded by angelic women, the Grail Maidens. Here, the dove of heaven bears a gold censer from which arose "a savour as if all the spice of the world had been there", recalling the spicy "greal" of Celtic myth. (THE DAMSEL OF THE SANC GRAIL BY DANTE ROSSETTI, CANVAS, 1874.)

SANGREAL (left), after inspiring the great quest in Britain, was borne back to Sarras by the three good knights, Galahad, Percival and Bors, and was celebrated in a Eucharistic Mass before ascending to heaven. (HOW THE GRAIL ABIDITH IN A FAR COUNTRY BY WILLIAM MORRIS, GLASS, C.1890.)

sinfulness of the times. Indeed, the mere presence of the holy vessel was enough to act as a challenge to most knights to pursue a path of goodness. On its unseen arrival at Camelot, the chivalrous Sir GAWAIN immediately vowed to seek out its home in order to see the Grail for himself. Many of the Knights of the Round Table made similar vows, much to the distress of King ARTHUR, who feared the loss of his best fighting men. But only Sir Galahad successfully completed the quest and died contented. After holding the Grail in his own hands, the young knight's soul was released from his body and "a great multitude of angels bore it up to heaven". That the Grail was the representation of the body and blood of Christ there can be no doubt, for Joseph of Arimathea administered it as part of the sacrament to Sir Galahad, "who had trembled when his mortal flesh beheld spiritual things". It is even stated that Sir Galahad was a descendant of the same Joseph, "the first Christian bishop".

There remains, nevertheless, a powerful charge of Celtic magic in this Christian myth. When "the Holy Grail covered with a white cloth" appeared at Camelot, the vessel filled King Arthur's hall with the most tasty smells, so that the Knights of the Round Table ate and drank as never before. It was, in fact, nothing less than a Celtic cauldron of plenty. When, at the end of the quest, the Grail became "Our Lord's body", the draught that Sir Galahad took from it at Joseph of Arimathea's request ensured his spiritual survival. Like a Celtic cauldron of rebirth, it allowed Sir Galahad to live on in a Christian otherworld. This obvious debt to Celtic mythology meant that the Church never fully embraced the Grail as a Christian symbol. The great popularity of Grail stories forced a degree of toleration, but clerics were always aware of its links with pre-Christian rites. (See also WONDROUS CAULDRONS; HEROIC QUESTS)

SCATHACH (whose name means "shadowy") was a warrior-princess in the Land of Shadows and tutor in the martial arts. One myth recounts that her most famous pupil was the Ulster hero CUCHULAINN. She taught him his famous battle leap and gave him the spear named Gae-Bolg ("Belly-spear"). Although it made a single wound on entry, once inside the body of one of Cuchulainn's enemies, thirty barbs opened to tear the stomach apart. UATHACH, the daughter of Scathach, was Cuchulainn's mistress during his year of training, and was unhappy that he wanted to fight her sister AOIFA. In the event, Cuchulainn was able to defeat Aoifa by trickery and made her his next mistress.

SCOTA

SCOTA was said to be the earliest known ancestor of the Scots. According to one version of the myth, she was the daughter of an Egyptian pharaoh. A wise teacher named Niul, who had settled in Egypt, became her husband and they had a child, Goidel, who gave his name to the Gaels. In another tradition, she was the wife of *MILESIUS* and was killed fighting the *TUATHA DE DANANN*.

SEARBHAN

SEARBHAN, in Irish mythology, was a *FOMORII* warrior, one of the ancient sea gods. This one-eyed, one-armed and one-legged fighter

guarded a magic tree, which no one dared approach. However, during the sixteen-year flight of *GRAINNE* and *DIARMUID UA DUIBHNE* from the *FIANNA*, the hard-pressed lovers managed to become friends with Searbhan and he allowed them to shelter in the branches of the magic tree, which made it difficult for *FINN MACCOOL* to find them. However, Searbhan and Diarmuid came to blows when Grainne attempted to eat some of the magic berries that grew on the tree, and the Fomorii warrior was slain.

SETANTA

SETANTA see *CUCHULLAIN*.

SUALTAM MAC ROTH

SUALTAM MAC ROTH, in Irish mythology, was the brother of *FERGUS MAC ROTH*. An Ulsterman, he accepted *CUCHULAINN* as his own son, although the hero's real father was the sun god *LUGH*. On

SEARBHAN (left), the surly one-eyed Fomorii giant, guarded a magic tree, squatting at its foot all day. The eloping lovers, Diarmuid Ua Duibhne and Grainne sheltered in its branches, but Grainne developed a craving for the tree's magic berries. This so enraged the giant that he and Diarmuid fought and the mighty Searbhan was slain with his own club. (ILLUSTRATION ANON.)

SUALTAM MAC ROTH'S (right) head rallied the Ulstermen to battle, even after his death. He had exhorted them in life without success, as they were weakened by Macha's curse. The cries of the severed head at last broke the spell and roused the men to fight. (ILLUSTRATION BY STEPHEN REID, 1910.)

the night of her wedding to Sualtam Mac Roth, *DECHTIRE* had swallowed a fly and fallen into a deep sleep. In this state she went to the otherworld with Lugh and there conceived Cuchulainn. While Cuchulainn was single-handedly defending Ulster against the invading forces of Queen *MEDB* of Connacht, Sualtam Mac Roth attempted to gather the men of Ulster who had been weakened by *MACHA's* curse. So desperately did he turn his horse that Sualtam cut off his own head with the sharp edge of his shield. But the severed head continued the call to arms long enough to rouse the warriors.

167

T

SUIBHNE GEILT, "the mad one", in late Irish mythology was a king cursed by St Ronan. One day King Suibhne was outraged to learn that, without his permission, Ronan was founding a church on his land. Although his wife, Eorann, tried to restrain him, the king rushed to the new foundation, seized the saint's psalter and threw it in a nearby lake. He then laid hands on St Ronan, when a messenger arrived to summon him to an ally's aid on the battlefield. Next day an otter returned the psalter unharmed. St Ronan thanked heaven for this and cursed Suibhne, who assumed the characteristics of a bird, leaping from trees for seven years before his reason returned.

When St Ronan heard about this recovery, he prayed that the king would not return to persecute Christians. So Suibhne was once again on the brink of madness as headless bodies and severed heads harried him. Another priest took pity on the tormented man and wrote down his sad tale, after which Suibhne "died a Christian and his soul ascended to heaven".

TARANIS, "the thunderer", was a Celtic sky god whom the Romans equated with their supreme deity Jupiter. The wheel, which is sometimes used as a symbol of the sun in Celtic art, here represents the electric light of a thunderbolt, symbolized by the trident, a three-pronged spear.
(ILLUSTRATION BY MIRANDA GRAY, 1994.)

TALIESIN was a prophetic bard who was gifted with all-knowing vision, which was symbolized by his shining brow. At the young age of thirteen, he already surpassed all of Arthur's bards in spiritual insight. He is portrayed here as a visionary spirit who was at one with the forces of nature. (ILLUSTRATION BY STUART LITTLEJOHN, 1994.)

TAILTU was the daughter of a ruler of the FIRBOLG and wife of Eochaidh Mac Erc, another Firbolg king. She was said to have cleared the forest of Breg so that it became a plain, a task which killed her. Because she was the foster-mother of the sun god LUGH, he declared that the festival of Lughnasadh be held in her honour, which took place on the first day of August. It was originally the occasion of a national sporting competition, not unlike the Olympic Games.

TALIESIN ("Shining Brow") was a Welsh wizard and bard and according to Welsh mythology he was the first person to acquire the skill of prophecy. In one version of his story he was the servant of the witch CERIDWEN and was named Gwion Bach. Ceridwen prepared a magic brew that, after a year of boiling, was to yield three drops of knowledge. Whoever swallowed these precious drops would know all the secrets of the past, the present and the future. As Gwion Bach was tending the fire beneath the cauldron, some of the hot liquid fell on his finger and he sucked it to relieve the pain (much like FINN MACCOOL when he was cooking the Salmon of Knowledge). The furious Ceridwen employed all her magic powers to pursue the boy. During the chase he transformed himself into a hare, a fish and a bird before being eaten by the witch in the form of a grain of wheat. Later Gwion Bach was thrown into the sea and was caught in a fish-trap and renamed Taliesin because of his radiant forehead. "I am old, I am new," he said. "I have been dead, I have been alive." (See also SAGES AND SEERS)

TARANIS (whose name means "Thunderer") was one of the few Celtic gods with whom the Romans identified and he was often equated with Jupiter. Monuments to Taranis have been found all over the Celtic world, from the Adriatic coast to the northern regions of Britain. Taranis is usually depicted with his symbol, the wheel. The word "taran" is still used in modern Welsh and Breton to mean thunder.

TEIRNON was lord of Gwent Is Coed and foster-father of PRYDERI. Teirnon owned a beautiful mare, and every year on the eve of the first of May the animal gave birth to a foal, which mysteriously disappeared. One year Teirnon decided to keep watch to see what would happen. A giant clawed hand came through the stable window and took the new-born foal. He hacked off the hand but heard a crying coming from outside and found a three-day-old baby boy lying on his doorstep.

Teirnon and his wife took the child in and raised him as one of their own, but as he grew, the resemblance to PWYLL became increasingly marked until they knew that he was the missing son of Pwyll and RHIANNON.

TEUTATES, also called Toutatis, was one of the Celtic gods mentioned by the Roman historian Lucan and is often equated with the god Mars. His name means "a people" or "a tribe" and so it may well be that the many inscriptions to him are actually dedicated to local deities of a region rather than to a single pan-Celtic figure.

TEIRNON, *watching the birth of a foal, was shocked to see a vast hairy arm thrust through the stable window. After hacking at the arm with his sword, Teirnon found a beautiful baby boy in the stable, whom he raised and who turned out to be the lost son of Rhiannon and Pywll, rulers of the realm. (ILLUSTRATION BY ALAN LEE, 1984.)*

to Cornwall, where King Mark waited to marry her. The ensuing tale relates the sad course of their love, separation and their deaths. The lovers' end was particularly touching. Having agreed to part, Tristan went to Brittany, but later was gravely wounded and sent for help from Iseult, who had once before cured him of a serious wound. So she sailed to Brittany with a magic cure. It had been agreed that the ship carrying Iseult would hoist a white sail to indicate that she was aboard. However, an incorrect report of a black sail caused Tristan to lose the will to live and he died of his wound. When Iseult was told of her lover's death she too quickly died, but of a broken heart. (See also CELTIC ROMANCE; SINGLE COMBAT)

THOMAS THE RHYMER see CELTIC OTHERWORLDS

TRISTAN, the nephew of King MARK of Cornwall, was one of the great lovers of medieval mythology. His name is said to have been given to him after his mother's death in childbirth. Of Breton origin, the story of Tristan and ISEULT was popular in Cornwall, Ireland and Brittany. A love potion prepared by Iseult's mother, the Irish queen, was the cause of their great love. Tristan and Iseult drank it accidentally when Tristan was escorting her

TRISTAN and Iseult (left), enchanted by a love potion, gaze at each other in rapture. In one legend, the two had fallen in love before sipping the potion, which only served to quash their scruples. The Victorian design captures the extreme nature of courtly love. (ILLUSTRATION BY EVELYN PAUL, 1900.)

TRISTAN humbly sought the Grail, even though he doubted his chances because of his illicit love for Iseult. At one stage in his quest, he found a splendid castle all alight and alive with song. Sadly, however, he was struck back by a burning beam of light, for only the purest could attain the Grail. (ILLUSTRATION BY EVELYN PAUL, C. 1900.)

TUATHA DE DANANN were "the people of the goddess Dana" in Irish mythology. They were the last generation of gods to rule Ireland before the invasion of the sons of *MILESIUS*, the ancestors of the present-day Irish. The Tuatha De Danann overcame the *FOMORII*, violent and monstrous sea gods, at the second battle of Magh Tuireadh largely because of their superior magic. They were said to have learned magic, crafts and knowledge in four marvellous cities of the north, Falias, Gorias, Finias and Murias. From these cities the Tuatha De Danann brought to Ireland four talismans: the Stone of Fal, which screamed aloud when the rightful king of Ireland placed his foot upon it; the magic sword of *NUADA*, their great war-leader, which was a weapon that could only inflict fatal blows; the spear or

TWRCH TRWYTH (below) was a boar that guarded three treasures between his ears which Culhwch sought to retrieve. Arthur's war-band hunted the boar, and here Mabon, the renowned hunter, skilfully snatches one treasure from between the boar's ears. (ILLUSTRATION BY ALAN LEE, 1984.)

TUATHA DE DANANN (above), an ancient race of Irish gods, went to live underground after their defeat by the Milesians. Beneath grassy mounds, each had his own sparkling sidhe, a subterranean court which glittered with wonders within. (ILLUSTRATION BY ALAN LEE, 1984.)

sling-shot of the sun god *LUGH*, who, as the slayer of *BALOR*, was the bringer of victory over the Fomorii; and the cauldron belonging to *DAGDA*, father of the gods, which was an inexhaustible pot that was capable of satisfying every appetite.

It is clear that the gods known in Ireland as the Tuatha De Danann were common to all Celtic peoples. Their names can be found in Welsh myths and in inscriptions on the continent of Europe. In Ireland they were not entirely lost with the advent of Christianity. Apart from having their exploits recorded by the monks who wrote down the Irish sagas, the Tuatha De Danann took up residence underground as the fairies. On the ancient Celtic feast of Samhain, celebrated on the last day of October to mark the new year, the De Danann were believed to allow mortals to enter their realm.

TUIREANN was the Irish father of three sons who killed Cian, father of the son god *LUGH*. To atone for this crime, Lugh demanded that the sons of Tuireann should perform a series of near impossible tasks, bringing back to Ireland such magical objects as a healing pigskin belonging to a king of Greece and a cooking spit from an undersea kingdom. When fulfilling their final labour they were badly wounded and Tuireann begged Lugh for the pigskin to cure his sons, but the god refused and they died.

TWRCH TRWYTH, in Welsh mythology, was a king who was turned into a gigantic boar for his sins. Between his ears he kept a comb, a pair of scissors and a razor. The retrieval of these objects was one of the hardest of the tasks that the giant Yspaddaden set *CULHWCH* who wanted to marry his daughter *OLWEN*. The boar was an important animal to the Celts and appears in many myths, as well as in statues and carvings. It represented both war and feasting.

UAITHNE was the god Dagda's inspired harpist. He had three equally gifted sons who played such sad music that on one occasion twelve men died weeping from sorrow. The Celtic bards accompanied their music with lyrics which perpetuated the legends down the generations.
(ILLUSTRATION ANON.)

UATH submitted three Irish heroes to a beheading contest to test their courage and find the champion of Ireland. The rules allowed a hero to behead the giant but only if he could return the favour on the next day. Only Cuchulainn had the courage to behead the giant and place his head on the block. (ILLUSTRATION BY JAMES ALEXANDER, 1995.)

UAITHNE, in Irish mythology, was the magic harp of the *TUATHA DE DANANN* god *DAGDA*. It was stolen by the *FOMORII*, the enemies of the De Danann. When Dagda discovered where it was, he called out to the harp to free itself. The harp responded by killing nine Fomorii and then singing Dagda's praises. Uaithne was also the name of Dagda's harpist.

UATH ("Horror") was the name of the water giant who challenged the three Irish heroes *CUCHULAINN*, Laoghaire and *CONALL* to a beheading contest. Each was invited to take an axe and chop off the giant's head, provided that he would then lay his own head on the block for the giant to decapitate. Only Cuchulainn rose to the challenge, and was proclaimed by the giant as the Irish champion. After the announcement Uath revealed himself to be *CU ROI*, the Munster king.

UATHACH was one of the lovers of the great Ulster hero and champion *CUCHULAINN*, and, according to Irish mythology, the daughter of the female warrior *SCATHACH*, who had been Cuchulainn's tutor in the martial arts. When Uathach served

UTHER PENDRAGON, Arthur's father, hit upon the incredible idea of having a round table at which 150 knights could see each other and sit without quarrelling. Turning to Merlin, he asked him to design a table "round in the likeness of the world".
(ILLUSTRATION ANON.)

the hero food, he forgot his own strength and accidently broke her finger while taking a dish from her hand. Her scream brought her previous lover to Uathach's immediate aid, but Cuchulainn easily slew him in the fight that followed and afterwards Uathach transferred her affection to the victor.

VORTIGERN, a fifth-century ruler of Britain, tried to build a grand castle, but the walls kept crumbling. The boy Merlin, a precocious seer, was consulted and revealed that two dragons battled beneath the site every night, destroying the castle walls.
(ILLUSTRATION BY ALAN LEE, 1984.)

URIEN, father of *OWAIN*, ruled Rheghed in north-west Britain. His courage and skill as a warrior were celebrated in many songs, including the work of *TALIESIN*. When the Angles invaded, Urien is said to have fought a successful campaign against them and besieged them on the island of Lindisfarne.

UTHER PENDRAGON (whose name means "dragon head") was *ARTHUR*'s father. According to late-British mythology, Uther was able to sleep with Igraine because he was disguised as her husband, Gorlois, Duke of Cornwall, and the result of their union was Arthur. The wizard *MERLIN* helped in this deception and later Uther killed Gorlois and married Igraine, while Arthur was taken by Merlin.

VORTIGERN was a British ruler who hired Jutish mercenaries, but as increasing numbers of Saxons came into Britain he fled to Wales. Here he tried to build a stronghold, but it kept collapsing. When *MERLIN* was consulted he said that a red dragon (the Saxons) battled with a white dragon (the Britons) beneath the fort and that the red dragon would eventually win.

NORSE
MYTHOLOGY

INTRODUCTION

THE MYTHOLOGY OF NORTHERN AND eastern Europe is essentially that of two main groups, peoples of Germanic and of Slavic descent. Today the former group includes Germans, Dutch, Danes, Swedes, Norwegians, Icelanders, English, and any of their extraction, while the Slavs are made up of Russians, Serbs, Croats, Bulgarians, Rumanians, Slovacs and Poles. Other peoples have also contributed to the mythological tradition of the region, such as the inhabitants of the Baltic shore: the Prussians, Lithuanians and Letts. Further north there are contributions from the Finns and the Lapps of Sweden and Norway. The northernmost people of all, the Lapps of Finland and their cousins, the Samoyeds of Russia, are actually the scattered remnants of the Uralians, an ancient group once spread right across the tundra of Europe and Asia. Their beliefs remained similar to those held by the tribespeople of Siberia until quite recent times. For the purpose of this book these traditions have been grouped together under the generic term, Norse.

It is a fact that the overwhelming bulk of mythology surviving from northern and eastern Europe is Scandinavian and Icelandic in origin. Most Slavic gods are not much more than names, and the little we know about their worship is usually as a consequence of its Christian termination. In Russia the conversion of Vladimir in 989 to the Orthodox faith involved the ransacking of pagan temples at Kiev. Fortunately, chroniclers of this event noted the strange worship accorded to the thunder god Perunu or Veles, the god of flocks. Without such passing testimony our scant knowledge would be almost nonexistent. Even so, there are difficulties with Vladimir's own pagan beliefs prior to his conversion to Christianity. He was of Swedish descent and the "Rus" state he ruled on the

River Dnieper was a by-product of Viking exploration. It is therefore likely that the Slavic thunder god Perunu had already absorbed much of Thor's mythology. Although a native hammer-god undoubtedly existed before the Vikings arrived in the 860s, the importance of northern warriors in Novgorod and Kiev made it inevitable that the Russian god would be identified with his Germanic counterpart. The strength of the Viking presence can be judged from the Arab traveller Ibn-Fadlan's account of the ship cremation of a "Rus" leader on the Volga river in 922.

In the Balkans the Slavs not only encountered Orthodox Christianity, but were later for a time under Islamic rule also. This long isolation from such Slavonic influences did not bode well for Balkan mythology. As the myths were never written down, the influence of Christianity and Islamic rule replaced the native story-telling. Of Baltic mythology next to nothing now exists, although some idea can be formed of the pantheon. The brutal truth is that European mythology has escaped the Baltic fate only where by historical accident it was written down. In the case of Celtic

ODIN, the leading warrior god of the Vikings, at left, bears the weapons of his warcraft, an axe and spear. The stylized tree depicted beside him symbolizes Yggdrasil, the World Tree. At centre is the thunder god Thor, wielding his fiery thunderbolt, Mjollnir; while at right, Freyr bears an ear of corn to represent his fertility. (TAPESTRY, 12TH CENTURY.)

mythology we are fortunate in the care taken by Christian monks in Ireland to record the ancient sagas. The classical heritage of Greece and Rome was preserved like that of the Celts in monastic libraries, after the Germanic peoples overran the western provinces of the Roman empire. And much of Germanic mythology would have been lost in its turn without the efforts of the Icelandic scholar and statesman Snorri Sturluson.

At the turn of the thirteenth century Snorri Sturluson wrote a handbook for poets on the world of the Germanic gods, providing detailed explanations of the old myths. He was recalling the sagas of the Viking era, approximately 750–1050, when a vigorous tradition formed around the heroic deeds of Odin, Thor and Freyr. Still untouched by Christianity, the restless and adventurous Northmen – the Danes, Norwegians and Swedes – put to sea in search of plunder and land. Viking warriors were largely organized in small bands or ships' crews, only joining together in temporary alliances for military expeditions, trading voyages or piracy. They might serve under a famous leader for a while, and then break up again, although on occasion they built up armies or large fleets of warships, like the forces that attacked France in 842 or invaded England in 866. Their magnificent ships and expert seamanship gave them mastery of rivers and seas, and enabled them to travel far and wide.

The Irish lamented the Viking onslaught most. "The sea spewed forth floods of foreigners over Ireland," noted the *Annals of Ulster*, "so that no harbour, no beach, no stronghold, no fort, no castle, might be found, but it was sunk beneath waves of northmen and pirates." In 836 the Vikings had decided to set up a permanent raiding base on the site of present-day Dublin.

It is hardly surprising that aggressive Viking

SIGURD *roasts the heart of the terrible dragon, Fafnir, and sucks his thumb which was splashed with the dragon's blood. On tasting the otherworldly blood, Sigurd gained the power to understand birdsong and learnt from the birds that Regin, his tutor sleeping by the fire, planned treachery.* (WOOD CARVING, 12TH CENTURY.)

warriors loved hearing about the exploits of one-eyed Odin. This chief of the Germanic gods exerted a special fascination as "father of the slain". He shared those who fell on the battlefield with Freyja, the goddess of fertility. He also inspired the frightful berserkers, the shield-biting fighters who rushed unheeding and naked into the fray. When the Danish king Harald Wartooth complained about Odin's fickleness, the way he gave luck in battle and then suddenly withdrew it again, the war god said "the grey wolf watches the halls of the gods". Gathering to Valhalla the heroic warriors slain in battle was the only policy Odin felt he could sensibly follow under the constant threat of Ragnarok, the doom of the gods. These dead warriors, the *Finherjar*, were desperately needed for the final battle on the Vigrid Plain, where nearly all would fall in an encounter between the gods and the frost giants. Odin himself was destined to be killed by the wolf Fenrir, the monstrous offspring of the fire god Loki and the frost giantess Angrboda. Whether Harald Wartooth accepted this as an adequate answer is uncertain, since Odin, who was acting as his charioteer, flung the old king down and slew him with his sword as he fell.

VALHALLA (below), the splendid, many-spired Hall of the Slain, housed Odin's phantom army of heroic warriors, gathered to fight at Ragnarok – the preordained doom of the gods. On the right, the massive World Serpent, Jormungand, was destined to overwhelm the world at Ragnarok. (ILLUSTRATION FROM THE PROSE EDDA, 1760.)

The "axe-age, sword-age", which was the age that would lead up to the catastrophe of Ragnarok, must have seemed like a description of contemporary times to the footloose Vikings. But for those who settled down as colonists, either as farmers or traders, an alternative god to worship was Thor, Odin's son. Although "allergic" to frost giants, Thor is represented in the sagas as an honest and straightforward person. He was very popular with Icelandic colonists, who had fled southern Norway to avoid the Odin-like activities of leaders like Erik Bloodaxe. Thousands of them revealed their allegiance in the choice of family name: Thorsten or Thorolf were most common. Thor was indeed a reassuring supernatural presence in both divine and human crises, be they encroachments by frost giants on gods, or local tyrants on farmers, or even overzealous Christian missionaries on pagan temples. Ever handy was his thunder-hammer Mjollnir, a magic instrument with powers of destruction, fertility and resurrection. It was hardly surprising then that Thor became a greater god than Odin at the close of the Viking era, just a century or so before Scandinavia was converted to Christianity.

LOKI (below), the fiery trickster god, was to begin with a mischievous and playful prankster, but he became so dark and twisted that his malice threatened the stability of the world and precipitated Ragnarok. Here, the troublesome god taunts the Rhine Maidens, who are grieving the loss of their Rhinegold. (ILLUSTRATION BY ARTHUR RACKHAM, C. 1900.)

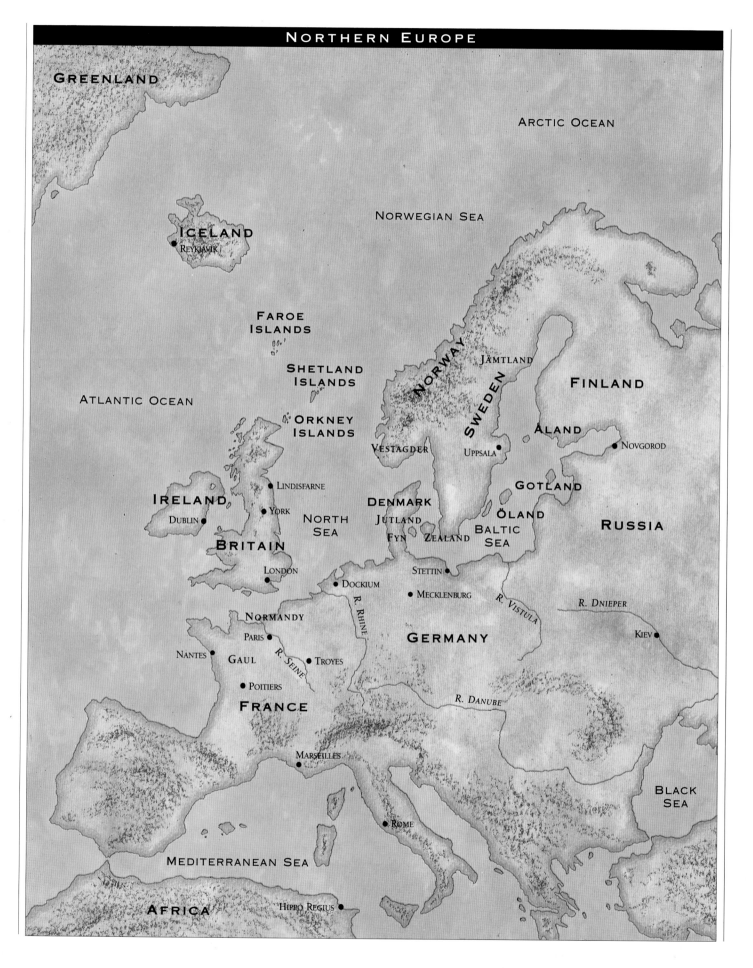

NORTHERN EUROPE

GREENLAND

ARCTIC OCEAN

NORWEGIAN SEA

ICELAND
● REYKJAVIK

FAROE
ISLANDS

SHETLAND
ISLANDS

ATLANTIC OCEAN

ORKNEY
ISLANDS

NORWAY

JÄMTLAND

SWEDEN

FINLAND

ÅLAND

● NOVGOROD

VESTAGDER

UPPSALA ●

● LINDISFARNE

GOTLAND

IRELAND

● YORK

DENMARK

ÖLAND

DUBLIN ●

NORTH
SEA

JUTLAND

RUSSIA

BALTIC
SEA

BRITAIN

FYN

ZEALAND

LONDON ●

● DOCKIUM

STETTIN ●

NORMANDY

● MECKLENBURG

R. VISTULA

R. DNIEPER

PARIS ●

R. RHINE

GERMANY

KIEV ●

NANTES ●

GAUL

R. SEINE

● TROYES

● POITIERS

FRANCE

R. DANUBE

MARSEILLES
●

BLACK
SEA

● ROME

MEDITERRANEAN SEA

AFRICA

● HIPPO REGIUS

A

AEGIR, or Eagor, was a Germanic sea god, the husband of *RAN* and father of nine daughters, the waves. He seems to have belonged to an older generation of the gods than either the *AESIR* or the *VANIR*, although no details of his descent survive. Aegir was sometimes depicted as a very old man with white hair and claw-like fingers. Whenever he rose from his underwater hall, he broke the surface of the sea for a single purpose, the destruction of ships and their crews. To ensure a calm voyage, prisoners would usually be sacrificed to Aegir before a Viking raiding party set sail for home.

One myth tells how the proud sea god was outwitted by *THOR*. Aegir had been ordered by Thor to brew some ale for the gods, but he pretended that he had no cauldron large enough for the task. In fact he disliked being told what to do. But undaunted, Thor acquired a vast cauldron from the frost giant *HYMIR*. It was so big that when he hoisted it onto his shoulders, the

AEGIR (above), a tempestuous and powerful god of the sea, resided in a glistening underwater palace from where he directed the swirling waves through his nine daughters, who were known as the billow maidens. The hissing, seething Nordic sea was called "Aegir's Brewing Kettle". (ILLUSTRATION BY JAMES ALEXANDER, 1995.)

AEGIR'S sister-wife, Ran, was famous for her drowning net, which she used to snatch unsuspecting sailors from the decks of ships and drag them down to the seabed. She entertained them in her coral caves, which were lit by gleaming gold and where mead flowed as freely as in Valhalla.
(ILLUSTRATION BY PETER HURD, 1882.)

handles reached his ankles. Hymir tried to stop Thor leaving with the cauldron, but the god's hammer saw off Hymir and his gigantic friends. As a result, a humiliated Aegir had to accept the cauldron and supply *ASGARD*, the home of the gods, with ale.

It was at a subsequent feast for the gods held by Aegir that *LOKI* showed how evil he had become when he insulted the assembled company and stabbed Aegir's servant Fimafeng.

THE AESIR, in Germanic mythology, were one branch of the family of the gods; the other branch were the *VANIR*. At one time there was a war between the younger Aesir and the older Vanir, which ended in a peace that left the Aesir dominant. Both branches had in fact grown weary of fighting, and were pleased to come to terms. In order to cement the peace, several of the leading Aesir went to live among the Vanir, while a number of important Vanir went to *ASGARD*, the Aesir's home.

The Aesir, under the leadership of *ODIN*, included his sons *BALDER* ("the bleeding god") and *BRAGI*, the god of eloquence; the justice god *FORSETI*, who resolved quarrels in a splendid hall supported by pillars of red gold and covered with a roof inlaid with silver; the fertility god *FREYR*, once a leading Vanir; the vigilant *HEIMDALL*, whose duty it would be to summon every living creature to *RAGNAROK*, the day of doom, with his horn; blind *HODR*, the unwitting killer of Balder; the trickster *LOKI*, god of fire and ally of the frost giants; the sea god *NJORD*, one of the gods exchanged with the Vanir; another of Odin's sons, *THOR*, whose mighty magic hammer was the only weapon the frost giants feared; the god of war *TYR*, a son of Hymir; *VILI* and *VE*, the brothers of Odin; and *VIDAR*, a son of Odin who was destined to avenge his father's death at Ragnarok.

The goddesses of the Aesir were *FREYJA*, the fertility goddess and twin sister of Freyr; *FRIGG*, Odin's wife; *SIF*, the wife of Thor; and *IDUN*, who was the keeper of the apples of youth.

Almost all the Aesir were to be killed at Ragnarok (the doom of the gods), when a terrible battle was destined to take place between the forces led by Odin, and the forces led by Loki.

ALBERICH see *ANDVARI*

ALVIS ("All Wise"), in Germanic mythology, was a dwarf who was outwitted by *ODIN*'s son *THOR*, the possessor of a magic hammer of irresistible force. In payment for the weapons Alvis had forged for them, the gods promised that he could marry Thor's daughter *THRUD*. However, Thor was displeased with the arrangement and so devised a test of knowledge to stop the dwarf from marrying his daughter. When Alvis came to *ASGARD*, Thor questioned him all night long because sunlight turned dwarfs to stone.

ALVIS, a dwarf famed for his wisdom, hoped to marry Thor's giant daughter, Thrud, but first he had to prove that his great wisdom made up for his small stature. Thor quizzed him and prolonged the test until sunrise when the first ray petrified Alvis who, like all dwarfs, turned to stone in daylight. (ILLUSTRATION BY JAMES ALEXANDER, 1995.)

*THE AESIR (left) were warrior-gods worshipped by heroes and kings. Very like Norsemen, they loved, fought and died with human feelings for, though divine, they were not immortal. Odin, seen here in horned helmet, behind the Vanir twins, led the heroic Aesir. (*THE NORTHERN GODS DESCENDING *by W Collingwood, canvas, c. 1890.)*

*ANDVARI'S (above) treasure trove was stolen by the gods Odin and Loki in order to pay a ransom. When they took his gold-making ring too, Andvari danced with rage and cursed the ring. At top, the three Norns examine the dark thread of destiny, while below, Hel awaits a new inmate. (*ILLUSTRATION BY F VON STASSEN, 1914.)*

ANDVARI, or Alberich, as he was known in later German legend, was a craftsman dwarf who lost his hoard of treasure to the fire god *LOKI*. On an expedition to Midgard (the land of men), Loki killed a sleeping otter with a stone. Carrying the dead otter, he, *ODIN* and *HONIR* came across a farm and offered to share the otter's meat with the household in return for a night's lodgings. To the horror of *HREIDMAR*, the farmer, the offering was none other than his own son *OTTER*. First of all, Hreidmar chanted a spell to weaken his guests and then his two surviving sons, *FAFNIR* and *REGIN*, bound them hand and foot. Odin protested their innocence and pointed out that they

would not have come straight to the farm had they known the otter was the farmer's son. So, eventually, Hreidmar settled on a death-price: enough gold to cover Otter's skin, inside and out. Because the flayed skin was endowed with magic powers, it was capable of being stretched to a great size and so no ordinary amount of gold could be accepted in compensation.

Loki was allowed by Hreidmar to seek this great treasure, while Odin and Honir (in some versions just Honir) remained at the farm as hostages. The fire god was not permitted to wear his sky-shoes, however, and these were also kept as security against Loki's return. Having borrowed the drowning-net

of Ran, wife of the sea god *AEGIR*, Loki descended through a maze of dripping tunnels to an underground lake, where he caught a large pike. This fish, like the otter before, turned out to be more than it first seemed. For it was in fact the dwarf Andvari, who was the richest of those who dwelt underground. Only because of Loki's terrible threats, Andvari surrendered all his immense hoard of gold, including his magic gold-making ring. But in his anger the dwarf laid a terrible curse on the ring which would cause the doom of whoever wore it. When Loki returned to the farm with the gold and Odin and Honir were released, he told Hreidmar of Andvari's curse and in this way

passed it on to the farmer. Indeed, Hreidmar was soon after killed by his son Fafnir, who then ran away with the cursed treasure.

The hero *SIGURD* was later persuaded by his foster-father Regin to pursue Fafnir, who had by this time become a dragon. The hero duly searched for the creature and eventually found it in its lair and slew it. However, when Sigurd realized that for the sake of the treasure Regin intended to kill him in turn, he made sure that he slew his foster-father first. Thus it was that Andvari's curse continued to cling to the stolen gold and brought about the death of all those who attempted to possess it. (See also *RINGS OF POWER*)

A

ANGRBODA (left) mothered a dreadful brood of monsters – a rotting girl, Hel; a savage wolf, Fenrir; and a giant serpent, Jormungand – who were banished by the gods. Here, Odin flings the serpent into the icy deep, while Angrboda guards her wolf-child. (ILLUSTRATION BY JAMES ALEXANDER, 1995.)

ANGRBODA, or Angerboda ("Distress-bringer"), in Germanic mythology, was a frost giantess. She was the mistress of *LOKI* and the mother of three monstrous offspring: the wolf *FENRIR*, the serpent *JORMUNGAND*, and a daughter named *HEL*. When the gods heard about this brood, they agreed that such creatures must be dealt with quickly. A group of gods broke into Angrboda's hall at night, bound and gagged her, and took her and Loki's children to *ASGARD*.

ODIN first banished Hel to the "world beneath the worlds" and there he put her in charge of all the inglorious dead. He then hurled Jormungand into the ocean, where the huge snake smashed through the ice and sank down into the depths. Odin was less certain what to do with Fenrir, so at first he decided that the gods should keep an eye on him at Asgard. However, when the *NORNS*, the goddesses of destiny, warned that the wolf would bring about Odin's death action was finally taken to bind Fenrir securely with a magic chain and keep him in captivity.

Although Angrboda's children were thus contained, Odin knew that the wolf Fenrir would break free at *RAGNAROK*, the day of doom, and destroy him. The sea serpent Jormungand also awaited the final conflict, like his sister Hel "surrounded by corpses and swirling death-mist" in the netherworld. A tenth-century Danish complaint about Odin's withdrawal of luck from brave warriors is answered in terms of Angrboda's brood. Odin is supposed to have said that "the grey wolf watches the halls of the gods". With this threat in mind, he had no choice but to gather to his side the greatest champions.

ASGARD, in Germanic mythology, was the divine stronghold of the *AESIR*, who were the younger and stronger branch of the family of gods. The other branch, the *VANIR*, lived in Vanaheim. Asgard's mighty walls were built by a stonemason, Hrimthurs, who named the hand of the fertility goddess *FREYJA*, plus

the sun and the moon, as his price for the eighteen-month task. At *LOKI*'s suggestion, *ODIN* set the seemingly impossible limit of six months for the construction of Asgard's walls. As a concession the stonemason was allowed to use his horse, the magic Svadilfari, to help him in the work. To the horror of the gods he had finished all the walls, except a gateway, three days before the time was up. So Loki transformed himself into a mare and beguiled the stonemason's stallion, thus preventing the completion of the job. The stonemason then revealed himself as a frost giant and *THOR* broke his skull with his hammer. It is ironic that the defences of Asgard should have been built by the labour of a frost giant, given the bitter enmity between the gods and the giants. Indeed, at *RAGNAROK* these two enemies were destined to meet in a battle of mutual destruction.

The idea of city walls that were built by giants is a widespread myth in Europe. The walls of Tiryns in southern Greece, for example, were believed to have been constructed by the Cyclopes, who were giant, one-eyed beings. There is also a story of a dispute over payment for the strengthening of Troy's walls by the gods Apollo and Poseidon and King Laomedon, which is not dissimilar to the above story concerning Asgard's walls. (See also *RAGNAROK*)

ASGARD's (left) walls were built by a giant stonemason, Hrimthurs, aided by his wondrous horse, Svadilfari. The gods gave him only six months to complete the work, hoping to avoid payment. He nearly finished on time but was thwarted by Loki's trickery. (ILLUSTRATION BY H HENDRICH, C. 1890.)

ASGARD, (above) the magnificent stronghold of the Aesir gods, shimmered on a plane above Midgard. Within, there were countless shining, glittering halls for each of the gods. Asgard was linked to Midgard by an ethereal pathway for the gods, a wondrous rainbow bridge called Bifrost. (ILLUSTRATION BY ALAN LEE, 1984.)

AUDHUMLA (below), the original cow, emerged from the primal ice at the dawn of time, and nourished the first frost giant, Ymir. She survived by licking ice from which she freed the first man, Buri. Here, while Ymir suckles her milk, Audhumla licks Buri free of the ice. (AUDHUMLA BY N A ABILGAARD, CANVAS, C. 1790.)

BABA YAGA (bottom right) was a Slavonic witch of monstrous size who preyed on travellers, devouring their flesh with a mouth that stretched from earth to hell. She was seen as a hunched hag, bearded, part-woman, part-tree. Here, perched on a rolling log, she propells herself forward with a pole. (ILLUSTRATION BY I BILIBIN, 1900.)

AUDHUMLA was the primeval cow in Germanic mythology. This creature was the first animal to emerge from *GINNUNGAGAP* ("the yawning emptiness") at the start of creation. From Audhumla's teats "flowed four rivers of milk", nourishment enough for *YMIR*, the first frost giant and the first live thing of all. From Ymir's children descended the frost giants, the implacable enemies of the gods. The cow herself seems to have survived on the goodness that she obtained from an icy salt lick. As she licked, first some hair appeared, then a head, and finally the whole body of a man, *BURI*. In time Buri had a son named *BOR*, who married Bestla, the daughter of a frost giant. Their sons were the first gods, *ODIN*, *VILI* and *VE*. These three battled against the frost giants and finally slew Ymir. As the giant fell the blood from his wounds flooded the land and drowned all his frost children, except for *BERGELMIR* and his wife who managed to escape.

BABA YAGA, sometimes Jezi Baba, is the hideous man-eating female demon of Slavonic tradition. According to some versions of her myth, her mouth is said to stretch from earth to the gates of hell. She lived in a strange house which had legs like a chicken's at each corner, and stood inside a fence made of human bones. When she wished to travel, it was believed that she flew in an iron kettle.

BALDER, sometimes Baldr or Baldur, was the son of *ODIN* and *FRIGG* and the "bleeding god" of Germanic mythology. His wife was Nanna and their son, *FORSETI*, was the god of justice.

As a young man, Balder was tormented by nightmares, all of which indicated that he was about to die. A sense of foreboding, therefore, settled over *ASGARD*, the home of the gods, as the divine inhabitants tried to understand the meaning of Balder's dreams. They were deeply puzzled because the gentle god least deserved to suffer such torments. So Odin rode his eight-legged steed *SLEIPNIR* to the land of the dead and by means of magic learned from a seeress there that Balder was to be killed by the blind god *HODR*, his own brother, with a branch. Although depressed by this news, Odin returned to Asgard and found that his wife Frigg had a plan to save Balder. The goddess

BALDER, a loving and gentle soul, spread light and goodwill wherever he went but, inevitably, evoked the envy of the bitter god Loki, who plotted his tragic death and imprisonment in Hel. This romantic portrayal captures the sacred, Christ-like goodness of the god.
(BALDER BY B FOGELBERG, MARBLE, 1840.)

travelled through the nine worlds and got each and every thing to swear an oath that it would do her son no harm. To Odin's relief this plan seemed to work. When the gods decided to test Balder's new invulnerability by throwing stones and spears at him with great force, he remained unharmed. All in Asgard were delighted except *LOKI*, the god of fire. He was so annoyed by Balder's escape from danger that he transformed himself into an old woman and visited Frigg's hall. In conversation with the goddess, Loki learned that she had received a promise of harmlessness from all things except the mistletoe, which was a plant too small and too feeble to bother about.

Armed with this information, Loki went off to cut some mistletoe. In his normal shape the fire god returned to the assembly of the gods and found everyone throwing things at Balder, except blind Hodr. Pretending to help Hodr enjoy the sport, Loki gave him the branch of mistletoe and directed his throw, with the result that the branch passed right through Balder, who immediately fell down dead. At Frigg's entreaty *HERMOD*, Balder's brother, was sent to *HEL* in order to offer a ransom for Balder. He used the eight-legged Sleipnir for the journey. While Hermod was away, the bodies of Balder and Nanna, who had died of grief, were placed on a pyre in a longship which was allowed to drift burning out to sea.

BALDER's body was laid on a pyre in his longship and he was then covered in treasure and decorated with flowers and thorns, the emblems of sleep. His ship was set aflame and pushed out to sea where it shone brightly, before sinking into darkness.
(FUNERAL OF A VIKING BY F DICKSEE, CANVAS, 1893.)

In the netherworld the brave Hermod found his brother Balder seated in a high position. When he asked for his release, Hel said Balder could leave only on condition that "everything in the nine worlds, dead and alive, wept for him". Messengers were sent out and soon even the stones were weeping. But THOKK, an old frost giantess, refused, saying, "Let Hel hold what she has." So upset were the gods at this refusal to mourn that it took some time for them to realize that Thokk was none other than Loki in disguise. Nevertheless, Balder remained with Hel.

Balder's good looks and early death recall the myths of the Egyptian Osiris and the Sumerian Tammuz, as well as that of Adonis, who was the dying-and-rising god the ancient Greeks adopted from the Phoenicians. For the Germanic peoples believed that the return of the wounded, dying Balder would occur in a new world, a green land risen from the sea, after RAGNAROK, the doom of the gods. Like the undead Celtic King Arthur, Balder was expected to return and rule over a world cleansed by catastrophe. It would seem that some of the initial appeal of Christianity in northern Europe was connected with the triumphant return of the risen Christ on Judgement Day. (See also RAGNAROK)

BALDR see *BALDER*

BALDUR see *BALDER*

BEOWULF was the Germanic hero who slew two water monsters. He was said to be the nephew of the king of Geats, whom some interpret as the Jutes. His story is set in Denmark. One night a dreadful creature known as *GRENDEL* came to the hall of King Hrothgar and ate one of the warriors sleeping there. Although invulnerable to weapons, Grendel was seized by Beowulf and held in a powerful grip, from which it could only

BEOWULF, seen here with raised drinking horn, gazes up at the gory trophy hanging from the splendid vault of Denmark's Victory Hall. The giant hairy hand belonged to the fearsome sea monster, Grendel, who had continually terrorized and devoured the Danes, until Beowulf tore the creature's arm right out of its socket. (ILLUSTRATION BY ALAN LEE, 1984.)

BEOWULF wrestles with a monstrous merwoman in the crystal cavern of her underwater den. Grieving for the death of her son, Grendel, slain by Beowulf, the merwoman fought with frenzy, but Beowulf battled calmly and took her by surprise. (ILLUSTRATION BY JAMES ALEXANDER, 1995.)

break away by losing an arm. Mortally wounded, the water monster fled to its home, deep in a nearby lake, and bled to death.

Delighted by this feat of courage and strength, King Hrothgar loaded Beowulf with gifts, since his kingdom had been rid of a menace. But neither the king nor the warrior reckoned on Grendel's mother, an even more dreadful creature. She returned to the attack and ate another sleeping warrior. In pursuit, Beowulf followed her into a lake and dived down to her cavernlike lair. A desperate struggle then took place and Beowulf lost his

trusty sword. Like Arthur, he was fortunate to find another magic weapon in the water and he used this to finish off Grendel's mother.

Having once again saved King Hrothgar's kingdom from danger, Beowulf returned home to southern Sweden, where his father ruled. Towards the end of his popular reign a dragon attacked his land. Going out with twelve followers to slay the fiery beast, Beowulf soon found himself almost on his own, for all his companions but one ran away in terror. Although he managed to kill the dragon, it was at the cost of his own life.

In contrast to the Celtic myths that describe combat with watergiants, the Germanic stories tell of heroes who face actual monsters rather than magical opponents. This is quite unlike the great Ulster hero and champion Cuchulainn's beheading contest with Uath, or Sir Gawain's with the Green Knight, for in these traditions their monstrous opponents were able to restore themselves to life after they had been decapitated.

BEOWULF, even in his old age, tackled firebreathing dragons. Yet neither his might nor his fabled armour, crafted by Wayland, could withstand the dragon's crushing teeth. Beowulf was mortally wounded in the combat, but he did not die before seeing the dragon's treasure released for his people. (ILLUSTRATION BY JAMES ALEXANDER, 1995.)

BERGELMIR, according to Germanic mythology, was the son of Thrudgelmir and the grandson of *YMIR*. When *ODIN*, *VILI* and *VE* killed Ymir and threw his body into the middle of *GINNUNGAGAP*, all the frost giants drowned in the giant's blood except Bergelmir and his wife. By using a hollowed tree trunk as a boat, they escaped to

BIFROST (above) was a gigantic rainbow causeway, reaching from the shining citadel of Asgard to the earthly realm of Midgard. Composed of fire, water and air, it shimmered with rainbow-coloured light in hues of red, blue and green. Over the ethereal arch, the gods moved to and fro. (ILLUSTRATION BY ALAN LEE, 1984.)

continue the race of giants, who never lost their hatred for the gods. At *RAGNAROK* the frost giants and the dead of *HEL* were destined to settle the final account for Ymir's dismemberment.

BIFROST, in Germanic mythology, was the flaming three-strand rainbow bridge between *ASGARD* and Midgard (heaven and earth respectively). It was said to have been built by the gods out of red fire, green water and blue air, and was guarded by the watchman god *HEIMDALL*. Every day the gods rode across the bridge to hold meetings at the well of *URD*.

BILLING, in Germanic mythology, was the father of *RIND*. According to some traditions, he was king of the Ruthenians, or Russians. So strong-willed was Rind that *ODIN* could not woo her, even though Billing approved of the god's suit. On the contrary, she treated the chief of the Germanic gods with undisguised contempt. Eventually, however, she gave way to his advances and she bore a son, *VALI*, who killed *HODR* with his bow and arrow.

BERGELMIR (below) and his wife were the only frost giants to escape drowning in the torrent of Ymir's blood that flowed from his mortal wounds. They journeyed in a hollowed-out tree trunk to the edge of the world where they founded the realm of Jotunheim and bred a new race of giants. (ILLUSTRATION BY NICK BEALE, 1995.)

BILLING (above) gazes in wonder at the glittering trinkets fashioned by the dwarf goldsmith Rosterus. Unknown to King Billing, the dwarf is Odin in disguise, who was intent on wooing the king's daughter, Rind. She was destined to bear Odin a son, Vali, who would avenge Balder's death. (ILLUSTRATION BY NICK BEALE, 1995.)

BOR was the son of *BURI*, husband of the giant Bestla and father of *ODIN*, *VILI* and *VE*. An ancient god, Bor lived in the time before the world had been made, when there was no earth, sky or sea, only mist, ice, fire and the gaping pit of *GINNUNGAGAP*. Bor's father-in-law, the giant Bolthur, also had a son who imparted his wisdom to his nephew Odin.

BRAGI was the son of *ODIN* and Gunnlod, a female giant, and was the Germanic god of poetry and eloquence. He was married to *IDUN*, the goddess who kept the magic apples of youth. When *LOKI* returned to *ASGARD*, after being instrumental in causing *BALDER*'s death, Bragi, who was never at a loss for words, told him that he was

BRAGI (above) was born in a glittering stalactite cave, where his mother, Gunnlod, guarded the Mead of Poetry, until seduced by Odin. The dwarfs gave the fair child a magical harp and set him afloat on one of their fine-crafted vessels from which he sang his poignant Song of Life which rose to the heavens. (ILLUSTRATION BY PETER HURD, 1882.)

THE BRISINGAMEN (below) was an exquisite necklace crafted by dwarfs so finely that it shone like liquid flame. The goddess Freyja, beside herself with longing, paid dearly for possessing the treasure. An emblem of the stars, it so enhanced her beauty that she wore it continually, night and day. (ILLUSTRATION BY J PENROSE, C. 1890.)

unwelcome company at their feast. Enraged, Loki called Bragi "the bragger", whereupon Bragi threatened to twist off Loki's head as the only sure method of stopping his lies. Although Odin tried to calm the gathering, the effect of Bragi's words on Loki was to make him even more threatening. He finally prophesied the destruction of the gods and then fled from Asgard.

Possibly Bragi was a late addition to the Germanic pantheon. It is not unlikely that Bragi was added through the divine elevation of a poet, since in Germanic courts poets were venerated second only to kings. Bragi was portrayed as an old, bearded man carrying a harp, and when oaths were sworn they were solemnized by speaking over a vessel called the Cup of Bragi.

BRISINGAMEN see RINGS OF POWER

THE BRISINGS, also known as the Bristlings, were the mysterious owners of a golden necklace, called the Brisingamen, that the fertility goddess *FREYJA* craved. To *ODIN*'s disgust she slept on four successive nights with the dwarfs Alfrigg, Dvalin, Berling and Grer in order to acquire it. When she returned to *ASGARD*, Odin accused her of debasing her divinity by paying such a price. As a penance he made her stir up war in Midgard, the world of men. Freyja and Odin shared those slain on the battlefield.

No agreement exists about the meaning of this strange myth, not least because the identity of the Brisings is unknown. It has been suggested that necklaces were the special adornment of mother goddesses, but this hardly does more than explain Freyja's attraction to this particular one. What seems more likely is that the sexual price Freyja paid for it represents the other side of love, namely, blind passion and lust. Nothing could stop her, not even Odin's great disapproval, when she desired something badly enough. The Brisingamen came to be identified so closely with Freyja that when *THOR* wished to disguise himself as the goddess to retrieve his hammer from *THRYM*, she lent it to him to make his costume convincing. (See also *TREASURES AND TALISMANS*)

THE BRISTLINGS see *BRISINGS*

BRUNHILD see *BRYNHILD*

BRYNHILD was a *VALKYRIE* who defied *ODIN* and so was banished to earth and imprisoned within a ring of fire. When *SIGURD* braved the fire and broke her charmed sleep, they fell in love. He gave her his ring, Andvarinaut, unaware of its curse. On his travels he was bewitched by Grimhild into betraying Brynhild, first by marrying Gudrun and then by helping Gunner win Brynhild. On discovering Sigurd's betrayal, Brynhild planned his death, but then killed herself in despair. (See also *THE VALKYRIES*; *TRAGIC LOVERS*)

BURI, in Germanic mythology, was the ancestor of the gods. He was released from the ice by *AUDHUMLA*, the primeval cow. One day Buri's hair appeared where she licked; on the second day, his head was free of ice; and, on the third, his entire body. He had a son, *BOR*, who married a frost giantess, and their sons were *ODIN*, *VILI* and *VE*.

BRYNHILD, one of the leading Valkyries, was punished by Odin for meddling with his will in warfare: The god put her to sleep and imprisoned her in a ring of fire, where she would remain until a peerless hero freed her. Only Sigurd braved the scorching fire, waking her from her enchanted sleep. (ILLUSTRATION BY ARTHUR RACKHAM, C.1900.)

NATURE SPIRITS

THE DRAMATIC LANDSCAPE of Scandinavia, with its electric skies, icy wastes and seething springs, was easily peopled with nature spirits. Such spirits roamed the mountains and snow slopes as fearsome frost, storm and fire giants, personifying the mysterious and menacing forces of nature. So great were the terrors of crushing ice and searing fire that the giants loomed large in the Norse myths as evil and ominous forces. Yet other less dramatic but no less important spirits were the invisible *landvaettir*, or land spirits, who imbued the land and guarded its welfare. Helpful and timid, the *landvaettir* easily took fright, shying away from Viking dragon ships. In the underground caverns, dark dwarfs unearthed glittering gems and metals, while light elves inspired the forests and lakes. In Slavonic myth, a host of vital forces filled the world and imbued the forests, fields and rivers with whirling spirits of nature.

THE FROST GIANTS (below) personified the icy terrors of the Nordic landscape. Mighty, menacing and numbing, the ice masses of the North were a constant threat to the Norsemen, much like the frost giants, whose undying enmity would overwhelm the gods at Ragnarok. In the interim, the frost giants sent freezing blasts to nip the buds of spring, or shook avalanches from their icy shoulders and brows. (RONDANE AT NIGHT BY H SOHLBERG, CANVAS, C. 1890.)

THE SUN (above), in one myth, was fashioned by the gods from a bright spark of fire. Its glowing orb was placed in a chariot, drawn by two white steeds and driven by the sun-maid, Sol. Fearing that the sun's heat might be harmful, the gods placed a shield, Svalin, or Cooler, in front of the golden car. In another myth, the gods gave a giant, Day, a chariot and horses to drive round the earth once every 24 hours. Day's horse, Shining Mane, lit up the earth and sky with the radiance of his shining hair. (SUN DISC, GILDED BRONZE, C. 1000 BC.)

RAN (left), a stormy spirit of the sea, reflected the shifting moods of the ocean, sometimes helpful, sometimes harmful. She gathered sailors in her drowning net and dragged them down to the depths of the sea. There, with her husband, Aegir, she entertained her victims in her gleaming coral caves, which were lit by the shining gold of the sea. Ran loved gold, named the Flame of the Sea, after the fluorescent quality of Nordic waves. Sailors seeking Ran's favour wisely pocketed some gold for the trip. (ILLUSTRATION BY ARTHUR RACKHAM, C. 1900.)

DARK DWARFS (below) were formed from maggots in the rotting flesh of the slain giant, Ymir. The gods thought them too ugly to be seen, however, and condemned them to a life underground. Like giants, they turned to stone in daylight, thus explaining the many smaller stones and rocks scattered across the Nordic landscape. The twin peaks of Trold Tindterne, for example, are two bands of warring dwarfs who forgot to retreat before sunrise. As dwarfs had a habit of whispering behind rocks, the mountain echoes were known as "dwarfs' talk". (ILLUSTRATION BY ALAN LEE, 1984.)

THE RHINE MAIDENS (above) were ethereal sprites who dwelt in lakes and rivers during the winter, emerging from the water to flit through the forests in summer. The river's colours reflected the nymphs' moods, turning black with grief when the Rhine Maidens lost their gold. Here, the Rhine Maidens berate their loss to the gods crossing the rainbow bridge above. (ILLUSTRATION BY ARTHUR RACKHAM, C.1900.)

ROCK AND STORM GIANTS personified the vast craggy mountains and storm clouds. Rocky chasms and outcrops were created by giants treading too heavily at the dawn of time. Best suited to mist and fog, the mountain giants, like dwarfs, were petrified by the light of day, which explains some fantastic rock formations, such as the Riesengebirge (right), formed by foolish giants who were caught outside at sunrise. Similarly, in Iceland the highest peaks are named Jokul which derives from Jotun or Giant.

(ILLUSTRATION BY NICK BEALE, 1995.)

E

DAZHBOG was the Slavic sun god, known as Dabog to the Serbs and Dazbog to the Poles. Son of Svarog, the god of the sky, and brother of *SVARAZIC*, god of fire, he was born again every morning and rode through the sky on his diamond chariot until he became an old man in the evening. In some versions he is married to *MYESYATS*, the moon, and quarrels between them are said to cause earthquakes.

DRAUPNIR see *RINGS OF POWER*

DIETRICH see *RINGS OF POWER*

EAGOR see *AEGIR*

THE EINHERJAR were the "heroic dead" of Germanic mythology. They were gathered from the battlefields by the *VALKYRIES*. In *VALHALLA*, the Einherjar formed *ODIN*'s private army, which he raised to fight at *RAGNAROK*, the doom of the gods. This was the final battle between the gods and the frost giants on the *VIGRID* Plain. Until then, these dead warriors would fight every day and feast every night, and any wounds they sustained were magically healed. (See also *THE VALKYRIES*)

FAFNIR slays his father, Hreidmar, because he is bewitched by the treasure trove stolen from the dwarf Andvari. The dwarf's cursed ring can be seen glittering on Hreidmar's forefinger as he writhes in the dust. Behind the warring pair, the gods gaze on in numb dismay. (ILLUSTRATION BY F VON STASSEN, 1914.)

FAFNIR, son of the magician *HREIDMAR*, was corrupted by the cursed ring Andvarinaut. Lusting after the fabulous ring-hoard, he slew his father, helped by his brother *REGIN*. Greed made him monstrous in nature and form, as he turned into a dragon to guard his hoard. The legend of his treasure drew many aspiring heroes to his lair in search of fame and fortune. Most met their deaths on the blasted heath outside his lair, but the youthful *SIGURD*, armed with his father's sword and guided by Regin, outwitted the dragon and won his ill-fated treasure.

FARBAUTI ("Cruel striker") was a giant and father of the fire god *LOKI*. According to one tradition, his wife was another giant, Laufey ("Tree island") who gave birth to Loki when hit by a lightning bolt unleashed by Farbauti. Little else is known of Loki's parents.

FENRIR, or Fenris, according to Germanic mythology, was the son of the mischief-making god *LOKI* and the frost giantess *ANGRBODA*. He was the devouring wolf, the beast of *RAGNAROK*, the doom of the gods. His was "an axe-age, a sword-age, a wind-age, a wolf-age, before the wrecking of the world". *ODIN*, the chief of the gods, was destined to become his victim.

Kidnapped by the gods and brought to *ASGARD* where they could keep an eye on him, Fenrir was so savage that only the war god *TYR* dared to feed him. At first Odin was uncertain about the wolf, but when the *NORNS*, the goddesses of destiny, warned him about his own fate, he decided that Fenrir should be restrained. No chain, however, was strong enough to hold the animal. Finally, the dwarfs made a magic fetter called Gleipnir from strange materials such as the roots of a mountain and bird's spittle. Although it seemed to be a silken ribbon, Fenrir would not have it round his neck unless one of the gods put his hand between his jaws as a pledge that it was as harmless as it seemed. Tyr was the only one prepared to risk his hand, and the other gods laughed when the wolf bit it off on finding that the chain could not be broken. Fenrir was then secured to a rock and his

THE EINHERJAR, or "heroic dead", were gathered up from the battlefield by the Valkyries who galloped over the fray, choosing the bravest heroes for Odin's ghostly army. A chosen hero saw a soaring Valkyrie just before the fatal blow. (THE RIDE OF THE VALKYRIES BY W T MAUD, CANVAS, C. 1890.)

mouth was kept open by a sword so he could not bite.

When freed from captivity at Ragnarok, Fenrir was a fearsome spectacle. His vast mouth gaped so wide that the lower jaw touched the ground and the upper one reached the sky, and Odin was swallowed by him.

FENRIS see *FENRIR*

FJALAR and his brother Galar, in Germanic mythology, were the wicked dwarfs who killed the wise man *KVASIR* in order to gain his magic powers. They mixed his blood with honey in a cauldron and made a mead that bestowed wisdom. But Fjalar and Galar lost the wonderful drink to Suttung, a frost giant whose parents they had also killed. Unlike the dwarfs, Suttung was boastful about his

FORSETI, the fair god of justice, was a Solomon-like force for peace. He sat in judgement in his golden hall, Glitnir, and settled the disputes of gods and men, allaying strife and resolving feuds. He never failed to reconcile even the bitterest foes. (ILLUSTRATION BY NICK BEALE, 1995.)

FENRIR (above), the wolf fathered by Loki, was so savage that the gods chained him to an underground rock. Only a magical cord was strong enough to bind him. Here, the brave god Tyr fetters Fenrir at the cost of his own hand, which he placed in the wolf's mouth as a sign of trust. (DIE, 8TH CENTURY.)

FJALAR (below) and his brother Galar slew the wise Kvasir and drained his blood to extract his wisdom. Two glistening bowls and the Kettle of Inspiration contained the magical fluid, which the brothers mixed with honey to produce the golden Mead of Poetry. (ILLUSTRATION BY JAMES ALEXANDER, 1995.)

acquisition and it was not long before the gods heard about the mead. ODIN himself decided that he would go to JOTUNHEIM, the land of the frost giants, and lay hold of the magic drink. Disguised as evil Bolverk, he journeyed to Jotunheim and persuaded the frost giant Baugi to tunnel through a mountain to where Suttung kept the mead under the care of his daughter Gunnlod. Once the hole was drilled, Odin changed his shape from Bolverk's to a snake, and slithered downwards to the hidden treasure as quickly as he could. Reaching the secret cave, he changed himself into a handsome one-eyed giant and for three days and nights he was Gunnlod's lover. The passionate giantess let Odin drink up every drop of the mead, before he turned himself into an eagle and flew back to ASGARD, the home of the gods. There he spat the mead into jars left empty for his return. Suttung gave chase as another eagle, but just failed to catch Odin.

In the account of Kvasir's death, it is clear that this is a myth about fermentation. To put the seal on their peace agreement the two branches of the gods, the AESIR and the VANIR, had spat into a jar, and it was from the spittle that Kvasir had been formed. Spittle, like yeast, causes fermentation, and so when Fjalar and Galar mixed Kvasir's blood with honey in a cauldron they created a magical mead. The connection between inspiration, poetry and wisdom and some form of potent drink occurs in several mythological traditions.

FORSETI was the Germanic god of justice, and was known to the Frisians as Forsite. He was the son of BALDER and Nanna. Both of his parents were killed, his father stabbed by a piece of mistletoe, thrown unwittingly by the blind god HODR, and his mother with a broken heart shortly after this tragic event. Although Forseti plays only a relatively small role in Germanic mythology, we are told in detail that his hall of Glitnir "had pillars of red gold and a roof inlaid with silver." There he sat in judgement and resolved strife.

F

FREYJA, the voluptuous, blue-eyed goddess of love, rode in a chariot drawn by cats, which were symbols of her warm affections. Accompanied by a flock of airborne love spirits, she toured heaven and earth in search of her roving husband, Odur, shedding tears of gold all the while.

(FREYJA BY N J O BLOMMER, CANVAS, 1852.)

FREYJA ("Lady"), sometimes known as Freya or Frea, was the daughter of the sea god *NJORD* in Germanic mythology and sister of *FREYR*. She was an important fertility goddess and a member of the *VANIR*, one of the two branches into which the Germanic gods were divided. After a war the Vanir seem to have been supplanted by the younger *AESIR*, who were led by *ODIN*. When peace was agreed between the two sides, Njord went with Freyr and Freyja to *ASGARD*, where they lived with the Aesir as a token of friendship.

Freyja's greatest treasure was the *BRISINGS'* necklace, which she obtained by sleeping with its four dwarf makers. Her beauty won her many admirers, including *OTTAR*, whom she changed into a boar. She was said to be a sorceress who could fly in a falcon's skin. Some traditions state that, on her arrival in Asgard, she taught the gods the spells and charms of the Vanir.

Both Odin and Freyja took an interest in the heroic dead, dividing the slain between them at the end of every battle. Odin's share went to live in *VALHALLA*, while Freyja's lived in her hall, Sessrumnir. It is possible that Freyja's lost husband Odur, or Od, of whom nothing is known but his name, was Odin. For she was the goddess of lust as well as love, a suitable partner for Odin who was the father of battles and the lover of destruction. (See also *SORCERY AND SPELLS*)

FREYR ("Lord"), sometimes Frey, was the twin brother of the Germanic fertility goddess *FREYJA*. Their father was *NJORD*, the god associated with the wind and the sea. Freyr, with *ODIN* and *THOR*, was one of the principal gods. He was mainly concerned with fertility, having control of sunlight, rain, fruitfulness and peace. His title of Skirr means "shining", and the name of the frost giantess he married, *GERDA*, derives from "field". As late as 1200, Freyr's statue in his temple at Uppsala, Sweden was noted for the size of its penis. Possibly for this reason the Romans had always identified him with Priapus, the virile son of Dionysus and Aphrodite. Although a member of the *VANIR* by descent, Freyr moved to *ASGARD* to live with the *AESIR*, the younger branch of the gods under the leadership of Odin, along with his father Njord and his

FREYJA (below) flew over the earth, sprinkling morning dew and summer sunlight behind her. She shook spring flowers from her golden hair and wept tears which turned to gold, or to amber at sea. She was so beautiful that she was wooed and pursued by all living creatures.

(ILLUSTRATION BY F VON STASSEN, 1914.)

FREYR (right), a gentle god of summer sun and showers, was lord of the fairy realm of Alfheim, home of the Light Elves. Here, he is sailing his ship, Skidbladnir, personifying the clouds. His flashing sword, symbolizing a sunbeam, fought of its own accord. (ILLUSTRATION BY JAMES ALEXANDER, 1995.)

sister Freyja, as a gesture of good-will that had been agreed at the end of the war between the Vanir and the Aesir.

Freyr's myth is about his woo-ing of Gerda, the daughter of the frost giant Gymir. When Freyr first saw Gerda he immediately fell in love with her, and because he did not know how to gain her affection he became ill. Njord became so worried about him that he asked his faithful servant Skirnir to find out what was amiss. Having learned of this love, Skirnir went to *JOTUNHEIM*, the land of the giants, taking two of Freyr's greatest treasures, his magic horse and his magic sword. The servant was instructed to bring Gerda back to Asgard, whether her father liked it or not. On reaching Gymir's hall, Skirnir tried to persuade Gerda to

FRIGG (below), a deity of the atmosphere, spun long pearly webs of cloud from her jewelled distaff which shone in the night sky as the constellation of Frigg's Spinning Wheel. Her heron plumes symbolize her discretion, while her keys signify her divine housewifery. (ILLUSTRATION BY NICK BEALE, 1995.)

declare her love for Freyr in return for "eleven of the apples of youth". She refused both this gift and Skirnir's second offer of one of Odin's arm-rings. Gerda's resolve was only strengthened further when Skirnir then threatened to decapitate her with Freyr's sword. Finally, Skirnir said that he would impose on her an unbreakable spell that would make her a permanent outcast and it was this that per-suaded Gerda to pledge herself to

the fertility god with an agreement to meet Freyr in a forest in nine days' time. In this way the passion of Freyr was fulfilled, though it cost him his horse and sword which he gave to Skirnir. At *RAGNAROK*, the doom of the gods, he sorely missed his mighty magic weapon, since it could fight giants on its own. (See also *TREASURES AND TALISMANS*; *TRAGIC LOVERS*)

FRICKA see FRIGG

FRIGG, also known as Frigga, Frija and Fricka, in Germanic mythology, was the daughter of Fjorgyn, goddess of the earth and atmosphere, wife of *ODIN*, the chief of the gods, and mother of *BALDER*. She has given her name to Friday. Frigg was a fertility goddess who "will tell no fortunes, yet well she knows the fates". When Balder dreamed of impending danger, Frigg extracted a promise from each and every thing, except the mistletoe, that no harm should happen to him. Apparently, the mistletoe appeared such a harmless

plant that she did not bother about it. This proved to be a mistake because the fire god *LOKI* got the blind god *HODR* to throw a branch of mistletoe at Balder which killed him. Frigg's subsequent effort to have her son released from the land of the dead also failed, because Loki refused to mourn on behalf of Balder. Thus it would seem that Frigg was a fertility goddess not unlike the Sumerian deity Inanna, though she lacked that goddess's ability to enter the netherworld.

Frigg has much in common with *FREYJA*. Although her role as consort of Odin shows her to be a devoted wife and mother, she too possesses a falcon skin and has a great passion for gold. It is quite possible that the two goddesses had their origins in a single earth-mother deity.

FRIGGA see FRIGG

FRIJA see FRIGG

FRITHIOF see TRAGIC LOVERS

GEFFINN see GEFION

FRIGG enjoyed the privilege of sitting beside her husband, Odin, on his fabulous throne, Hlidskialf, from where the divine pair could view the nine worlds, witnessing events present and future. A paragon of silence, she never revealed her foreknowledge. (ILLUSTRATION BY H THEAKER, C. 1920.)

GEFION, also known as Gefinn and Gefjon, was a Germanic goddess of fertility akin to *FREYJA*, the sister of the fertility god *FREYR*, and *FRIGG*, the wife of *ODIN*. Appropriately for a goddess of agriculture, Gefion's name is connected with "giving". She was usually imagined as a virgin and as the protector of virgins after their deaths. However, *LOKI* accused Gefion of selling herself, like Freyja, for a necklace.

Her myth concerns ploughing and doubtless recalls the ancient ritual of ploughing a token strip of land each spring. Gefion, disguised as an old beggar, managed to trick King Gylfi of Sweden out of a great tract of land. In return for her hospitality, the king offered Gefion as much of his kingdom as she could plough with four oxen during one day and one night. With the aid of her four giant sons, transformed into oxen, she cut from the mainland the whole island of Zealand, part of present-day Denmark.

GEIRROD was a frost giant, the father of two daughters, *GJALP* and Greip, and was one of *THOR*'s most formidable enemies. It happened that *LOKI*, a constant companion of Thor, had taken the form of a hawk and was captured by Geirrod. The only way Loki could avoid death was to promise to bring Thor to Geirrod's hall without his magic belt and magic hammer which protected the god against frost giants.

Because Thor trusted Loki he went with him to Geirrod's hall. Fortunately, they rested on the way at the home of a friendly giantess named *GRID*, and she warned Thor about the plan while Loki was asleep. She also lent the god her own magic belt of strength, magic iron gloves and magic staff. Thus equipped, Thor arrived at their destination, with Loki hanging as usual on his belt. Geirrod was not at home, but the giant's servants received the visitors. It was not long, though, before Geirrod's two

GEIRROD's (left) immense body, slain by Thor, lay in the City of the Not-Dead, shrouded in cobwebs. Beyond the sleeping giant sparkled the Chamber of Treasures full of jewels and weapons. Here came the Danish hero, Thorkill, years later, on a raid for his king. (ILLUSTRATION BY NICK BEALE, 1995.)

GEFION (above), disguised as a beggar, ploughed a vast field in Sweden with four giant oxen, her supernatural sons. They dragged the tilled field to the coast and floated it across the sea to Denmark, where it formed the island of Zealand. (ILLUSTRATION BY JAMES ALEXANDER, 1995.)

daughters tried to kill the slumbering Thor by lifting up his chair and dashing out his brains on the ceiling. But with the aid of Grid's staff, Thor succeeded in driving the chair downwards and crushed the frost giantesses instead. However, Geirrod himself then appeared in the hall and using a pair of tongs he picked up a red-hot iron ball and threw it at Thor, who caught it in Grid's iron gloves. Angered beyond measure by this extremely discourteous action, Thor threw the still hot and smoking ball back down the hall, straight through an iron pillar and deep into Geirrod's stomach. After this, the thunder god laid about the frost giant's servants with the magic staff.

GERDA, in Germanic mythology, was a beautiful frost giantess and daughter of the giant Gymir, who reluctantly became the wife of *FREYR*, the fertility god. Although initially resistant to the idea, she was persuaded to marry by Freyr's faithful servant *SKIRNIR*, when he threatened to recite a terrible spell. This spell would have made Gerda so ugly than no man would ever come near her again. She would be transformed into "a sight to make the blood run cold". So it was that Gerda met Freyr in a forest after nine nights, representing the nine months of the northern winter. The Aurora Borealis was believed by some to be the radiance of Gerda. (See also *TRAGIC LOVERS*)

GINNUNGAGAP, in Germanic mythology, was a "yawning emptiness" at the time of creation, which lay between the realms of fire and cold. As the warm air from the south met the chill of the north, the ice of Ginnungagap melted and from the drops was formed *YMIR*, the frost giant, and *AUDHUMLA*, the primeval cow. By licking the ice, Audhumla uncovered *BURI*, ancestor of the gods. Buri's three grandsons, *ODIN*, *VILI* and *VE*, killed Ymir and took his body to the centre of Ginnungagap. There they made Midgard, the world of men, from his body. Ymir's flesh became the earth, his bones the mountains, his teeth rocks and stones, his hair the trees and his blood turned into the lakes and seas. The brothers used his skull to form the sky, with four dwarfs named Nordi, Sudri, Austri and Westri holding up the corners.

GJALP ("Howler") was a frost giantess, daughter of *GEIRROD*, who, along with her sister Greip, tried to kill *THOR*, the Germanic thunder god. When Thor, accompanied by the fire god *LOKI*, came to the hall of Geirrod, Gjalp did what she could to harm the visitors. Even before their arrival she added a torrent of her menstrual blood to a river in order to drown Thor and Loki. A well-aimed stone stopped Gjalp and sent her howling home. However, she and Greip then tried to ram the head of sleeping Thor against the rafters by suddenly raising his chair. The thunder god woke just in time to force the chair downwards by using a magic staff. Its massive weight broke the backs of the two giantesses and they died in agony on the floor.

GERDA (above), a frosty beauty, inspired the love of Freyr who sent Skirnir to win her hand. Although he offered her the apples of youth, and revealed his master's glowing portrait reflected in water, she remained unmoved until forced by threat of magic to consent. (ILLUSTRATION BY H THEAKER, C. 1920.)

GJALP (right) stirs up a river into a great flood, engulfing Thor as he wades across. Thor managed to stem the torrent by striking Gjalp with a boulder. He then heaved himself ashore by grasping a mountain ash named "Thor's Salvation". (ILLUSTRATION BY JAMES ALEXANDER, 1995.)

GINNUNGAGAP (right), the primal abyss at the dawn of creation, lay between the icy north and fiery south. Twelve swirling streams gushed into its vacuum and froze into massive ice blocks. In the south, fiery sparks slowly melted the ice, and from the icy droplets slowly emerged a frost giant. (ILLUSTRATION BY NICK BEALE, 1995.)

G

GRENDEL, a man-devouring monster, met his match in the fearless warrior Beowulf, who seized the creature's hairy limb in a vice-like grip and wrenched it from its socket. Howling with pain and rage, Grendel fled back to his watery lair and bled to death. (ILLUSTRATION BY ALAN LEE, 1984.)

GRENDEL was the name of a water monster which was invulnerable to weapons and troubled the kingdom of King Hrothgar of Denmark. One night Grendel, "grim and greedy, brutally cruel", came to the royal hall and ate a sleeping warrior, but a visiting warrior, BEOWULF, held one of the monster's arms in a vice-like grip. In the fierce struggle that ensued, Grendel's arm was torn off and he ran away and bled to death in his watery lair. It was in this lair that, later, Beowulf killed the monster's mother. Grendel's head was so large that when Beowulf brought it back as a trophy to King Hrothgar, he needed the assistance of four men to carry it.

GRID was a kindly frost giantess who helped the Germanic thunder god THOR in his struggle against GEIRROD. Thor had been lured by LOKI, the fire god, into danger without the protection of his magic belt of strength and his magic hammer. Grid loaned Thor her own belt, iron gloves and unbreakable staff to face Geirrod. In some traditions she is said to have borne ODIN a son, the silent god VIDAR, and to have made for him a special shoe which enabled him to stand in the mouth of the wolf FENRIR.

GRIMHILD see SORCERY AND SPELLS

GROA, according to Germanic mythology, was a seeress and the wife of Aurvandil, whose frozen toe THOR turned into a star by throwing it up into the sky. Exactly who this Aurvandil, or Aurvandill, was remains uncertain, though it has been suggested that he may have been a fertility god of the wetlands. Groa herself tried by magic to remove whetstone fragments from Thor's head after his fight with the frost giant HRUNGNIR. They had come from Hrungnir's sharp-edged, three-cornered stone when it had collided with Thor's hammer in mid-air. So excited was Groa, however, by Thor's news about the star and the return of her lost husband that she unfortunately failed to finish the spell, and this was why a few fragments of whetstone remained in Thor's head. Some time after her death, Groa was roused from the grave by her son, Svipdrag, who needed her advice on how he could win the love of the beautiful Menglad.

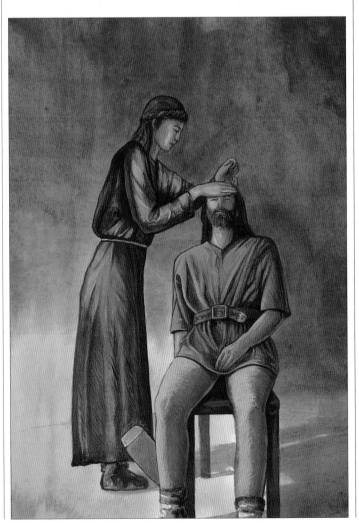

GUNGNIR was the magic spear belonging to ODIN, the leader of the Germanic gods. It was forged by dwarfs, the sons of Ivaldi, at the same time as a wig of spun gold, which the fire god LOKI ordered as a replacement for the golden hair of THOR's wife SIF. Mischievous Loki had cut off her beautiful locks as a joke. Having made the wig, the dwarfs decided to please the gods by using the furnace to make a ship for FREYR and, for Odin, a spear that managed to be both strong and slender, and never missed its mark. It was required in Viking custom that a spear should be thrown over the heads of an enemy before battle commenced, as an entreaty for Odin's aid. When the god hung himself on the cosmic tree YGGDRASIL for nine nights in order to obtain wisdom, he was, just like Christ, stabbed with a spear. (See also TREASURES AND TALISMANS)

GUDRUN see THE VALKYRIES

GUNNER see NORSE HEROES

HARBARD ("grey-beard"), in Germanic mythology, was a surly boatman. Wishing to cross a deep river, the god THOR summoned Harbard to ferry him over, only to be met by insults. Thor could think of no response to Harbard's abuse other than anger, but the boatman remained away from the bank. In his fury, Thor failed to notice that Harbard was his father ODIN. The meeting between the two gods reveals their different characters: Odin, the deceitful troublemaker and braggart; while Thor is hot-tempered but honest.

GROA, a gifted healer, chants charms over Thor in order to loosen the stone splinters lodged in the god's forehead. Feeling relief and gratitude, Thor rashly revealed that her long-lost husband was alive. The happy news so excited Groa that she forgot her spells and so left a splinter in Thor's head. (ILLUSTRATION BY NICK BEALE, 1995.)

GUNGNIR (above) was the name of Odin's spear; both slender and strong, it was unswerving in its flight. The weapon was so sacred that oaths were sworn on its point. Dvalin, the dwarf, forged its head, and Odin made the staff, carving it with magic runes. (ODIN BY R FOGELBERG, MARBLE, C. 1890.)

HEIMDALL

HEIMDALL, or Heimdalr, was the son of nine mothers and the watchman for the Germanic gods. Originally, he may have been an omniscient sky god. He could hear the sound of grass and wool growing, and see for over a hundred miles. He stood upon BIFROST, the three-strand bridge that linked ASGARD and Midgard (heaven and earth respectively). There he stood ready to blow his horn Gjall at the onset of RAGNAROK, during which he was to be the last to fall in single combat with LOKI. Heimdall's name may be related to the concept of a "world tree", as he was thought to be the supreme watchman perched at its top, above the highest rainbow. He disguised himself as RIG, the mortal who established the three social groups: the nobles, the peasants, and the enslaved. Disguised as Rig, the god visited in turn three houses in Midgard and fathered handsome children for the nobility, sturdy children for the peasants and ill-favoured children for the slaves.

HEIMDALR see HEIMDALL

HEIMDALL (right), bright guardian of the Bifrost Bridge, was ever alert, sleeping less than a bird. Gifted with special sight and hearing, he could see for 100 miles by night or day, and hear grass growing on the hillside. With his curved herald's horn, he would summon the gods to Ragnarok. (ILLUSTRATION BY NICK BEALE, 1995.)

GUNGNIR's (below) spear shaft was carved from the sacred wood of Yggdrasil. After gaining wisdom at the World Tree, Odin broke off a bough, and fashioned a perfect staff from its holy wood. Here, the one-eyed, all-seeing god peers through the boughs of the sacred ash. (ILLUSTRATION BY ALAN LEE, 1984.)

TREASURES AND TALISMANS

THE MOST CELEBRATED CRAFTSMEN of the Norse world were wise and gifted dwarfs who laboured underground in caverns studded with gems. With superhuman artistry and secret wisdom, they fashioned fabulous treasures and talismans for gods and heroes. Some of their creations were exquisitely beautiful, such as the Brisingamen necklace; others were supernaturally powerful, such as the silken thread which fettered the fierce wolf, Fenrir. Most indispensable were the gods' wondrous weapons – Thor's boomerang hammer, Mjollnir, and Odin's infallible spear, Gungnir. The tireless dwarfs were also innovative engineers who crafted a collapsible, flying ship for Freyr and a sword that fought of its own accord once drawn. Most amazing of all, perhaps, were their living treasures, the gold-bristled boar, Gullinbursti, and Sif's golden hair which grew naturally. Some precious marvels were created by nature, such as the golden apples of youth. Among mortals, only Volund the smith could match the dwarfs in artistry and craft while, among sorcerers, the Finnish Ilmarinen excelled in magical craft and produced a peerless talisman, the Sampo.

IDUN'S (left) golden apples kept the gods eternally young. The fabulous fruit tree was tended and guarded by the three wise Norns who allowed only Idun, the deity of Spring, to pick the magic fruit. Yet such precious gifts were coveted by the giants who sought to strip the gods of their vigour and youth. Here, the giant Thiassi, disguised as a bird, carries Idun and her apples off in an ill-fated attempt to steal the gods' elixir of life. (ILLUSTRATION BY H THEAKER, C. 1920.)

THE BRISINGAMEN (above) necklace was crafted by four dwarfs with such artistry that it glittered like a constellation of stars in the night sky. Around Freyja's lovely neck it became an emblem of the fruits of the heavens and earth. She, in her turn, produced treasures for the earth whenever she cried, and Freyja wept profusely, especially during her search for her husband, Odur. When her tears fell on rock, they turned to gold, but tears shed at sea turned to amber. (FREYJA BY N J O BLOMMER, DETAIL, CANVAS, 1852.)

MJOLLNIR (left), Thor's wondrous hammer, was never far from his grasp, as seen here in this characteristic pose of the god with his hammer clutched close to his heart. The Mjollnir was used as a fiery thunderbolt, launching shafts of lightning, and as a weapon for smashing giants' skulls. It was a talisman of both creativity and destruction, and was used to hallow both birth and death ceremonies. (BRONZE, 10TH CENTURY.)

GUNGNIR (right), Odin's great spear, never missed its mark. The spear shaft was fashioned by Odin from the sacred ash of Yggdrasil and carved with the god's magic runes. Just as valuable was Odin's fabulous ring, Draupnir, which produced eight similar gold rings every nine days, an everlasting source of wealth and power. (ILLUSTRATION BY H HENDRICH, C. 1906.)

THE SAMPO (below) was forged by Ilmarinen, the Eternal Hammerer of Finnish myth, who hammered out the sky at the dawn of time. Over three days, the talisman was fashioned mysteriously from one swift quill, milk of the fertile cow, a grain of barley and the fleece of a summer lamb. So out of the magical flames of the forge the Sampo was created; it consisted of a flour mill, salt mill and money mill, ensuring lasting prosperity and power. Here, the master smith looks intently into the furnace to see what the fire has produced. (THE FORGING OF THE SAMPO BY A GALLEN-KALLELA, CANVAS, C. 1852.)

WONDROUS LONGSHIPS (above) belonged to both Freyr and Thorstein. The god's ship, Skidbladnir, was crafted by the dwarfs. A personification of the clouds, it glided across land, sea and air. Although massive enough to convey all the gods and an entire host, it could be folded up and pocketed like a handkerchief. Thorstein's fabulous dragon boat, Ellida, was a gift from the sea god, Aegir. Shaped by swelling planks which grew together in the form of a winged dragon, Ellida raced with the whistling wind and outstripped the eagle. The floating fortress was famed far and wide. (ILLUSTRATION BY I J BILIBIN, C. 1900.)

HEL was the daughter of trickster *LOKI*, the fire god, and the frost giantess *ANGRBODA*. She was ruler of the Germanic netherworld (also called Hel), to which she had been banished by *ODIN*, the chief god. Once there, however, her powers were stronger than Odin's, for when Odin's son *BALDER* was killed Hel refused to return him to his parents. Her brothers, *FENRIR* the wolf and *JORMUNGAND* the serpent, were as terrifying as she, though it was Hel and her ghastly home which were adopted by the Christians as the name for their realm of eternal damnation.

The unpleasantness of Hel's realm stands in marked contrast to the pleasurable and enviable after-life that was enjoyed by the heroic dead who dwelt in Odin's wondrous hall *VALHALLA*. However, Hel's subjects were little more than silent attendants of the semi-decomposed queen. She was only partly decomposed because she had the face and body of a living woman, but her thighs and legs were those of a corpse. Hel's throne was known as the Sick Bed and her subjects were "all who died through sickness and old age".

HERMOD leaps bravely into misty Hel on his vain mission to seek Balder's release from death. The great noise made by the hero and his eight-hoofed horse Sleipnir when they crossed the crystal Gioll Bridge, provoked the grim guardian, Modgud, to complain irritably that Hermod must be alive. (ILLUSTRATION BY PETER HURD, 1882.)

HEL, the grim goddess of the dead, listens unimpressed to Hermod's plea to release the much-loved god Balder from her dismal realm. Behind her, kneeling, there are rows of her sad subjects – souls of the old, sick or criminal who suffered ceaseless cold, pain and hunger in their cheerless, dreary home. (ILLUSTRATION BY JAMES ALEXANDER, 1995.)

HERMOD, in Germanic mythology, was the son of *ODIN* and *FRIGG*, and brother of *BALDER*. Rather like the Greek god Hermes and the Roman Mercury, he acted as a divine messenger. Hermod also shared these gods' interest in the dead, for it was he who was sent to *HEL* after Balder's death to ask for his brother's release. He rode there on Odin's famous horse, the eight-legged *SLEIPNIR*. When Hel refused to let Balder go until everything wept for him, Hermod was allowed to take back to *ASGARD* the arm-ring which Odin had fastened to Balder's body as a memento.

Hermod nearly met his own death on a journey to Midgard, the land of men. He was sent there by Odin to consult a Finn named Rossthiof about his worries concerning the future. He was saved by magic, however, and returned to reassure his father as best he could.

HIMINBRIOTER see *HIMINRJOT*

HIMINRJOT, or Himinbrioter, ("Sky Bellower") was the head of a gigantic black ox. The ox belonged to *HYMIR* with whom *THOR* went fishing for *JORMUNGAND*, the sea serpent. Thor had no trouble in breaking Himinrjot's neck, despite the animal's vast size, and used its head to bait his hook. Jormungand rose for this delicacy, but the head stuck in his throat. Thor would have landed the prize had not the sight of the serpent rising from the depths of the sea terrified Hymir. In the confusion that ensued Hymir was able to cut the great sea serpent free.

HOD see *HODR*

HODR, sometimes Hodur or Hod, the son of *ODIN* and *FRIGG*, was the blind god of Germanic mythology. In the Icelandic tradition, Hodr unintentionally killed his brother *BALDER*. When Balder was troubled by dreams of his coming death, his mother Frigg exacted a promise from each and every thing not to do her son any harm. A sole exception was the mistletoe, a plant the goddess considered to be too insignificant. The trickster god *LOKI* learned about the mistletoe, however, and guided Hodr's hand when he threw it at his brother. The branch of mistletoe went straight through Balder, who fell down dead. Once it became clear that Balder would have to stay in the land of the dead, Hodr was sent to join him as a punishment. In a very different version of the story, Hodr and Balder are rivals for the hand of Nanna, and Balder is portrayed as a hateful figure. Their conflict is finally resolved when Hodr kills Balder with a magic sword. This Danish version shows the brothers in a very different light.

HERMOD (below) spurs his fabulous steed to assail the barred gate of Hel. Within, Balder can be seen waiting stoically beside an alarming creature, who is possibly one of the starved inmates of Hel. Balder, who knew the future well, knew that he was destined to remain in cheerless Hel for ever. (ILLUSTRATION FROM THE PROSE EDDA, 1760.)

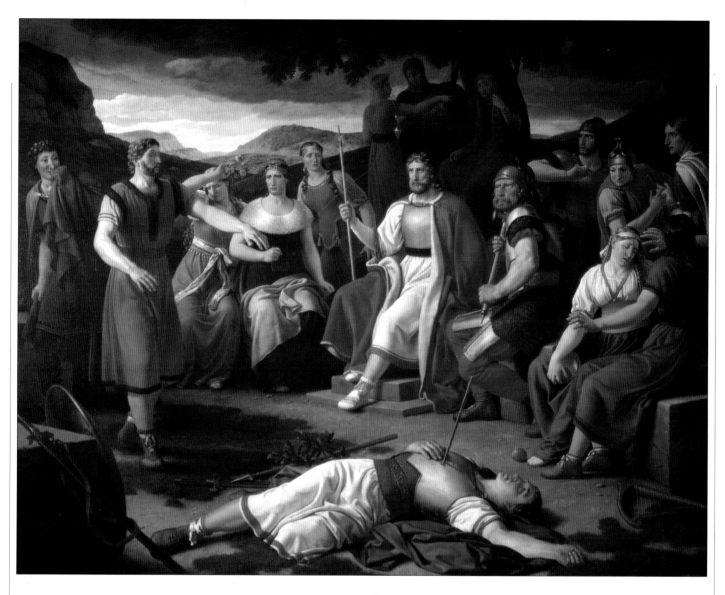

After *RAGNAROK*, the doom of the gods, "Balder and Hodr return from the world of the dead", reconciled, to a new earth. That these two sons of Odin are mentioned together here shows their importance in Icelandic mythology. First there is Balder, handsome and kind, almost too good for the world. He represents the positive side of his father's nature, as the god of magic and inspiration. The second brother, Hodr, is the opposite of Odin's foresight. Instead, he represents his blind spot, the side of his nature that takes delight in

death. Not for nothing was Balder slain by his blind brother in a game that involved throwing potentially dangerous objects.

HODUR see HODR

HOENIR see HONIR

HOGNI and his brother, Gunner, befriended the hero *SIGURD*, who owned a famous but ill-fated fortune generated by a magic ring called Andvarinaut. Under the ring's spell, Sigurd had unwittingly betrayed the Valkyrie *BRYNHILD*. She asked the brothers for help, and, bewitched by the curse, they arranged Sigurd's death. However, when Hogni and Gunner inherited Sigurd's fortune, they in turn were doomed and suffered at the hands of the Atli who coveted the gold. (See also *NORSE HEROES*)

HONIR, or Hoenir, according to Germanic mythology, was a member of the *AESIR* group of gods and brother of *ODIN*, the chief god. Apart from a terrible inability to make up his mind, his other prominent characteristic was said to be his long-leggedness. Sent to live among the *VANIR* as a token of goodwill after peace was agreed between the two warring branches of the gods, Honir unfortunately proved to be a grave disappointment to his new companions, who became increasingly angry at the way he appeared always to rely on his fellow Aesir, the wise *MIMIR*, when it came to making decisions of any kind. The Vanir therefore killed Mimir and sent his head back to the Aesir. In some versions of the Germanic creation story, it was believed that Honir was the god who gave humans their senses.

HREIDMAR, or Reidmar, according to Germanic mythology, was a magician-farmer and the father of *REGIN*, *FAFNIR* and *OTTER*. When Otter, who was a shape-changer, was killed accidentally by *LOKI*, Hreidmar demanded to be compensated and told Loki to obtain enough gold to cover Otter's flayed skin, inside and out. The wily fire god seized the dwarf *ANDVARI*'s treasure, but the dwarf placed a curse upon it. Hreidmar was so pleased with the gold that he did not worry about the curse. But his second son, Fafnir, came to covet the treasure and killed him for it. Fafnir changed into a dragon to guard the gold and Regin asked *SIGURD* to slay him and recover the treasure, but he was killed as well.

HRUNGNIR, in Germanic mythology, was the strongest of the frost giants and owner of a powerful stallion named Gullfaxi, or Golden Mane. He encountered *ODIN* on one of the god's journeys through the nine worlds and challenged him to a horse race. Mounted on eight-legged *SLEIPNIR*, Odin won a narrow victory over Hrungnir on Golden Mane. By this time, the two had ridden to *ASGARD*, the divine stronghold, where Hrungnir was invited to rest before returning to *JOTUNHEIM*, the land of the giants. But Hrungnir drank too much strong ale and became arrogant. He even threatened to carry *VALHALLA*, the hall in which the honoured dead lived with Odin, off to Jotunheim on his back and to kill

HRUNGNIR (left), a mighty frost giant with a stony heart and skull, foolishly balances on his stone shield, believing that his expected foe, Thor, plans to attack him from below. Fully exposed to the impact of Thor's crushing hammer, the giant tries to deflect the hammer with his whetstone. (ILLUSTRATION BY JAMES ALEXANDER, 1995.)

HUGI (above) outstrips his rival Thialfi, an athletic warrior, competing in a contest of skills between gods and giants. Try as he would, Thialfi could not outrun his frosty rival who gathered speed at every step for, unknown to Thialfi, Hugi was an illusion symbolizing Thought, ever faster than action. (ILLUSTRATION BY JAMES ALEXANDER, 1995.)

all the gods, except *FREYJA* and *SIF*. At this point the giant-slayer *THOR* returned and waved his magic hammer at Hrungnir, but the frost giant, understanding that he would be easily killed without his own weapons, challenged Thor to a duel on the border between Asgard and Jotunheim. No one had met the thunder god in single combat before. Thor accepted eagerly, even though Hrungnir's head, heart and shield were made of stone.

When the frost giants heard about the forthcoming duel, they were both proud and anxious: proud that Hrungnir had challenged Thor, but anxious lest the god slay the most powerful of their number. So they made out of clay a man so huge that the thunder god would shake with fright when he first caught sight of him. The heart of a dead mare was used to animate the clay giant, whom they called Mist Calf. Alongside Mist Calf stood Hrungnir, awaiting the arrival of Thor. The frost giant knew that he had to avoid his opponent's hammer, and he held his sharp whetstone in readiness. As soon as Thor was in range, he hurled his magic weapon at Hrungnir, who swiftly launched his own sharp-edged, three-cornered stone in Thor's direction. The weapons met in mid-air. Although the hammer shattered the whetstone and went

on to crush Hrungnir's skull, a number of stone fragments lodged in Thor's head and he was also pinned beneath one of the fallen Hrungnir's legs. After this heroic incident, Thor became known as "Hrungnir's skull splitter".

HUGI ("Thought"), in Germanic mythology, was a young frost giant who outran *THOR*'s human servant *THIALFI* in a race. The story of Thor's journey to the stronghold of *UTGARD* in the land of the frost giants is full of magic. The race between Hugi and Thialfi was but one incident in this strange adventure, which shows Thor to be an ineffectual strong man in the face of cunning spells. Throughout the journey the trickster *LOKI*, the god of fire, had cause to remind Thor of the superiority of brain over brawn. At one point Thor, Loki, Thialfi and his sister *ROSKVA* inadvertently slept in the thumb of an empty glove belonging to the enormous frost giant *SKRYMIR*, mistaking it for a vast hall. When he woke, Skrymir warned them that at Utgard there were giants even greater than he. Sure enough, when the travellers reached Utgard, they were unable to see the top of its battlements

without pressing the crowns of their heads on the napes of their necks. Inside the great fortress Thor and his companions failed in a number of tests, the thunder god himself being wrestled down on one knee by an "old, old woman". He also failed to empty a drinking horn, only to learn afterwards how its other end was in the sea. At the end of their adventure, however, the travellers saw that Skrymir and Utgard were no more than magic creations sent out by the frightened frost giants to mystify mighty Thor.

HUGINN ("Thought") and Muninn ("Memory") were the ravens of *ODIN*, the chief Germanic god. In order to be informed about events in the nine worlds, Odin sent the ravens out every day to see and hear all that happened there. They would then return to rest on Odin's shoulders and tell him what they had observed.

HYMIR ("Dark One") was a frost giant and, according to some traditions, father of the war god *TYR*. Hymir had an enormous cauldron, so deep that it could brew ale for all the gods. Without this huge vessel, there was no way that the sea god

AEGIR could offer hospitality to *ODIN* and his companions, so Tyr and *THOR* were sent to fetch it. When they arrived at Hymir's hall, Tyr's mother advised them to hide until she had explained their presence. Hymir found them and offered them a meal, though he felt uneasy. Thor astonished the assembled company by eating two whole oxen by himself. The next day their host suggested they go fishing if they wanted to eat again. Together they put to sea in Hymir's boat, Thor baiting his colossal hook with the head of *HIMINRJOT*, the giant's black ox. When the sea monster

JORMUNGAND took this bait and Thor set about its head with his hammer, Hymir shook with terror. In the confusion Jormungand tore itself free of the great hook and sank bleeding beneath the surface of the waves. Two whales had to suffice for food instead.

Back in Hymir's hall, relations between host and guest quickly deteriorated into violence. Goblets were thrown before Thor left with the gigantic cauldron. When Hymir and some frost giants attempted to follow him in order to regain the cauldron, Thor used his hammer to such effect that all were killed.

HUGINN (left), one of Odin's fabulous ravens, whose name means Thought, was an airborne gatherer of news. Along with his brother raven, Muninn, or Memory, he flew through the nine worlds collecting information. They would then fly back to Odin and whisper the latest news into his ear. (ILLUSTRATION FROM THE PROSE EDDA, 1760.)

HYMIR and Thor (below) forage for food on a fated fishing trip. Thor's tantalizing bait attracted the monstrous water serpent, Jormungand, which delighted the god who battled furiously with his giant catch. When the struggle threatened to capsize the boat, however, Hymir, in fear, cut the line. (ILLUSTRATION FROM THE PROSE EDDA, 1760.)

I

IDUN, Idunnor or Iduna, was, in Germanic mythology, the goddess who guarded the apples of youth. She was the wife of *BRAGI*, the god of poetry. When *LOKI*, the fire god, was captured by the frost giant *THIASSI*, he had to promise to steal the apples from Idun to secure his release. On his return to *ASGARD*, therefore, Loki told Idun that he had discovered apples of much better quality growing nearby, and so the goddess trustingly accompanied him into the forest, where, in the shape of an eagle, Thiassi awaited his prey. He took Idun and her apples in his claws and flew to *JOTUNHEIM*, the land of the frost giants. The loss of the apples at first caused the gods to become weak and old, with bleary eyes and loose

IDUN guarded a fabulous fruit tree, which produced life-giving apples. Here, she hands out her precious gifts to the ever-youthful gods from her inexhaustible casket. The mythic tradition of the golden apple, symbolizing immortality and fertility, can be found in both ancient Greek and Celtic cultures. (ILLUSTRATION BY J PENROSE, C. 1890.)

skin. Then their minds began to weaken, as a general fear of death settled on Asgard. At last *ODIN* gathered his remaining strength and found Loki. By threat of magic he compelled Loki to bring back Idun and her apples.

Loki flew to Jotunheim as a falcon, changed Idun into a nut and carried her home. The frost giant gave chase as an eagle, but he was burned to death by fires placed along the tops of Asgard's mighty walls. Loki then restored Idun to her true shape and she gave magic apples to the ailing gods. (See also *TREASURES AND TALISMANS*)

IDUNA see *IDUN*

JORMUNGAND (left), the serpent son of Loki, was hurled into the icy ocean by Odin. There he grew to such a monstrous size that he encircled Midgard and threatened sailors throughout the oceans. Here, the World Serpent rises to a bait of ox head, dangling from Thor's fishing line. (ILLUSTRATION FROM THE PROSE EDDA, 1760.)

JOTUNHEIM (right), the home of the frost giants, was a snow-covered wasteland on the ocean edge, possibly near the North Pole. It was a realm of mists, blizzards and roaring winds. From here the frost giants directed blasts of wind to nip the buds of spring. (ILLUSTRATION BY NICK BEALE, 1995.)

IDUNNOR see *IDUN*

INGEBORG see *TRAGIC LOVERS*

JEZI BABA see *BABA YAGA*

JORMUNGAND, in Germanic mythology, was the serpent son of *LOKI*, god of fire, and the frost giantess *ANGRBODA*, and brother of *FENRIR* and *HEL*. *ODIN* arranged for these monstrous children to be kidnapped and brought to *ASGARD*. He then threw Jormungand into the ocean, where he grew so long that he encircled the earth, and was known as the Midgard Serpent. At *RAGNAROK* Jormungand was to come on to the earth and be slain by *THOR*. (See also *RAGNAROK*)

JOTUNHEIM was the land given to the frost giants by *ODIN* and his brothers at the Creation. With its stronghold of *UTGARD*, it was one of the nine worlds sheltered by the cosmic tree *YGGDRASIL*. The others were *ASGARD*, the home of the

AESIR, one branch of the gods; Vanaheim, the home of the *VANIR*, the other branch of the divine family; Alfheim, the land of the light elves; Nidavellir, the land of the dwarfs; Midgard, the home of humankind; Svartalfheim, the land of the dark elves; *HEL*, the realm of the unworthy dead; and cold Niflheim beneath Yggdrasil's roots. A mountainous region of freezing cold, Jotunheim was variously described as being inside Midgard, the land of mortals, or over the sea.

JUMALA was the creator god of Finnish mythology and their supreme deity. Very little is known about him, except that the oak tree was sacred to him. He was later replaced by Ukko, also a supreme god, but a deity of the sky and the air, who allowed the rain to fall. Ukko's wife was Akka, which suggests a link with *MADDER-AKKA*, the creator goddess of the Lapps.

KIED KIE JUBMEL was a stone god worshipped by the Lapps, the northernmost people of Europe. Reindeer were sacrificed to Kied Kie Jubmel as late as the seventeenth century to ensure success in the hunt. He seems to have been regarded as "lord of the herds". Among the Swedes he was known as Storjunka, or "Great Lord".

KREIMHILD see *TRAGIC LOVERS*

LEMINKAINEN (above) was slain and dismembered during one of his exploits. But his magician mother gathered him up and restored him to life. Here she calls upon a bee to bring life-giving honey from beyond the highest heaven. (LEMINKAINEN'S MOTHER BY A GALLEN-KALLELA, CANVAS, C.1890.)

KULLERVO see *SORCERY AND SPELLS*

KVASIR was a wise man in Germanic mythology. His name means "spittle" and recalls his creation when the gods spat into a jar to mark the end of conflict between two branches of the divine family, the *VANIR* and the *AESIR*. The Aesir then took the jar and Kvasir was made from the spittle. Renowned for his great wisdom, he travelled the world and wherever he went people stopped what they were doing to listen to him. He was killed by two dwarfs, *FJALAR* and Galar, who wanted his wisdom. They mixed his blood with honey in order to make a wonderful mead which gave the gift of poetry to everyone who drank it.

LEIB-OLMAI ("Alder man") was a Lapp bear god. At bear festivals hunters used to sprinkle their faces with an extract of alder bark. As the protector of bears, Leib-Olmai required certain prayers before he would allow any man to kill a bear.

LEMINKAINEN ("Lover") was one of the heroes of Finnish epic. As a child, he was bathed by his mother three times in one summer night and nine times in one autumn night to ensure that he would become a wise adult, gifted

KVASIR (right), a character endowed with wondrous wisdom, was created from the spittle of the gods. He travelled the world inspiring gods and mortals with his sense and wisdom. After his death his blood was used to make a mead of inspiration. (ILLUSTRATION FROM THE PROSE EDDA, 1760.)

with a talent for song. A carefree young man, many of his adventures involve the pursuit of women and he accompanied *VAINAMOINEN* on a journey to the land of Pohja in search of wives. His most dangerous exploit was an attempt to kill the swan of *TUONI*, the god of the dead. Failing to protect himself with magic, he was torn apart by Tuoni's son and his remains were scattered in the river. But his magician mother put his body back together again and restored him to life. (See also *NORSE HEROES*)

NORSE HEROES

THE VIKINGS were famed for their fighting spirit, facing death and doom with vigour and courage. Their hardy heroism was doubtless shaped by the crushing Nordic climate, but also by a stoic fatalism. While accepting the inevitability of death on the field and doom at the end of the world, the Norsemen fought with undiminished spirit. For the Vikings, word-fame was everything, redeeming and surviving a hero's death. After death, the bravest heroes went to Valhalla where they awaited the fated and fatal showdown at Ragnarok. No less than the heroes, the Norse gods were heroic, facing doom at Ragnarok with fighting spirit. Finnish heroes were quite as determined and brave in their way, though perhaps less grand and stoic. Armed with magical forces, they battled with incantations rather than force of arms. For the Finns, death was not always final: Leminkainen had more than one life, while aged Vainamoinen could always slip out of a tight corner by shifting shape.

GUNNER AND HOGNI (left), the Nibelung brothers, died gallantly though neither lived a flawless life. Drawn into the web of tragedy woven by a cursed ring, they slew the peerless hero Sigurd, and hoarded his gold. When seized by Atli, who coveted their gold, they refused to surrender under threat of death. Hogni died laughing as his heart was cut out; and Gunner, here, cast into a serpent's pit with bound hands, played his harp with his feet, defying death to the last.
(WOOD CARVING, 12TH CENT.)

THOR (right), supernaturally strong and armed with the magical Mjollnir, was a formidable foe. Being neither immortal nor invulnerable, he fought with a fearless spirit, slaying giants with effortless ease and reckless rage. Along with some of the other gods, Thor was destined to die heroically at Ragnarok, after putting up a fierce fight and slaying his arch-foe, the World Serpent. (THOR AND THE GIANTS BY M E WINGE, CANVAS, DETAIL, C. 1890.)

SIGURD (above), the most famous of Iceland's heroes, slew the terrible dragon, Fafnir. Armed with his father's invincible sword, Sigurd hid in a hole in the dragon's slime track and, as Fafnir slithered across on his daily trip to the foul forest pool, thrust his sword into its belly. The bloated creature had grown increasingly monstrous in shape and character; all the better to guard his cursed treasure. Although Sigurd's heroic deed won him fame and fortune, his life from then on was blighted by the curse that came with the ill-fated treasure. (ILLUSTRATION BY ALAN LEE, 1984.)

SIGMUND THE VOLSUNG (right) proved his heroic status by drawing forth a magical sword thrust into the Branstock oak by Odin. With this sword he won fame throughout Scandinavia, but also provoked the envy of his brother-in-law, Siggeir, who resolved to slay all the Volsungs. All ten sons were tied to forest trees, prey to the beasts of the forest. Only Sigmund escaped, by biting off a wolf's tongue, and sought vengeance for his kinsmen. (ILLUSTRATION BY P WILSON, C. 1900.)

L

LESHY (left), spirit of the forest, though he appeared in the shape of a man, cast no shadow where he walked and could easily camouflage himself among his forest trees, sometimes as small as a leaf, sometimes as tall as the tallest tree. A jealous guardian of his leafy realm, he loved to lead trespassers astray. (ILLUSTRATION BY M VON SCHWIND, C. 1860.)

LIF (right) and her mate, Lifthrasir, took shelter at the end of the world in the sunlit branches of the cosmic ash tree, Yggdrasil. After the earth had been purged by fire and flood, the young couple climbed down and a new age dawned, a fresh green age in which they were destined to repopulate the world and so renew the human race. (ILLUSTRATION BY NICK BEALE, 1995.)

THE LESHY, also known as Lesovik and Lesiye, was the Slavonic spirit of the forest who led travellers and hunters astray in the woods. Although human in form, he had a long green beard and cast no shadow. His chief attribute, however, was his ability to change size: he could become as small as a mouse or as tall as the highest tree. Every October the Leshy went into a kind of hibernation, disappearing from his woodland home until the following spring, when he would return wilder and noisier than ever.

LESIYE see THE LESHY

LESOVIK see THE LESHY

LIF and Lifthrasir ("Life" and "Eager for Life") were the man and woman who were to hide in the cosmic ash tree YGGDRASIL at RAGNAROK, the doom of the gods. They were destined to survive this catastrophe and then repopulate a new world, which would rise from the sea like a volcanic island. "The bellowing fire will not scorch them; it will not even touch them, and their food will be the morning dew. Through the branches they will see a new sun burn as the world ends and starts again."

LIFTHRASIR see LIF

LODDFAFNIR, in Germanic mythology, was a man who learned the wisdom of the gods. He visited the Well of URD, where the gods held their daily assembly, and stayed in VALHALLA, ODIN's hall. His myth comprises a retelling of the knowledge he gathered there. It is an interesting mixture of commonsensical advice about good conduct and superstitions concerning the avoidance of witchcraft.

LOKI, sometimes Lopt, was the Germanic fire god and son of the giants FARBAUTI and Laufey. He was a mischief-maker, trickster and shape-changer, and grew progressively more evil until eventually the gods bound him in a cave until the coming of RAGNAROK, the end of the world. Boredom was a problem for Loki, who "was tired of the string of days that unwound without a knot or a twist in them".

The fact that his parents were giants may help to explain his tendency towards evil deeds. He

LOKI helped to precipitate a cycle of violence by callously slaying Otter for his fur. To appease Otter's father, Loki stole a dwarf's treasure, invoking his bitter curse. Here, Loki helps Odin quieten the raging dwarf, while at the top, Otter's brothers see a weeping Norn, which was an omen of doom. (ILLUSTRATION BY F VON STASSEN, 1914.)

simply could not help playing tricks and exposing the gods to danger, although it was often his quick-wittedness that afterwards saved them. Loki, for instance, brought about the loss and return of *IDUN* and her apples of youth. Without these magic fruit, the gods were subject to the ravages of time like everyone else. On occasion Loki was even prepared to risk serious harm to his companion *THOR*, the thunder god. When Loki led Thor unarmed to the hall of the frost giant *GEIRROD*, only the loan of weapons from the kindly frost giantess *GRID* saved the thunder god. Loki tricked his friend because the price of his own release by Geirrod had been delivery of the thunder god into his power.

Yet it was Loki who devised the novel scheme to get back Thor's magic hammer after it was stolen by dwarfs and passed into the hands of the frost giant *THRYM*. The price for the hammer's return, Loki discovered, was the hand of *FREYJA*, the fertility goddess. He therefore persuaded Thor to go to Thrym dressed in Freyja's clothes. When Thrym took out the magic hammer, Thor seized it and laid low all the frost giants present.

Loki was married twice, first to the giant *ANGRBODA* and then to *SIGYN*, with whom he had two sons, *VALI* and Narvi. His monstrous children by Angrboda were *FENRIR*, *JORMUNGAND* and *HEL*, ruler of the underworld: all fearsome representatives of the evil side of his nature. Even after he brought about the death of *ODIN*'s son *BALDER*, the gods continued to tolerate his presence in *ASGARD*. But when he arrived at *AEGIR*'s feast and began to torment everybody present with insults and sneers, their patience came to an end.

To escape their wrath Loki changed himself into a salmon. From his high seat in Asgard, however, Odin located the fish and mounted an expedition to catch it. Loki was then placed in a dark cave. His son Vali was changed into a wolf, who immediately attacked his brother Narvi and killed him. Narvi's intestines were then used to bind Loki beneath the dripping mouth of a venomous snake. In this dreadful prison, the god awaited Ragnarok. Then he was to emerge to lead the army of evil in their final battle with the gods, when Loki would meet his own end at the hands of *HEIMDALL*. (See also *RAGNAROK*)

LOPT see *LOKI*

LUONNOTAR (which probably means "Daughter of Nature") was the creator goddess of the Finns. At the beginning there was only Luonnotar "all alone in a vast emptiness". Later she floated for centuries on the cosmic ocean, until one day a bird made a nest on her knees and began to hatch some eggs. But the goddess became excited and upset the nest, with the result that from the broken shells of the eggs the heavens and the earth were formed. The yolks became the sun, and the whites the moon. Scattered fragments of these eggs were transformed into the stars. Afterwards Luonnotar fashioned the continents and the seas, and gave birth to *VAINAMOINEN*, the Finnish hero.

MADDER-AKKA and her male companion Madder-Atcha were, according to the Lapps, the divine couple who created humankind. Madder-Atcha was responsible for the soul and Madder-Akka for the body. The child they made was then placed in the womb of its earthly mother. Their three daughters were involved with procreation as well. Sarakka supported women during childbirth; if a male child was to be born, Juksakka ensured that the baby changed from its originally female gender, while Uksakka, who lived underground, looked after the interests of the new-born child. See also *JUMALA*.

LOKI (above), the trickster god, was at first just a playful prankster, but became so dark and twisted that the gods realized he was evil and resolved to imprison him. Loki was eventually bound to a rock, with his face exposed to the fiery drops of a snake's venom. (ILLUSTRATION BY D PENROSE, C. 1870.)

LUONNOTAR (below), a primal goddess, grew restless in the heavens and slipped into the cosmic sea, where she drifted until an eagle built a nest on her knee. When she accidentally upset the nest, its eggs broke and formed the earth and sky, sun, moon and stars. (ILLUSTRATION BY NICK BEALE, 1995.)

MAGNI ("Mighty") was the son of *THOR*, the Germanic thunder god, and the giantess Jarnsaxa, and brother of Modi. After his duel with *HRUNGNIR*, the strongest of the frost giants, Thor fell wounded to the ground, as fragments of whetstone had lodged in his head. He was also unable to move because one of Hrungnir's lifeless legs pinned him to the ground. Even worse, Thor wetted himself when he noticed the clay giant Mist Calf. Insult was nearly added to injury when, at the age of three years, Magni proved strong enough to free his father Thor, even though none of the gods had been able to shift Hrungnir's leg. "It's a pity I didn't come sooner," Magni commented. "If I had met this giant first, he would be fallen to my bare fists." Although *ODIN* was rather put out by young Magni's intervention, Thor showed his gratitude by giving the young frost giant Hrungnir's magnificent horse, Golden Mane. After *RAGNAROK*, the doom of the gods, Magni and Modi together would inherit Thor's magic hammer, *MJOLLNIR*.

MATI SYRA ZEMLYA ("Moist Earth Mother") was the Slavonic earth goddess. Archaeological evidence suggests that her worship may have originated in the basin of the River Don as much as 30,000 years ago. Believed to possess the ability to predict the future and to settle disputes wisely, she was an object of veneration up to the early years of the twentieth century, when Russian peasant women were still performing elaborate rites in order to summon her presence to protect them from disease.

MENU, or Menulis, was the Baltic moon god. The sun was imagined as the goddess *SAULE*, the patroness of green snakes. The Letts believed that the stars were the children of Menu and Saule. The Morning Star, however, was said to have been the child of a love affair between Saule and *PERKUNO*, the thunder god. For this reason the moon god, in shame and anger, avoided his spouse, and appeared only by night, while the sun goddess was happy to be seen all through the day.

MAGNI and his brother, Modi, stride across the sunlit Plain of Ida at the dawn of a fresh green age, after the world destruction of Ragnarok. Magni ("Mighty") swings Thor's sacred hammer, while Modi ("Courage") follows behind. (ILLUSTRATION BY JAMES ALEXANDER, 1995.)

MATI SYRA ZEMLYA was invoked by Slavic farmers at harvest time. They entered their fields at dawn and blessed the earth with libations of hemp oil. Bowing to the east, west, north and south, they invoked the primal deity, each time soaking the earth with oil. (ILLUSTRATION BY NICK BEALE, 1995.)

MENULIS see *MENU*

MIMIR, in Germanic mythology, was a wise god sent by the *AESIR* to the *VANIR* in order to seal the peace after these two branches of the divine family tired of war. Because the Vanir felt that they had been cheated, they cut off Mimir's head and sent it back to the Aesir. *ODIN*, however, smeared the severed head with herbs so that it would never rot. He then recited a charm over it to restore its power of speech. Later, Mimir's head was placed by Odin to guard a magic well under the root of the cosmic tree *YGGDRASIL*. To gain Mimir's wisdom, which comprised "many truths unknown to any other person", Odin gave one of his eyes for permission to drink at the well.

MJOLLNIR was the magic hammer of the Germanic thunder god *THOR*. Made by the dwarfs Brokk and Eitri, it was an instrument of destruction, fertility and resurrection. In Thor's hands Mjollnir was the gods' certain protection against their enemies, the frost giants. That is why the gods were so worried when the frost giant *THRYM* stole it. The price for its return was the hand of *FREYJA*, the fertility goddess. Dressed in Freyja's clothes and accompanied by the trickster god *LOKI*, Thor went to Thrym's hall. Since it was customary to ask a blessing on any marriage by placing the hammer on the knees of the bride, Thrym ordered it to be brought out. But no sooner had Thor got hold of Mjollnir than he jumped up and crushed the frost giant's skull with a mighty blow.

Mjollnir's powers as a restorer of life were revealed on a journey made by Thor to the frost giants' stronghold of *UTGARD*, when he used it to reconstitute from skin and bones two goats which had been eaten the night before. The magic hammer was also used at funerals. When the fire was lit round the pyre of *BALDER* and

MIMIR serves Odin a draught from his wondrous Fountain of Wisdom. The price demanded for this privilege was one eye, symbolizing the sacrifice of one view for another, greater vision. Odin's eye floated in the fountain, a symbol of the full moon, beside the crescent moon of Heimdall's horn. (ILLUSTRATION BY NICK BEALE, 1995.)

Nanna, Thor raised his hammer and chanted certain magic words to consecrate the ceremony.

After *RAGNAROK*, the day of doom and the end of the world, ownership of Mjollnir passed to Thor's sons *MAGNI* and Modi. (See also *TREASURES AND TALISMANS*)

MOKKURALFI, or Mist Calf,

was a gigantic clay giant. He was made from the clay bed of a river by frost giants in order to terrify *THOR*, the thunder god. This occurred just before Thor met *HRUNGNIR*, the strongest of the frost giants, in single combat. Mist Calf was animated by the heart of a mare, but it proved inadequate for the task. Though the creature towered into the clouds, it was very slow-moving

and its legs were vulnerable to attack. On the day of the duel, Thor killed Hrungnir but wet himself at the sight of Mist Calf. His human servant *THIALFI* was less impressed, however, and swung his axe at the clay giant's legs. When Mist Calf toppled backwards, his fall shook *JOTUNHEIM*, the land of the frost giants.

MUNDILFARI was a man who

offended *ODIN*. When Odin, along with his brothers *VILI* and *VE*, carved the world out of the carcass of *YMIR*, the original frost giant, they solved the problem of its illumination by using sparks and glowing embers from the sun, moon and stars. Mundilfari, who lived in Midgard, had a son and a daughter so handsome and beautiful that he called one Moon and the other Sun. The gods were angered by this comparison. Odin snatched the brother and sister from Midgard and turned them into constellations to guide the real heavenly bodies on their daily and nightly journeys across the sky.

MJOLLNIR (left), symbolizing Thor's thunderbolt, glowed red-hot at the mallet end, and could only be held by an iron gauntlet. It was not just destructive, but also creative and hallowed weddings and births. The exquisite, whirling patterns of Viking art beautifully depict the blazing eyes of the god. (SILVER PENDANT, 10TH CENTURY.)

MUNDILFARI (below) named his lovely children after the sun and moon, angering the gods with his arrogance. The children were made to drive the heavenly chariots across the sky. At left, the moon is drawn by All-Swift, while two eager steeds, Early Waker and Rapid Goer, pull the larger sun chariot. (ILLUSTRATION BY GLENN STEWARD, 1995.)

N

MYESYATS was the moon deity of Slavonic myth. Some traditions represent him as the cold, bald-headed uncle of the sun god *DAZHBOG*. In others, Myesyats is a beautiful woman, the consort of Dazhbog and mother by him of the stars. Every spring the divine pair are remarried, but in the autumn Dazhbog leaves his bride and only returns to her after the cold winter months have passed.

NERTHUS was a Germanic goddess, whose cult was described by the Roman writer Tacitus in the first century AD. According to him, she was an important mother goddess who had a sacred grove on a Frisian island. At regular intervals Nerthus travelled inland along a recognized route, her image placed in an ox cart and attended by a priest. During these sacred journeys peace was expected to prevail because "all iron was put away". At a certain lake the goddess bathed,

NERTHUS rides in a triumphal procession, during her biannual fertility festival. Bedecked with flowers, her chariot was drawn by two heifers, which symbolized primal motherhood and abundance. The people honoured her by laying aside all iron tools and weapons and donning festive dress. (ILLUSTRATION BY JAMES ALEXANDER, 1995.)

and afterwards slaves who had helped in this ritual were drowned in Nerthus' honour. Sacrifice by drowning was a practice also favoured by the ancient Slavs in eastern Europe. The name of the goddess may have meant "power-ful one" because it refers to strength. Quite possibly Tacitus was describing a local cult of *FREYJA*. Some versions of the myths of *ASGARD*, home of the gods, suggest that Nerthus was sister and wife to *NJORD*, the sea god, and mother of Freyja and *FREYR*.

NIDHOGG, in Germanic mythology, was the dragon living at one of the three roots of the cosmic tree *YGGDRASIL*. The freezing mist and darkness of Niflheim, which was the lowest of the nine worlds, was

NIDHOGG (left), a gruesome dragon, dwelt in icy Niflheim and, when not devouring corpses, it habitually nibbled the root of Yggdrasil, the cosmic tree. Here, a stag browsing on the leaves of Yggdrasil is in its turn nipped by Nidhogg, reflecting the life and death struggle at the root of the universe. (WOOD CARVING, 8TH CENTURY.)

where the dragon lived, ripping corpses apart and eating them. Between mouthfuls he would send the squirrel Ratatosk up the cosmic tree on an errand of insult, for the agile animal periodically disturbed two birds, an eagle and a hawk, who were perched at the very top. When momentarily tired of the taste of dead flesh, Nidhogg would gnaw at the root of Yggdrasil itself, presumably hoping to inflict damage on the cosmos in some way. Both Yggdrasil and Nidhogg were destined to survive the final catastrophe of *RAGNAROK*, the doom of the gods and the end of the world. Neither fire nor flood could deter the dragon from its ceaseless feasting on the vast and inexhaustible supply of dead.

NJORD was the Germanic sea god, a member of the divine race of *VANIR* and father of the fertility gods *FREYR* and *FREYJA*. When peace was agreed between the *AESIR* and the Vanir, the two branches of the divine family, Njord, Freyr and Freyja came to live with the Aesir as a sign of goodwill. According to some versions of the myth, the mother of Freyr and Freyja was Njord's own sister *NERTHUS*, but

NJORD (below) lines up with the gods to have his feet inspected by Skadi, who was obliged to choose a husband from the shape of his feet. When Skadi picked Njord, she found that she had won a sweet, old sea god with passions quite opposite to her own, and so she soon took to her chilly hills alone. (ILLUSTRATION BY J HUARD, 1930.)

NJORD calmed the storms raised by the tempestuous god, Aegir. A gentle soul, Njord loved his sunlit coves and creeks, home of his sacred seagulls and swans. Popular with sailors and fishermen, he aided ships in distress, blew favourable winds and caused summer showers.

(ILLUSTRATION BY JAMES ALEXANDER, 1995.)

since the Aesir disapproved of marriage between brother and sister, Nerthus did not accompany her husband and children to Asgard.

Njord's second marriage was to the frost giantess SKADI, who chose him on the basis of his beautiful feet. However, the couple could not agree about where they should live. Njord found Skadi's home in JOTUNHEIM, the land of the frost giants, too cold and barren, while Skadi disliked the noise and bustle of shipbuilding around Njord's hall of Noatun in Asgard. After nine nights in each place they decided to live apart. Skadi went back to her favourite pastime of hunting on skis and the weather-beaten Njord returned to a life at sea. The apparently unbridgeable gap between them probably reflects more than personal taste. Njord was certainly seen as a god of fertility, since he provided to those who worshipped him not only safe voyages at sea, but also wealth and good fortune in the form of land and sons. Skadi's associations were quite different, however. She came from a range of frozen mountains, where heavy clouds masked the sun and harsh rocks made the ground as barren as death. In her wild and unforgiving land, where nothing was able to grow or prosper at all, there was hardly any scope for humankind.

NORNIR see THE NORNS

THE NORNS, also known as the Nordic Fates, decided the destinies of both gods and mortals as they wove the Web of Fate. Here, at left, wise old Urd reads from the scroll of the past, while young Verdandi symbolizes the present, and veiled Skuld clasps her closed scroll of the future.

(ILLUSTRATION BY JAMES ALEXANDER, 1995.)

THE NORNS, or Nornir, were the Germanic fates, the goddesses of destiny. The original Norn was undoubtedly URD ("Fate"). The Well of Urd, which was situated under one of the roots of the great cosmic tree YGGDRASIL, was the site where the gods held their daily assembly. The two other Norns known by name are Verdandi ("Present") and Skuld ("Future"). It was believed that the Norns decided the destinies of gods, giants and dwarfs, as well as of humankind. The Anglo-Saxons called Urd by the name of Wyrd, and in England there was maintained a belief in the tremendous powers of the three sisters long after the arrival of Christianity. For instance, in Shakespeare's tragic play *Macbeth*, the Three Sisters on "the blasted heath" obviously owed something to the Norns.

A clear parallel of the Norns are the Moerae, or "Fates", encountered in Greek mythology. As in the Germanic mythic tradition, they were seen as three sister goddesses: Klotho ("The Spinner"), Lachesis ("The Decider") and Atropos ("The Inevitable"). It would seem more than possible that the Norns were also originally thought of as spinners. However, in Germanic mythology the Greek and Roman concept of the Fates spinning an individual length of yarn for each mortal life does not appear.

THE VALKYRIES

VALKYRIES WERE ORIGINALLY SINISTER SPIRITS of slaughter, dark angels of death who soared over the battlefields like birds of prey, meting out fate in the name of Odin. Chosen heroes were gathered up and borne away to Valhalla, the heavenly abode of Odin's ghostly army. In later Norse myth, the Valkyries were romanticized as Odin's shield-maidens, virgins with golden hair and snowy arms who served the chosen heroes everlasting mead and meat in the great hall of Valhalla. On the battlefield, they soared over the host as lovely swan-maidens or splendid mounted Amazons. This far more appealing portrayal was further developed in the Volsung Saga and *Niebelungenlied*, where the heroine, Brynhild or Brunhild, was a beautiful, fallen Valkyrie. Idealized Valkyries were infinitely more vulnerable than their fierce predecessors, and often fell in love with mortal heroes. Swan-maidens, especially, were at risk as they might easily be trapped on earth if caught without their plumage.

MOUNTED VALKYRIES *(left) soared over the battlefield through storm clouds on flying steeds. Their pearly mounts personified the rain clouds, spraying dew and hoar frost over a thirsty earth. The flying Amazon, here, expresses the swift, irrevocable force of fate and the finality of death.* (THE VALKYRIE BY STEPHEN SINDRING, MARBLE, C. 1900.)

VALKYRIES *(left) were originally demons of death who ravaged the battlefields or stormy seas, weaving the web of war, like the bloodthirsty Morrigu of Celtic myth. Behind the grisly image lay the ghastly necessity of death and revenge. The Valkyries' grim mission was reflected in their menacing names, such as Shrieking, Screaming or Raging. This striking modern portrayal captures the ancient vision of the Valkyries as wild and gleeful spirits of disorder and destruction, astride bat-like dragons.* (THE RIDE OF THE VALKYRIES BY KARL ENGEL, CANVAS, C. 1860.)

ODIN (above) commanded the Valkyries, who dispatched his will on the battlefield without question. In a unique case of rebellion, the heroic Valkyrie, Brynhild, defied Odin by helping her half-brother, Siegmund, against his will. In penance, Brynhild was condemned to lie defenceless on a hilltop until claimed by a mortal. Later the god relented and softened his punishment by putting Brynhild to sleep in a ring of fire, protected against all but the bravest hero. (ODIN AND BRUNHILD BY F LEEKE, CANVAS, C. 1890.)

GUDRUN (above) fell in love with a mortal hero, Helgi. When Helgi died, Gudrun wept so much that he called from his grave, imploring her to stop crying, for each tear she shed so his wounds flowed. Soon after, Helgi's spirit rose to Valhalla where the lovers dwelt. Here, Gudrun gathers up the slain to swell the ghostly army which Helgi led at Ragnarok. (ILLUSTRATION BY K DIELITZ, C. 1890.)

A SERVING VALKYRIE (above) holds out a horn of plenty to welcome the chosen heroes to Valhalla. By the sixth century, the Valkyries were already being portrayed in a softer light as helpful handmaidens of Odin, gathering up the slain and serving the heroes in Valhalla. Clad in flowing robes and with long golden hair caught up in a bun, this gracious maiden helpfully offers a brimming horn of mead – a welcome sight for the weary warrior. (SILVER GILT, PENDANT, 6TH CENTURY.)

VALHALLA, (left), the glittering and magnificent Hall of the Slain in Asgard, the home of the gods, was built to house Odin's huge army of heroes who were gathered to fight at Ragnarok, the preordained doom of the gods. A Viking's paradise in every way, the splendid hall gleamed with walls of polished spears and vaults of shining shields. At the long benches, decorated with glowing chain mail, warriors wined and dined everyday on ever-flowing mead and everlasting meat, served by the lovely Valkyries. The heroic host, which was amassed over the centuries, must have been massive; to feed such an army the cook, Andhrimnir, stirred a mighty cauldron, called Eldhrimnir, in which he prepared an inexhaustible boar stew. (VALHALLA BY MAX BRUCKNER, CANVAS, 1896.)

O

ODIN, also known as Woden or Wotan, was the chief god of Germanic mythology, the son of *BOR* and grandson of *BURI*. He was particularly favoured by the Vikings and rose to prominence in the eighth and ninth centuries. These seafarers and raiders were attracted by Odin's love of battle as the "father of the slain", for in *VALHALLA*, an immense hall in the divine fortress of *ASGARD*, the one-eyed god was said to preside over the *EINHERJAR* ("glorious dead"). At this period it seems that Odin displaced *TYR*, whom the Romans had identified as the sky god of the north European peoples. Tyr retained his interest in war, but

Odin was looked upon as the inspiration for hard-bitten warriors. He alone had the power to inspire men in battle to a state of berserk rage in which they feared nothing and felt no pain. The terrible berserkers would rush naked into the fray, biting the edges of their shields in a maddened frenzy. Odin's name means something akin to "fury" or

ODIN (left), the highest of gods, sits on his exalted throne, Hlidskialf, which was a mighty watch-tower overlooking the nine worlds. Hovering nearby are his tireless ravens, the airborne news reporters, Huginn and Muninn, while at his feet crouch his pet wolves, Geri and Freki, omens of good luck. (ODIN BY E BURNE-JONES, C. 1870.)

"madness". It indicates possession, as in the battle-frenzy exhibited by the Irish hero Cuchulainn.

That Odin became the foremost god shows how important warfare always was in Germanic tradition. It should be noted, however, that he did not embody martial esctasy himself; rather he inspired it in a devious manner. Odin was ever

ODIN (below), as the Wild Huntsman, leads the heroic host on a ghostly hunt through the stormy midnight sky. In the roar and rumble of the storm clouds, Norsemen fancied they heard Odin's phantom riders sweep across the sky, dark omens of doom. (THE WILD HUNT OF ODIN, BY P N ARBO, CANVAS, 1872.)

ready to stir up strife, and on one occasion commanded the fertility goddess *FREYJA* to "find two kings and set them at each other's throats" so that their vassals would wade through torrents of blood on the battlefield. The Danish King Harald was supposed to have been instructed in tactics by the god and granted many victories. In his final battle, though, Odin took the place of the king's charioteer and drove Harald to his death. When asked about such withdrawals of luck, Odin used to reply that "the grey wolf watches the halls of the gods". Gathering to Valhalla heroic warriors slain in battle was the only policy he could adopt under the constant threat of *RAGNAROK*, the doom of the gods. These Einherjar were desperately needed for the final battle on the *VIGRID* Plain, where nearly all would fall in a struggle between the gods and the frost giants. Odin himself was to be killed by the wolf *FENRIR*, the monstrous offspring of the fire god *LOKI* and the frost giantess *ANGRBODA*.

Besides his authority over the battlefield and the glorious dead, Odin was a god of magic and wisdom. As the oldest of the gods, the first-born son of Bor, he was treated by the other gods as their father. Shifty-eyed and flaming-eyed he might be, but Odin also had a strongly positive side to his character as the most learned god. His conflicting negative and positive aspects are indeed very similar to those of the Hindu god Shiva, the great destroyer-saviour of Indian mythology. For Odin's love of wisdom was so profound that he was prepared to sacrifice himself to plumb its depths. Odin was often portrayed as a grey-bearded old man with one eye, his face hidden by a hood or a broad-brimmed hat, because he had cast an eye into *MIMIR*'s well in return for a drink of its "immense wisdom". He gained insight in another way by hanging himself for nine days from *YGGDRASIL*, the cosmic tree. This

voluntary death, and his subsequent resurrection by means of magic, gave Odin greater wisdom than anyone else.

It is possible that the obvious parallel between this myth and the Crucifixion gave Christianity a head-start in northern Europe. Odin's own worship appears to have gone into decline in the early eleventh century, at the close of the Viking age. Violent times were passing as Viking colonists settled down as peaceful farmers and traders. But during the Vikings'

ODIN (below), in a timeless battle scene, clasps his wife longingly, before diving into the fray. Armed for battle in eagle helmet and blue tunic, symbolizing the sky, he is armed with his infallible spear, Gungnir, and his wondrous ring Draupnir, which was the symbol of his power and wealth. (ODIN'S LEAVE-TAKING BY F LEEKE, CANVAS, C. 1875.)

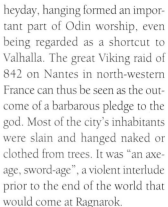

ODIN (above), a god of vision, sacrificed one eye for a draught of Mimir's Fountain of Wisdom. His single eye symbolized the radiant all-seeing sun, while his lost eye, floating in Mimir's well, signified the full moon. Odin hung himself from Yggdrasil, the cosmic tree for nine days, to learn the secrets of the dead. (BRONZE RELIEF, C. 1950.)

heyday, hanging formed an important part of Odin worship, even being regarded as a shortcut to Valhalla. The great Viking raid of 842 on Nantes in north-western France can thus be seen as the outcome of a barbarous pledge to the god. Most of the city's inhabitants were slain and hanged naked or clothed from trees. It was "an axe-age, sword-age", a violent interlude prior to the end of the world that would come at Ragnarok.

In addition to *FRIGG*, his wife in Asgard, Odin had many other wives, and he fathered a number of children. Among those said to be his sons were *THOR*, *BALDER*, *HODR*, and *VALI*.

Odin kept himself informed about the affairs of the nine worlds with two faithful ravens. As Vikings at sea sent out ravens in search of land, Odin's own ravens *HUGINN* and Muninn flew about and then "whispered into his ears every scrap of news which they saw or heard tell of". The birds' names mean "thought" and "memory" respectively. Because of his wisdom and his knowledge of events, Odin was oppressed by the approach of Ragnarok. Just as the cycle of Germanic mythology started with a cosmos awash with the blood of the original frost giant *YMIR*, when Odin and his brothers *VILI* and *VE* carved the world of men out of his dead body, so the final scene was to be a battlefield, where the gods were predestined to gush out their own blood. Ragnarok, the doom of the gods, began with the death of Odin's son Balder and the realization by the gods that in Loki, the god of fire, they had tolerated the growth of evil. There was nothing that Odin could do to prevent the catastrophe. His only consolation was the foreknowledge that his resurrected son Balder would be worshipped in his stead in a new age and a new land which would rise from the sea. (See also *THE VALKYRIES*; *SORCERY AND SPELLS*; *RINGS OF POWER*; *RAGNAROK*)

P

OTTAR was disguised as a boar by his divine lover, Freyja. Here, Freyja rides him to the seer Hyrdla, seeking proof of Ottar's kingship. The seer imparted to Ottar his family tree with some Memory Beer to help him recite it correctly in a contest for the throne. (ILLUSTRATION BY JAMES ALEXANDER, 1995.)

OTTAR was the human lover of *FREYJA*, the Germanic fertility goddess, and was said to be a distant descendant of the hero *SIGURD*. The warrior caught the goddess's attention through grand sacrifices. He built a stone altar and turned it into glass by the constant heat of the fire he used in preparing his bloody offering. Freyja transformed him into a boar so that she could keep him with her in *ASGARD*, the home of the gods. She even used the disguised Ottar as a mount. Ottar may have been a leader of a warrior band, a lover pleasing to Freyja who shared those fallen in battle with Odin. In the myth it is suggested that he is related to the berserkers, warriors who, "howling and foaming in frenzy, left a trail of terror and leaped like wildfire over land and sea"

OTTER, in Germanic mythology, was the son of the magician-farmer *HREIDMAR*. When the fire god *LOKI* killed him by mistake, for he had taken the shape of an otter, Hreidmar demanded compensation. The otter's flayed skin was to be covered inside and out with gold. Loki succeeded in taking as much gold as he needed from the dwarf *ANDVARI*, and insisted that he also be given a ring which

Andvari tried to conceal. Andvari cursed both the ring and the gold, saying that whoever owned them would be destroyed by them. Loki put the ring on his own finger and returned to Hreidmar with the gold. There was enough to cover the whole skin, except for one whisker; so Loki was compelled to hand over the ring as well, and the curse passed to Hreidmar.

PATOLLO was the Baltic war god, the equivalent of Germanic *ODIN*, the one-eyed god of battle, magic, inspiration and the dead. He was depicted as an old man with a long green beard and death-like pallor, wearing a turban. His sacred objects were the skulls of a man, a horse and a cow.

Patollo was the chief god of the Baltic region. He bestowed good fortune and, like Odin, he took it away whenever he had a desire to taste human blood. At some point before the advent of Christianity Patollo seems to have taken on a more pronounced role in respect of the dead. This would explain why Christian missionaries immediately identified him with the Devil.

PERKONIS see *PERKUNO*

PERKONS see *PERKUNO*

PERKUNAS see *PERKUNO*

PERKUNO (which probably meant "striker"), known as Perkunas in Lithunia, Perkons or Perkonis in Latvia, was the Baltic thunder god. He was obviously connected with the Slavic god *PERUNU*, although Perkuno was the standard European god of the storm. He was depicted as an angry-looking middle-aged man with a fiery face and a curly black beard. An order of priests is known to have maintained a perpetual fire as part of Perkuno's worship.

Baltic mythology appears to have possessed three main gods, not unlike the Germanic trio

OTTER was turned into an otter by his father to catch fish for dinner. Here, he nibbles a salmon with his eyes closed to avoid seeing his dinner diminish with each mouthful. Blind to the world, he was easy prey for Loki who coveted the otter's fine fur. (ILLUSTRATION BY NICK BEALE, 1995.)

worshipped at Uppsala in Sweden. There the war god *ODIN*, the thunder god *THOR* and the fertility god *FREYR* were revered, whereas at Romowe in Prussia, Baltic peoples gave worship to *PATOLLO*, Perkuno and *POTRIMPO*. The young, beardless god Potrimpo was the Baltic Freyr; grim Patollo was the Baltic Odin; and the Baltic Thor was Perkuno, as quick to anger as the giant-killing Germanic thunder god. A late account of the Balts even supposes a migration from Sweden in the sixth century.

Unfortunately, next to nothing of Baltic mythology has survived, apart from the names of gods and goddesses. It is of considerable interest, therefore, that Perkuno

appears in a surviving myth about *SAULE*, the sun goddess, and the moon god *MENU*. According to this tale, the moon chose not to appear in the sky with the sun because of Perkuno, who had an affair with Saule. Their love-child was the Morning Star. Whereas the sun goddess carried on as if nothing had happened and continued to show herself to all humankind during the day, Menu made himself visible only by night.

PERUN see *PERUNU*

PERUNU, known as Pyerun in Russia, Piorun in Poland and sometimes Perun, was the Slavic thunder god. He was the chief god and a creator god. At Kiev in Russia he had an important temple until the tenth century. Perunu's supremacy was ended by Vladimir, the ruler of Kiev who was later raised to the sainthood. After living the typical life of a Slavic prince, with numerous wives and mistresses, Vladimir

"tired of the desire for women" and sought a new way of living. He sent out ambassadors to witness the religious ceremonies of both the Catholic and Orthodox churches, as well as those of the Jews and

PERUNU roamed the thundery sky on his millstone, flashing shafts of lightning from his thunderbolt. In his effigy at Kiev, he appeared with a silver head and golden moustache. He was transformed into St Elijah with the arrival of Christianity, (ILLUSTRATION BY NICK BEALE, 1995.)

Moslems. His choice fell on the Byzantine form of Christianity and thereafter the Russians and the Greeks shared the same form of Christian worship.

Prior to this conversion in 988 though, the "Rus" owed more to north-western Europe, for the establishment of the Russian state resulted from Viking trade and settlement on its great rivers. The Viking leader Oleg had captured Kiev in 882 and raised its status to "mother of Russian cities". With this Germanic influx, it is hardly surprising that there are obvious parallels between Perunu and *THOR*. Oleg was referred to as a "wizard". It seems quite likely that Thor provided the native Slavic thunder god with a developed mythology, since surviving details of Perunu's worship suggest that he was originally believed to be an aid to agriculture. Indeed, rain-making ceremonies are known to have involved a chaste girl, naked and decked with flowers, dancing in a magic circle. Whirling and drinking seem to have been important in his Russian worship.

PERKUNO can be seen here riding with his divine companions: on the left, young Potrimpo, crowned with fruitful wheat; next, veteran Patollo bears a skull symbolizing his affinity with war and death, while his horned turban recalls his sacred cow. Perkuno, at right, flashes his lightning. (ILLUSTRATION BY JAMES ALEXANDER, 1995.)

PERUNU, as a fertility god, wandered over the earth, spreading summer sun, chasing away clouds and melting the snow. A god with a social sense, he bombarded the lands of the wicked with hailstorms. The oak, his sacred tree, was burned in his honour. (ILLUSTRATION BY NICK BEALE, 1995.)

Elsewhere in Europe the Slavic peoples also revered Perunu, as place names still indicate. In Slovenia there is Perunji Ort, in Croatia Peruna Dubrava, in Bulgaria Perin Planina, and in Poland Peruny as well as Piorunow. According to Procopius, secretary to the Greek general Belisarius in the sixth century, the Slavs worshipped above all the god of lightning, and sacrificed cattle and other animals to him. In Russian folklore the memories of Perunu's great skill with the thunderbolt can doubtless be found in stories that tell of dragon-slaying and other supernatural deeds that required enormous strength.

PIORUN see *PERUNU*

POTRIMPO was the Baltic god of fertility and the equivalent of the Germanic fertility god *FREYR*, though he was also associated with rivers. He was depicted as a happy young man without a beard and crowned with ears of grain.

PYERUN see *PERUNU*

R

RAGNAROK was the doom of the Germanic gods. After a terrible winter lasting three years, a final battle would be fought between the gods and the frost giants on the *VIGRID* Plain. On the side of *ODIN* and the gods were ranged the "glorious dead" who had fallen in battle and were taken to live in *VALHALLA*; while with the fire god *LOKI* and the frost giants fought the "unworthy dead" from *HEL* (the Germanic netherworld), plus the fearsome wolf *FENRIR* and the sea monster *JORMUNGAND*. There was nothing that the chief god Odin could do to prevent this catastrophe. His only consolation was the foreknowledge that Ragnarok was not the end of the cosmos. After he had been killed by Fenrir, *THOR* had been overcome by Jormungand, and most of the other gods had died in the mutually destructive encounter with the frost giants, a new world was destined to "rise again out of the water, fair and green".

Before the battle two humans, *LIF* and Lifthrasir, had taken shelter in the sacred tree *YGGDRASIL* and they emerged after the carnage was over to repopulate the earth. Several of the gods also survived, among them Odin's sons *VIDAR* and *VALI*, and his brother *HONIR*, Thor's sons Modi and *MAGNI*, who inherited their father's hammer, and *BALDER* who came back from the dead.

Ragnarok held a great appeal for the Vikings, whose onslaught on western Europe is still the stuff of legend. Once they understood the effectiveness of the *standhogg*, the short, sharp shore-raid against the richer lands to the west and south, then, as Alcuin remarked in the eighth century, "no one is free from fear". In 793 the British offshore monastery of Lindisfarne was sacked and St Cuthbert's church was spattered with the blood of the monks. "Never before in Britain," Alcuin lamented, "has such terror appeared as this we have now

RAGNAROK (above) was foreshadowed by a chilling Fimbul winter. Sol and Mani grew pale with fear; blizzards swept down from the peaks and icebergs towered over the frozen earth. Loki broke free from his bonds and set sail with the fiery host. (ILLUSTRATION BY JAMES ALEXANDER, 1995.)

RAGNAROK's (left) war raged on the icy Plain of Vigrid. Here, Odin wrestles with the snarling wolf, Fenrir, while Thor slays the monstrous world serpent, Jormungand, though dying from its fatal venom. At left, Loki wrestles with the bright god, Heimdall, and both gods die in the conflict. (ILLUSTRATION BY JAMES ALEXANDER, 1995.)

suffered at the hands of the heathen." But for the Vikings it was like Ragnarok, "an axe-age, a sword-age". It was a rehearsal for the "wind-age and wolf-age before the world is wrecked". Although Christianity did eventually come to the Germanic peoples of northern Europe, their preoccupation with a cosmic catastrophe did not fade altogether. The Last Judgement exercised their minds during the Middle Ages. It may well have been that behind the Nazis' resolve to fight on in World War Two lay a folk memory of Ragnarok.

RAN see *NATURE SPIRITS*

REGIN and his brother *FAFNIR* slew their father, the magician *HREIDMAR*, while under the spell of a cursed ring, Andvarinaut, which made them covet their father's gold. While Fafnir turned into a dragon in order to protect his gold, Regin settled down as a smith in the royal Danish household. There he tutored the young hero *SIGURD* and urged him to overcome Fafnir, which he did. But, equally as corrupted by the curse as his brother, Regin then plotted to murder Sigurd. However, he reckoned without the young hero's insight: Sigurd was forewarned by the birds and killed Regin first.

REIDMAR see *HREIDMAR*

RHINE MAIDENS see *NATURE SPIRITS*

RIG was the name assumed by the Germanic god *HEIMDALL* when he created the three categories of men: the slave or *thrall*; the free peasant or *karl*; and the noble or chieftain, known as *jarl*. Though usually imagined as the watchman of the gods, scanning the horizon for the final frost giant attack at Ragnarok, Heimdall was also identified with Rig, or "king". According to Rig's myth, the god once approached the lowly dwelling of an old couple,

Ai and Edda (literally "great-grandfather" and "great-grandmother"). After introducing himself as a lone wayfarer, Rig was given coarse food to satisfy his hunger and a place in the bed between them when it was time to sleep. Rig stayed three nights and gave them good advice. Nine months afterwards Edda bore a son, Thrall, who was black-haired and ugly, with rough skin, thick fingers, short nails, swollen knuckles, long heels and bent back; but he was strong. Thrall took as his wife an equally ungainly person, a drudge with crooked legs, dirty feet, sunburned arms and a big nose. Their many children included boys like Noisy, Roughneck and Horsefly, as well as girls such as Lazybones, Fatty and Beanpole. From these ill-favoured children descended the thralls, the enslaved labourers of the oppressed class. Eddar's son Thrall himself perfectly sums up the back-breaking toil of his oppressed class, weighed down with generations of hard labour.

Rig visited a second house, warm and better furnished. Inside

RIG wandered throughout the earth, visiting its people and fathering three classes of men, the thralls or serfs, karls or freemen and jarls or earls. Here, Rig sups with aged rustics in their seashore hut, gazing with pride at his first mortal child, Thrall, who was a born labourer and father of the serfs. (ILLUSTRATION BY NICK BEALE, 1995.)

he encountered an industrious couple, Afi and Amma (literally "grandfather" and "grandmother"). The well-dressed pair were spinning and weaving: Afi prepared a loom, Amma spun a thread. Once again Rig shared their table and bed, gave good advice and departed after three nights. Nine months afterwards Amma bore a son, Karl, who was red and fresh and bright-eyed. Karl took to wife Snor (meaning "daughter-in-law") and their children included boys named Strongbeard, Husbandman and Smith, and girls called Prettyface, Maiden and Capable. Together they ran farms and were free.

A third dwelling Rig stayed at was a splendid hall belonging to Fadir and Modir ("father" and "mother"). While Fadir attended to his bow and arrows, Modir saw to her own looks and clothes. After a large meal, accompanied by fine conversation and drink, Rig slept between his well-off hosts. He stayed three nights and gave good advice. Nine months afterwards Modir bore a son, Jarl, who was fair-haired and handsome, with a bright cheek and an eye as piercing as a serpent's. When he grew to manhood, Jarl could use bow, spear, sword and shield; he could ride and swim and hunt expertly. One day Rig returned and greeted Jarl as his special son, imparting wisdom and telling him how to claim his lands. In obedience to the

REGIN reforges the shards of Sigurd's wondrous sword, Gram. Once mended, the sword was so strong and sharp that it split the iron anvil in two. With it, Sigurd slew Regin's brother, Fafnir, who had turned himself into a dragon so that he could guard his gold. (WOOD CARVING, 12TH CENTURY.)

RIG next visited a thrifty farmhouse where he was hospitably entertained by Amma and Afi. Rig stayed for three days and fathered a fine sturdy, blue-eyed boy, named Karl, who grew up to be a natural farmer. Here, Karl and his wife, Snor, can be seen working their fruitful land. (ILLUSTRATION BY NICK BEALE, 1995.)

god, Jarl rode through the world, fighting and slaying, seizing booty and distributing treasure to his free followers. At last he married Erna ("lively"), a fair and wise noblewoman, and she bore him twelve sons. One of these learned magic so well that he could prevent forest fires, control storms and cure the sick. It was said that he excelled even Rig in understanding and almost became a god. The implication is that in his person he combined the roles of priest and king.

The myth of Rig sheds light on the structure of Viking society. In contrast with the Celts, the other main tribal people of pre-Christian Europe, the Germanic tribes of Scandinavia and northern Europe had already lost a priestly class by the time we encounter their mythology. As Julius Caesar noted, the ancient Germans had no equivalent of the druids and cared little for ritual. They found religious significance in the depths of forests. But the Romans, and later the Vikings' victims, were in no doubt about the Germanic love of warfare and the role of the armed retainer, the sturdy free peasant, in battle.

219

SORCERY AND SPELLS

SORCERY AMONG THE NORSEMEN was a unique and precious art practised essentially by Odin and the Vanir deities of nature, but also by dwarfs and some privileged mortals, usually women. Although distinguished heroes, such as Sigurd, were blessed with magical weapons, they usually lacked any magical powers. Odin, the arch-sorcerer, developed his skills over a lifetime of search and sacrifice, much like a mortal shaman. Ever thirsty for wisdom and power, he wandered the nine worlds as a vagrant, clad in a blue mantle and slouch hat, gathering and garnering every snippet of information he could find. After hanging himself on the World Tree, he learnt the secrets of the dead and restored himself to life. By contrast, the heroes of Finnish myth were often gifted from birth with astounding magical powers and arcane wisdom. The wise wizard, Vainamoinen, was a born sage and sorcerer, while debonair Leminkainen was bathed as a baby to imbue him with wisdom and sorcery. Equipped with a repertoire of sacred songs, the Finns penetrated to the roots of life. Finnish sorcerers were so famous that in medieval times Norwegian kings forbade people to sail to Finnmark for the purpose of consulting magicians.

KULLERVO curses Ilmarinen's wicked wife who had taunted him beyond endurance, giving him a dry loaf for his lunch, stuffed with a rock which shattered his family knife. In response, he turned her gentle cows into bears which devoured her at the milking. Kullervo, a tortured soul, unloved from birth, responded to the world's sleights with distorted malice. Gifted with powerful sorcery, he punished his enemies beyond their crime. (THE CURSE OF KULLERVO BY A GALLEN-KALLELA, CANVAS, C. 1850.)

VAINAMOINEN (above) fends off the griffin perched on his ship. The monster was the sorceress, Louhi, who had turned herself into a metallic bird. She was after the talisman, the Sampo. Just as she reared to strike the final blow, Vainamoinen raised his rudder and crushed her talons. The Sampo was broken and scattered, but Vainamoinen gathered some fragments and partly restored its power. (DEFENCE OF THE SAMPO BY A GALLEN-KALLELA, CANVAS, 1852.)

KULLERVO (above), doomed from birth, set out on his last journey, piping loudly on his cow horn, his mother's Blackie dog running behind. En route he passed a blasted stretch of green where he had unwittingly despoiled his long-lost sister. Here the meadow grasses bemoaned the maiden's terrible fate. Feeling the crushing weight of guilt and a lifetime of bitterness, Kullervo eventually threw himself on his sword. Although a powerful sorcerer, Kullervo was denied love throughout his life and never learnt the way of things. (KULLERVO BY A GALLEN-KALLELA, CANVAS, C. 1850.)

FREYJA (right) was renowned for her magical crafts, along with the other Vanir deities of fertility and nature. She was the first to teach the warrior Aesir the practice of seior or magic. Seior was useful but could be dangerous, giving its practitioners foreknowledge and power over life and death, love and intelligence. Odin quickly learnt all that Freyja could teach him and, ever thirsty for knowledge, surpassed the Vanir in magic arts. In later myth, Freyja was identified with Idun, goddess of Spring who guarded the magic apples of youth, seen here. (ILLUSTRATION BY ARTHUR RACKHAM, C. 1910.)

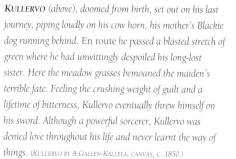

A RING OF FIRE (far left) encircled the Valkyrie, Brynhild, protecting her in an enchanted sleep from all but the bravest. Only Sigurd dared the fiery circle of flames to win the sleeping beauty. His fearless spirit carried him through, mysteriously unharmed, as predicted by the birds whose song he understood. (ILLUSTRATION BY H THEAKER, C. 1920.)

GRIMHILD (left), Queen of the Niebelungs, was famed and feared for her magic. With her spells and potions, she could erase a person's memory and control his will. When she offered unsuspecting Sigurd her magic mead, he forgot his love for Brynhild and instead fell in love with Grimhild's daughter, Gudrun. (ILLUSTRATION BY ARTHUR RACKHAM, C. 1910.)

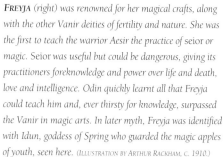

S

RIND (above), a cool Nordic princess, became ill with a mystery malady and was nursed back to health by Odin in disguise. The old nurse, Vecha, restored Rind to health, first by bathing her in a hot bath. The warm water thawed her frozen heart and symbolized the melting of the frozen rind of earth. (ILLUSTRATION BY NICK BEALE, 1995.)

THE RUSALKI (right) dwelt in rivers and lakes. The southern sprites were pearly beauties who lured travellers with their sweet song. During Rusalki Week, which was at the start of summer, they emerged from the rivers to dwell and dance in the forests, enriching the grass in their wake.
(ILLUSTRATION BY ALAN LEE, 1984.)

RIND, in Germanic mythology, was the daughter of King BILLING and the mistress of ODIN, who pursued her in various disguises. Their love led to the birth of VALI, the child who was to avenge the death of BALDER. In one version, Odin was deposed as king of the gods for forcing Rind to submit simply in order that he might father a son.

ROSKVA was a farmer's daughter who became a servant of the god THOR. When Thor stopped at her father's house and asked for food and shelter they were too poor to provide meat, so Thor offered his own goats on the condition that no bones were broken. But Roskva's brother THIALFI broke one of the thigh bones and when Thor came to resurrect the goats one of them had a limp. The enraged god was only pacified by the promised service of Roskva and Thialfi, who travelled with him thereafter.

THE RUSALKI were water nymphs and can be found in both Slavonic and Russian mythology. They were thought to be the spirits of drowned girls. During the winter months, they lived in the great rivers of eastern Europe, taking on different forms in different regions. For instance, in the Rivers Dnieper and Danube, in south-eastern Europe, they were commonly pictured as beautiful, siren-like creatures who would attempt to lure unsuspecting passers-by into the water with their magical song. In the northern regions, in contrast, the water nymphs were considered to be malevolent, unkempt and unattractive creatures, who would grab travellers from the river banks and drag them down into the river and drown them. During the summer, when the rivers were warmed by the sun, the Rusalki came out of the water on to the land and lived in the cool of the forests.

SAMPO see *TREASURES AND TALISMANS*

SAULE was the Baltic sun goddess and, according to one tradition, the mistress of the thunder god PERKUNO. She was worshipped by Lithuanians, Prussians and Letts before they were converted to Christianity. Her worship took the form of looking after a harmless green snake. Every house kept one: under the bed, in a corner, even under the table. Apart from ensuring a household's wealth and fertility, the kindness shown to the snake was regarded as a guarantee of Saule's generosity. To kill a snake was an act of sacrilege. The sight of a dead one was believed to bring tears to the eyes of the sun goddess. Even after the conversion of the Lithuanians to Christianity in the fifteenth century – they were the last people to be Christianized on the continent – the peasants continued to revere green snakes. It was long held that seeing one in the countryside meant that either a marriage or birth would follow.

Saule was imagined as pouring light from a jug. The golden liquid which she generously gave to the world was the basis of life itself, the warmth so necessary after the cold north-eastern European winter. Another fragment of myth about Saule concerns the Baltic equivalent of the Greek Dioscuri, who were the divine twins Castor and Polydeuces. The unnamed Baltic twins are said to have rescued Saule from the sea and built a barn in which the goddess could rest.

SIEGFRIED see *SIGURD*

SIEGMUND see *TRAGIC LOVERS*

SIF was the wife of THOR, the Germanic thunder god, and the mother, by a previous marriage, of Uu, god of archery and skiing. She is the subject of a strange myth in which the trickster LOKI, the god of fire, one night cut off her beautiful golden hair, probably a representation of ripe corn and therefore fertility. Next morning Thor was beside himself with rage at Sif's distress. When Loki protested that it was only a joke, Thor demanded to know what he was going to do about it, and the fire god said he would get the dwarfs to weave a wig as a replacement.

So Loki asked the sons of Ivaldi to make a wig from spun gold. The completed piece of work was quite remarkable, for it was so light that a breath of air was enough to ruffle its skeins and so real that it grew on her head by magic. Thinking to get the gods even more into their debt, the sons of Ivaldi used the remaining heat in their furnace to construct a collapsible ship named *Skidbladnir* for the fertility god FREYR and a magic spear called GUNGNIR for ODIN. On his way back to ASGARD, the stronghold of the gods, crossing the underground

SAULE (above), the Baltic sun goddess, poured golden light from her heavenly height through the summery clouds down to the earth below. The snake on her crown symbolizes her fertility and abundance. The Morning Star, her child, flashes above her. (ILLUSTRATION BY JAMES ALEXANDER, 1995.)

SIF (above right) was famous for her gold, flowing hair, symbolizing ripe harvest corn. When Loki cut off her locks her misery represented the winter season when the cornfields are reduced to stubble. Here, Loki lurks menacingly behind the dreaming beauty. (ILLUSTRATION BY NICK BEALE, 1995.)

SIGNY (right) Queen of Gotaland, rushes down the glacial fjord to greet her kinsmen. She warns them of an ambush planned by her vengeful husband, Siggeir, a sore loser, who bitterly resented her brother Sigmund's victory in a magical sword contest. (ILLUSTRATION BY JAMES ALEXANDER, 1995.)

caverns where the dwarfs lived, Loki also met the dwarf brothers Brokk and Eiti. They were so jealous of the workmanship that had gone into the wig, the boat and the spear that Loki persuaded them to make something better; he even staked his own head on their inability to do so. As a result, the dwarf brothers fashioned the magic hammer known as *MJOLLNIR*, the scourge of the frost giants.

The gods were delighted with the treasures Loki and Brokk had brought back. However, Brokk demanded Loki's head. The gods would not agree, but they had no objection to Brokk sewing up Loki's lips with a thong when Thor dragged the god back home after he tried to flee, which caused Loki to plan a revenge against Thor. (See also *TREASURES AND TALISMANS*)

SIGMUND see *NORSE HEROES*

SIGNY, in Germanic mythology, was the unfortunate daughter of *VOLSUNG*, supposedly a descendant of *ODIN*. Married against her will to the Gothic king Siggeir, she tried to warn her father and her ten brothers about Siggeir's plot against them, but they were ambushed in a forest and bound to a fallen tree. Each night a wolf devoured one of them in turn, until only her youngest brother Sigmund was left alive. Signy got a slave to smear Sigmund's face with honey so that the wolf would lick him instead of biting him. Sigmund was thus able to catch the wolf's tongue in his teeth and overcome the beast.

Signy helped Sigmund to plot revenge. She even slept with him in disguise and bore a son named Sinfiotli. When Sinfiotli grew up she placed him in Sigmund's care, but they were both captured by Siggeir. A magic sword freed them and killed Siggeir and his sons. Signy chose to die herself in the burning Gothic palace, but not before she had told Sigmund the truth about Sinfiotli's parentage.

SIGRYN see *SIGYN*

SIGUNN see *SIGYN*

SIGURD, or Siegfried as he was known in German, was a northern Germanic hero similar to the Celtic King Arthur. He was the foster-son of *REGIN*, the smith at the court of King Hjalprek in Jutland, who sent him to recover a fabulous hoard of gold. Regin's father *HREIDMAR* had first acquired this treasure, which once belonged to the dwarf *ANDVARI*. To get their hands on the gold Regin and his brother *FAFNIR* had then killed Hreidmar, but Fafnir wanted the treasure for himself and turned into a dragon to guard it. By cunningly stabbing the monster from underneath, Sigurd succeeded in slaying Fafnir, thus apparently gaining both dwarfish wealth and wisdom, since Fafnir was said to have understood the language of birds. When he realized that Regin intended to kill him for the gold, Sigurd slew him before carrying it away himself. (See also *NORSE HEROES*; *TRAGIC LOVERS*; *RINGS OF POWER*)

SIGYN, also known as Sigunn or Sigryn, in Germanic mythology, was the faithful wife of the fire god *LOKI* and mother of his sons Narvi and *VALI*. Once the gods realized that in Loki they had allowed the growth of evil in their midst, they

SIGURD (above) watches with fascination as Regin forges the broken shards of his father's wondrous sword, a gift from Odin. The conquering sword would help Sigurd in his destined mission to slay the dragon, Fafnir, guardian of a fabulous but ill-fated treasure. (SIEGFRIED IN THE FORGE OF REGIN BY W VON HANSCHILD, FRESCO, 1880.)

SIGURD (right) confronts the fire-breathing dragon, Fafnir, and slays him, winning fame and a fateful fortune. On the advice of his mentor, Regin, he roasted the creature's heart, licking some spilt blood from which he learnt the speech of birds. (SIEGFRIED AND FAFNIR BY H. HENRICH, CANVAS, 1906.)

SIGURD (above) exults in his wondrous new weapon, anticipating victory over his frightful foe, Fafnir. Equipped with the sharpest blade and nerves of iron, the eager hero set off excitedly on his first quest. This striking portrayal highlights the youthful idealism of the zealous Nordic hero. (ILLUSTRATION BY ARTHUR RACKHAM, C. 1900.)

bound him in a cave. First they took hold of three slabs of rock, stood them on end and bored a hole through each of them. Then the entrails of Loki's son Narvi were employed as a rope which bound the fire god to the stones. When the gods had tied the last knot, the entrails became as hard as iron. To ensure Loki's discomfort the frost giantess *SKADI*, *NJORD*'s wife, fastened a snake to a stalactite above the god's head and there he was to remain until *RAGNAROK*.

SKADE see *SKADI*

SKADI, a cool and independent huntress, roamed the mountains on her snow shoes. A spirit of winter, she was far happier on her icy slopes than in her husband's sunlit coves. A deity of hunters and mountain climbers, she guided their sleighs over the snow. (ILLUSTRATION BY JAMES ALEXANDER, 1995.)

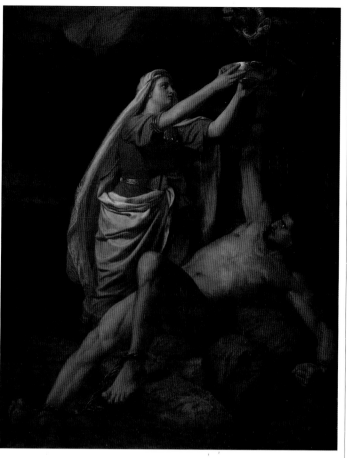

SIGYN (above), the devoted wife of Loki, stood by him even after he had been banished to an icy prison. There she lessened his pain by catching the fiery venom dribbled by a serpent tied above his face. When she went to empty the bowl, he writhed in agony, shaking the earth. (LOKI AND SIGYN BY M E WINGE, CANVAS, C. 1890.)

Despite all that her husband had done, Sigyn remained true to him and did what she could to lessen his suffering by catching the venom dripping from the snake in a wooden bowl. However, whenever she went away to empty its poisonous contents, the venom fell on Loki's head and caused him to twitch violently. According to the Vikings, it was these compulsive movements that accounted for earthquakes.

SKADI, or Skade (which means "destruction"), was a figure in northern Germanic mythology. She was the wife of the sea god *NJORD* and daughter of the frost giant *THIASSI*. When the gods of *ASGARD* killed her father for stealing *IDUN*'s apples, Skadi armed herself and went to the gods' stronghold to seek compensation. Refusing an offer of gold, she demanded a husband and a bellyful of laughter. This was agreed, provided that Skadi chose her husband by his feet only. Thinking that the most shapely feet must surely belong to handsome *BALDER*, *ODIN*'s son, Skadi made her choice only to discover that she had picked Njord. The merriment was provided by *LOKI*, who tied his testicles to a goat. As the couple were unable to stand the conditions in each other's homes, Njord and Skadi decided that it was best to live apart. Her relationship with the gods continued, however, and it was she who placed the venomous snake above Loki's head when the gods eventually imprisoned the troublesome god in a cave.

SKIRNIR (above) gallops through a fiery ring guarding the icy home of Gerda, a frost giantess. On a mission to win Gerda for his gentle master, Freyr, Skirnir bears gifts of life-giving apples, a multiplying ring, Draupnir, and a glowing portrait of Freyr, captured in his drinking horn. (ILLUSTRATION BY GLENN STEWARD, 1995.)

SKIRNIR ("Shining") was a servant of *FREYR*, the Germanic god of fertility. When Freyr wished to marry the frost giantess *GERDA*, he promised Skirnir his horse and his sword and sent him to *JOTUNHEIM*, the land of the frost giants. Skirnir had some difficulty in persuading Gerda to agree to the match, however. Eleven apples of youth, the magic fruit that kept the gods young, were no temptation to her. Nor was one of Odin's arm-rings. Gerda showed no fear when Skirnir threatened to behead her, but she began to panic the moment he started to recite a powerful spell. It promised to deny her any joy or passion, for the beautiful frost giantess was to be transformed into a loveless outcast, a companion of the "unworthy dead". As a result of this threatened fate, Gerda at last consented to meet Freyr and so Skirnir received his promised rewards. On another occasion, Skirnir acted in his role as messenger by going to the dwarfs on Odin's behalf to order a magical fetter so that Odin could restrain the terrible wolf *FENRIR*.

SKOLL, in Germanic mythology, was a wolf that pursued the sun in her flight across the sky. At *RAGNAROK*, the doom of the gods, Skoll was destined to seize the sun between his jaws and swallow her. Just before this happened, though, the sun would give birth to a daughter as beautiful as herself and this new sun would warm and illuminate the new earth risen from the sea, "fresh and green", following the catastrophe. Another wolf, named ·Hati, chased after the moon. Both creatures were said to be the sons of a giantess living in Iron Wood.

Ravenous dogs often threatened to eat the heavenly bodies in the myths of northern parts of both Europe and Asia. Chinese families today still bang cooking utensils to frighten "the dog of heaven" during a lunar eclipse.

SKOLL (below), a fierce wolf, symbolizing Repulsion, chased the sun across the sky, from dawn to dusk. Skoll's sole aim in life was to overtake and devour the heavenly orb, plunging the world into primordial darkness. (ILLUSTRATION BY GLENN STEWARD, 1995.)

SKRYMIR, a massive frost giant, acts as mountain guide to Thor and his party, pointing out the shortest route to Utgard, the citadel of the frost giants. The travellers struggled on through snow drifts, unaware that Skrymir was in fact only a giant illusion sent to thwart and mislead them. (ILLUSTRATION BY NICK BEALE, 1995.)

SKRYMIR ("Vast") was an extra large frost giant in Germanic mythology. So huge was he that on a journey through the land of giants *THOR* and *LOKI*, along with their servants *THIALFI* and *ROSKVA*, inadvertently slept in the thumb of Skrymir's empty glove, thinking it was a hall. When Thor later tried to hammer in the skull of the sleeping Skrymir, the frost giant awoke in the belief that either a leaf or an acorn had dropped on his brow. Afterwards it dawned on Thor and his companions that Skrymir was a gigantic illusion, a magic creation sent out by the frost giants in order to prevent them from reaching *UTGARD*, the giants' citadel.

SLEIPNIR ("Glider"), was the eight-legged horse ridden by *ODIN*, the chief of the Germanic gods. This fabulous creature was the offspring of an unusual union between Svadilfari, a stallion of great strength, and *LOKI*, the shape-changer, who had disguised himself as a mare. Sleipnir could travel over sea and through the air, and was swift enough to beat any other horse in a race. At *RAGNAROK*, Sleipnir was the horse that carried Odin into battle.

SOL see *NATURE SPIRITS*

SURT ("Black"), in Germanic mythology, was a fire giant with a flaming blade who would set the cosmos alight at *RAGNAROK*. He was identified with the fire god *LOKI*. At Ragnarok Surt was to rise from Muspell, the land of flame, and fling fire in every direction. The nine worlds were to become raging furnaces as gods, frost giants, the

SLEIPNIR (above), the fabulous eight-hoofed (or some say, eight-legged) steed of Odin, certainly deserved his name "Glider" for he slipped through cloud, sea or earth with equal ease. Sleipnir's hooves rumbled in the storm clouds when Odin travelled across the sky as god of the winds. (ILLUSTRATION BY GLENN STEWARD, 1995.)

SVANTOVIT (right), the four-headed war god of the Slavs, guarded the world on four sides. His stone effigy at Rugen was worshipped before battle. As a deity of fertility, plenty and destiny, he bore a horn of plenty and rode a horse of divination. A white horse was kept in the temple for ritual divination. (ILLUSTRATION BY NICK BEALE, 1995.)

SURT (below), a fierce fire giant, rose from the furnace of Muspell at Ragnarok to lead his fiery hordes against the divine host. With his flaming sword, he set the nine worlds ablaze, burning them to blackened cinders which sank beneath the boiling ocean only to rise again fresh, green and new. (ILLUSTRATION BY JAMES ALEXANDER, 1995.)

dead, the living, monsters, dwarfs, elves and animals were all to be reduced to ashes. Then the earth would sink into the sea, before rising again, fresh and green. It may be that the view of the end of the world as an immense conflagration was influenced by the volcanic nature of Iceland, from where many of the written myths originated. In 1963–7, a new island, formed by a volcanic eruption off the coast of Iceland, was named Surtsey after the god Surt.

SVANTEVIT see *SVANTOVIT*

SVANTOVIT, also known as Svantevit, was the war god of the Slavic peoples of central Europe. His temple at Arcona on the Baltic island of Rugen was destroyed by King Valdemar of Denmark and his Christian adviser Absalon in 1169.

The building contained a four-headed statue of Svantovit that was nearly thirty feet in height. Multiple heads were indeed a feature of the Slavic pantheon. It is thought that Svantovit may also have been worshipped as a supreme deity and seen as a father to other gods.

Prior to the Danish destruction of the temple in the Christian era, the worshippers of Svantovit at Arcona believed that the god would mount a sacred white horse and ride out at nights against those who denied his divinity. In the morning the horse was often discovered to be covered in sweat. Omens for success in war were read from the behaviour of the sacred horse as well. Human sacrifices, which were a widespread custom throughout the Germanic and Slavic peoples, were made to Svantovit before any great undertakings, .

SVARAZIC, sometimes Svarozic or Svarogich (which probably meant "hot" or "torrid" – a meaning that can still be found today in the Romanian language), was the Slavic fire god, especially of the fire that was used to dry grain. He was the son of Svaroz, or Svarog (who was identified with the Greek smith god Hephaistos) and the brother of *DAZHBOG*. The fire god was depicted wearing a helmet and carrying a sword, and on his breast was a black bison's head. Human sacrifices were made to Svarazic, including, after his capture in 1066, the German bishop of Mecklenburg. In some traditions, Svarazic was identified with the flame of lightning.

SVAROGICH see *SVARAZIC*

SVAROZIC see *SVARAZIC*

TRAGIC LOVERS

TIMELESS TALES OF TRAGIC LOVE are common everywhere, yet rarely so stark and bleak as in Norse mythology. Sometimes a curse lies at the root of the trouble, as in the tale of Sigurd and Brynhild, where a cursed ring wrecks the lives of several pairs of doomed lovers. Sometimes the trials of love symbolize the battles of nature. Sigurd, for instance, might be seen as a sun lord who, armed with a sunbeam, dispels darkness; while his lover, Brynhild, symbolizes the dawn-maiden whose path he crosses only at the start and close of his shining career. In other tales, obstacles simply serve to test the lovers' honour and courage, as when Frithiof faithfully guards his sleeping rival, Sigurd Ring. In their love affairs, the gods seem luckier than mortals, though friction is rife, if short-lived, as when Odur flees Freyja or Skadi lives apart from Njord. Such conflict might symbolize seasonal changes: Njord's sunny love can only hold wintry Skadi for three months of the year. By contrast, in the heart-warming tale of the summer god, Freyr, he wins his frosty bride by sheer warmth of love which melts her icy heart.

SIEGMUND and Sieglinde (left), were siblings who grew up apart, both enduring tragic fates, before meeting by chance and falling in love. Here, the lovers exchange secret glances while in the company of Sieglinde's suspicious husband, Hunding, who plans to slay Siegmund in a duel. When Siegmund wins, he and Sieglinde enjoy brief love before dying, one on the battlefield, the other in childbirth. The child of their sad union is the great hero, Sigurd. (ILLUSTRATION BY F LEEKE, C. 1895.)

INGEBORG (above), in the sanctuary of Balder's temple, stops spinning and pines for her lover, Frithiof. Cloistered by her watchful brothers, she was denied contact with Frithiof, who was considered beneath her royal status. Yet when Frithiof broke the sanctity of the temple to rescue Ingeborg, she refused to flee with him, believing herself honour bound to obey the wishes of her royal brothers. (INGEBORG'S LAMENT BY F N JENSEN, CANVAS, C. 1830.)

FREYR (left), a gentle summer god, caught a glimpse of the radiant frost giantess, Gerda, from afar and at once fell in love, but doubted his chances until his decisive servant, Skirnir, set off to woo the girl for his master. Gerda remained unmoved until she was forced by threat of magic to at least consent to a meeting with Freyr. Once in the company of the fiery god, Gerda's icy heart thawed. Freyr appears here as a dreamy summer god, bearing his wheat, with his boar at his feet, emblems of fruitful harvest. (FREYR BY E BURNE-JONES JONES, CANVAS, C. 1870.)

KREIMHILD (right) wakes from a nightmare in which she dreamt that a lovely white falcon was struck in flight by two black eagles. Her mother interprets the dream to mean that Kreimhild will eventually fall in love with a peerless prince – who is symbolized by the white bird – and that he will be killed by two murderers – the black eagles. Indeed, some years later the dream came true as Kreimhild fell in love with the great hero Sigurd, later slain by her two brothers, Gunner and Hogni, who were acting under the influence of a curse. Here, Kreimhild is depicted telling her mother about her dream, while below a bard, a poet and a Christian pontiff ponder the meaning of the Teutonic epic, the Niebelungenlied. (THE LEGEND OF SIEGFRIED BY F PILOTY, WOOD, C. 1890.)

FRITHIOF and Ingeborg (left) are at last united in Balder's temple. The childhood sweethearts had been thwarted by Ingeborg's hostile brothers. While Ingeborg was forced into a marriage with an old chieftain, Sigurd Ring, Frithiof roamed the high seas in misery. When his undying love drove him home, he waited honourably until the old king died before at last winning his bride. (FRITHIOF AND INGEBORG BY J A MALMSTROM, CANVAS, C. 1840.)

BRYNHILD and Sigurd (above) find peace together at last after a romance wrecked by a web of intrigue and vengeance. After pledging his love to Brynhild, Sigurd was bewitched into marrying Gudrun. Brynhild, in her turn, was unwittingly tricked by Sigurd into marrying Gunner. When Brynhild discovered Sigurd's apparent betrayal, she cried out for vengeance. Sigurd was slain and Brynhild, overcome by grief, killed herself to be laid to rest beside him. (THE FUNERAL PYRE BY C BUTLER, CANVAS, 1909.)

T

TANNGNOST (meaning "Tooth-gnasher"), in Germanic mythology, was the name of one of the two billy goats which pulled *THOR*'s chariot. The other was named Tanngrisnir ("Tooth-grinder"). The rumble of the chariot was heard by people on earth as the sound of thunder. Like the magic boar of *VALHALLA*, which could be eaten one day and reappear alive the next, Thor's goats provided an end-less supply of meat as long as, after cooking, all their bones remained intact. Thor would then wave his magic hammer over the skin and bones and the goats came alive.

TAPIO was the Finnish forest god, who, along with his wife Meilikki and his son Nyyrikki, was believed to ensure that woodland game remained in plentiful supply. He had a dangerous side to his nature, however, as he enjoyed tickling or smothering people to death. His daughter Tuulikki was a spirit of the wind. Tapio is often portrayed as wearing a cloak of moss and a bonnet of fire.

THIALFI and his sister *ROSKVA* were the children of a farmer and servants of the Germanic thunder god *THOR*. When Thor and *LOKI* were travelling through Midgard they stopped at the farmhouse and Thor provided goats for supper on condition that all the bones be kept intact. Because Thialfi had not had a satisfying meal for a long time, he ignored this instruction and split a thigh bone to get at the marrow. Next morning, when Thor used his magic hammer to restore the goats to life, the thunder god noticed

TANNGNOST and Tanngrisnir (left) were a pair of goats who pulled Thor's chariot across the sky, creating the clatter and rumble of storm clouds. Thor alone among the gods never rode, but either strode or drove his goat-drawn chariot. (THOR AND THE GIANTS BY M E WINGE, CANVAS, C. 1890.)

TAPIO (above), a green god of the Finnish forests, dwelt in the depths of the green-wood, clad in moss, and growing a fir-like beard. Along with other sylvan deities, he was lord not just of forest plants, but also of forest beasts and the herds of woodland cattle. (ILLUSTRATION BY JAMES ALEXANDER, 1995.)

that one animal was lame. He was so enraged that he threatened destruction of the farm and de-manded compensation. He was placated only when Thialfi and Roskva were given to him as his servants. Although Thialfi lost a running contest to *HUGI* during Thor's visit to the frost giant strong-hold of *UTGARD*, his master was outwitted by magic in several chal-lenges too. In another myth Thialfi deserved Thor's gratitude when he toppled the enormous clay giant Mist Calf, which had caused Thor to panic with fear. He also fetched aid for the wounded thunder god after his duel with *HRUNGNIR*, the strongest of the frost giants.

THIASSI, or Thiazi, in Germanic mythology, was a frost giant and the father of *SKADI* who stole from the goddess *IDUN* the apples of youth. It was really *LOKI*'s fault that this event occurred. Disguised as an eagle, the giant grabbed hold of the god and, to secure his own release from Thiassi, Loki promised to deliver the goddess and her magic apples into the frost giant's hands. The effect upon the gods was immediate. Without Idun's apples to eat each day, they grew anxious and old. In this crisis Odin alone had the determination to rally enough strength to plan a recovery. The gods captured the trickster Loki, and made him fly as

THIALFI (left) and his sister, Roskva, accompanied Thor on a fabulous journey to Jotunheim. En route, they sheltered in a giant's glove, until woken by his gusty snores. Here, Thor batters the giant's head, hoping to silence his snores, while Thialfi and Roskva gaze on in dazed disbelief. (ILLUSTRATION BY NICK BEALE, 1995.)

THIAZI see *THIASSI*

THOKK was the callous frost giantess of Germanic myth. After the popular god *BALDER*'s unfortunate death, *HEL,* the queen of the "unworthy dead", said that she would allow him back to the land of the living on the condition that "everything in the nine worlds, dead and alive, weeps for him". Messengers were therefore sent out to ensure that everything mourned and were satisfied that they had achieved their aim. On their way back to *ASGARD*, however, they found Thokk in a cave, and when they explained their mission the giantess replied that she had no use for Balder and added, "Let Hel keep what she holds." Some versions of the myth maintain that Thokk was none other than *LOKI*.

THIASSI (left), a frost giant, disguised as an eagle, pestered Odin, Honir and Loki on a trip to Midgard. At one point Thiassi swooped down and scooped up the gods' dinner pot. Enraged, Loki lunged at the eagle with his staff but became stuck fast to the bird. (ILLUSTRATION BY PETER HURD, 1882.)

a falcon to Thiassi's hall in order to bring back Idun and her apples. This Loki was able to accomplish, but the frost giant almost thwarted the plan by turning himself yet again into an eagle and flying after the god. He very nearly caught up with Loki, but as Thiassi flew over *ASGARD* his wings were set alight by fires that the gods had placed on top of the stronghold's high walls. The giant could no longer fly and so fell to the ground, burned to death by the flames.

Eventually, Thiassi's daughter Skadi came to Asgard to seek compensation for her father's death. When her demands had been satisfied, Odin took Thiassi's eyes from his cloak and threw them into the sky as stars. "Thiassi will look down on all of us," he said, "for as long as the world lasts."

THOKK, alone among all the creatures in the nine worlds, refused to shed a single tear for Balder, so destroying his one chance of escape from Hel. Around bitter Thokk all creation weeps – the leaves, stones and snow itself – mourning the loss of the much-loved Balder. (ILLUSTRATION BY NICK BEALE, 1995.)

THOR was the Germanic thunder god. He was the son of ODIN, the chief god, and Fjorgyn, the goddess of earth. When the Anglo-Saxons eventually adopted the Roman calendar, they named the fifth day Thursday after Thor, for this was the day belonging to Jupiter, the Roman sky god and peer of the hot-tempered, red-headed Thor, along with the Greek Zeus and the Hindu Indra. His name means "thunder" and his magic hammer, MJOLLNIR, may once have meant "lightning". Among Icelanders and Norwegians family names like Thorsten recall the name of the god, for these farmers had little sympathy with the footloose Vikings who worshipped Odin, the father of the slain. The Icelandic colonists, who had fled southern Norway to escape the aggression of Danish and Swedish rulers, preferred honest Thor, the powerful but straightforward opponent of the frost giants.

Yet Thor, the bitter enemy of the frost giants, was in many aspects not unlike a giant himself. He was exceptionally strong, very

THOR, in his most popular guise as champion of the gods, was a tireless warrior and giant-slayer. With his red-hot hammer and belt of strength, which doubled his power, he was a formidable foe. Here, the thunder god swings his fiery missile. (ILLUSTRATION BY ARTHUR RACKHAM, C. 1900.)

large – his frequent companion LOKI, the fire god, usually attached himself to Thor's belt – energetic and had an enormous appetite, which allowed him to eat a whole ox at one sitting. And, of course, there was his relish for a contest, a trial of strength. Two goats drew Thor's great chariot across the sky: their names were Tooth-grinder and Tooth-gnasher. His magic weapons were a hammer, really a thunderbolt; iron gauntlets, which he used to handle the red-hot hammer shaft; and a belt that increased his strength. MJOLLNIR, the hammer, was the handiwork of two dwarfs, the sons of Ivaldi. It had a huge head and a short handle and always hit its target.

Thor was the mightiest of the Germanic gods and their staunch protector against the frost giants. At RAGNAROK, the doom of the gods,

he was destined to be killed by the poisonous venom of the sea serpent JORMUNGAND, although not before Thor had killed the monster. Before he was slain by this terrible son of Loki, however, Loki and he had many adventures together.

These adventures were often dangerous for Thor, especially when Loki led the thunder god into danger as a price for his own freedom. Such was the case with their visit to the hall of the frost giant GEIRROD. Having been captured by Geirrod when Loki was in the shape of a hawk, he could avoid death only by making a promise to deliver an unarmed Thor into the frost giant's hands. Because Thor enjoyed Loki's company and was so trusting, he let the fire god lead him to Geirrod's hall without the protection of his hammer, gloves and belt. But on the

edge of JOTUNHEIM, the land of the frost giants, Thor and Loki spent the night with GRID, a friendly giantess. Grid warned Thor about Geirrod's hatred of the gods. She told him that he would be especially pleased to avenge the death of HRUNGNIR, the strongest of the frost giants whom Thor had killed in a duel. The thunder god still had a piece of this dead frost giant's throwing stone stuck in his head to prove it, so Thor was most grateful at Grid's loan of her own belt of strength, iron gloves and unbreakable staff.

Crossing a torrent of water and blood near the frost giant's hall proved difficult, until Thor blocked the source of the blood with a well-aimed stone. It struck GJALP, Geirrod's daughter, whose menstrual outpouring had swollen the river. Even then, the two gods were swept away, as Thor lost his footing and Loki clung desperately to the belt of Grid that the thunder god was wearing. Happily, Thor succeeded in grabbing a mountain ash overhanging the flood and scrambled ashore on the opposite bank.

Soon Thor and Loki arrived at Geirrod's hall, where servants grudgingly received them. The owner was nowhere to be seen, so Thor sat down in a chair to await his return. Snatching a nap, he was surprised when he dreamed he was floating in the air. Thor opened his eyes and saw that his head was about to be rammed against the ceiling. Quick as a flash, he used Grid's staff to push against the ceiling, with the result that the chair came down hard enough to crush Gjalp and Greip to death. These two daughters of Geirrod had been

of such enormous size that Thor would be struck by terror on seeing him. Named MIST CALF, the clay giant was animated by the heart of a mare and, slow moving though he was, clouds gathered round his towering head. On the day of the duel Thor wet himself at the sight of Mist Calf, although his chario-teer had the good sense to topple the clay giant by attacking his legs with an axe. Mist Calf's fall shook Jotunheim, the land of the frost giants. In the fight with Hrungnir it was Thor who came off best, although the thunder god was left

THOR's (left) hammer was a symbol of creative and destructive power and a source of fertility, renewal and good fortune. As Christianity swept north, the sign of the cross often fused with the sign of the hammer, as in this charm, containing a cross within a hammer. (SILVER, 10TH CENT.)

pinned to the ground by one of the dead frost giant's legs and with a piece of whetstone lodged in his head. None of the gods could release Thor and it was fortunate that his own three-year-old frost giant son MAGNI turned up after the fight. The son of the frost giant-ess Jarnsaxa, a mistress of Thor, Magni also told his flattened father how he could have dealt with Hrungnir with his bare fists. Thor was delighted to see Magni's strength and gave him the dead frost giant's steed Golden Mane as a reward, much to Odin's

THOR (below), the thunder god, ruled the storms and tempests. With eyes ablaze and hair aflame, he bears his red-hot hammer in its iron gauntlet. As his bronze chariot made a racket like the clash and clatter of copper kettles, he was nicknamed the Kettle Vendor. (ILLUSTRATION BY JAMES ALEXANDER, 1995.)

thrusting it upwards. Then the frost giant returned and tried to kill Thor as well. Using a pair of tongs, he launched a red-hot iron ball at Thor, but the thunder god caught it deftly in the iron gloves he had been given by Grid, and returned the compliment by throwing it back at the giant. The iron ball passed through an iron pillar before tearing a hole in Geirrod's belly. Afterwards Thor smashed the skulls of all the servants.

The frost giant mentioned by Grid, the powerful Hrungnir, had fallen in single combat with Thor. Foolishly, the frost giant challenged Odin to a horse race but then, as a guest at the gods' stronghold of ASGARD, he drank too much and insulted the gods. When Thor returned at this point the giant challenged Thor to a duel.

The frost giants did what they could to aid Hrungnir in the forth-coming fight. They built a clay giant

annoyance. "You should not give a horse to the son of a giantess instead of your own father," complained Odin.

Another famous adventure in Jotunheim concerns the visit of Thor and Loki to the stronghold of *UTGARD*. On the way the thunder god passed through Midgard, the land of people, and gained two human servants named *THIALFI* and *ROSKVA*, a brother and sister. It happened that Thialfi disobeyed an instruction of Thor when they dined together at his parents' farm. Thor told everyone to be careful with the bones of some goats they were eating. But hungry Thialfi split a thigh bone to get at the marrow, before throwing the bone on the goat skins in a corner. Next morning, when Thor used his magic hammer to restore the eaten goats to life, the thunder god noticed that one of them was lame. As compensation and in order to prevent him from slaying the household, Thialfi and Roskva pledged themselves as Thor's servants.

As Thor, Loki, Thialfi and Roskva neared Utgard, they spent one night in an empty hall. It was so big that several of the halls in Asgard, the home of the gods, could have fitted inside it at the same time. Later they realized that the hall was in fact the thumb of a frost giant's empty glove. It belonged to *SKRYMIR*, whose name means "vast". Blows delivered by a frustrated Thor to Skrymir's sleeping head were dismissed by the giant as either a leaf or a twig brushing his brow during the night. On their arrival at Utgard, the travellers were just as amazed at the stronghold's dimensions. While Thor said that size was of no importance – "the bigger they are, the heavier they fall" – Loki was more thoughtful. Inside Utgard huge frost giants eyed the four guests. Their leader at first ignored them, but finally acknowledged "little" Thor. Then he devised a series of games in which Loki, Thialfi and Thor all failed to shine. First the fire god lost an eating contest. A second event saw Thialfi easily outpaced in a foot-race. Then successively Thor lost a drinking contest, managed to lift only one paw of a cat, and, most embarrassing of all, was easily wrestled down on to one knee by "an old, old woman".

Once Thor admitted on leaving Utgard that they had come off second best, the leader of the frost giants revealed that he had used spells to gain the advantage. He told them how Loki had actually been pitted against wildfire, and Thialfi against his own thought, while Thor had tried to swallow the

ocean, lift the massive sea serpent Jormungand and wrestle with old age. As soon as this message was delivered, Utgard vanished. Only then did it dawn on Thor that Skrymir and Utgard were illusions, vast creations sent out by frightened frost giants. But it gave Loki some satisfaction to learn that brain had indeed triumphed over brawn.

Even Thor had to admit that on certain occasions Loki's cleverness was necessary to hold the frost giants in check. Such a moment in time was when Mjollnir, Thor's magic hammer, fell into their hands after it was stolen by the dwarfs. Its new owner, the frost giant THRYM, demanded as the price of the hammer's return the hand of FREYJA, the fertility goddess. Loki got Thor to dress in Freyja's clothes and go to Thrym's hall instead. Despite his god-like appetite, Thor was passed

THOR (above) impulsive as ever, confronted mighty Skrymir with his tiny hammer, bashing him over the head to silence his snores, but to no avail. Each time the giant woke he scratched his brow and nodded off again. Later, Thor learnt that Skrymir had been an illusion. (ILLUSTRATION BY J HUARD, 1930.)

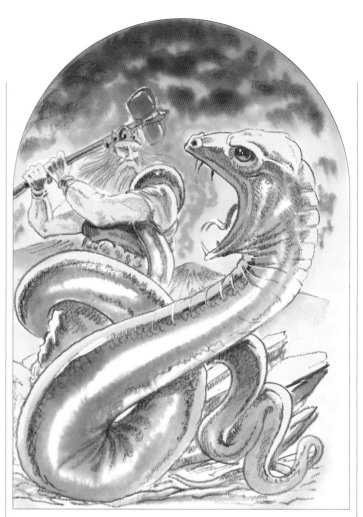

THOR (left) and his party visited the icy citadel of Utgard, the stronghold of the frost giants, where they underwent a series of allegorical tests. Thialfi was outstripped by the speed of Thought, Loki out-eaten by Wildfire, and Thor overcome by Age. Here, Thor fails to drain a horn brimful of the ocean. (ILLUSTRATION BY JAMES ALEXANDER, 1995.)

THOR (above) wrestles with Jormungand in their final combat at Ragnarok. Trapped within the serpent's crushing coils, Thor smashed its ugly head with a fatal blow of his hammer; he then staggered back nine paces and drowned in the flood of venom flowing from the beast's gaping jaws. (ILLUSTRATION BY JAMES ALEXANDER, 1995.)

off by his "bridesmaid" Loki as a blushing bride, and an excited Thrym handed over Mjollnir. The ensuing massacre did a great deal to restore Thor's fierce reputation, which had been tarnished by the god having to dress like a woman.

Mjollnir was the sole protection of the gods against the frost giants. It was the thunderbolt which terrorized them prior to the catastrophe of Ragnarok. Apart from its destructive side, the hammer had other magic powers over fertility and death. It seems to have had the ability to restore animal life. It also hallowed marriage, for otherwise Thrym would not have been so ready to place Mjollnir between

Thor's knees when the thunder god was disguised as Freyja. But throughout the myths relating to Thor we are never unconscious of its unlimited destructive powers. For it was the thunder god's purpose to quell the enemies of the gods – "to smash their legs, break their skulls, and crush their backs". Like his Hindu equivalent Indra, Thor was the scourge of evil and in Germanic mythology this could only mean frost giants. Loki's eventual siding with these grim opponents is therefore one of the saddest events to befall Thor, for the two gods "both enjoyed each other's company". (See also NORSE HEROES; RAGNAROK)

RINGS OF POWER

AMONG THE VIKINGS, the ring was a potent symbol of power, fortune and fame. A gift of honour and form of currency, it was also sometimes a royal heirloom, such as the Swedish Sviagriss. The magical rings of Norse myth were also symbols of destiny and, in their bleakest form, symbols of doom. One famous example was the cursed ring, Andvarinaut, which blighted many lives. Another ring of doom was Thor's Domhring, formed by a circle of stone statues surrounding a punishment pillar in front of his temple. The Domhring possibly symbolized the inevitability of retribution. Much more joyous and fabulous rings were Odin's astounding Draupnir which literally dripped eight similar gold rings every nine days; or Thor's Oath Ring, a symbol of fair play and good faith. The rings of heroes inevitably brought wealth and power, but not always happiness and sometimes tragedy, if corrupted by greed. Yet the pure rings of Orthnit, Wolfdietrich and Dietrich were symbols of a ring-lord's circle of power and everlasting fame.

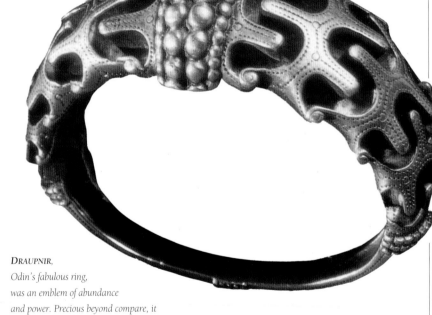

DRAUPNIR,

Odin's fabulous ring,

was an emblem of abundance

and power. Precious beyond compare, it

dripped eight similar gold rings every ninth night, consolidating his vast wealth and dominion over the nine worlds. Draupnir was crafted by the dwarf, Sindri, while his brother, Brokk, pumped the bellows. In an extravagant gesture of grief, Odin cast the ring upon Balder's funeral pyre, but later retrieved it when Hermod ventured to Hel. The return of the ring symbolized the promise of fertility after winter bleakness. Here, the dwarf Sindri fashions the magnificent ring with fire and arcane magic in his underground forge. (ILLUSTRATION BY ALAN LEE, 1984.)

THE GOLD RING among the Vikings was a precious token of power, fame and fortune. Sometimes bequeathed as an heirloom, it was also often buried with the ring-lord for the journey to the otherworld, such as this burial treasure. Exquisitely wrought, the ring's clear, bold lines express the vigour and strength of Viking craft. (GILT SILVER, 10TH CENTURY.)

ALBERICH (above), a dwarf of the Niebelungenlied, forged a ring of power from the Rhinegold stolen from the Rhine Maidens. News of the gold robbery and ring of power incited gods and giants alike to action. The giants Fafner and Fasolt demanded the ring in payment for building Valhalla, and carried off Freyja as a hostage. In the border, the gods, Odin, Frigg, Loki, Freyr and Thor all search despairingly for the hidden treasure. (ILLUSTRATION BY F VON STASSEN, 1914.)

DIETRICH (above), a Gothic hero, won a wondrous ring from the dwarf, Laurin, who ruled a fabulous underground kingdom lit by gems. After various battles and intrigues, Dietrich overcame the wily dwarf, and claimed his magical gold ring as well as a girdle of strength, a cape of invisibility, a magical sword and a vast ring-hoard. Laurin's ring was the very one owned by Dietrich's great-grandfather, the Emperor Wolfdietrich. Here, Dietrich breaks into Laurin's enchanted, ever-flowering rose garden, before winning the ring treasures. (ILLUSTRATION BY ALAN LEE, 1984.)

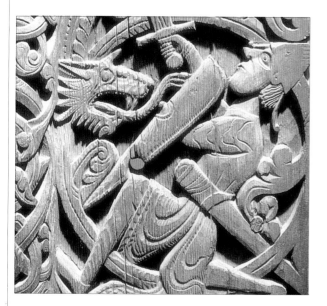

SIGURD (right) won the cursed ring, Andvarinaut, after slaying its dragon guardian, Fafnir. Although innocent himself, he suffered from the ring's web of doom. After falling in love with the splendid Valkyrie, Brynhild, he was bewitched by Grimhild into betraying Brynhild by marrying Gudrun. When his memory returned, he suffered from guilt and grief. Sigurd's gold in turn evoked the envy of the Nibelung brothers who slew him, urged on by a vengeful Brynhild, seeking to assuage her honour. As the hero breathed his last, he died calling to Brynhild. (ILLUSTRATION BY ARTHUR RACKHAM, C. 1900.)

THE RING ANDVARINAUT wove a fortune of gold much like Draupnir, but was tainted by the bitter curse of Andvari. Hreidmar, who had demanded the ring as wiergold from Loki, was the first to suffer from the curse by falling at the hands of his son, Fafnir, who lusted after the gold. Next, Fafnir turned himself into a monstrous dragon to guard the ring-hoard. When the youthful hero Sigurd (above) slew the dragon, he inherited the fabulous ring-hoard, but with it a terrible curse. (WOOD CARVING, 12TH CENTURY.)

T

THRUD, in Germanic mythology, was the daughter of the thunder god *THOR* and his wife *SIF*. She was promised to the dwarf *ALVIS* as a payment for his handicraft. But Thor prevented the dwarf from claiming Thrud by keeping him talking until morning, when the sunlight turned Alvis into stone.

THRYM, in Germanic mythology, was the frost giant who came to acquire *THOR*'s magic hammer. The gods were at a loss because only this weapon could protect them against the frost giants. When Thrym said he would exchange the hammer for the fertility goddess *FREYJA*, the fire god *LOKI* persuaded Thor to go to the frost giant's stronghold disguised as the bride in order to recover the hammer. Loki also went along in the form of a maidservant. Thus the unusual pair arrived at Thrym's hall. Even though the frost giant was quite suspicious about his bride-to-be, Loki cleverly managed to talk him into producing the hammer, which Thor then used to lay low all the frost giants in sight.

THRYM (left), a daring storm giant, stole Thor's sacred hammer, causing panic at Asgard. Here, the giant broods on his rocky hilltop overlooked by Loki, disguised as a falcon, and scouting the icy wastes in search of the hammer, buried eight fathoms down. (ILLUSTRATION BY JAMES ALEXANDER, 1995.)

TIR see *TYR*

TIWAZ see *TYR*

TRIGLAV was a three-headed god of the Slavs living in central Europe. At Stettin in present-day Poland, Triglav once boasted four separate temples. These were maintained by war booty, one tenth being the amount due to the god at the end of a campaign. The best temple at Stettin housed a black horse for Triglav's use. In the twelfth century Christianity arrived and Triglav's statues were broken and their multiple heads sent to the Pope in Rome as curiosities.

TUONI was the Finnish god of the dead, who lived in the dark land of Tuonela, from which few travellers return. With his wife Tuonetar he had several children who were deities of suffering, including Kipu-Tytto, goddess of illness. One of the few heroes who managed to escape from Tuonela was *VAINAMOINEN*. After successfully crossing the river that marked the border of Tuonela, he was received there by Tuonetar, who gave him beer to drink. But while her visitor slept, her son created a vast iron mesh across the river so that Vainamoinen could not return that way and would be trapped forever. But when he woke, the hero changed into an otter and swam easily through the net.

TUONI guarded the dark realm of Tuonela on the banks of a black river. When Vainamoinen visited Tuoni in search of magic charms, he was trapped by a vast iron net, flung across the river; but the hero changed into an otter and slipped through. (ILLUSTRATION BY NICK BEALE, 1995.)

TYR (left), famed for his bravery and might, was assigned the task of feeding Fenrir, the fierce wolf-son of Loki. Yet Fenrir kept on growing, stronger and fiercer every day, until all-seeing Odin realized the danger and the gods decided to bind the beast underground. (ILLUSTRATION BY J HUARD, 1930.)

TYR (above left), a popular sword god, was invoked before battle, honoured with sword dances, and had his rune engraved on blades. He lost his right hand in a fight with Fenrir, but was just as skilful with his left, and at Ragnarok slew the hell-hound Garm. (ILLUSTRATION BY JAMES ALEXANDER, 1995.)

URD (above), a wise Norn, personified the past, while her sisters represented present and future fate. The Norns warned the gods of future evil and drew lessons from the past. Urd fed two swans on the Urdar pool who gave birth to the swans of the world. (ILLUSTRATION BY JAMES ALEXANDER, 1995.)

TYR, also known as Tiv and Tiwaz, was the Germanic war god, and the son of *ODIN* and his wife *FRIGG*. The Anglo-Saxons usually called him Tiw and gave his name to Tuesday (Tiwesdaeg in Old English). He was closely associated with Odin and, like that god, received sacrifices of hanged men. It is not unlikely that Tyr was an early sky god whose powers were later passed to Odin and Thor. *GUNGNIR*, Odin's magic spear, may once have belonged to Tyr, since it was customary for the Vikings to cast a spear over the heads of an enemy as a sacrifice before fighting commenced in earnest, and over recent years archaeologists have found numerous splendidly ornamented spears dedicated to Tyr.

The myth of Tyr relates to the binding of the wolf *FENRIR*. This monstrous creature had grown so powerful that the gods decided to restrain it. No ordinary chain was strong enough, and before Fenrir would consent to a magic one being placed round his neck, Tyr had to put his hand in the wolf's mouth as a sign of goodwill. When the wolf discovered the chain could not be broken, he bit off Tyr's hand. Although Tyr was in agony, the other gods just laughed. The downgrading of Tyr may not be unconnected with the loss of a hand. A Celtic god by the name of Nuada was forced to give up the leadership of the Irish Tuatha De Danann ("the people of the goddess Dana") after he lost a hand at the first battle of Magh Tuireadh. But Tyr was still able to fight at *RAGNAROK*, during which it was destined that the hound Garm, which stood at the gates of *HEL*, acting as watchdog to the land of the dead, was to leap at Tyr's throat and they would kill each other.

URD, or Wyrd (meaning "Fate" or "Past"), was one of three sisters who were the Germanic fates and were known as the *NORNS*. The two other sisters were Verdandi ("Being" or "Present") and Skuld ("Necessity" or "Future"). Urd gave her name to the well that was situated beneath one of the roots of *YGGDRASIL*, the cosmic tree, and that was where the gods would hold their daily meeting. As was also the case in Greek mythology, the gods were not superior or beyond the influence of the fates. Indeed, Urd warned the chief of the Germanic gods, *ODIN*, that he was destined to be killed by the terrible wolf *FENRIR* at *RAGNAROK*, the doom of the gods.

V

UTGARD ("Outer Place"), in Germanic mythology, was the huge giants' stronghold in *JOTUNHEIM*, where *LOKI*, *THOR* and Thor's servant *THIALFI* found themselves in contests against unequal opponents. Loki failed to consume more food than wildfire; Thialfi could not keep pace as a runner with thought; and Thor was unable to drink the sea dry, pick up the sea serpent *JORMUNGAND* or wrestle old age. When they left, the gods realized that Utgard was an illusion made by the frightened frost giants to deter Thor, their greatest enemy.

VAFTHRUDNIR, in Germanic mythology, was a wise frost giant. He was believed to have gained his impressive store of wisdom by consulting the dead. Possibly like *ODIN*, the chief of the gods, who voluntarily hanged himself for nine nights on *YGGDRASIL*, the cosmic tree, in order to become wise, Vafthrudnir had also temporarily died. Seeking to test his knowledge against the giant's, Odin decided to journey to Vafthrudnir's land in disguise. There he challenged the gigantic "riddle-master" to match their knowledge of the past, the present and the future. After an impressive display on the part of both Odin and Vafthrudnir, the giant was eventually defeated by a quite unanswerable question, when the god asked the giant what he had whispered to his dead son *BALDER* before he lit the pyre on which he lay. It is implied in the story that Odin's foreknowledge allowed him to assure Balder of future resurrection and worship on the new earth, "risen out of the water, fresh and green", after *RAGNAROK*, the doom of the gods and the end of the world.

UTGARD, *the icy citadel of the frost giants, was carved out of snow blocks and glittering icicles. The Norse poets, who knew all about the terrors of the ice of their northern homes, inevitably portrayed the evil giants in just such a harsh realm, where numbing cold froze the muscles and paralysed the will. (ILLUSTRATION BY ALAN LEE, 1984.)*

Now Vafthrudnir recognized Odin and admitted that no one could tell what the god had whispered into the ear of the dead Balder. The frost giant's last words were: "So I have pitted myself against Odin, always the wisest."

VAINAMOINEN, the chief hero of Finnish epic, was the son of a primal goddess, *LUONNOTAR*. He was always depicted as a vigorous and sensitive old man, who from birth possessed the wisdom of the ages, for he was in his mother's womb for at least thirty years. As the champion of the Kalevala (which means "the fatherland of heroes"), Vainamoinen was gifted with extraordinary magical powers. He was less lucky in love, however. When he sought a bride from among the women of Pohja, he was promised one of Louhi's daughters if he made the magic talisman, the Sampo. He gave the task to his comrade Ilmarinen and so Louhi's daughter was married to Ilmarinen instead. But the bride was killed and the magic talisman stolen, so Vainamoinen and Ilmarinen, joined by *LEMINKAINEN*, set off to find the Sampo. After several great adventures, they succeeded in recovering it. However, Louhi raised a great storm and, in the form of a griffin, descended onto their ship. Only the swift action of Vainamoinen saved them, but during the storm the Sampo was lost to the winds. When the storm had passed, Vainamoinen collected all the scattered pieces together and was able to restore some of the talisman's former power. With his mission completed, Vainamoinen built a ship and embarked on an endless voyage. (See also *TREASURES AND TALISMANS*; *SORCERY AND SPELLS*)

VAINAMOINEN (above), a peerless mage, was also a gentle, humane hero. A tireless explorer, he journeyed across the known world and, alone among heroes, returned from the underworld. At the end of his life, he set sail in a copper boat and embarked on a voyage without end. (VAINOMOINEN BY A GALLEN-KALLELA, CANVAS, C. 1890.)

VAINAMOINEN (below) courts reluctant Aino in her father's grove. Promised to the old man against her will by her brother, she drowned herself rather than marry, only to wind up as a salmon on his fishing line, before leaping back into the river and returning to her human form. (THE AINO TRIPTYCH BY A GALLEN-KALLELA, CANVAS, C. 1890.)

The newly fallen joining the residents in Valhalla had to enter by a door called Valgrind ("the sacred barred-gate of the slain"). Even before they reached this entrance, they must pass several obstacles, including a fast-running river of air. Once in Valhalla "the men killed in war" were miraculously cured of their wounds and were able to indulge endlessly in the pleasures of feasting and fighting. The meat of a magic boar was prepared as wonderful stew in an inexhaustible cauldron. The same boar was eaten day after day through a process of resurrection. Mead was provided from the teats of a goat. It was said that every day the Einherjar put on their armour, went to the practice ground and fought each other. If killed, they were restored to life. At midday they returned to Valhalla and started drinking. Such an existence for a Viking helps to explain Odin's popularity in Denmark, southern Norway and Sweden, the regions where most of the raiding expeditions came from.

VALHALLA'S Valkyries – beautiful battle-maidens – welcomed the chosen slain with open arms. At other times, Odin's sons, Hermod or Bragi, received the heroes, conducting them to the foot of Odin's throne; while Odin himself rose to greet the bravest Vikings at the gate. (ILLUSTRATION BY E WALLCOUSINS, C. 1920.)

VALHALLA was a Viking's paradise where chosen heroes fought and feasted from dawn to dusk. Wounds healed overnight, and mead and meat flowed freely. The hectic round of combat ensured that heroes stayed in fighting form, fit for the final battle at Ragnarok. (ILLUSTRATION BY W B DRACK, 1900.)

VALHALLA (above), the Hall of the Slain, was built in the shimmering grove of Glesir. Encircled by strong outer walls, the magnificent hall glittered with precious metals, its walls were built of spears and its roof of shining shields. This starlit scene evokes a sense of the untold wonders that lie within. (ILLUSTRATION BY F VON STASSEN, 1914.)

VALHALLA, or Valholl, in Germanic mythology, was the hall of the *EINHERJAR* ("heroic dead"), those warriors slain on the battle-field and chosen by *ODIN* himself as his followers. Built in *ASGARD* by Odin, Valhalla was enormous. It had over five hundred doors, each wide enough to allow up to eight hundred men to march through abreast. These wide doors were designed to allow the chosen warriors to pour forth at the first sign of *RAGNAROK*, the doom of the gods. Then they were destined to fall again, alongside the gods, in a great battle on the *VIGRID* Plain.

Odin was known as the father of the slain and he was the host who presided over Valhalla, and daily sent out the *VALKYRIES* to add to the number of the dead. In Valhalla the Valkyries would carry food and drinks for the Einherjar.

Ragnarok was always given as the reason for creating Valhalla. When asked about his habit of giving luck to a warrior in a battle and then suddenly taking it away, Odin said that "the grey wolf watches the halls of the gods": that is to say, the gods were constantly threatened by Ragnarok, the catastrophe in which they would die in mutual destruction with the frost giants and the forces of evil. The gathering of the "heroic dead" in Valhalla was the only way the gods could prepare to face their own fate, no matter how vain the attempt would prove to be. At least Odin's men, caught up in a berserk fury, could be guaranteed to tear into the enemy ranks in one last battle. (See also *THE VALKYRIES*)

VALHOLL see *VALHALLA*

VALI was one of the few bright young gods to survive Ragnarok. Destined from birth to avenge Balder's death, he grew at an amazing rate, reaching manhood in a single day and rushing off with uncombed hair to slay Hodr. Here, he is portrayed striding across the new earth after Ragnarok. (ILLUSTRATION BY NICK BEALE, 1995.)

VALI was the son of *ODIN* and *RIND* and was destined to kill blind *HODR* in revenge for his unwitting murder of *BALDER*. Fulfilling a prophecy, he grew from a baby to manhood in a single day and rushed off to kill Hodr. Along with his half-brother *VIDAR*, he survived *RAGNAROK*. Another Vali was one of the unlucky sons of *LOKI*.

THE VALKYRIES ("female choosers of the slain") were *ODIN*'s battle- or shield-maidens. They rode over battlefields and selected the *EINHERJAR* ("heroic dead") who would go to *VALHALLA*. They probably derived from something more dreadful than the attendants of Valhalla, and must have originally been the goddesses of slaughter itself, wild Amazon-like creatures who took great delight in the severed limbs and bloody wounds of battle. Something of this early terror can be imagined in an account of the battle of Stamford Bridge, King Harold's victory over the Norwegians shortly before his defeat by the Normans at Battle in 1066. A soldier in the Norwegian army dreamt of a Valkyrie before the battle. He thought he was on the king of Norway's ship, when he beheld a great witch on an island, with a fork in one hand to rake up the dead and a trough in the other to catch the blood. (See also *THE VALKYRIES*; *RAGNAROK*)

VALKYRIES (above), Odin's martial maidens, alighted on the battlefield to select the bravest warriors for Valhalla, the idyllic abode of Odin's ghostly army. Although quite charming in Valhalla, on the battlefield the Valkyries became sinister spirits of slaughter, goading heroes to their death. (THE VALKYRIES BY G VON LEEKE, 1870.)

VALKYRIES (below) rode through the stormy sky on magnificent pearly steeds, personifying clouds, and whose soaking manes sprayed the earth with fertile frost and dew. They also scoured the seas, snatching sailors from ships, or sometimes beckoning from the strand. (THE RIDE OF THE VALKYRIE BY H HERMAN, CANVAS, C. 1890.)

RAGNAROK

RAGNAROK WAS THE preordained doom of the gods, and the climax of the cosmic drama. The seeds of doom were sown at the dawn of time when the world and its first creatures emerged from the violent extremes of ice and fire. Inherently fragile, the universe was beset by forces of destruction and flawed from the outset. The inevitable climax was precipitated by a series of disasters. Loki, a catalyst of evil, spawned three fearsome monsters against whom the gods were ultimately powerless. Consumed with hate, Loki went on to slay Balder, symbol of goodness and beauty. Beyond Asgard, the enmity of the hostile giants gathered momentum until, at Ragnarok, all the world's destructive forces burst forth in cataclysmic disaster. Apocalypse is a common mythical theme, but the Norse vision is starker than most and unique in the loss of its gods. In one hopeful version, some gods survive and the earth emerges fresh and green, purged by flood and fire. Ragnarok casts a dark shadow over the Norse myths, yet also highlights the heroism of gods and heroes.

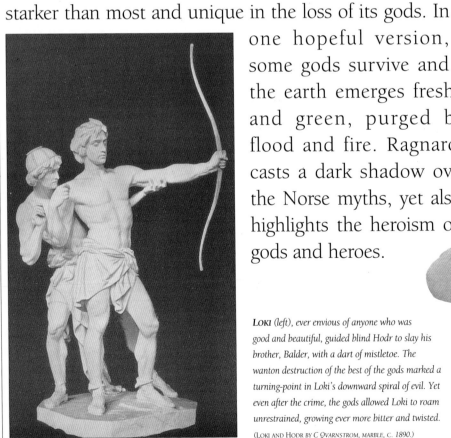

LOKI (left), ever envious of anyone who was good and beautiful, guided blind Hodr to slay his brother, Balder, with a dart of mistletoe. The wanton destruction of the best of the gods marked a turning-point in Loki's downward spiral of evil. Yet even after the crime, the gods allowed Loki to roam unrestrained, growing ever more bitter and twisted. (LOKI AND HODR BY C QVARNSTROM, MARBLE, C. 1890.)

THE MIGHT OF THOR (above) and his hammer, Mjollnir, symbolized the foremost defence of the gods against the threat of the giants and the doom of Ragnarok. Yet Thor's sustained might proved ultimately inadequate to withstand the combined onslaught of giants and monsters. At the end, however, Thor rid the world of the giant monster, Jormungand, before dying himself from its venom. (THOR BY B FOGELBERG, MARBLE, C. 1890.)

JORMUNGAND (above) was one of the evils threatening the survival of the Norse world. Along with his monster siblings, Fenrir and Hel, Jormungand epitomized darkness and destruction. The massive serpent lurked in the ocean depths, circling the world in a stranglehold. Coiled in upon itself, this striking snake motif recalls the World Serpent curled around Midgard with its tail in its mouth, until it burst forth at Ragnarok. (BROOCH, 7TH CENTURY.)

LOKI (above) gate-crashes Aegir's feast and ridicules the gods with his sardonic wit, undermining and humiliating each in turn. None can either match or silence him, until Thor enters and threatens Loki with his hammer. Odin, at the right, looks on in speechless sorrow, recognizing the signs of Ragnarok. (AEGIR'S FEAST BY C HANSEN, CANVAS, C. 1861.)

ODIN (left), despite all his wisdom and power, was powerless to prevent the imminent doom of the gods. Yet he tried everything to fend off the fateful moment. Here, he carves magic runes on his spear, setting out rules of conduct for giants and dwarfs, gods and mortals. Odin learnt the wisdom of the runes from the dead when hanging from the sacred Yggdrasil in voluntary self-sacrifice. He also paid for wisdom with one eye at Mimir's well. Yet all his spies and sources only reinforce his own foreknowledge of doom. (ILLUSTRATION BY F VON STASSEN, 1914.)

AT RAGNAROK (above) the mighty walls of Asgard, home of the Aesir gods, were destroyed and the heavenly Bifrost Bridge was set alight by Surt, the fearsome flame giant. Jormungand, the gigantic World Serpent, burst from the seething ocean and engulfed the Vigrid Plain, spewing venom in all directions. Fenrir broke his bonds and roamed the earth with his savage brood, spreading death and destruction. The wolves swallowed the sun and moon, and even Yggdrasil itself shuddered. Over the whirling seas, Loki sailed with his giant host, while his daughter Hel rose from misty Niflheim with her pale army of the dead, and the assembled host issued forth over the Vigrid Plain. At the very end, Surt set all the nine worlds ablaze and the earth sank beneath the boiling ocean. (ILLUSTRATION BY ALAN LEE, 1984.)

THE VALKYRIES (left), Odin's formidable martial shield-maidens, gathered up the heroic slain from the battlefield and ferried them to Valhalla where they kept in fighting form until Ragnarok. By raising a heroic army, Odin determined to put up a fighting stand against the enemy host at Ragnarok. (THE RIDE OF THE VALKYRIES ANON.)

THE VANIR were the older of the two branches of the Germanic family of gods and were fertility deities. They lived at Vanaheim, far from *ASGARD*, the fortified residence of the *AESIR*, the younger branch, who were primarily war gods. Myth relates how the Vanir and the Aesir fought for supremacy not long after creation. After the Aesir had won, peace was sealed by an exchange of gods and goddesses. The Vanir sent to Asgard the sea god *NJORD* and his twin son and daughter *FREYR* and *FREYJA*, and also *KVASIR*, who was believed to be second to none in his wisdom. The Aesir despatched to Vanaheim long-legged *HONIR* and wise *MIMIR*.

At first Honir and Mimir were welcomed and accepted by the Vanir, but the gods gradually came to the conclusion that they had got the worst of the exchange with the Aesir. The problem was the terrible indecisiveness of Honir, which reached embarrassing proportions whenever Mimir was absent. To the Vanir it seemed that Mimir was not only Honir's voice but also his brain, so in anger they cut off Mimir's head and sent it back to Asgard. Although this did not rekindle the conflict, it effectively caused a rift between the Aesir and the Vanir which greatly reduced the mythological significance of the Vanir, so they slowly faded into the background.

The distinction between the older Vanir and the younger Aesir was uncertain even in Viking times. When the sagas were collected in the late twelfth century, there was speculation about the origins of the two groups. The Icelander Snorri Sturluson thought that the name of the Aesir recalled their homeland in Asia, and that *THOR* was the grandson of King Priam of Troy and *ODIN* his descendant in the twentieth generation, while the Vanir were originally inhabitants of the land by the River Don, formerly called Vanaquisl. Today, however, these theories have been discounted.

THE VANIR, deities of fertility, wealth and health, were worshipped by farmers. The three main Vanir gods, Njord (centre) and his lovely twins, Freyja and Freyr, were all gentle, benign spirits of nature, who nourished the earth and seas, and granted fair weather and good harvests. (ILLUSTRATION BY JAMES ALEXANDER, 1995.)

VE, in Germanic mythology, was one of the sons of *BOR* and the brother of *ODIN* and *VILI*. At the beginning of creation the primeval cow *AUDHUMLA* sustained herself by licking the ice and from her ample teats flowed enough milk to feed the frost giant *YMIR*, the first living creature. He is described as being utterly evil. However, Audhumla's licking also uncovered *BURI*, the grand-father of Ve. All the gods were descended from Buri, because his son Bor married the frost giantess Bestla and had three sons – Odin, Vili and Ve.

Although the blood of the frost giants and the gods intermingled, the implacable enmity between them could not be denied or resolved, for it went right back to the killing of Ymir. Odin, Vili and Ve disliked Ymir and his growing band of frost giants. Eventually, their dislike turned to hatred and they slew Ymir, making the world in *GINNUNGAGAP* (the "yawning emptiness") from the giant's body.

Afterwards the three brothers found on the seashore two fallen trees, an ash and an elm. From the wood they made first man and then woman. Odin breathed into them the spirit of life; Vili gave them intelligence and emotion; and Ve added the ability to see and hear. In some versions of the creation myth, Ve is known as Lodur or Lothur.

THE VANIR were famed for magic and foresight of which the macho Aesir were a little suspicious, except for Odin who, ever eager to increase his knowledge, rapidly absorbed the Vanir arts. Here, the fruitful Vanir twins follow Odin and Frigg over the Bifrost Bridge, with Thor and Loki in the rear. (ILLUSTRATION BY F VON STASSEN, 1914.)

VIDAR *(above), a strong, silent and solitary god, lived alone in a leafy palace deep in his primal forest. He personified the imperishable forces of nature, and was one of the few gods destined to survive Ragnarok. He slew the wolf Fenrir with his iron-shod foot.*

(ILLUSTRATION BY NICK BEALE, 1995.)

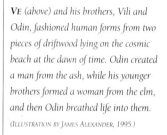

VE *(above) and his brothers, Vili and Odin, fashioned human forms from two pieces of driftwood lying on the cosmic beach at the dawn of time. Odin created a man from the ash, while his younger brothers formed a woman from the elm, and then Odin breathed life into them.*

(ILLUSTRATION BY JAMES ALEXANDER, 1995.)

VELES *guarded cattle and flocks for the Slavs. Especially popular with farmers, he survived into the nineteenth century, when Russian farmers still honoured him in the harvest fields by curling the ears of one sheaf of corn (see right), symbolizing the god's curly hair and beard.*

(ILLUSTRATION BY NICK BEALE, 1995.)

VELES, or Volos, was the Russian god who had authority over flocks and herds. It was customary to swear oaths in the names of Veles and *PERUNU*, who was the thunder god. When Vladimir, ruler of Kiev, was baptized into the Orthodox faith in 988, he had a statue of Veles thrown into the River Dniepner. In Russian folklore, however, the god of flocks survives. For instance, at harvest time the ears of the last sheaf of corn are still

woven into a plait known as "Veles' beard". Also in Russian Orthodox tradition, Veles was incorporated into the Christian faith by identifying him with St Blasius, who was a shepherd and martyr from Cappadocia. Prayers offered to this saint are expected to protect and increase flocks of sheep and goats.

VIDAR was the silent and solitary god of Germanic mythology. He was the son of *ODIN* and the frost giantess *GRID*, and lived in a place called Vidi, where all was quiet and peaceful. It was Vidar's destiny to avenge his father's death at *RAGNAROK*, the doom of the gods and the end of the world. When the terrible wolf *FENRIR* had overcome Odin in a fierce and bloody struggle and swallowed him, Vidar stepped forward, smashed one of his well-shod feet against the wolf's lower jaw, and then with both hands he forced the upper jaw open till the ravenous beast's throat was torn asunder. It is more than likely that the meaning of Vidar's own name refers in some way to this ripping in half of evil.

V

VIGRID, in Germanic mythology, was the name of a plain that was destined to be the scene of the final conflict between the gods and the frost giants. There at *RAGNAROK* the two sides and their allies would engage in mutual destruction. A huge expanse of land, Vigrid was said to stretch 120 leagues in every direction. Even so, it was predicted that the assembled hosts would cover it completely.

VILI, in Germanic mythology, was the son of *BOR* and Bestla and the brother of *ODIN* and *VE*. At the beginning of creation he helped his brothers to slay the frost giant *YMIR* and form the world from his carcass. When they later created the first man and woman from wood, Vili's contribution was sharp wits and feeling hearts. Odin gave them the breath of life, while Ve added the powers of sight and hearing. In one Icelandic poem Vili is given the name *HONIR*.

VLKODLAK was the Slavic wolf-man. More a figure of folklore than mythology, he exists because of the ancient respect accorded to the ravenous wolf, which in the forests of northern and eastern Europe was the animal most feared. According to Germanic mythology, the chief god *ODIN* was destined to be killed by the wolf *FENRIR* at *RAGNAROK*, the doom of the gods.

VOLOS see *VELES*

VOLSUNG was the subject of a late Germanic myth. He was said to be a descendant of *ODIN*. When Signy, Volsung's only daughter, was married against her will to the Gothic king Siggeir, a one-eyed stranger appeared among the wedding guests. It was Odin, chief of the Germanic gods. He stuck a sword deep into an oak and told the company that the weapon would belong to the man who pulled it out. Whoever wielded the sword could never be defeated.

THE VIGRID PLAIN (above) *was mapped out as the battlefield of Ragnarok. When Heimdall sounded the call to battle, the warring hosts converged from all corners of the earth; gods and heroes poured over the Bifrost Bridge, while Loki and the fiery host swarmed in from the swirling seas.*
(ILLUSTRATION BY JAMES ALEXANDER, 1995.)

Out of courtesy Volsung invited his son-in-law Siggeir to try his luck first. But Siggeir did not succeed. Nor was anyone else able to pull out the sword, except the youngest of Volsung's sons, Sigmund. When Siggeir offered to buy the magic weapon, Sigmund refused to part with it at any price.

This refusal made the Gothic king really angry. Despite Signy's

VOLSUNG's (below) *great hall, built around a sacred oak, was the scene of a magical event when Odin appeared one night and thrust a sword, hilt-deep, into the great oak. He challenged the heroes to pull it out, offering the divine gift to the winner. Sigmund was the much-envied champion.*
(ILLUSTRATION BY ALAN LEE, 1984.)

warning, Volsung and his ten sons walked into Siggeir's trap when they accepted an invitation to visit his court. They were ambushed on the way and left in the forest, bound to a fallen tree. Each night a wolf came and ate one of them, until only Sigmund was left alive. Signy succeeded in rescuing him.

As a result, Siggeir wrongly believed that no one had escaped the attentions of the wolf. He relaxed his guard and Signy was able to bury her family and help Sigmund. It took a long time to prepare a revenge, however. First of all Signy tried to have her own sons trained by Sigmund, but they lacked courage. A second attempt to reinforce her brother involved incest. Without his knowledge, Signy slept with him and bore Sinfiotli, a warrior with double Volsung blood. When Sinfiotli grew up, Signy sent him to her brother to be trained as a warrior.

Although Sigmund and Sinfiotli were captured by Siggeir, the magic sword secured their release and allowed them to take revenge on the king and his sons. Afterwards Sigmund returned home, and had another son, *SIGURD*, known in German legend as Siegfried.

VOLUND see *WAYLAND*

WAYLAND was the smith god of the Anglo-Saxons. The son of a sailor and a mermaid, he was renowned for making coats of mail and swords. In Scandinavia he was known as Volund, or Volundr, and in Germany as Wielund.

Wayland's myth is a story of revenge. King Nidud of Sweden cut Wayland's leg sinews and placed him and his forge on a remote island. The smith god avenged this mutilation by killing Nidud's two sons, who came to see his treasures, and sending their heads studded with precious jewels and mounted on silver to King Nidud. He may also have raped Nidud's daughter, but this is not certain.

WAYLAND's (above) smithy was visited not just by warriors seeking arms, but by noblewomen wanting dainty trinkets of purest gold. Wayland was also a craftsman on the grand scale, designing a fabulous Icelandic maze, known as Volund's House. (WHALEBONE CARVING, 8TH CENTURY.)

WAYLAND (below), captive on a desolate island, laboured in his underground forge, fashioning wondrous ornaments and weapons for his oppressive master, Nidud of Sweden. Like Daedalus, Wayland fashioned wings and flew away to freedom. (WIELAND BY MAX KOCH, WATERCOLOUR, 1904.)

WAYLAND (above right) and his brothers chanced upon three Valkyries bathing in a lake. They took their plumage left on the bank and kept them on earth for nine years, until they escaped. Fashioning wings for himself, Wayland flew after his wife, Alvit, to Alfheim. (ILLUSTRATION BY H THEAKER, 1900.)

Afterwards Wayland is said to have flown to VALHALLA, like the Greek inventor Daedalus, on wings he had made for himself. Near Uffington in Wiltshire, a long barrow has ancient associations with Wayland, and is locally known as his smithy. His lameness parallels that of Hephaistos, the Greek smith god whose injury had two different explanations. In one version it was claimed that his limp was the result of his having interfered in a violent quarrel between his parents, Zeus and Hera. So annoyed did Zeus become that he flung his son out of Olympus and let him fall heavily on the island of Lemnos. A second explanation tells how Hephaistos was born a dwarfish figure with a limp. Hera even tried to drown him, but he was saved by sea nymphs. The latter version of the myth is most relevant to Wayland. In Germanic mythology the master craftsmen were mainly dwarfs, and Wayland's own mother was a mermaid. It is interesting to note that Lemnos was an island with volcanic activity, like the remote island to which Wayland had been banished.

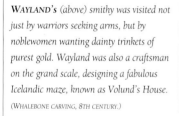

WIELAND see WAYLAND

WODEN see ODIN

WOTAN see ODIN

Y

YGGDRASIL, or Yggdrasill, (which means something like "dreadful mount") was the cosmic ash tree in Germanic mythology. Its name is a reference either to the gallows or *ODIN*'s horse. Not only did Odin hang himself on Yggdrasil for nine nights in order to learn wisdom, but sacrificial hangings from gallows trees were also a favourite Viking way of worshipping the god. An archaeological find that reveals the extent of this ghastly ritual is the Tollund Man, found in a Jutland peat bog in 1950. The corpse was so well preserved that it was possible to deduce that he was a prisoner of war who had been sacrificed as a thank-offering after a battle.

The parallel between Odin's voluntary death on Yggdrasil and

YGGDRASIL (right) the World Tree, lay at the heart of the universe. Here, the whirling patterns of Viking art strikingly capture the swirling vitality at the centre of life. A stag browses on its evergreen foliage while a serpent nips the stag's neck, reflecting the life and death struggle at the root of life. (WOOD CARVING, 8TH CENTURY.)

YMIR (below) was the first creature to emerge from the primal wastes of ice in the yawning abyss of Ginnungagap at the dawn of creation. As fire from the south melted ice from the north, the icy droplets fused to form a massive frost giant. As he slept, his sweat formed other frost giants. (ILLUSTRATION BY NICK BEALE, 1995.)

the Crucifixion remains striking. Odin was also pierced with a spear and, like Christ, cried out before he died. Although it is possible that the Crucifixion was known at the time that the Odin myth was recorded, there is little doubt that his hanging on the cosmic tree had pre-Christian origins and derived from ancient pagan worship. Odin had long been the god of the spear, the god of the hanged.

Yggdrasil is described as the largest and most stately tree ever to have grown. Its branches overhung the nine worlds and spread out above the heavens. It was supported by three great roots: one descended to *JOTUNHEIM*, the land of the giants, where *MIMIR*'s well stood; the second ended in foggy Niflheim, close by the spring of Hvergelmir, where the dragon *NIDHOGG* gnawed the root from below whenever it tired of chewing corpses; the last root was embedded near *ASGARD*, the stronghold of the gods, beneath *URD*'s well, where the gods held their daily assembly. Water was taken from the well each day by the *NORNS*, the three fates, Urd, Skuld and Verdandi, and mixed with earth as a means of preventing Yggdrasil's bark from rotting. An eagle perched on the very top of the cosmic tree

was daily harassed by a squirrel named Ratatosk, who brought unpleasant comments and insults up from the dragon Nidhogg. Another bird in its branches was a cock, sometimes referred to as "Vidofnir the tree snake".

The idea of a cosmic tree is common in the myths of the northern parts of both Europe and Asia. It was thought of as the backbone of the universe, the structural support of the nine worlds. In Ireland, however, the sacred tree acquired a different role. Although always associated with otherworld splendour, the musical branches of Irish mythology acted as cures for

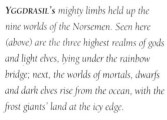

YGGDRASIL's mighty limbs held up the nine worlds of the Norsemen. Seen here (above) are the three highest realms of gods and light elves, lying under the rainbow bridge; next, the worlds of mortals, dwarfs and dark elves rise from the ocean, with the frost giants' land at the icy edge.

(ILLUSTRATION FROM NORTHERN ANTIQUITIES, 1847.)

YGGDRASIL (right) filled the known world, taking root not only in the dark depths of Niflheim (bottom), but also in Midgard and Asgard. Its topmost boughs reached heaven, while its lowest root touched hell. It was generally thought of as the structural support of the universe.

(ILLUSTRATION BY ALAN LEE, 1984.)

sickness and despair. In a number of tales these magic branches of silver or gold were brought by messengers from otherworld lands. Thus the fabulous voyage of Bran began with the sound of music that caused him to fall asleep. It came from a branch of silver with white blossoms, which a beautiful lady took away after telling of the delights of her world beyond the sea. Hints of such magic are also present in Germanic mythology. The obvious example must be the apples belonging to the goddess *IDUN*. Only this magic fruit prevented the gods from growing old. They were clearly the gift from

another sacred tree. How much trees were once revered can be seen from the reactions to early Christian missionaries like St Boniface. In the eighth century he cut down sacrificial trees, to the terror of the Frisians, until he himself was felled at Dockum by an outraged pagan.

YGGDRASILL see *YGGDRASIL*

YMIR, in Germanic mythology, was the first living creature. He was a frost giant who emerged from the ice in *GINNUNGAGAP* ("the yawning emptiness"). He was evil and the father and mother of all frost giants, who first came from the sweat of

his armpit. Ymir fed on the milk of the primeval cow *AUDHUMLA*. He was slain by the brothers *ODIN*, *VILI* and *VE*, who were the grandsons of *BURI*, whom Audhumla had licked free of the ice.

Growing tired of the brutality of Ymir and his ever-increasing band of frost giants, Odin, Vili and Ve took up arms. They slew Ymir and then drowned all the frost giants in his blood, with the exception of *BERGELMIR* and his wife, who managed to escape by sailing on a hollowed tree trunk.

Odin, Vili and Ve then threw Ymir's carcass into Ginnungagap. His flesh became the earth, his

unbroken bones mountains, his teeth and jaw rocks and boulders, his blood rivers, lakes and the sea, and his skull the sky, which was held up at its four corners by dwarfs. Sparks were used to make the sun, the moon and the stars.

Such an extremely violent creation myth is by no means unique. The Babylonian champion of the gods, Marduk, slew the chaos-dragon Tiamat with raging winds and an arrow, before splitting her carcass into two parts. One he pushed upwards to form the heavens, the other he used to make a floor above the deep, the emptiness at the bottom of the universe.

251

PICTURE ACKNOWLEDGEMENTS

The Publishers gratefully acknowledge the following for permission to reproduce the illustrations indicated.

INTRODUCTION

Archiv für Kunst und Geschichte, London: 6, 5, 7T, 7B.
Ateneum, Helsinki, The Central Art Archives: 2.

CLASSICAL MYTHOLOGY

Archiv für Kunst und Geschichte: 12, 13BL, 14B, 15T, 16T, 18L, 19T, 20 (all), 21L, 23, 24, 30 (all), 34BR, 34TR, 35, 36L, 38TR, 39T, 40R, 41T, 41BR, 43R, 44TR, 45, 47T, 48TL, 49TL, 50BL, 52TR, 53 (all), 55 (all), 56T, 57T, 58BR, 59T, 59B, 60BR, 61TR, 62T, 63T, 64T, 65T, 66T, 66BR, 67T, 68B, 69BR, 70R, 72T, 74TL, 75, 76, 78B, 79B, 80T, 81TM, 82T, 83 (all), 87T, 87B, 88B, 89T.
The Bridgeman Art Library/Bristol Museum and Art Gallery: 84B/Kunsthistorisches Museum, Vienna: 77B/The National Gallery, London: 85BL/Galerie Estense, Modena: 85BR.
Board of Trustees of the National Museums and Galleries on Merseyside (Walker Art Gallery): 63B.
E. T. Archive: 31TR, 50TR, 51BR, 68T, 85TL.
Fine Art Photographic Library: 74BR.
Alan Lee: 44BR.
Manchester City Art Galleries: 17B, 52BL.
Scala, Florence: 29TL.
The Tate Gallery, London: 42T.

CELTIC MYTHOLOGY

Archiv für Kunst und Geschichte, London: 93T, 113T, 114B, 121T, 123BR, 132L, 133BL, 133BR, 140L, 148B, 160.
Birmingham Museums and Art Gallery: 101T, 120BR, 135, 141L, 151B, 157T, 167T.
The Bodleian Library: 139TL.
The Bridgeman Art Library: 94BR/Phillips Fine Art: 90/Lady Lever Art Gallery, Port Sunlight: 94L/Private Collection: 128R/Bibliothèque Nationale: 133T/Phillips Fine Art 136B/City of Edinburgh Museums and Art Galleries: 138TR/Private Collection: 141L/Giraudon: 155T.
E. Davison: 119L.
Dundee Art Galleries and Museums: 103T, 104B, 131T, 142BL.
Fine Art Photographic Library: 92, 102T, 103B, 104T, 124BL, 126B, 140R, 142BL, 166BL.
Glasgow Museums: Art Gallery and Museum, Kelvingrove: 115T.
Yvonne Gilbert: 148ML.
Miranda Gray: 102BL, 128BL, 144T, 146BL, 168B.
King Arthurs Great Halls, Tintagel: 100T, 134TL, 134TR, 137TL, 151TR.
Alan Lee: 105 (all), 106T, 107R, 108R, 111B, 125L, 125R, 132R, 137TR, 141TR, 141BR, 143T, 145TL, 146T, 147L, 149TL, 149BR, 150TM, 153R, 156 (both), 157BL, 157BR, 158 (all), 159BR, 161 (all), 162 (both), 164L, 165L, 169T, 170 (both), 171BR.
Stuart Littlejohn: 114T, 115BL, 130BR, 168T.
Manchester City Art Galleries: 101B.
Danuta Meyer: 107L, 145B, 164R.
National Galleries of Scotland: 99L, 110, 118B, 122T.
Courtesy Susan Russell Flint: 146BR.
The Tate Gallery, London: 134B.
Courtesy of the Board of Trustees of the Victoria and Albert Museum: 150BL, 166.

NORSE MYTHOLOGY

Ateneum, Helsinki, The Central Art Archives: 197BL, 203T, 220R, 221TL, 221 TR, 241B.
Archiv für Kunst und Geschichte, London: 179R, 181R, 188BL, 190B, 197BR, 206TL, 206BR, 215B, 234, 229TR, 237TL, 237BL, 242TL, 242BR, 243T, 245ML, 246B, 249B.
Arnamagnaean Institute, Copenhagen: 176L, 202BL, 203BR.
Bildarchiv Preussischer Kulturbesitz: 224T.
The Bridgeman Art Library/Bonhams: 179L/Royal Library, Copenhagen: 198BR, 201 (both).
Jean Loup Charmet: 197TR, 224B.
Christies Images: 212T, 229BR.
E. T. Archive: 186T, 213B.
Fine Art Photographic Library: 188T, 243BR.
Alan Lee: 181T, 183T, 184T, 194T, 195B, 205T, 222TR, 236BL, 237TR, 240, 245MR, 251TR.
Manchester City Museums and Art Galleries: 192B.
Nasjonalgalleriet, Oslo: 186B, 214B.
National Museum Stockholm: 182T, 190T, 196R, 215T, 230BL.
Statens Museum fur Kunst, Copenhagen: 181B, 199T, 245TR, 248B.
Werner Forman Archive: 174, 210BL, 250TR/National Musuem, Copenhagen: 236BR/Statens Historiska Museum, Stockholm: 189TL, 197TL, 205, 209BL, 213TR, 245TL/Thjodminjasafin, Reykjavik: 233/Universitetets Oldsaksamling, Oslo: 175.

INDEX